RCL23

GOVERNORS STATE UNIVERSITY LIBRARY

W9-BDS-954

3 1611 00309 3165

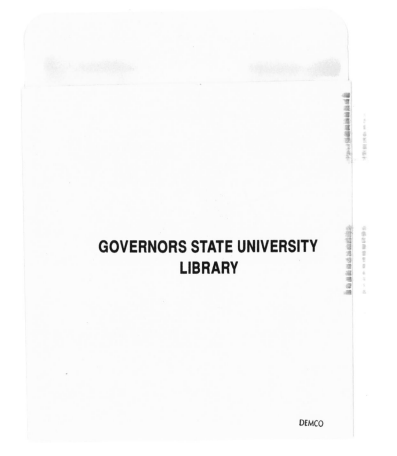

GOVERNORS STATE UNIVERSITY
LIBRARY

DEMCO

# TOUCH AND INTIMACY IN FIRST WORLD WAR LITERATURE

The First World War ravaged the male body on an unprecedented scale, yet fostered moments of physical intimacy and tenderness among the soldiers in the trenches. Touch, the most elusive and private of the senses, became central to war experience. War writing is haunted by experiences of physical contact: from the muddy realities of the front to the emotional intensity of trench life, to the traumatic obsession with the wounded body in nurses' memoirs. Through extensive archival and historical research, analysing previously unknown letters and diaries alongside close investigative readings of literary writings by figures such as Owen and Brittain, Santanu Das recovers the sensuous world of the First World War trenches and hospitals. This original and evocative study alters our understanding of the period as well as of the body at war, and illuminates the perilous intimacy between sense experience, emotion and language in times of crisis.

SANTANU DAS is a British Academy Postdoctoral Fellow at Queen Mary College, University of London and a former Research Fellow at St John's College, Cambridge.

# TOUCH AND INTIMACY IN FIRST WORLD WAR LITERATURE

SANTANU DAS

*Queen Mary College, University of London*

GOVERNORS STATE UNIVERSITY
UNIVERSITY PARK
IL 60466

CAMBRIDGE
UNIVERSITY PRESS

CAMBRIDGE UNIVERSITY PRESS
Cambridge, New York, Melbourne, Madrid, Cape Town, Singapore, São Paulo

Cambridge University Press
The Edinburgh Building, Cambridge CB2 2RU, UK

Published in the United States of America by Cambridge University Press, New York

www.cambridge.org
Information on this title: www.cambridge.org/9780521846035

© Santanu Das 2005

This book is in copyright. Subject to statutory exception
and to the provisions of relevant collective licensing agreements,
no reproduction of any part may take place without
the written permission of Cambridge University Press.

First published 2005

Printed in the United Kingdom at the University Press, Cambridge

*A catalogue record for this book is available from the British Library*

ISBN-13 978-0-521-84603-5 hardback
ISBN-10 0-521-84603-X hardback

Cambridge University Press has no responsibility for the persistence or accuracy of URLs for external
or third-party internet websites referred to in this book, and does not guarantee that
any content on such websites is, or will remain, accurate or appropriate.

R
478
.W65
D37
2005

*in memoriam*
*Subhas Ghosal*
*1924–1998*
*Kajal Sengupta*
*1931–2006*

'In every touch more intimate meanings hide.'
  Rupert Brooke, 'Town and Country', *The Collected Poems*, 65

'I have not seen any dead. I have done worse. In the dank air I have perceived it, and in the darkness, felt.'
  Wilfred Owen, *Collected Letters*, 429

'My hands could instantly tell the difference between the cold of the harsh bitter night and the stealthy cold of death.'
  Mary Borden, *The Forbidden Zone*, 124

'Language is a skin: I rub my language against the other. It is as if I had words instead of fingers, or fingers at the tip of my words. My language trembles with desire.'
  Roland Barthes, *A Lover's Discourse*, 73

# Contents

# Figures

# Acknowledgements

My deepest gratitude is to Dame Gillian Beer who supervised the thesis on which this book is based. Gillian has known the work intimately in its various forms. Her great capacity for pleasure in language, astuteness as a reader and constant generosity have made working with her an inspiring experience, and I have benefited immensely from her advice and warm support. Throughout, I have been indebted to the kindness and goodwill of the Master and Fellows of St John's College, Cambridge. They elected me to a research fellowship and made the writing of this book possible. The Cambridge Commonwealth Trust and the Cambridge English Faculty have also helped me at critical moments.

John Kerrigan has been a powerful presence since my undergraduate days: he read Chapter 3 with his usual forensic care and his intellectual encouragement, kindness and practical advice over the years have been very important. Jon Stallworthy has been extremely generous with his time and learning, and a supportive friend of the book from its initial stages. David Trotter was always open-handed with knowledge and expertise, and his insightful comments pushed my thoughts forward while revising the thesis as a book. Trudi Tate has shown a sustained interest in the project and been a great interlocutor: many thanks to her and to Supriya Chaudhuri for reading several chapters at short notice and for their valuable criticism; and to Michèle Barrett and Mary Jacobus for their warm encouragement and generous support.

Fran Brearton and Laura Marcus read the typescript for Cambridge University Press, and I am grateful for their detailed engagement with the work and criticism of the most constructive kind; thanks are also due to the anonymous third reader. Alison Hennegan and Sarah Cain kindly heard or read early versions of some chapters while Stefan Goebel, John Pegum and Mike Roper involved me in conversations on nailed bodies, trench journals and maternal relations respectively. Clémence O'Connor and Emma Wagstaff helped me with the French translations and

Bernhard Malkmus with German. Ari Reimann provided some useful references. My special thanks to my editors at Cambridge University Press – Ray Ryan and Maartje Scheltens – for their efficiency and understanding, and for evolving the process of editing into one of friendship.

My warm thanks to the staff of St John's College library, the University Library and the English Faculty Library, Cambridge and the British Library, London for their kind assistance which made the research possible. I am particularly indebted to the staff of the Imperial War Museum, London for their helpful and courteous service, and for permission to use some of their documents, photographs and paintings; to the copyright holders of different private collection of letters for their kind permission to use them in the book; to Jon Stallworthy and the Wilfred Owen Estate for allowing me to quote from the manuscript poems of Wilfred Owen and to Oxford University Press to quote from Owen's *Collected Letters*; and to the University Library, Cambridge to quote from a typescript version of Siegfried Sassoon's 'The Last Meeting'.

In a book about intimacy, it is a great pleasure to be able to acknowledge some of my close friends as some of its most enthusiastic readers: Robert Macfarlane, Ralph O'Connor, Toby Smith and Hugh Stevens commented acutely on large portions of the book, often at very short notice. They pointed me to areas which needed more work as well as to a whole world beyond it: long walks by the river, cava, battlefield tours (thanks, Toby!) and endless chats have been all parts of the process which helped the thesis to grow into a book. Hugh made important suggestions for the section on Rosenberg and kept me entertained with music, ballet and fine food: I am very grateful for the quality of his affection and attention. Subha Mukherji was also always there, providing support and infusing academia with a spirit of fun; my thanks to her and to Debdulal Roy for many memorable hours and dinners together.

Warm thanks to Amit Chaudhuri, Barnita Bagchi, Shantimoy and Ranjana Mukherji, Aroon and Anima Basak, Yota Batsaki, Andreas Bücker and Barnali Ghosh for drawing me into their different worlds, and to my teachers in Calcutta, at Presidency College and Jadavpur University; and particularly to Lina Guha Roy. Finally, I would like to thank my parents, especially my dear mother for continuing to place every interest of mine above her own. Their phone calls and e-mails continue to sustain me. Without the love and support of my father and my mother – and of course Sasha – it would have been very difficult to undertake this research. The book is dedicated to the memory of two remarkable people: Kajal Sengupta who lit up our days at Presidency College, Calcutta, and my beloved uncle Subhas Ghosal.

Several portions of this book have been published: a version of Chapter 3 in *Modernism/Modernity*, 9, 1 (January 2002), and reprinted in *The Kiss in History*, ed. Karen Harvey (Manchester: Manchester University Press, 2005) and *The Book of Touch*, ed. Constance Classen (Oxford: Berg, 2005), and portions of Chapters 5 and 6 in *Textual Practice*, 19, 2 (June, 2005).

# Abbreviations

Quotations from the following works are cited in the work through these abbreviations.

IWM     Imperial War Museum, London.

CP&F    *Wilfred Owen: The Complete Poems and Fragments*, ed. Jon
        Stallworthy, 2 vols. (London: Chatto and Windus, Hogarth
        and Oxford University Press, 1983).

CL      *Wilfred Owen: Collected Letters*, ed. Harold Owen and John
        Bell (London: Oxford University Press, 1967).

CW      *The Collected Works of Isaac Rosenberg: Poetry, Prose, Letters,
        Paintings, and Drawings*, ed. Ian Parsons (London: Chatto
        and Windus, 1984).

FZ      Mary Borden, *The Forbidden Zone* (London: William and
        Heinemann, 1929).

GWMM    Paul Fussell, *The Great War and Modern Memory* (Oxford:
        Oxford University Press, 1975).

PP      *The Poetry and Plays of Isaac Rosenberg*, ed. Vivien Noakes
        (Oxford: Oxford University Press, 2004).

SE      *The Standard Edition of the Complete Psychological Works of
        Sigmund Freud*, translated from the German under the
        General Editorship of James Strachey, 24 vols. (1953–74).

UF      Henri Barbusse, *Under Fire*, translated from *Le Feu* (1918)
        by W. Fitzwater Wray (1919; London: Dent, 1965).

WTWY    Irene Rathbone, *We That Were Young* (1932; New York:
        The Feminist Press, 1989).

# Introduction

'touch is the spirit and rule of all'[1]

Ten blindfolded soldiers move haltingly in a single file across the twenty-foot-long canvas in John Singer Sargent's *Gassed* (1918–19), each touching the man in front (Figure I.1).[2] What each soldier perceives is what the hand feels – rucksack, rifle or the rough uniform-clad body in front. The hand not only grasps or clutches; it enables the soldiers to think and plan the next step forward, gathering a cluster of disabled men into a neat line. The sense of touch defines space and guides the rhythm of their movement, as if new eyes have opened at the tip of the fingers. Sound is implicitly there, in the form of noises of the football match played in the distant background or the flock of aeroplanes whirring above the parallel file of soldiers towards the top right-hand corner of the painting. But rushes of sound are subsumed into the tactile continuum joining the figures in the file as well as those heaped on the ground. Painting, like surgery, requires a rare co-ordination of the eye and the hand. Every fresh brushstroke is a guiding and manoeuvring of touch on the canvas just as each little movement of the blindfolded soldiers in the painting is sensed through the hand. The interruption of the chain by the fourth soldier from the end as he temporarily falls out of line draws attention to the centrality as well as the nakedness of the hand. The gesture is raw: the human subject is cast as a set of anxious, vulnerable limbs, groping in a dark world.

In contrast to the leg of the player about to kick the ball in the army match, the third soldier lifts his foot far higher than is needed as he tries to negotiate the duckboard: blindness is inscribed most powerfully at a point where touch is anticipated as collision but is actually absent. The

1 Gordon Bottomley, 'A Hymn of Touch', *Poems and Plays* (London: The Bodley Head, 1953), 46.
2 John Singer Sargent, *Gassed*, oil on canvas, courtesy of the Imperial War Museum, London.

Figure I.1. John Singer Sargent, *Gassed*, 1919. Oil 2290×6100 mm. Imperial War Museum, London.

exaggerated gesture dramatises the disjunction between our optical sense of space and the soldiers' tactile perception. In 'The Fleeting Portrait', Virginia Woolf recalls how '"Gassed" at last pricked some nerve of protest, or perhaps of humanity'. Referring to the raised foot, Woolf notes, 'This little piece of over-emphasis was the final scratch of the surgeon's knife which is said to hurt more than the whole operation'.[3] In Woolf's evocative account – as she plays on the relation between the surface of the canvas and the surface of the skin – the body of the painting and that of the viewer meet and move under the artist's hand: the 'little piece of over-emphasis' acts like the Barthesian 'punctum', pricking the skin set between the viewer and the painting, and subjectivity bleeds.

Sargent was commissioned to do a large painting for the Hall of Remembrance depicting the 'fusion of British and American forces'.[4] Trying to find a worthy subject, Sargent, along with his old friend Henry Tonks, travelled to France in July 1918 and, after spending some time as Earl Haig's guest, joined the Guards Division under General Fielding near Arras. On 11 September 1918, he wrote to his friend, Charteris, 'The nearer to danger the fewer and the more hidden the men – the more dramatic the situation the more it becomes an empty landscape'. Of the three night-scenes he goes on to describe, one engrosses him: 'a harrowing sight, a field full of gassed and blindfolded men'.[5] The scene was the aftermath of a mustard gas attack in which the 99th Brigade and the 8th Brigade of the 3rd Division were caught. It is narrated in greater detail by Tonks: 'Gassed cases kept coming in, led along in parties of about six just as Sargent has depicted them, by an orderly. They sat or lay down on the grass, there must have been several hundred.'[6] Later, while spending a week in a hospital tent at Ypres, Sargent was further exposed to 'the chokings and coughing of gassed men, which was a nightmare'.[7] Yet, such horrors are largely absent in the painting. Sargent's emollient contours and colours aestheticise the soldiers: they are tall,

3 Virginia Woolf, 'The Royal Academy', in *The Essays of Virginia Woolf*, vol. III, *1919–1924*, ed. Andrew McNeillie (London: Hogarth, 1988), 92–3. Also see Evan Charteris, *John Sargent* (London: William Heinemann, 1927), 213–16; Richard Cork, *A Bitter Truth: Avant-Garde Art and the Great War* (New Haven: Yale University Press, 1994), 219–22. For a suggestive theoretical exploration of blindness in art, see Jacques Derrida, *Memoirs of the Blind: The Self-Portrait and Other Ruins*, trans. Pascale-Anne Brault and Michael Naas (Chicago: University of Chicago Press, 1993).
4 Alfred Yockney to John Sargent, 26 April 1918, John Sargent File, 1918–1924, First World War Artists' Archive, 284 A/7, 170, Imperial War Museum, London (hereafter abbreviated IWM).
5 The letter is quoted by the Hon. Evan Charteris in his biography, *John Sargent*, 214.
6 Henry Tonks to Yockney, 4 October 1918, Sargent File, IWM.
7 Sargent to Isabella Stewart Gardner quoted in Charteris, *John Sargent*, 216.

blond and athletic, moving with solemn dignity, as in a sculpted frieze. The sky is strangely tranquil. The pinkish glow of the setting sun, coming from no particular direction, holds the soldiers, and stills them in our minds in a moment of numbed serenity. The most striking feature in the painting is the strange use of light: the spectacle of blindness is repre-sented through the drama of chiaroscuro. The trance-like figures seem to be moving in an imaginary space amidst the scattered light, as if replaying a scene from one of the traumatic war-dreams that haunt First World War writings, and which Freud used as one of the starting points for *Beyond the Pleasure Principle* (1920).

The sense of finale is particularly evident when compared to Bruegel's more macabre *The Parable of the Blind* (1568) to which Sargent's painting clearly refers. In Sargent's world, there is an eternal wait for the piles of bodies crowding the ground, for the casualty station can treat only a handful of them. Yet the sense of desolation is balanced by an Owenesque sense of community as the soldiers on the ground, 'leaning on the nearest chest or knees / Carelessly slept'.[8] The homoerotic undertones of war that Owen evokes would not be lost on this society artist who painted portraits of fashionable women for his living, and often did nude studies of young working-class men for pleasure.[9] If we look at the figures on the ground, we do not know where one figure ends and the other begins: the folds of colour and fabric hold within them the contours of the bodies as they touch and blend in a world of sensuous contact and comfort. The young boy in the right-hand corner gulps down water to alleviate the effects of mustard gas. Sargent's draft sketch (Figure I.2) shows the gentleness of the orderly through a double movement: he swivels round to clasp the elbow of the soldier behind him (this second figure is not in the sketch but is in the final painting) while supporting, at the same time, the limp figure in front of him in a gesture that recalls the taking down of the body of Christ. The world's first major industrial warfare ravaged the male body on an unprecedented scale but also restored tenderness to touch in male relationships. Instead of evoking the wasted landscape, as in Nash's *The Menin Road* (1919) or depicting horror, as in

8 Wilfred Owen, 'Spring Offensive', *Wilfred Owen: The Complete Poems and Fragments*, 2 vols., ed. Jon Stallworthy (London: Chatto and Windus, Hogarth and Oxford Univeristy Press, 1983), 192; hereafter abbreviated *CP&F*.

9 The most notable example is the *Nude Study of Thomas E. Mckeller*. See Trevor Fairbrother, *John Singer Sargent: The Sensualist* (New Haven: Yale University Press, 2001), especially the album of figure studies (Folios 1–30), 181–212.

Figure I.2. John Singer Sargent, *Study for Gassed*, 1918–19. Imperial War Museum, Artists' Archives.

Otto Dix's *Dead Sentry* (1924), Sargent distils the pity of war into a moment of blindness and touch.

*

This book examines the central importance of the sense of touch in the experience of the First World War and its relation to literary representation. The writings of the First World War are obsessed with tactile experiences: from the horrors of the 'sucking mud' that recur in trench diaries, journals and letters to the 'full-nerved, still warm' boys of Owen, Nichols and Sassoon to the ordeal of bandaging wounds described in memoirs of the women nurses. In the foreword to the *Collected Works* of Isaac Rosenberg, Siegfried Sassoon, singling out 'Break of Day in the Trenches' for special praise, notes, 'Sensuous frontline existence is there, hateful and repellent, unforgettable and inescapable'.[10] The aims of

10 Siegfried Sassoon, 'Foreword', reprinted in *The Collected Works of Isaac Rosenberg*, ed. Ian Parsons (London: Chatto & Windus, 1979), ix; hereafter, Rosenberg, *CW*.

my study are both recuperative and literary: it seeks to recover and analyse the 'sensuous' world of the trenches and the war hospitals as lived by the men at the front and the women nurses, and to show how the texture of such experience is fundamental to, and provides new ways of under-standing, First World War literature and art. If, in some contemporary discussions, the body has become a linguistic trace in the maze of signification,[11] *Touch and Intimacy* draws attention to its physicality, to the material conditions which produced the literature. Vision, sound and smell all carry the body beyond its margins; tactile experience, by con-trast, stubbornly adheres to the flesh.[12] At once intense and diffuse, working at the threshold between the self and the world, touch can be said to open up the body at a more intimate, affective level, offering fresh perspectives on certain issues that repeatedly surface in war writings and have become central to contemporary cultural thinking: ideas of space and boundaries, questions of gender and sexuality or the concept of trauma ('neurasthenia' or 'shell-shock', as it was known at the time). The immediate post-war years were also the time when touch was being conceptualised by men such as Havelock Ellis in *Sexual Selection in Man* (1920) and Sigmund Freud in *The Ego and the Id* (1923). Though tightly focused on the First World War, the larger intention of the book is to provide an intimate history of human emotions in times of crisis – to explore the making and unmaking of subjectivity through the most elusive and private of the senses.

The First World War is remembered and represented as a time of darkness. The eyes of the soldiers I write about are not gassed or banda-ged but open and disorientated in the night. Burgoyne, in his diary, describes the world of the trenches as 'dark as Hades and wet'; David Jones, in *In Parenthesis* (1937), writes about 'the stumbling dark of the blind, that Bruegel knew about – ditch circumscribed'.[13] The reference manual *British Trench Warfare 1917–1918* issued for the soldiers by the War Office stressed in a section titled 'Training in Night Work' how

11 The classic instance is Judith Butler's *Gender Trouble* (New York: Routledge, 1990), a question that Butler herself addresses at the very beginning of *Bodies That Matter: On the Discursive Limits of 'Sex'* (1993): 'What about the materiality of the body, *Judy?*' At the same time, there has also been a powerful impulse towards 'corporeal feminism', associated with Luce Irigaray, Adrienne Rich and Julia Kristeva.

12 See Maurice Merleau-Ponty, *Phenomenology of Perception* trans. Colin Smith (1962; London: Routledge, 2002), 368–9.

13 *The Burgoyne Diaries*, ed. Claudia Davidson (London: Thomas Harmonsworth, 1985), 10; David Jones, *In Parenthesis* (London: Faber, 1937), 31.

essential nocturnal duty was to trench life.[14] In *The First Hundred Thousand* (1915), Ian Hay notes, 'The day's work in the trenches begins about nine o'clock the night before'; the French writer, Ferdinand Céline, corroborates, 'Everything that's important goes on in the darkness'.[15] Amidst the dark, muddy, subterranean world of the trenches, the soldiers navigated space, as I argue in the first two chapters, not through the safe distance of the gaze but rather through the clumsy immediacy of their bodies: 'crawl' is a recurring verb in trench narratives, showing the shift from the visual to the tactile.

After three weeks at the front, Owen writes to his mother, 'I have not seen any dead. I have done worse. In the dank air, I have <u>perceived</u> it, and in the darkness, <u>felt</u>.'[16] Touch is considered to be the more apt register for recording the horrors than sight; the sense of violation is at once more acute and personal. And a month before his death on the Oise-Sambre Canal Bank, he writes to Siegfried Sassoon:

. . . the boy by my side, shot through the head, lay on top of me, soaking my shoulder, for half an hour.

Catalogue? Photograph? Can you photograph the crimson-hot iron as it cools from the smelting? This is what Jones's blood looked like, and felt like. My senses are charred.

Owen tries to evoke the perilous intimacy of the moment by drawing on the eye ('crimson-hot iron') but soon the visual gives way to the tactile. The moment is recalled differently to his mother: 'Of whose blood lies yet crimson on my shoulder where his head was – and where so lately yours was'.[17] Horror, pity, maternity and a diffuse eroticism are fused and confused in that 'half an hour' of bodily contact, defying the established categories of gender and sexuality. On the other hand, Donald Hankey, who was killed on the Somme in October 1916, evokes the ideal of the Christian officer through a careful detail: 'If a blister [on the foot] had to be lanced, he would very likely lance it himself. . . . It seemed to have a touch of the Christ about it, and we loved and honoured him the more.'[18] Between Owen's account of horror and Hankey's idealisation

---

14 *British Trench Warfare 1917–1918: A Reference Manual* (1917; London: IWM, 1997), 11.
15 Ian Hay, *The First Hundred Thousand: Being the Unofficial Chronicle of a Unit of 'K 910'* (London: William Blackwood, 1915), 245; Ferdinand Céline, *Journey to the End of the Night*, trans. Ralph Manheim (1932; London: John Calder, 1988), 62.
16 *Wilfred Owen: Collected Letters*, ed. Harold Owen and John Bell (London: Oxford University Press, 1967), 429; hereafter abbreviated *CL*. The two words are underlined in the original letter.
17 *CL*, 581, 580.
18 Donald Hankey, *A Student in Arms* (London: Andrew Melrose, 1918), 60.

of daily routine, a whole new world of physical contact was opening up between men. Owen's repetition of the word 'felt' also raises an issue that will confront us repeatedly in relation to its neighbour 'touch': though referring primarily to the sensation ('<u>perceived</u>'), 'felt' gathers its full significance in relation to the emotional world it contains, hovering at the threshold between the sensory and the psychic, bringing together the body and the mind.

Two broad questions will frame the argument of this book. First, I shall explore why the sense of touch seems to be so crucial to the experience of the First World War, and the profound, if at times necessarily oblique, ways in which it affects the subjectivities of soldiers and nurses. Second, I shall highlight the urgent need within war writings to find a literary language around this particular sense which gets charged with new intensities of meaning. Starting with a variety of archival and testimonial material – letters, diaries, journals, trench newspaper accounts – I move on to examine how imaginative writing of the period repeatedly dwells on moments of tactile contact and the ways in which these processes of touch – whether in a context of disgust, tenderness, pain – are gathered into the creative energies of a text, conceptualised within a novel, a poem or a short story. If such writing provides special insights into the phenomenological and emotional world of the First World War, its analysis will show literature's close engagement with the realm of the senses.

In the incomplete Preface to his intended collection of poems, Owen refashioned poetry as testimony. The relationship between touch and testimony is a particular concern of this study, especially in the case of the women who were called upon to nurse the men and whom Owen so uncharitably excluded ('for you may touch them not'). Yet, it is precisely in this forbidden zone of physical contact that Mary Borden, an American nurse who served in Belgium and France, would locate her work, establishing the authority and authenticity of her touch: 'My hands could instantly tell the difference between the cold of the harsh bitter night and the stealthy cold of death'.[19] If Dr Elsie Inglis was famously told to 'Go home and be still' when she volunteered her medical services in August 1914, Borden would boldly lay claim to bodily knowledge, traditionally associated with the male experience of war. The book explores the pressures of memory and culture that underpin this kind of physical

---

19 Mary Borden, *The Forbidden Zone* (London: William Heinemann, 1929), 124; hereafter abbreviated Borden, *FZ*.

testimony. At the outbreak of the war, thousands of women, trained to be genteel Edwardian ladies, ventured into France, Belgium, Serbia and Mesopotamia to nurse the war-wounded. The direct relation posed by Owen between combat experience and war knowledge has in the past privileged a particular construction of war that largely marginalised women and civilians. Over the last two decades, however, a number of feminist critics such as Higonnet, Marcus and Tylee have powerfully drawn attention to the war experience of women, fundamentally affecting the way in which we 'reconceptualise war – and therefore the vocabulary of war'.[20] *Touch and Intimacy* shows that women's writings are essential to an understanding of warfare and continues the process of recovery through examination of archival and literary material, shifting the idea of trauma, traditionally associated only with the figure of the shell-shocked soldier, onto the neglected figure of the nurse. However, as Trudi Tate usefully reminds us in *Modernism, History and the First World War* (1998), it is not always helpful to treat gender as the 'final point of inquiry'.[21] Instead of viewing trauma exclusively through the lens of gender (which remains an important category of analysis), or solely as a representational crisis, this study also addresses the relation of gender to the witnessing of the body in pain and the 'charred' senses of the young nurses.

In 1929, John Brophy, while putting together an anthology of war writings, used as his criterion for inclusion accounts only 'by men who waged and suffered it, not vicariously, but with their own bodies'.[22] The combat model, inherited partly from the war poetry of Sassoon and Owen ('except you share / With them in hell'), was elaborated in its most evocative and influential form by Paul Fussell in *The Great War and Modern Memory* (1975) and much subsequent war criticism has an oedipal relation to this grand narrative.[23] The chief problem with Fussell's

---

20 Margaret Higonnet, 'Not So Quiet in No-Woman's Land', in *Gendering War Talk*, ed. Miriam Cooking and Angela Woollacott (Princeton: Princeton University Press, 1993), 208.

21 Trudi Tate, *Modernism, History and the First World War* (Manchester: Manchester University Press, 1998), 5.

22 John Brophy (ed.), *The Soldier's War: A Prose Anthology* (London: Dent, 1929), x. This view was aggressively advanced the same year in France by Norton Cru in his 700-page *Temoins*, published in a shortened English version as *War Books: A Study in Historical Criticism*, ed. and trans. Stanley J. Pincetl, Jr. and Ernest Marchand (San Diego: San Diego University Press, 1976).

23 Paul Fussell, *The Great War and Modern Memory* (Oxford: Oxford University Press, 1975). Given the various and valid charges brought against it – its sexist and elitist bias, its formulation of too neat a rupture between a pre-war and a modern, ironic consciousness – it is worth noting that it still forms a point of return, described by one of its most astute critics, Daniel Pick, as 'compelling' and 'deeply evocative', in *War Machine: The Rationalisation of Slaughter in the*

account, as has often been pointed out, was that it became the *defining* narrative of the First World War, confining it narrowly to the trench experience of a group of educated, mostly middle-class British officer-writers. This bias has been challenged in recent years by the 'second wave' of war criticism which has been marked by two important trends: interdisciplinarity and diversification of concern, with an emphasis on detail. 'There were others who suffered, whose voices we must also attend', notes Jay Winter whose *Sites of Memory, Sites of Mourning: The Great War in European Cultural History* (1995) has been seminal to the reconceptualisation of the First World War in recent years.[24] Over the last decade or so, scholars have uncovered further areas of interest: the experience of women and of male civilians; the war on the Eastern Front; the recovery of the colonial war experience; the ordeal of the conscientious objectors, military deserters, labourers, stretcher-bearers and medical staff.[25] This diversification has been a much-needed and welcome development. At the same time, it would be unfortunate if, as a hasty reaction against a previous generation of critics who laid an exaggerated emphasis on the soldier-writer as representing the 'truth of war', it led us to disparage or dismiss the trench narratives. The trench accounts, it is true, cannot be used as the only narrative of the war or turned into a metaphor for twentieth-century consciousness but, instead of simply challenging them, it is time that we try to understand and analyse 'why those repeated images persist'.[26] They have continued to inspire writers from Susan Hill and Jennifer Johnston in the 1970s to Sebastian Faulks and Pat Barker in the 1990s. On 4 August 2004, to mark the ninetieth anniversary of England's entry into the war, only four of

---

*Modern Age* (New Haven: Yale University Press, 1993), 4. Two works to develop Fussell's thesis of 'modernist' consciousness are Modris Eksteins, *Rites of Spring: The Great War and the Birth of the Modern Age* (New York: Bantham Books, 1989) and Samuel Hynes, *A War Imagined: The First World War and English Culture* (London: Bodley Head, 1991).

24  Jay Winter, 'Shell-shock and the Cultural History of the Great War', *Journal of Contemporary History*, 35, 1 (2000), 10–11. In *Sites of Memory, Sites of Mourning* (Cambridge: Cambridge University Press, 1995), Winter through a wide array of sources analyses a complex traditional vocabulary of mourning, powerfully challenging Fussell's modernist thrust.

25  Major works, relevant to my study, are mentioned in the respective chapters. For a survey of recent historical works, see Gail Braybon (ed.), *Evidence, History and the Great War: Historians and the Impact of 1914–18* (Oxford: Berghahn Books, 2003), 1–29; for an overview of literary criticism, see James Campbell, 'Interpreting the War', in *The Cambridge Companion to the Literature of the First World War*, ed. Vincent Sherry (Cambridge: Cambridge University Press, 2004), 261–79; hereafter abbreviated *Cambridge Companion*.

26  Sharon Ouditt, 'Myths, Memories, and Monuments: Reimagining the First World War', in *Cambridge Companion*, 245.

the surviving twenty-three veterans were able to come to the Cenotaph: as they honoured their fallen comrades, a crowd of around 1,000 people broke into spontaneous applause and some even wept.[27] These last survivors curiously affect even those of us who have been alerted to the problematic ideology of 'combat gnosticism'.[28]

The present work brings together men and women, combatants and nurses, in the belief that all are important to an understanding of the war experience. Since bodily experience is my theme, I have concentrated on men and women for whom the material conditions of everyday life – the immediate, sensory world – were altered radically by the war and often came to define their subjectivities: private, officer, stretcher-bearer, ambulance driver and nurse. Allen, in *Toward the Flame*, notes, 'The feel of warm bodies, and blood, the quiet patience and confidence of the men, brought a realisation of life in that hour that I shall never forget'; coming out of the operating theatre 'with my hands covered with blood', Vera Brittain realises that she will never be the same person again.[29] I have focused on men and women within the zone of horror in order to examine the physical and emotional aspects of such encounters – their relation to human subjectivity and literary form – without any attempt to idealise these experiences and I write with full awareness that this is only one of the many narratives of the war.[30] While the sensory impressions are central to the iconography of the First World War, here I have tried to understand them in their historical, emotional and literary contexts and to analyse why and how they continue to haunt us. I read diary entries, journals and memoirs by ordinary soldiers and nurses alongside published works by writers such as Owen, Sassoon or Brittain in order to retain contiguity between daily life in the trenches and the hospitals and literary writing, as well as to have a more broad-based view, to find out how daily

---

27 'The Last Survivors', *The Independent*, 5 August 2004, 1.
28 James Campbell, 'Combat Gnosticism: The Ideology of First World War Poetry Criticism', *New Literary History*, 30 (1999), 203–15.
29 Hervey Allen, *Toward the Flame: A War Diary* (London: Victor Gollancz, 1934), 57; Vera Brittain, *Testament of Youth* (1933; London: Virago, 1999), 215–16.
30 If the experiential dimension has unfortunately been used in the past to marginalise certain groups of people, in recent years, civilian war experiences of both men and women have been powerfully addressed. See Tate, *Modernism*; Paul Delany, *D. H. Lawrence's Nightmare: The Writer and His Circle in the Years of the Great War* (Sussex: Harvester, 1979); Margaret Darrow, *French Women and the First World War: War Stories of the Home Front* (New York: Berg, 2000); Debra Rae Cohen, *Remapping the Home Front: Locating Citizenship in British Women's Great War Fiction* (Boston: Northeastern University Press, 2002).

experiences affect different groups of people and in turn inhabit different kinds of discourse.

In the last few years, whether as backlash against the increasing abstraction of poststructuralist thought or theory's belated acknowledgement of the phenomenological tradition, there has been a sudden swell of interest in the senses. Within literary criticism, there has been a move towards a more physical understanding of past literatures and cultures, whether through ideas such as mess within a particular period, or through affective close reading of poetry.[31] In *The Book of Skin* (2004), Steven Connor has drawn attention to the 'contemporary fascination with the powers of the skin', whether it is through the 'erotics of texture, tissue and tegument' in certain strands of critical and cultural theory, or more generally, in 'modern experience' – in practices such as cosmetic care, body-piercing and tattooing.[32] In his influential essay on museum culture, 'Resonance and Wonder' (1990), Stephen Greenblatt points out the 'resonance' that certain material objects of the past hold for us – the threadbare fabric of an old chair or a vase broken by Marcel Proust – not because of their aesthetic value but because 'of use, the imprint of the human body on the artefact'; more recently, he has suggested how historical anecdotes and vignettes provide for him 'touch of the real', giving insights into 'the contact zone', the 'charmed space where the *genius literarius* could be conjured into existence'.[33] *Touch and Intimacy* shares the twin impulse towards the material and the testimonial, but grounds them both in the world of the senses.

In the early decades of the twentieth century, the typewriter severed the writer's hand from the act of writing.[34] In today's world of computers, there is no tangible relationship between the hand that taps at the keyboard and the final printed page: technology rather than death seems to give the lie to any universal validity for Keats's 'this warm scribe my

---

31 The two books I have in mind are David Trotter, *Cooking With Mud: The Idea of Mess in Nineteenth-Century Art and Fiction* (Oxford: Oxford University Press, 2000) and Susan Stewart, *Poetry and the Fate of the Senses* (Chicago: University of Chicago Press, 2003). See also Sara Danius, *The Senses of Modernism: Technology, Perception, and Aesthetics* (Ithaca: Cornell University Press, 2002); Elizabeth D. Harvey (ed.), *Sensible Flesh: On Touch in Early Modern Culture* (Philadelphia: University of Pennsylvania Press, 2003); Eve Kosofsky Sedgwick, *Touching Feeling: Affect, Pedagogy, Performativity* (Durham, NC: Duke University Press, 2003).

32 Steven Connor, *The Book of Skin* (London: Reaktion, 2004), 9–10.

33 Stephen Greenblatt, *Learning to Curse: Essays in Early Modern Culture* (New York: Routledge, 1990), 172 (161–83); 'Touch of the Real', *Representations*, 59 (Summer 1997), 29 (14–29).

34 See Martin Heidegger, *Parmenides*, trans. Andre Schuwer and Richard Rojcewicz (Bloomington: Indiana University Press, 1992), 81–2.

hand'.[35] But the relationship between the two remains infrangible in the world of the archives. We leaf through manuscripts, each alone, in palpable relation to past lives, past bodies. Some of the letters draw attention to the physical conditions of writing: 'I am now sitting in our tent half-dressed writing this, the rain is coming through a bit & that accounts for the blots'; similarly, Rosenberg writes, 'You must excuse these blots. I'm writing from pandemonium with a rotten pen.'[36] In the diary of Private A. Reid, the date 'Sunday 29th July, 1917' is carefully inscribed in anticipation of the day's record but only a blank space exists: Reid was killed before the day ended (Figure I.3). An empty page thus exposes the 'truth of war' more devastatingly than all the words that have gone before.[37] Lieutenant Ingle, writing at 7 pm on 30 June 1916 (the night before the Somme offensive), seemed to have a sense of foreboding. The final entry in his diary reads like a covenant, 'This ends the diary before the push as I must pack up. Ever yours, Ro.': he was killed at 7:15 the next morning.[38] Archival work requires the handling of documents as well as reading. As we open the dark brown pocket notebook of H. Gladstone, two loose pages – a hand-drawn map and a little diagram of a clock face with some Morse code signals – fall out of a curious little flap (Figure I.4). At the end of the little leather-bound and gold-edged diary of T. Dalziel, started originally in Dumdum, Calcutta, is tucked the tiny pencil that Dalziel had used to record his daily experiences in France (Figure I.5).[39] The much-creased Protection Certificate and Certificate of Identity of Arnold Simson lies on top of his war notebook (Figure I.6). G. W. Hayman writes to his 'dearest Marie' two letters patterned in the form of kisses (Figure I.7).[40] In fact, our complex encounter with 'meaning and materiality'[41] is deeply felt as we go through the documents of the nurses in the Imperial War Museum archives. We find not just a variety of written responses to the war but certificates, metal badges, photographs, postcards and ribbons. The material tokens of

---

35 'The Fall of Hyperion: A Vision', in *John Keats: The Poems*, ed. David Bromwich (London: Everyman's Library, 1992), 351.
36 J. Fraser, 'Letters', IWM 86/19/1; Rosenberg, IWM PP/MCR/C38.
37 A. Reid, 'Diary', IWM 87/8/1.
38 R. G. Ingle, 'Diary', IWM 77/96/1.
39 H. Gladstone, 'Diary', IWM 86/2/1; T. Dalziel, 'Diary', IWM 86/51/1.
40 A. Simson, 'First World War Note Book', IWM Misc. 41, Item 731; G. W. Hayman, 'Papers', IWM, 87/51/1.
41 Susan Stewart, *On Longing: Narratives of the Miniature, the Gigantic, the Souvenir, the Collection* (Durham, NC: Duke University Press, 1993), 44.

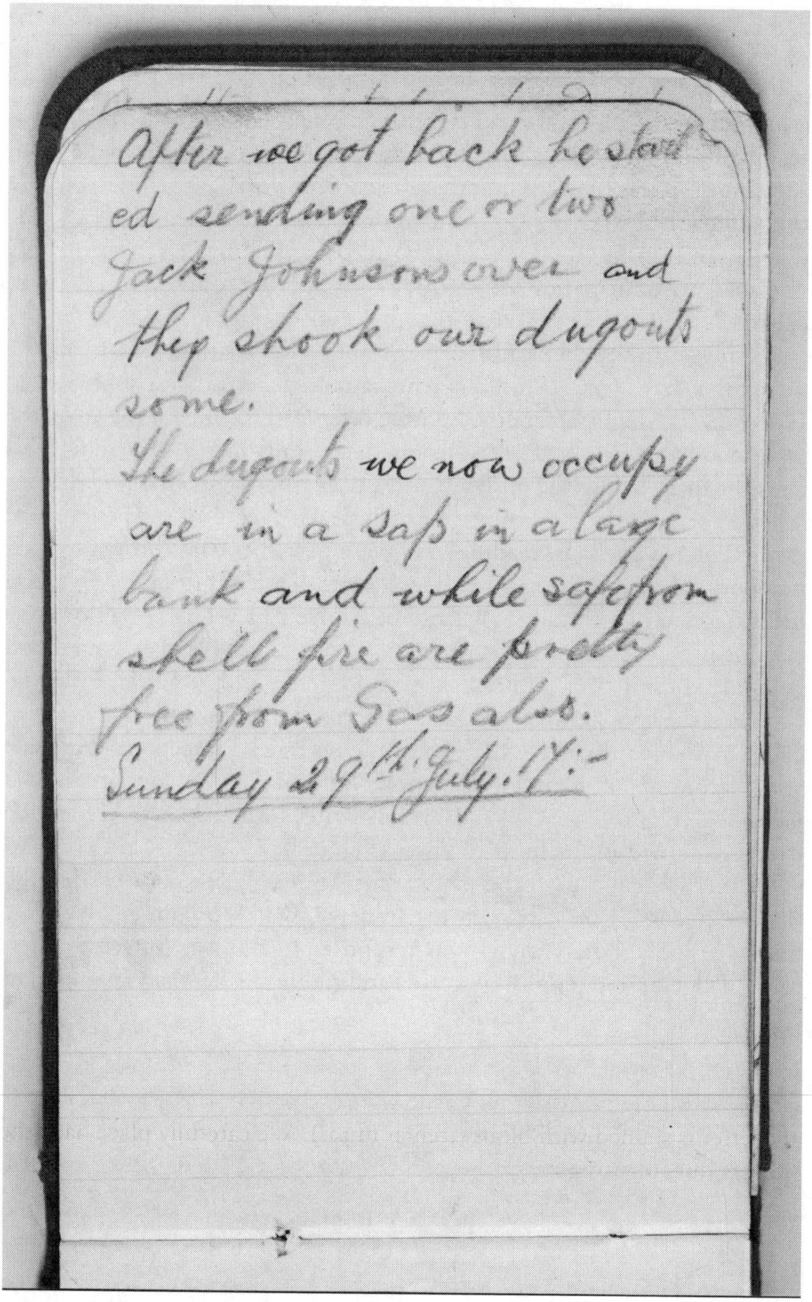

After we got back he started sending one or two
Jack Johnsons over and
they shook our dugouts
some.
The dugouts we now occupy
are in a sap in a large
bank and while safe from
shell fire are pretty
free from Gas also.
Sunday 29th July 17:--

Figure I.3. The final entry from the diary of A. Reid, 87/8/1, IWM (DOC).

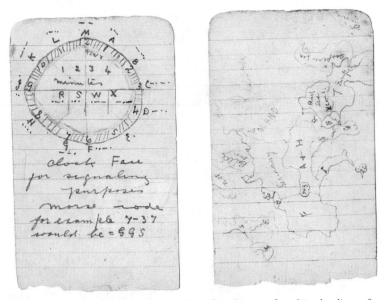

Figure I.4. A hand-drawn map and clock-face diagram found in the diary of
H. Gladstone, 86/2/1, IWM (DOC).

memory, they show not only the extent of women's participation in the
war but also the enduring meaning of the war years for them.[42]

Opening the file of Private George Bennett, it is hard to know what to
examine first: a Certificate of Employment, giving regimental details; a
Certificate of Transfer and a Certificate of Identity, torn at the edges; a
soiled Field Service postcard stamped 16 November 1915, reporting ad-
mission to hospital; and a fragile envelope, marked 'On Active Service'
and stamped 16 December 1916, addressed to Mrs Bennett (Figure I.8).[43]
As we try to take the letter cautiously out of the envelope, our fingers
encounter something leafy and crumbly: it is a bunch of blue and white
flowers, the dried stalks still green, pressed onto the letter. 'Some flowers
from outside our hut', Bennett had lovingly written to his wife in
smudged blue ink on the regiment paper as he pressed the flowers, and
the letter is stained with blobs (trench mud?). We carefully place back the
flowers our intrusive fingers have pulled out of the envelope: the process
is intimate and unsettling.

42 See 'Nurse's Autograph Book World War I', IWM Misc. 24 Item 464; Ruth Whitaker, IWM, 76/
123/1 for an interesting collection of documents and objects.
43 G. H. Bennet, 'First World War Papers', IWM Misc. 265.

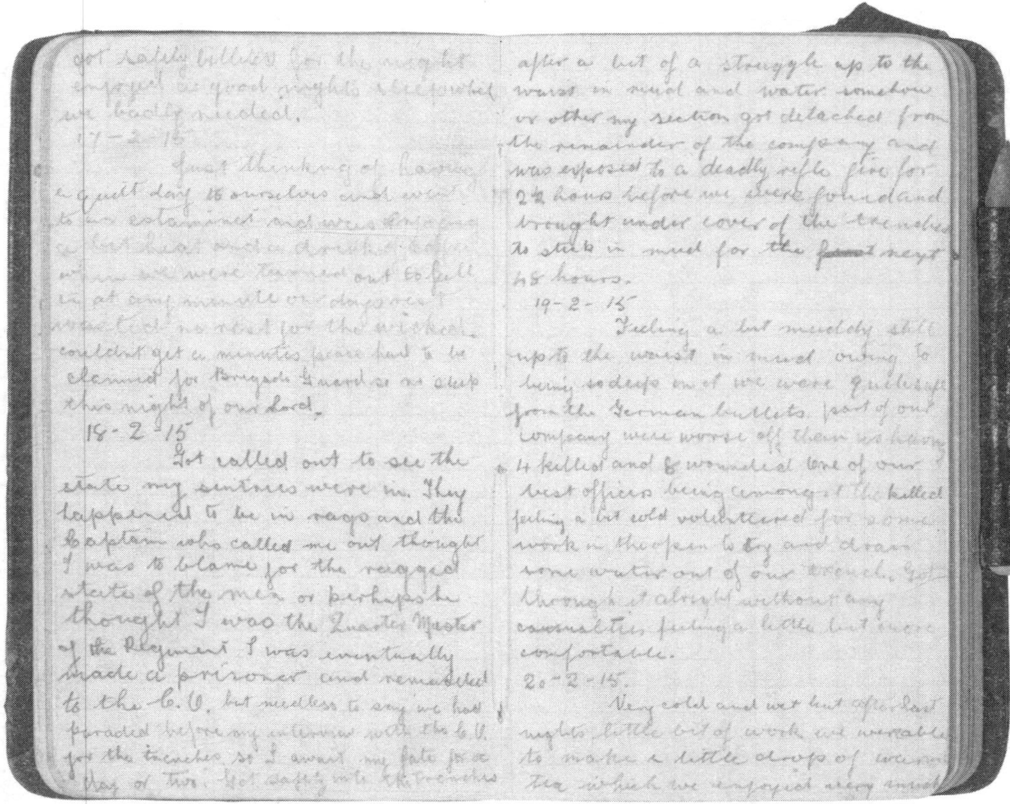

Figure I.5. A page from the diary of T. Dalziel, 86/51/1, IWM (DOC).

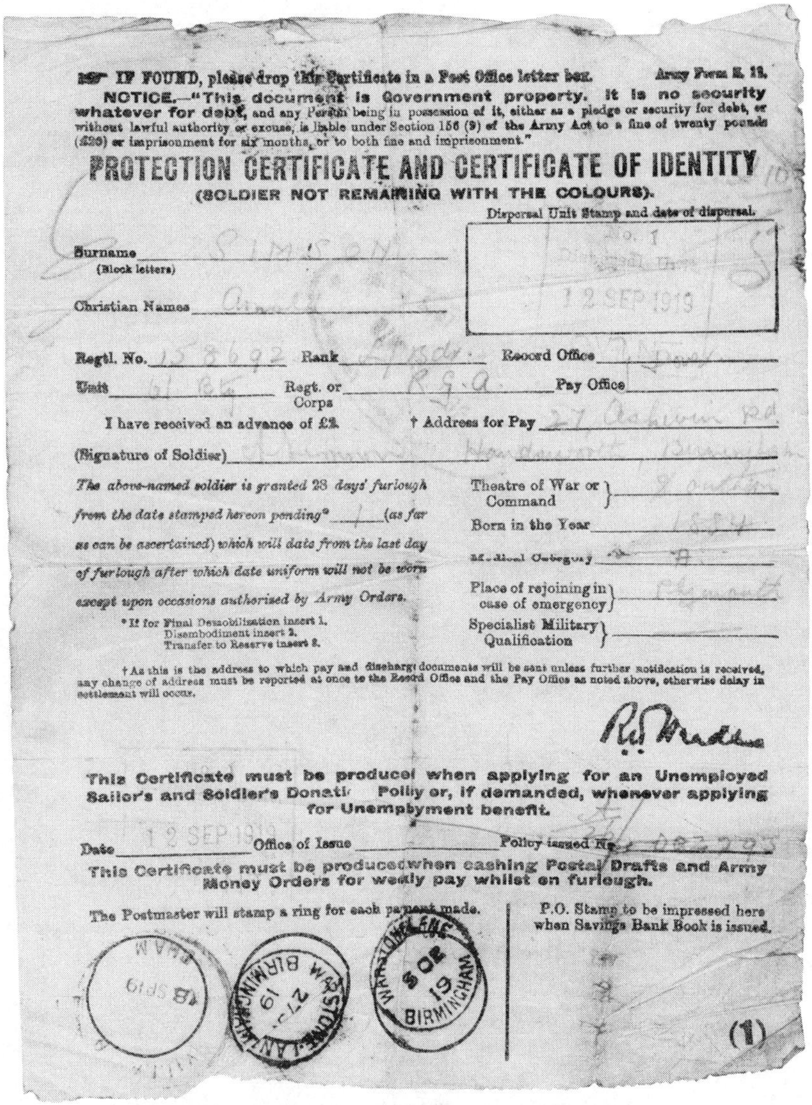

☞ IF FOUND, please drop this Certificate in a Post Office letter box. Army Form Z. 11.

NOTICE.—"This document is Government property. It is no security whatever for debt, and any Person being in possession of it, either as a pledge or security for debt, or without lawful authority or excuse, is liable under Section 156 (9) of the Army Act to a fine of twenty pounds (£20) or imprisonment for six months, or to both fine and imprisonment."

PROTECTION CERTIFICATE AND CERTIFICATE OF IDENTITY

(SOLDIER NOT REMAINING WITH THE COLOURS).

Dispersal Unit Stamp and date of dispersal.

No. 1 Dispersal Unit

12 SEP 1919

Surname (Block letters) SIMSON

Christian Names Arnold

Regtl. No. 158692 Rank Gnr.

Record Office

Unit 61 Bty Regt. or Corps R.G.A.

Pay Office

I have received an advance of £2. † Address for Pay 27 Ashview Rd.

(Signature of Soldier)

*The above-named soldier is granted 28 days' furlough from the date stamped hereon pending* 1 (as far as can be ascertained) which will date from the last day of furlough after which date uniform will not be worn except upon occasions authorised by Army Orders.*

* If for Final Demobilization insert 1.
Disembodiment insert 2.
Transfer to Reserve insert 3.

Theatre of War or Command

Born in the Year 1884

Medical Category A

Place of rejoining in case of emergency

Specialist Military Qualification

† As this is the address to which pay and discharge documents will be sent unless further notification is received, any change of address must be reported at once to the Record Office and the Pay Office as noted above, otherwise delay in settlement will occur.

This Certificate must be produced when applying for an Unemployed Sailor's and Soldier's Donation Policy or, if demanded, whenever applying for Unemployment benefit.

Date 12 SEP 1919 Office of Issue Policy issued No.

This Certificate must be produced when cashing Postal Drafts and Army Money Orders for weekly pay whilst on furlough.

The Postmaster will stamp a ring for each payment made.

P.O. Stamp to be impressed here when Savings Bank Book is issued.

WARSTOCK LANE BIRMINGHAM

(1)

Figure I.6. Protection Certificate and Certificate of Identity of Arnold Simson, Misc. 41, Item 731, IWM(DOC).

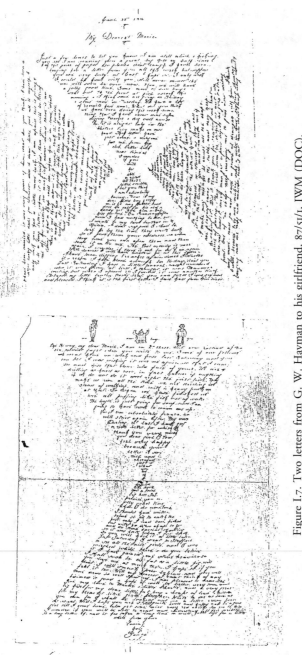

Figure I.7. Two letters from G. W. Hayman to his girlfriend, 87/51/1, IWM (DOC).

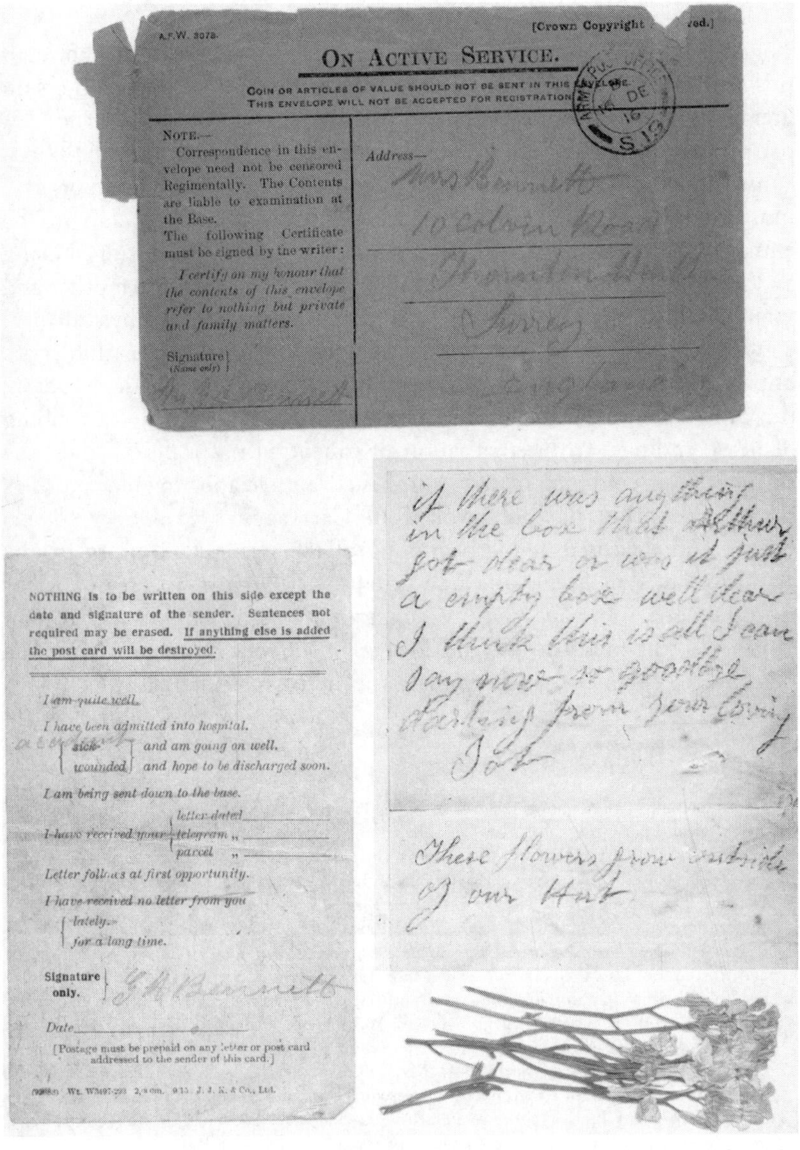

Figure I.8. Envelope, trench post-card and letter from G. H. Bennett to his wife, with some pressed flowers, Misc. 265, IWM (DOC).

*

Touch is the most intimate and elusive of the human senses: it is through this sense that we have access to the reality of our own bodies, the skin literally giving us 'both the shape of the world and our shape in it'.[44] A person may be born blind, deaf and mute but in order to live, the skin – constituting 20 per cent of the body weight and the largest human organ – must respond to touch, which is the earliest sense to develop in the embryo. Different kinds of bodily contact – holding, caressing, kissing and feeding – underlie the first communications between the mother and infant, and these tactile processes are fundamental to our physical, psychological and social development. Language is born as the child cries out to the mother for contact and comfort; language breaks down before the experience of physical pain, felt as hammering, burning, throbbing of nerve endings, an internalisation of touch; and as a person dies, the skin becomes cold and inert.[45] Our visual appreciation regularly brings the tactile within its fold, evoked in Caravaggio's *Doubting Thomas* (1602), and theorised at the beginning of the twentieth century by the art historian Alois Riegl who drew attention to 'haptic' vision in ancient Egyptian art.[46] In *The Senses Considered as Perceptual Systems* (1968), James Gibson put forward the idea of a '"haptic" system': 'It is the perceptual system by which animals and men are *literally* in touch with

44 Steven Connor, *Skin*, 36. Some major works to address the issue of touch and human subjectivity are Merleau-Ponty, *Phenomenology of Perception*; Ashley Montagu, *Touching: The Human Significance of the Skin* (New York: Columbia University Press, 1971); Didier Anzieu, *The Skin Ego*, trans. Chris Turner (New Haven: Yale University Press, 1989). More recently, Jacques Derrida has written on the subject in *Le Toucher: Jean-Luc Nancy* (Paris: Galilée, 2000), but the English translation (Stanford University Press, 2005) is forthcoming. See also Laura U. Marks, *Touch: Sensuous Theory and Multisensory Media* (Minneapolis: Minnesota University Press, 2002) and Constance Classen, ed., *The Book of Touch* (Oxford: Berg, 2005).

45 For some insightful approaches to questions of touch and literary subjectivity, see Gillian Beer, 'Four Bodies on the Beagle: Touch, Sight and Writing in a Darwin Letter', in *Textuality and Sexuality: Reading Theories and Practices*. ed. Judith Still and Michael Worton (Manchester: Manchester University Press, 1993), 116–32; Maud Ellman, 'Skinscapes in Lotus Eaters', in *Ulysses: (En)Gendered Perspectives*, ed. Kimberly Derlin and Marilyn Reizbaum (Columbia, SC: South Carolina University Press, 1999), 51–65: and Angela Leighton, 'Touching Forms: Tennyson and Aestheticism', *Essays in Criticism*, 52, 1 (January 2002), 56–75.

46 Alois Riegl (1858–1905) used the phrase 'haptic' plane in *Late Roman Art Industry*, first published in 1901 (Rome: Giorgio Bretschneider Editure, 1985, trans. Rolf Winkes). In an article of 1902, he explained that while the phrase 'tactile' vision was too literally 'touching', 'physiology has long since introduced the more fitting designation "haptic" (from *haptein – to fasten*)'. See Margaret Iversen, *Alois Riegl: Art History and Theory* (Cambridge, Mass.: MIT Press, 1993), 9. The *OED* defines the word 'haptic' (from the Greek word meaning able to come into contact with, to fasten) as 1. Of, pertaining to the sense of touch or tactile sensations; 2. Having a greater

the environment'.[47] Language is full of references to touch: all our words are in some way an attempt to *reach out* to people. We speak of being 'in touch' with our friends or being in 'safe hands'; we refer 'warmly' to our loved ones, are 'touched' and 'moved' by people or experiences, we 'jump out of our skin' in fright and some things get 'under our skin'. Fundamental to our ideas of the self, touch is almost impossible to express: that is perhaps why the entry under touch is one of the longest in the *Oxford English Dictionary*. One is reminded of Diderot's blind man who famously said that if he were granted a wish, it would not be for eyesight but for a pair of arms that would be long enough to reach out to the moon.[48]

Indeed, there is something quite unearthly in the immensity of its reach: we get to know through touch alone – or at times in close conjunction with vision or sound – size, texture, temperature, weight, hardness/softness, viscosity, depth, flatness, movement, composition and space.[49] The cutaneous layers also point to what lies within. Kicking, kissing, clinging, caressing, hitting, hugging, holding, shoving, stroking, soothing: changes in gestures and dermal pressure alert us to the complexity of our emotional and affective life, govern our relationship to other beings, both human and animal. It is this inclusiveness that paradoxically leads to the denigration of touch in the hierarchy of the senses. 'The primary form', notes Aristotle in *De Anima*, 'is touch, which belongs to all animals': some animals have all or certain of the senses, 'others only one, the most indispensable, touch'. Two particular questions trouble him: is touch one sense or a 'group of senses' for 'what can be tasted is always something that can be touched'; moreover, is the flesh the organ or the medium of touch, does it lie inward or not? Touch not only confuses the distinction between the different sense organs by spilling onto taste but seems to challenge the very principle underlying it: 'Every sense seems to be concerned with a single pair of contraries, white and black

---

dependence on sensations of touch than on sight. The *OED* notes the first use of the word in 1890; *Mind*, 48 (1939) associates it with 'tactile aesthetics' that combines 'touch' with 'kinaesthetic experiences'. See also Trotter, 'Stereoscopy: Modernism and the "Haptic"', *Critical Quarterly*, 46, 4 (2004), 38–58.

47 James J. Gibson, *The Senses Considered as Perceptual Systems* (London: George Allen & Unwin, 1968), 97. He further notes: 'The haptic system, then, is an apparatus by which the individual gets information about both the environment and his body. He feels an object relative to the body and the body relative to the object'. Gibson explores the idea through different experiments (97–115).

48 Denis Diderot, 'Letter on the Blind for the Use of Those who See', in *Thoughts on the Interpretation of Nature and Other Philosophical Works* (Manchester: Clinamen Press, 1999), 153.

49 Ruth Finnegan, *Communicating* (London: Routledge, 2002), 197.

for sight, sharp and flat for hearing, bitter and sweet for taste; but in the field of what is tangible we find several such pairs, hot cold, dry moist, hard soft, &c'.[50] The earliest commentary on touch happens to be one of the most acute. In fact, his tantalising metaphor of an 'air-envelope growing around the body' resonates in the twentieth century with Anzieu's complex, psychoanalytic account of the skin ego as a psychic 'envelope' which develops as a phantasmatic counterpart to the body.[51] The immediate impetus for Anzieu's work was Freud.

In *The Ego and The Id* (1923), Freud suggests an integral relation between the formation of the ego and processes of touch. In a footnote added to the text in 1927, Freud noted, 'The ego is ultimately derived from bodily sensations, chiefly from those springing from the surface of the body. It may thus be regarded as a mental projection of the surface of the body.'[52] Following Freud, there has been work on the relationship between touch and human subjectivity from different disciplines. Touch, to Merleau-Ponty, is a powerful example of the reversibility of the flesh. In *The Visible and the Invisible* (1964), he gives his classic account of the 'double sensation' – of the right hand touching the left hand – arguing that touch unfixes our categories of the subject and the object, transitivity and intransitivity. This sense of contact and mutuality has been developed with lyricism by feminists such as Irigaray and Kristeva who relate it to a lost, forgotten world, often associated with the mother; in recent critical discourse, touch is valorised as going beyond Cartesian dualism, non-teleological, infinitely expansive.[53] Yet the association of the tactile with the feminine is reminiscent – or a radical reconceptualisation – of Sartre's evocation of slime at the end of *Being and Nothingness*: 'The gluey, the sticky, the hazy etc. . . . all reveal to him modes of prepsychic and pre-sexual being which he will spend the rest of his life explaining'.[54] I shall engage with Sartre's text in the first chapter in

50 Aristotle, 'On the Soul (De Anima)', *The Complete Works of Aristotle*, ed. Jonathan Barnes (Princeton: Princeton University Press, 1984), 658, 659, 672.
51 Anzieu, *The Skin Ego*. To him, just as the skin is an envelope, shielding the entrails from the world, the 'skin ego' contains, defines and protects the psyche and he enumerates its nine functions. Anzieu's ideas have been developed suggestively by Naomi Segal in her forthcoming book, *Consensuality*.
52 Sigmund Freud, *The Standard Edition of the Complete Psychological Works*, ed. and trans. James Strachey *et al.* (London: Hogarth, 1953–74), XIX, 26. Hereafter Freud, *SE*.
53 Luce Irigaray, *An Ethics of Sexual Difference* (1984), trans. Carolyn Burke and Gillian C. Gill (Ithaca: Cornell Univeristy Press, 1993); Julia Kristeva, *Proust and the Sense of Time*, trans. Stephen Bann (London: Faber, 1993). For a survey of the various philosophical and psychoanalytic discourses on touch, see the introduction to Harvey (ed.), *Sensible Flesh*, 1–21.
54 Jean-Paul Sartre, *Being and Nothingness: An Essay on Phenomenological Ontology*, trans. Hazel E. Barnes (1943; London: Routledge, 1989), 612.

context of First World War trench mud, though visceral horror rather than 'tactile fascination' with slime will determine my critical focus. The aim of that chapter is not a Sartrean reading, but rather to facilitate a dialogue between phenomenological writing and war literature.

What are the relations between touch and warfare? Modern techno-logical warfare may be said to represent the ultimate de-personalisation and perversion of this intimate sense as bodies are ripped apart by in-dustrial weaponry. As early as 1832, Clausewitz, in *On War*, used the concept of 'friction' to distinguish 'real war' from 'war on paper', under-lining its physical, contingent reality and portraying it as 'movement in a resistant medium': 'Just as a man immersed in water is unable to perform with ease and regularity the most natural and simplest movement, that of walking, so too in war, with ordinary powers, one cannot keep even to the line of mediocrity'.[55] Clausewitz's metaphor was realised in the First World War trenches as they were often literally inundated with water which, mixed with mud, impeded the simplest movement. An officer of the 19th London Regiment at Ypres Salient in December 1916 recorded that it took him three hours to walk just 400 yards.[56] Central to an understanding of the perceptual processes of the First World War soldier are the peculiar conditions of underground warfare, an area explored by Eric Leed in his important study, *No Man's Land: Combat and Identity in World War I* (1979). Trying to understand the 'transformations of per-sonality' in trench warfare, Leed notes: 'The impact of war upon the human sensorium of combatants is the point where one must begin to understand the necessity of illusion, fantasy, and myth'.[57] He concentrates primarily on two sensory modalities or changes: curtailment in the field of vision, creating an atmosphere of anxiety and uncertainty, and a sudden, massive expansion in noise, associated with chaos and the supernatural. The first two chapters of my study develop the phenomenological aspect of Leed's study but move the focus from vision and sound to the sense of touch, and connect the sensory world of war to literary and cultural history. Moreover, the visual topography of the everyday world, I shall argue, was replaced by the haptic geography of the trenches and mud was a prime agent in this change. In an atmosphere of darkness, danger and

---

55  Carl Von Clausewitz, *On War*, ed. and intro. Anatol Rapoport (1832; Harmondsworth: Penguin, 1982), 165.
56  Quoted in Jon Ellis, *Eye-deep in Hell: Life in the Trenches 1914–1918* (London: Croom Helm, 1977), 44.
57  Eric Leed, *No Man's Land: Combat and Identity in World War I* (Cambridge: Cambridge University Press, 1979), 117. Hereafter Leed, *NML*.

uncertainty, sights, sounds and even smells are encountered as material presences against the flesh. This becomes evident in the varying use of the word 'thickly': Owen's 'thick green light'; Barbusse's 'smell thickly' of earth; Jünger's 'thickened' sound of explosions; Ford's 'thick darkness'.[58] Close analysis of how such moments are represented in the writings of the time, both literary and historical, will help us to understand better what Sassoon called the 'texture' of trench-life, or in the words of a recent theorist, the 'thickness' of experience.[59]

If touch, as in Jünger and Barbusse, is related to heightened processes of perception, situations of crisis also foster unique moments of intimacy. Consider the following two accounts, the first from the memoirs of Henry Williamson who fought in the war, and the second from the memoirs of Mary Britnieva, a young Anglo-Russian nurse:

[I saw] a Saxon boy half crushed under a shattered tank, moaning 'Mutter, Mutter, Mutter', out of ghastly grey lips. A British soldier, wounded in the leg, and sitting near by, hearing the words, and dragging himself to the dying boy, takes his cold hand and says: 'All right, son, it's all right. Mother's here with you.'[60]

Suddenly he raised himself: 'Hold me, Sestritza,' he said in a frightened voice, 'hold me tight, it is coming!' I put my arms round him holding him up with all my strength. 'Now kiss me, Sestritza,' he said. I kissed him. Then slowly he made the sign of the cross, and in a few moments he was dead.[61]

In spite of the very different contexts, both accounts insist on the closeness of the writing to personal experience. In each, as words fail and life ebbs away, the body moves in to fill the void: touch becomes the final antidote against the desolation of death, overriding political hostility or norms of professional behaviour.

The dying cry of the boy and the reciprocal gesture of the British soldier show, beyond the poignancy of the moment, the central presence of the mother in the emotional lives of these men: indeed, it was to their mother that the men wrote most often, as with Wilfred Owen who wrote 554 letters to his mother.[62] Similarly, the very words 'Hold me,

---

58 'Dulce Et Decorum Est', in Owen, *CP&F*, 140; Henri Barbusse, *I Saw It Myself* (New York, 1928), 19, quoted in Leed, *NML*, 80; Ernst Jünger, *Storm of Steel*, trans. Michael Hofmann (1920; London: Allen Lane, 2003), 161 (hereafter abbreviated Jünger); Ford Madox Ford, *A Man Could Stand Up*, Part III of *Parade's End* (1924–8; Manchester: Carcanet, 1997), 563.
59 Merleau-Ponty, *Phenomenology*, 503.
60 Henry Williamson, *The Wet Flanders Plain* (1929; Norwich: Glidden Books, 1987), 18.
61 Mary Britneva, *One Woman's Story* (London: Arthur Barker Ltd, 1934), 18–19.
62 See Mike Roper, 'Maternal Relations: Moral Manliness and Emotional Survival in Letters Home during the First World War', in *Masculinities in Politics and War: Rewritings of Modern History*,

Sestritza' ('little sister') rather than just 'Sestra' ('sister') or the more formal 'Sestra Miloserdiya' ('gracious sister', as nurses were called in Russia) show how the nurse–patient relationship is transformed into a personal familial bond: the last desperate clinging onto another human being becomes life's last stand against the terror of the unknown. The final kiss of blessing is as much an act of resignation as of charity. Though gender operates within both these acts, they are equally informed by a recognition of human vulnerability, empathy and caritas.

Masculinity, camaraderie and eroticism have been the subject of intense discussion in First World War studies, explored in recent years by Joanna Bourke in *Dismembering the Male: Men's Bodies, Britain and the Great War* (1996).[63] A recurring sentiment in war letters, diaries and memoirs is that comradeship made life bearable in the trenches: men nursed each other when ill; provided support in times of crisis; during the long winter nights in the First World War, they were even known to curl up under a common groundsheet as the snow thickened and the guns roared.[64] In *The Sexual History of the First World War* (1930), Magnus Hirschfeld recounts an episode uncannily similar to Williamson's account: here, a German infantryman holds 'a bottle to the lips of the delirious dying [English boy] who kept on crying, "Mother, are you here"' and 'softly stroked the feverish eyebrow of the youth'.[65] How far can such gestures be understood through the then contemporary concept of the 'urning soul', as Hirschfeld tried to do, or through the more recent insights provided by queer theory? It is important in this regard to remember that amidst daily death and degradation, the body was primarily an object of pain rather than that of desire. This is not to deny the homoerotic intensity of trench life, evident in the works of Sassoon and Owen, but to suggest that romance and eroticism in the trenches have to be attuned to a different emotional key, taking place against the hovering presence of danger and death. Touch helps to open

ed. S. Dudink, K. Hagerman and J. Tosh (Manchester: Manchester University Press, 2004), 295–315.

63 See also Adrian Caesar's provocative literary study, *Taking it Like a Man: Suffering, Sexuality and the War Poets* (Manchester: Manchester University Press, 1993); and Sarah Cole, *Modernism, Male Friendship and the First World War* (Cambridge: Cambridge University Press, 2003).

64 A. J. Abraham, 'Memoirs of a Non-hero', 1914–18, IWM P191, 14–15. See Joanna Bourke, *Dismembering the Male: Men's Bodies, Britain and the Great War* (London: Reaktion, 1996), 124–70.

65 Magnus Hirschfeld, *The Sexual History of the World War* (1930; New York: Cadillac, 1946), 121.

up to our understanding the ambiguous zone between diffuse homoeroticism and more conscious acts of homosexual intention. Touch is also
aligned to emotions such as pity, vulnerability or maternity. I am here
arguing for a more nuanced understanding of gender and sexuality.
Chapter 4 examines the poetry of Wilfred Owen who describes this
intense homosocial world with particular power; I focus on representations of the hand in his poetry and trace the connections between sound,
eros and violence.

The hand is a recurring trope in the memoirs of the nurses, being the
usual point of contact with the injured male body. Hands dress wounds,
clean instruments, habitually comfort, may even cause fresh pain, are
often disgusted and in rare moments of leisure, the hand writes its varied
life. 'You are continually doing things', writes Borden, 'with your
hands'.[66] The touch of the nurse does not have the history of comradeship
or of shared adventure, as between men; in fact, it is the gap between
the two worlds that constantly troubles the young nurse. Vera Brittain
writes about 'that terrible barrier of knowledge by which War cut off the
men who possessed it from the women who, in spite of the love that they
gave and received, remained in ignorance', a sentiment echoed by Rose
Macaulay: 'We are shut about by guarding walls'.[67] However, as Tylee has
noted, 'it was the construction of reality of the War that came between
men and women'.[68] Nursing became one of the experiential modes
through which such a perceived 'barrier' could be bridged: not just over
gender but at times over political hostilities, as when a Prussian officer
held out his 'emaciated hand' to Brittain and said, 'I tank you, Sister'.[69]
The revisionist literary historians Gilbert and Gubar refashioned the war
as a 'climactic episode in some battle of the sexes' in the 1980s, arguing
that women felt liberated, psychologically, financially and even sexually,
but subsequent feminist critics have challenged this thesis, highlighting
the traumatic aspects of the war for women as well.[70] The memoirs of the

66 Borden, *FZ,* 124.
67 Brittain, *Testament,* 215; Rose Macaulay, 'Picnic', in *The Virago Book of Women's War Poetry and
Verse,* ed. Catherine Reilly (London: Virago, 1997), 67.
68 Claire Tylee, *The Great War and Women's Consciousness: Images of Militarism and Womanhood in
Women's Writings 1914–1918* (Basingstoke: Macmillan, 1990), 55.
69 Brittain, *Testament,* 376.
70 Sandra Gilbert's influential article 'Soldier's Heart: Literary Men, Literary Women, and the Great
War', part of her book *No Man's Land* (New Haven: Yale University Press, 1988) first appeared in
*Signs* (1983) and was reprinted in Margaret Higonnet *et al.* (eds.), *Behind the Lines: Gender and the
Two World Wars* (New Haven: Yale University Press, 1987), 197–226. Her thesis has been
powerfully attacked by Tylee in '"Maleness Run Riot": The Great War and Women's Resistance
to Militarism', *Women's Studies International Forum,* 11, 3 (1988), 199–210.

nurses capture at once the exhilaration of service and the agony of witnessing. The hand might be said to mediate between these twin worlds; it reached out also to forbidden zones of the male anatomy. The material effects of war thus confronted the woman nurse-writer with a linguistic and social challenge, dramatised in Evadne Price's *Not So Quiet* (1930).[71] But there lay a deeper emotional and ethical crisis: the limits of empathy when the nurse was faced with the absoluteness of physical pain.

Touch has a particular relationship to time and representation. The visual appearance of a person can be preserved through photography; recorded voices may speak from beyond the grave; smell and taste, more difficult to re-create, have been successfully simulated in recent years. But touch dies with the person, impervious to technology and preservation, as if the soul lodged in the skin. Photography inhabits the realm of vision just as telephones, phonographs or record players do the world of sound. Touch, on the other hand, seems to break the chain of signification in that it cannot be directly represented. Photographs are the most common means of preserving memory: they steal moments back from the past but in the process can still familiar figures in an impersonal and public gaze – as in the photograph of the boy killed in France in Katherine Mansfield's short story 'The Fly'. Language, less immediate than a photograph or a voice, is often a more personal medium to remember the dead. Consider the following action of Sassoon, scribbled in his little notebook a day after the death of his 'dear' David:

So, after lunch, I escaped to the woods above Sailly-Laurette, and grief had its way with me in the sultry thicket. . . . And I lay there under the smooth bole of a beech-tree, wondering, and longing for the bodily presence that was so fair.

Grief can be beautiful, when we find something worthy to be mourned. To-day I knew what it means to find the soul washed pure with tears, and the load of death was lifted from my heart. So I wrote his name in chalk on the beech-tree stem, and left a rough garland of ivy there, and a yellow primrose for his yellow hair and kind grey eyes, my dear, my dear. . . .

> For you were glad, and kind and brave;
> With hands that clasped me, young and warm;[72]

Memory of the beloved reverts to the intimacy of the caress. Literary pastoral provides Sassoon with a ritual of mourning: Keatsian sensuousness flows into and fuses with homoerotic longing and loss. Inscribing the

71 See Higonnet, 'Not So Quiet', 205–26.
72 Siegfried Sassoon, *Diaries 1915–1918*, ed. Rupert Hart-Davies (London: Faber, 1983), 44–5.

name on the beech-tree has its root in absence and in longing, in the desire to touch a body that can no longer be touched. Yet the chalk-mark and the flowers will fade or wilt; in contrast, the diary, re-recording the moment, still exists, bearing traces of the hand that David had clasped, 'young and warm'. In *A Lover's Discourse*, Roland Barthes notes, 'I enwrap the other in my words, I caress, brush against, talk up this contact'.[73] Towards the end of the entry, almost resenting closure, Sassoon breaks into verse, as if suddenly realising that only poetry can capture and preserve what is longed for so poignantly and is irretrievably lost: the mutuality of the embrace. In a line subsequently excised from the printed version of his elegy for David entitled 'The Last Meeting', Sassoon writes, 'Who waits to feel my fingers touch his face', evoking through verse the primacy of the body and the privacy of the gesture.[74]

Trench poetry is obsessed with moments of physical intimacy: 'I clasp his hand', 'your hands in my hands', or Arthur Newberry Choyce's more suggestive 'That his fingers were stiff and cold / Which I had clasped warm, last night – / Encouraging'.[75] Choyce's uncanny echo of the closing lines of Sassoon's diary entry shows how touch, of all the senses, is the most acute bearer of private knowledge and emotion. When I touch a loved person, s/he touches me in turn, transmitting, through the responsiveness of live flesh, care and attention. The idea of touch is key to myths and legends of resurrection.[76] For tactile perception involves not just experience of the object but the experience of the experience itself. It is this reciprocity of the gesture that death takes away. Trench poetry might be seen as a phantasmatic space within which the returned soldier-poets would continue to reach out to their dead comrades, infusing them with the warmth they had once known.

*

Within the sphere of literary criticism, there has been much admirable work on First World War writings. If humanistic readings of war poetry by men such as Silkin and Bergonzi marked the earlier stages of war criticism, in recent years, literature has been brought out of the 'parenthesis' of wartime and aligned more closely to its intellectual and cultural

---

73  Roland Barthes, *A Lover's Discourse*, trans. Richard Howard (1978; Harmondsworth: Penguin, 1990), 73.

74  Sassoon, 'The Last Meeting'. The line, excised from the printed version, can be found in a rough draft of the poem in Cambridge University Library, E. J. Dent, MSS Add. 7973, S/75.

75  Raymond Heywood, 'My Pal', Robert Nichols, 'Casualty', Arthur Newberry Choyce, 'A May Morning', all quoted in Martin Taylor, *Lads: Love Poetry of the Trenches* (London: Duckworth, 1989), 95, 99, 96.

76  See Stewart, *Poetry and the Fate of the Senses*, 160–78.

contexts, often with a pan-European focus, as in Tate's *Modernism, History and the First World War* (1998), or more recently, in *The Cambridge Companion to the Literature of the First World War* (2004). The two most concentrated areas of enquiry have however been the sphere of gender, in connection to women's experience (male sexuality has been less talked about), and the war's relation to modernism. The sensory world, by contrast, has received limited attention, though the senses regularly feature as an experiential basis in writing, even when the women writers and the modernists write war 'slant'.[77] If Paul Virilio in *War and Cinema: The Logistics of Perception* (1984) had turned the war into a somewhat disembodied experience through the various technologies of vision, Jane Marcus underlined the messy corporeality of the body at war in the context of the women ambulance drivers, exploring the relation between trauma and the constant sound of bombardment.[78] But the 'common' sense – touch – has been largely ignored in war criticism, as if the all-pervasiveness of the sense has rendered it irrelevant. Yet, the world of the trenches is felt most acutely through the skin. 'The elemental forces of wet and cold', wrote Jünger, did more damage to the resistance of troops than artillery; for him, the difference between seeing the trenches and actually inhabiting them was like the difference between seeing a cavity in one tooth and feeling it with the tongue.[79]

What is the relation between touch and literary form? Discussing the nature of art about two decades after the war in which he had served as a private in the Royal Welch Fusiliers, David Jones wrote: 'Ars is adamant about one thing: she compels you to do an infantryman's job. She insists on the *tactile*.'[80] Consider the following passage from *In Parenthesis*, describing the most common ordeal of the soldier:

Sodden night-bones vivify, wet bones live. . . .

Nothing was defined beyond where the ground steepened just in front, where the trip-wire graced its snare-barbs with tinselled moistnesses.

Cloying drift-damp cupped in every concave place.

77 Higonnet *et al.*, *Behind the Lines*, 15.
78 Marcus, 'Corpus/Corps/Corpse', Afterword to Helen Zenna Smith, *Not So Quiet. . .Stepdaughters of War* (New York: The Feminist Press, 1989), 241–300. More recently, David Trotter has drawn attention to the sense of smell and its relation to disgust in the combat novels in 'The British Novel and the War', in *Cambridge Companion*, 34–56.
79 Jünger, 172; quoted in Leed, *NML*, 125.
80 David Jones, 'The Utile', in *Epoch and Artist: Selected Writings*, ed. Harman Grisewood (London: Faber, 1959), 183.

It hurts you in the bloody eyes, it grips chill and harmfully and rasps the sensed membrane of the throat; it's raw cold, it makes you sneeze – christ how cold it is.[81]

Here, syntax and style capture the act rather than the object of perception: wetness and coldness acquire meaning only in relation to sentient flesh, collapsing the distinction between surface and depth as, with sensuous intensification, the perceptual processes become visceral states of being: 'night-bones', 'wet bones'. The syntactical compression – Jones's double-words – closes the gap between objects of the world and the way they impinge on our consciousness: 'trip-wire' or 'snare-barbs' are not just metallic 'things' but carry certain meanings and threats in terms of human mobility and entrapment, bearing traces of the body imagined as spiked upon the 'tinselled moistnesses' of the night. This constant movement between sense experience and meaning hints at a mode of representation where temperature and texture are profoundly expressive of the subjectivity that feels them. Similarly, the expletive 'bloody eyes' (rather than 'poor' or 'sore' eyes) is at once a piece of trench realism, an example of transferred epithet ('bloody' cold) and indicative of the sense of bodily alienation brought about by pain. The use of anaphora and polysyndeton helps to trace its tortuous passage through the body while the extra word 'sensed' underlines the sense of exposure, carrying forward the hiss of the sibilant verbs ('hurts', 'grips', 'rasps') to combine with 'n' ('membrane') and making itself finally heard in 'sneezed': the materiality of language evokes the 'raw' body at war. If Sassoon's war satires exemplify a particular kind of war writing that lays claim on the sensuous for political reasons, Jones's prose remains one of the most luminous examples of such experience being integrated into the tissue of language.

Trauma and testimony have been powerful fields of enquiry in recent times to such an extent that the cultural and art critic Hal Foster notes a shift within contemporary art and theory 'from reality as an effect of representation to the real as a thing of trauma'.[82] Freud's theorisation of trauma, as we know, came in the wake of the First World War: the repetitive nightmares of the shell-shocked soldiers made Freud look for something *beyond* the pleasure principle. In fact, Freud's description of trauma as a 'break' through the protective psychic 'shield', 'membrane' or 'envelope' draws upon the vocabulary of touch as an index of the

81 Jones, *In Parenthesis*, 60–1.
82 Hal Foster, *Return of the Real: The Avant-Garde at the End of the Century* (Cambridge, Mass.: October, 1996), 146; see also Shoshana Felman and Dori Laub, *Testimony: Crises of Witnessing,*

intimate, or the exposed.[83] Yet, this relation between touch and trauma has largely gone unnoticed; even in some of the most acute discussions on the subject, the experience of the flesh has often been sacrificed to the representational crisis that trauma induces. The First World War soldiers knew the connection between the two, often to their own peril, as in the final stanza of Ivor Gurney's 'To His Love':

> Hide that red wet
> Thing I must somehow forget.[84]

Memory here is like a sharp weapon that cuts through both consciousness and literary form: shell-shocked, gassed and confined in a mental asylum, Gurney must – and could not – forget the viscera of war. In spite of the falling metre, 'wet' sticks at the end of the line and in our minds, acting as a formless noun until it spills on to the next line. The pastoral fabric ('Masses of memoried flowers') rips apart before the imagined touch of the abject. W. H. R. Rivers in *Instinct and the Unconscious* (1920) mentions the nervous breakdown of a young officer who was 'flung down' by an explosion so that his face struck the abdomen of a German several days dead. Before losing consciousness, the soldier realised that 'the substance which filled his mouth and produced the most horrible sensations of taste and smell was derived from the decomposed entrails of an enemy'.[85] Rivers regarded this case as incurable: horror cut deeper than fear or grief. This is an extreme example but the memoirs of the nurses are haunted by the sight, smell and touch of exposed flesh. While much attention has been paid to the war neuroses of the soldiers – from the war issues of *The Lancet* to Paul Lerner's *Hysterical Men: War, Psychiatry and the Politics of Trauma in Germany 1890–1930* (2003) – the experience of the nurses may lead us to reconceptualise contemporary notions of trauma through moments of contact with the damaged body.

In this study, I have concentrated on the experiences primarily of two groups of people – soldiers and nurses – for they constantly draw attention to the physicality and immediacy of experience. At the same time, the

*Psychoanalysis and History* (London: Routledge, 1992); Cathy Caruth, *Unclaimed Experience: Trauma, Narrative, and History* (Baltimore: Johns Hopkins University Press, 1996).

83 Sigmund Freud, 'Beyond the Pleasure Principle', vol. XVIII (1920–22) in *SE*, 29, 27.

84 'To His Love', in *Ivor Gurney: Selected Poems* ed. George Walter (London: Dent, 1996), 9. Gurney's friend F. W. Harvey – the subject of the poem – was mistakenly believed to be dead: he was a prisoner of war. See Stallworthy, *Anthem*, 148–9.

85 W. H. R. Rivers, *Instinct and the Unconscious: A Contribution to a Biological Theory of the Psycho-Neuroses* (Cambridge: Cambridge University Press, 1920), 192.

comparative framework allows us to discover the different ways in which the war affects men and women, combatants and non-combatants. I mainly discuss the experience of the Western Front as most of my writers served in this area. The focus is largely on English war writings, though I have drawn on both French and German material (usually in translations of the period)[86] to gain a broader European perspective and to examine certain common grounds across national and cultural boundaries. In doing so, the study explores whether European war writings similarly exhibit an urge towards the tactile as an impetus to literary creativity and the ways in which the war experience intersects with indigenous intellectual and cultural patterns, such as German sexology at the turn of the century, or the rise of Sartrean phenomenology in post-war France. There are also examples of inter-cultural transfer, as when Barbusse's *Le Feu* (1916) was translated by Fitzwater Wray, and was read by Owen in the English translation, inspiring 'The Show'; or when Evadne Price wrote the feminist counterpoint *Not So Quiet. . .* in 1930 to Remarque's war novel. Within English writing, I have drawn on a variety of sources, mostly from the period or immediately afterwards. I am interested in how different kinds of writing address a common historical experience, and the ways they raise questions about memory, narrative and genre.

The book has three parts and each part comprises two chapters. In the first chapter of each part, I draw on different kinds of historical material, both archival and published, and set them in dialogue with more self-conscious literary works. In the second chapter of each part, I concentrate on English literary texts (apart from 'Haptic geographies' in Chapter 2). The first part examines the muddy underground world of the trenches and how it affects the subjectivity of the soldiers. Part II studies the theme of male intimacy, with specific reference to the 'dying kiss', and then focuses on the tactile aesthetics of Wilfred Owen. Part III considers the experiences of the women-nurses through private and published material, and finally reads closely three 'operation-scenes'. Commenting on Rosenberg's 'Break of Day in the Trenches', Sassoon also noted that the poem had a 'poignant and nostalgic quality' that for him eliminated 'critical analysis'.[87] This study argues that one of the ways to gain an imaginative access to 'sensuous' war experience is through an appreciation *and* analysis of the literature of the period, through finding out why and how these writings lay claim on the most intimate of the senses.

86 The notable exception is Jünger, *Storm of Steel*, in which case I use the 2003 translation by Michael Hofmann.
87 Sassoon, 'Foreword', in Rosenberg, *CW*, ix.

# PART I

## *Trenches*

One of the nameless dead. Q 11688. Photograph courtesy of Imperial War Museum.

CHAPTER I

# Slimescapes

On 26 March 1917, in a front-line newspaper, some soldiers drew attention to what they thought to be the greatest reality of the Great War:

At night, crouching in a shell-hole and filling it, the mud watches, like an enormous octopus. The victim arrives. It throws its poisonous slobber out at him, blinds him, closes round him, buries him. . . . For men die of mud, as they die from bullets, but more horribly. Mud is where men sink and – what is worse – where their soul sinks. . . . Hell is not fire, that would not be the ultimate in suffering. Hell is mud.[1]

The extended image of the octopus is not merely a literary trope: the series of active verbs – blinds, closes, buries – hints at a hallucinatory quality on the level of perception, registering the threat of mud through the sense of touch. It captures the fear and bewilderment of the soldiers when human geography is suddenly changed, a reassuring visual universe is replaced by a mysterious tactile one and human life is at risk. Mud confuses the categories of solid and liquid. Moreover, it clings to the human body, defying its own inert nature and giving the impression of malevolent agency. The image of the octopus with enormous, glutinous tentacles suggests a progressive sense of suffocation: not the searing consciousness of burning in hell-fire, as associated with myths of afterlife, but that of being gradually choked and smothered. The passage reveals how sense perception is often a product of the interplay between cognition, knowledge, memory and language.[2] But the hallucinatory tone is soon abandoned in favour of the most literal statement: 'Mud is where men sink'. Burial in mud does not merely undercut the conventional heroism or

---

1  *Le Bochofage*, 26 March 1917. The translation used is from Stéphane Audoin-Rouzeau, *Men at War 1914–1918: National Sentiment and Trench Journalism in France during the First World War*, trans. Helen McPhail (Oxford: Berg, 1992), 38. Also refer to the fascinating collection of English trench newspapers, *Wipers Times 1916–18* (London: Peter Davies, 1973).
2  See Andrew Ortony (ed.), *Metaphor and Thought* (Cambridge: Cambridge University Press, 1993), 1.

martyrdom granted by shot or shell that forms a meaningful war narrative. More terrifyingly, it denies a narrative of human transcendence: 'what is worse – where their soul sinks'.

Dissolution of this too solid flesh in mud is an absurd image of matter consuming human form. Wilfred Owen, writing to his mother from the front, uses the same simile: 'the ground was not mud, not sloppy mud, but an octopus of sucking clay, 3, 4, and 5 feet deep' while the sculptor Gaudier-Brzeska takes up the end of that metaphor: 'now it's the third circle of Dante's Inferno. We have to stand in ditches with a foot of fluid mud at the bottom for four days.'[3] This vivid imagining of mud – something usually inert and anomalous – as a definite malevolent force might seem to have an exaggerated, almost paranoid, component but in the trenches of the Western Front, mud did actually have powers over life and death. Trooper Sam Goodman, in a letter, describes how 'I found myself sinking in the mud. I was passed [*sic*] my waist in it & I hadn't the strength to shout for assistance.' Tom Macdonald observes, 'The Salient in winter was like Dante's Inferno. Shell holes full of slime, mud every-where. Many men were wounded and trying to get back to Dressing Stations slipped in holes and were drowned.'[4] Captain Philip Christison, 6th Battalion, Cameron Highlanders, remembers a waterlogged country choked with 'dead men and animals, the stench of which made us retch'. Disgust and nausea give way to danger and horror as 'the leading NCO slipped off the track into a huge shell crater full of water' and 'could not be got out as the sides of the crater were just glutinous mud'. He mentions how 'in the blinding rain in the dark, heavily weighted men would slip into a shell crater and drown in gas contaminated mud often unheeded by their comrades. I found I lost three in this way when we reached the front line.'[5] Boyd Orr recalls that, in the winter of 1916–17, soldiers 'were liable to stumble into a shell-hole, and with the weight of their equipment sink like a stone to the bottom where rescue was impossible'. On a 'pitch black night', he remembers losing forty men who drowned in shell-holes.[6] Like the formless phenomenon that was its cause, the dread could not be

---

3  Owen, *CL*, 427; Gaudier-Brzeska's letter is quoted in Cork, *Bitter Truth*, 77. Ilana R. Bet-el, in *Conscripts: Lost Legions of the Great War* (Gloucestershire: Sutton, 1999) notes, 'Mud is indispensable to the imagery of the First World War . . . one of the few mythologised images actually rooted in fact' (88).

4  Sam Goodman, 'Papers', IWM, 97/26/1. Goodman became unconscious but was spotted and hauled out by two comrades. Tom Macdonald, 'Memories of 1914–1918 Great War', IWM 76/213/1.

5  Philip Christison, 'Memoirs', IWM, 82/15/1, 68, 65.

6  Boyd Orr, *As I Recall* (London: Macgibbon & Kee, 1966), 71.

contained within familiar psychological contours: it combined disgust and horror with a sense of almost metaphysical bewilderment. Like mud's own endless stretches, the complex feeling it elicited was endlessly expressed in a variety of tropes and names – *la melasse, la gadoue, la gadouille, la mouscaille* – reaching an all too realistic and tragic climax in the battle of Passchendaele.

The experience of trench mud was one of the most powerful encounters of the human subject with the immensity and chaos of inert matter. The present chapter examines the extraordinary psychic anxiety it generated and the ways in which it haunted the lives, memories and narratives of the soldiers. The subterranean, muddy world of the trenches confronted the soldiers, I shall argue, with the threat, both physical and psychic, of *dissolution into formless matter* at a time when modern industrial weaponry was eviscerating human form: it brought the soldiers to the precipice of non-meaning in a world that was already ceasing to make sense.[7] Burial in the mud was one of the nightmares that the soldiers commonly suffered from. There has been much theoretical interest in the relation between bodily margins and human subjectivity, the two most influential works on the subject being Mary Douglas's anthropological treatise, *Purity and Danger* (1966) and Julia Kristeva's psychoanalytical study, *Powers of Horror: An Essay on Abjection* (1982). In her classic study of how society maintains order and identity through a ritual of prohibition and taboo, Douglas alerts us to the fact that 'all margins are dangerous'. Our mistake, Douglas notes, is to treat 'bodily margins in isolation from all other margins' and she argues, with reference to Israelite culture, that 'the threatened boundaries of their body politic would be well mirrored in their care for the integrity, unity and purity of the physical body'.[8] To Kristeva, on the other hand, the threat to autonomy

---

7  Georges Bataille put the concept of the *informe* (formless) on the critical map in December 1929 in the 'dictionary' provided by the journal *Documents*. The purpose of this dictionary, Bataille stated, was not to give 'the meaning of words, but their tasks': 'Thus *formless* is not only an adjective having a given meaning, but a term that serves to bring things down in the world'. ('Formless', in *Visions of Excess: Selected Writings, 1927–1939*, ed. and trans. Allan Stoekl (Minneapolis: University of Minnesota Press, 1985), 31.) My use of the word 'formlessness' is different, having none of the ideologically subversive or celebratory connotations of Bataille. In the context of the First World War trenches, formlessness becomes a terrifying material reality. The two most sustained and stimulating explorations of art and literature through ideas of formlessness and mess respectively are Yves-Alain Bois and Rosalind Krauss, *Formless: A User's Guide* (New York: Zone, 1997) and David Trotter, *Cooking with Mud: The Idea of Mess in Nineteenth-Century Art and Fiction* (2000).

8  Mary Douglas, *Purity and Danger: An Analysis of the Concepts of Pollution and Taboo* (1966; London: Routledge, 1984), 121, 124.

goes back to the primordial maternal lining, the suffocating presence of
the mother. Bodily fluids are examples of what she calls the 'abject': it
is that which is excluded in the process of constituting the subject and
yet can never be got rid of, hovering 'at the border of my condition as a
living being'.[9]

While both works provide insights into the dangers, social or psychic,
hovering around liminal states, it is important to note that in the trenches,
mud was an actual physical threat: 'powers' or motions of horror were
often replaced by actual horror as men floundered and drowned. Secondly, there were active medical dangers relating to the questions of
hygiene and contamination. Soldiers standing in the muddy trenches
often suffered from trench foot; moreover, as an article in *The Lancet*
pointed out, the mud often contained some bacilli which, coming in
contact with open wounds, would result in the dreaded gas gangrene.[10]
These material facts add a new dimension to the psychic anxiety and
symbolic threat lurking around bodily margins and help us to understand
the unique conditions of trench life. More recently, David Trotter in
*Cooking With Mud: The Idea of Mess in Nineteenth-Century Art and
Fiction* (2000) has powerfully explored Victorian literature and culture
through ideas of mess and contingency.[11] Contingency would play a
central role in this modern industrial war where life would depend for
the next four years on the random direction of a shell.

What happens when mud becomes an actual material condition of life,
ubiquitous and constant, threatening to suck in the subject? 'We spend
most of our time pulling each other out of mud', writes Isaac Rosenberg

9  Julia Kristeva, *Powers of Horror*, 3. For discussion on abjection, see Bois and Krauss, *Formless*,
   235–40. For an alternative model through the emotion of disgust, see William Ian Miller, *The
   Anatomy of Disgust* (Cambridge, Mass.: Harvard University Press, 1997).
10 See C. Nepean Longridge, 'A Note on the Cause and Prevention of Trench Foot', *The Lancet*, 13
   January, 1917: 1, 62–3. Trench foot was caused by having stood for hours, even days on end,
   without being able to remove wet socks or boots. The feet would gradually go numb, turn red or
   blue, and in extreme cases, gangrene would set in. In the course of the war, 74,711 British troops
   were admitted to hospitals in France with trench foot or frost bite. This was the second largest
   number of admissions for any particular condition, though only forty-one men actually died
   from it. Jon Ellis, *Eye-Deep in Hell: Life in the Trenches, 1914–1918* (Glasgow: Fontana, 1977, 48–
   9). For gas gangrene, see Colonel Sir Almroth E. Wright, 'Conditions which Govern the Growth
   of the Bacillus of "Gas Gangrene", *The Lancet*, 6 January 1917: 1, 1–9.
11 Part of the excitement of Trotter's project lies in its attempt to draw us out of our narcissistic
   cocoon and re-centre our critical attention from subjects onto objects. See also David Trotter,
   'The British Novel and the War', in *Cambridge Companion*, 34–56. He argues that for the
   middle-class officer, the experience of the trenches 'was Victorian philanthropy's last hurrah (or
   last gasp)' and explores the productive uses made of fear and disgust in some of the combat
   novels (*Cambridge Companion*, 46, 50–1).

from the trenches.[12] The accounts of both Douglas and Kristeva have a phenomenological component which is reminiscent of Jean-Paul Sartre's description of slime at the end of *Being and Nothingness* (1943):

That sucking of the slimy which I feel on my hands outlines a kind of continuity of the slimy substance in myself. These long, soft strings of substance which fall from me to the slimy body (when, for example, I plunge my hand into it and then pull it out again) symbolize a rolling off of myself in the slime.[13]

Sartre further notes: 'so long as the contact with the slimy endures, everything takes place for us as if sliminess were the meaning of the entire world'. In the trenches of the First World War, this literally *was* the case: in Sassoon's words, 'naked sodden buttocks, mats of hair, / Bulged, clotted heaps slept in the plastering slime'.[14] If in the First World War experience of trench mud, we have a perverse historical validation of what Sartre meant by 'revenge of the In-itself', it is possible that the collective trauma of the trenches was dredged up, and fed into Sartre's extraordinary evocation of slime, especially when in the text he quotes from Jules Romains's First World War narrative *Preface to Verdun* (1938).

Starting with different kinds of material – letters, diaries and oral records – I shall move on to consider both the prose and poetry of the period in order to explore the muddy geography of the Western Front.[15] I have used the phrase 'slimescapes' for two reasons. Though the words 'mud' and 'slime' both occur in trench narratives, often interchangeably (and following my authors, I use both words), it is important to remember that trench mud was not only mud but was also compounded of organic wastes, industrial debris, iron scraps and even rotting flesh, all dissolving into what Sassoon calls 'plastering slime'. Ford's hero Tietjens, as he digs into the mud, observes, '*Slimy*, not greasy!'[16] Second, in addition to establishing its immediate physical presence, I shall examine

12 Rosenberg, *CW*, 267.
13 Jean Paul Sartre, *Being and Nothingness*, trans. Hazel E. Baines (1943; London: Routledge, 1989), 609–10. The word Sartre uses is 'visqueux'. The translator Hazel Barnes notes: 'I have consistently used the word "slimy" in translating because the figurative meaning of "slimy" appears identical in both languages' (604).
14 Sassoon, 'Counter-Attack', *Collected Poems*, 68.
15 Paul Fussell has called this landscape the 'troglodyte' world (*GWMM*, 36–74) while Eric Leed has drawn attention to this 'landscape suffused with ambivalence' as well as to the peculiarities of 'war in the labyrinth (*NML*, 20, 73–114); see also Allyson Booth, *Postcards from the Trenches: Negotiating the Space Between Modernism and the First World War* (New York: Oxford University Press, 1996), especially 'The Shapes of Countries' (67–103).
16 Ford Madox Ford, *Parade's End*, Part III (*A Man Could Stand Up*) (1926; Harmondsworth, Penguin, 1982), 638. Italics in original.

how slime becomes a 'scape' in these writings: war literature reveals a mode of thinking about mud, a way of giving linguistic shape to form-less matter.[17] This is particularly evident in the works of Barbusse, Sasssoon, Blunden and Jones. One of the questions the chapter will address is what happens to literary structures and rules of genre when too much matter seeps into the narratives. 'Slimescapes' suggest both the territorial expanse of the mud and its overwhelming presence in the consciousness of the soldiers and writers. The next section explores how this deluge of mud came about and the perceptual and emotional crisis it engendered, altering the soldier's relation to his own self, the war and the world.

### 'A REAL MONSTER THAT SUCKED'

The famous Western Front that stretched for 450 miles from the Swiss border to the North Sea was a stretch of parallel, zig-zagging trenches – a combination of earthworks, dug-outs and funk-holes – where thousands of soldiers remained cooped up for four years and sought protection against industrial weaponry. There had been trenches in previous wars, notably at Sebastopol during the Crimean War, but they were not as extensive, nor was the stalemate as long drawn-out as in the First World War.[18] While the Germans had the advantage of higher and drier ground such as Hill 60, two miles south-west of Ypres, and the Wytschaete–Messines Ridge, for the English the whole line from the coast to La Bassée was almost uniformly bad. As soon as the British soldiers would start to dig, they would usually find water two or three feet below the surface. In fact, around Nieuport, the terrain was little more than one big flood, the tide only being controlled by a complex series of locks, dams and canals.[19]

Ian Hay's 'first hundred thousand' rode through blue skies and sunlit days, but soon it began to rain. Between 25 October 1914 and 10 March 1915, there were only eighteen dry days; in March 1916, the rainfall was the heaviest for thirty-five years. In 1917, around Ypres and Passchendaele, at

---

17 The *OED* defines 'scape' (substantive): 'A view of scenery of any kind, whether consisting of land, water, cloud, or anything else. Also as the second element of combinations. Formed in imitation of *landscape*'. See also P. Dansereau, *Inscape and Landscape: The Human Perception of the Environment* (New York, 1973).

18 See Trevor Royle, *The Great Crimean War, 1854–1856* (London: Little, Brown and Company, 1999), especially 'Trench Warfare', 389–400.

19 Ellis, *Eye-deep in Hell*, 10–12. For details on trench warfare, see John Keegan, *The First World War* (London: Hutchinson, 1998); Tony Ashworth, *Trench Warfare 1914–18: The Live and Let Live System* (London: Macmillan, 1988).

Figure 1.1. Attempting to pull a field-gun out of the mud, IWM, Q 5938.
Photograph courtesy of Imperial War Museum.

the height of the third battle of Ypres, it began raining on 30 July and continued for the whole of August.[20] As the 17/King's Liverpool Battalion trudged through Shrewsbury Forest on the opening day of the battle, its commander noted at noon, 'Rain Starts'.[21] Moreover, industrial weaponry, particularly long-range artillery and landmines, deformed the landscape, throwing up fountains of mud and water. The greater part of the Western Front turned into a giant cess-pool: when ordered to consolidate an advanced position, an officer sent back: 'It is impossible to consolidate porridge'.[22] The mud did not just clog rifles; the swamps bogged down field guns (Figure 1.1); after a day of heavy fighting, it slowed down the rescue operation, as stretcher-bearers struggled through the mud (Figure 1.2). T. Dalziel wrote in his diary on 19 February 1915 that he was 'still up to the waist in mud' while on 19 October 1916,

20  For rain and the Passchendaele offensive, see Robin Prior and Trevor Wilson, *Passchendaele: The Untold Story* (New Haven: Yale University Press, 1996), 97–110.
21  17/Kings Liverpool Battalion, 'Precis of Operations – 30th July to 3rd August 1917', 30 Division War Diary May–Aug. 1917, War Office Papers, Public Record Office, Kew, WO 95/2312.
22  Quoted in Ellis, *Eye-deep in Hell*, 45.

Figure 1.2. Stretcher-bearers struggling through the mud, Q 5935. Photograph courtesy of Imperial War Museum.

W. R. Acklam noted that 'everything is one slimy mass of mud'.[23] Such accounts recur in the memoirs: Thomas Penrose Marks notes how his companion fell into a shell-hole filled with the 'filthiest mud' and 'sank inches each minute'; Alexander McKee in *Vimy Ridge* recalls a man who was trapped in mud for forty-six hours.[24]

If the First World War is described as the end of illusion for a whole generation of young men, mud can be said to be the beginning of that end. The process of disillusionment began at a daily intimate level, often in the attempt to find one's footing or one's boots. Fritz Voigt in *Combed Out* (1920) chooses to devote two full pages to the arduous process: 'My left foot had sunk deeply into the slush. I pawed the mud with my right in order to find the duckboard. . . . It came out with a loud, sucking squelch, but I felt it was leaving my boot behind. I let it sink back again and then freed it with a twist of the ankle.'[25] The fate of the foot in the mud is

---

23 T. Dalziel, 'Diary', IWM, 86/51/1; W. R. Acklam, 'Diary', IWM, 83/23/1.
24 Thomas Penrose Marks, *The Laughter Goes from Life: In the Trenches of the First World War* (London: William Kimber, 1977), 16; Alexander McKee, *Vimy Ridge* (London: Souvenir Press, 1966), 57.
25 F. A. Voigt, *Combed Out* (1920; London: Jonathan Cape, 1930), 24.

directly linked to the soldier's new relation to his body and the war. In the daily round of civilian life, excepting cases of illness or pain, one's consciousness is usually disembodied. 'If it is true that I am conscious of my body via the world' writes Merleau-Ponty, the body is also 'the unperceived term in the center of the world'.[26] The mud of the Western Front irrevocably altered this assumption, stressing the materiality and vulnerability of the flesh: it is no longer a privileged 'third term', understood tacitly against the double horizon of external and bodily space. In *The Middle Parts of Fortune* (1929), Manning's anti-hero Bourne begins his war ordeal by missing his foothold and slipping into a shell-hole. Writing horror was not alien to the genre of war poetry (though not horror on the scale of the first Somme offensive), but writing filth was. Fear and mortality were written, tinged with Georgian ardour, into Rupert Brooke's 'Safety'; but daily degradation was not. Mud divested the soldiers of the cloak of cleanliness and heroism that Victorian ideology and war propaganda had wrapped round them: soldiers realised that they were not 'swimmers into cleanness leaping' but rather 'houseflies upon a section of flypaper'.[27]

Verticality, to Sigmund Freud, was a sign of human evolution. In *Civilization and Its Discontents* (1930), he observes that 'the fateful process of civilization would thus have set in with man's adoption of an erect posture'. He further notes that, over time, there has been a 'diminution of the olfactory stimuli' as man slowly raised himself from the ground and assumed 'an upright gait'.[28] The process would also coincide with the diminution of tactile stimuli, as the body gradually lifted itself from the ground, the final points of contact being the two feet: the world would now largely be 'beheld' through the safe distance of the gaze.[29] The geography of the trenches however removed the gap built into our perceptual relation with the world. *Creep, crawl, worm, burrow*: these were the usual modes of movement during a night patrol in no man's land or while rescuing the war-wounded in order to avoid being detected. Sassoon in *Memoirs of an Infantry Officer*, recalls 'crawling

---

26 Merleau-Ponty, *Phenomenology*, 94.
27 Brooke, 'Peace', *Collected Poems* (London: Sidgwick and Jackson, 1929), 144; Wyndham Lewis, *Blasting and Bombardiering: An Autobiography (1914–16)* (1937; London: John Calder, 1982), 161.
28 Freud, 'Civilisation and Its Discontents', *SE*, xxi, 99.
29 See Bois and Krauss, *Formless*, especially the illuminating sections on 'Gestalt' and 'Horizontality' (89–103). Krauss explores how the art of Jackson Pollock and Andy Warhol involves an act of looking *down*, a movement towards the horizontal and the material, and how this perceptual shift affects the viewer's relation to the work of art.

among shell-holes in the dark', and later, on a rescue mission, having 'crawled along with mud-clogged fingers'; Barbusse, in *Light*, notes 'I had to worm myself, bent double' or 'I had to crawl, flat on our bellies'; in O'Flaherty's *Return of the Brute*, a soldier notes, 'It's the crawling around in mud that's killing us'.[30] Patrick MacGill, who served as a stretcher-bearer, captures the sense of absolute horizontality: 'Another soldier came crawling towards us on his belly, looking for all the world like a gigantic lobster which had escaped from its basket'.[31] 'The last kind of unclean animal', observes Mary Douglas in her analysis of the 'abominable' creatures, 'is that which creeps, crawls or swarms upon the earth' – and she associates it with the 'realm of the grave, with death and chaos'.[32] 'Crawling' for Douglas is an 'indeterminate' form of movement for it confuses the usual categories of walking, swimming or flying. Underlying the conceptual transgression that she points out, there is a perceptual crisis: the absolute lowering of the body on the ground allies seeing with the 'baser' senses of touch and smell. The trench mud thus challenged the vertical organisation of bodily Gestalt, and marked a regression to the clumsy horizontality of beasts. Rat, mole, earthworm and snail are recurrent similes that are used in trench narratives to describe the soldiers.

Stephen Kern in *The Culture of Time and Space 1880–1918* notes that the Great War shook belief in human progress and evolution.[33] The fear of dissolving into slime was one of the chief causes of this loss of belief. The war, Gertrude Stein noted, 'makes things go backward as well as forward'.[34] The vast stretches of mud exemplified this 'vertiginous notion' of time: it swallowed up tanks, made them look 'like some gigantic hippopotamus puffing and bellowing through a reedy swamp', taking soldiers back to some 'dim prehistoric age'.[35] The act of going down into the

---

30 Sassoon, *Memoirs of An Infantry Officer* (1930; London: Faber and Faber, 1965), 12, 21; Barbusse, *Under Fire* and *Light*, trans. Fitzwater Wray (London: Dent, 1919), 509, 483; Liam O'Flaherty, *Return of the Brute* (London: Mandrake Press, 1929), 162. Also see Leed who quotes Robert Michaels, an Austrian cavalry captain: 'Modern combat is played out almost entirely invisibly . . . . He cannot fight upright on the earth but must crawl into and under it' (*NML*, 19–20).
31 Patrick MacGill, *The Great Push* (London: Herbert Jenkins, 1917), 74.
32 Douglas, *Purity and Danger*, 56.
33 Stephen Kern, *The Culture of Time and Space 1880–1918* (London: Weidenfeld and Nicolson, 1983), 291.
34 Gertrude Stein, *Wars I Have Seen* (1945; London: Brilliance Books, 1984), 5.
35 Arthur Jenkin, *A Tank Driver's Experiences: Or Incidents in a Soldier's Life* (London: Elliot Stock, 1922), 135; Frank Mitchell, *Tank Warfare: The Story of the Tanks of the Great War* (1933;

bowels of the earth was like going back in time as well. And yet, 'the reedy swamp' was itself the product of industrial modernity, the result of long-range artillery and mines. Thus mud on the Western Front represented the paradoxical nature of time during the Great War: itself the result of the latest technology (combined with bad weather), it looked back to some primeval chaos.

But there lay a deeper anxiety: the world might not only dissolve into slime but draw man into its chaotic indifferentiation. Consider the following extract from the memoir of Lewis-gunner Jack Dillon:

Now the mud at Passchendaele was very viscous indeed, very tenacious, it stuck to you. Your puttees were solid mud anyway. When you took your puttees off you scraped them and hoped for the best; you couldn't put them on again. But it stuck to you all over, it slowed you down. . . . The mud there wasn't liquid, it wasn't porridge, it was a curious kind of sucking kind of mud. When you got off this track with your load, it 'drew' at you, not like a quicksand, but a real monster that sucked at you.[36]

The description bears witness at once to the trauma of experiencing a hostile world through the skin and the fabled consistency of the Passchendaele mud. The acute memory of tactile horror exceeds the material, literal referent – liquid, porridge, quicksand – and can, like the octopus simile in the opening letter, only resort to the imaginative. The verbs Dillon uses – stuck, suck, drew – are strikingly congruent with Sartre's description of slime: 'I open my hands, I want to let go of the slimy and it sticks to me, it draws me, it sucks at me'.[37] The aggressive agency of the trench mud – its leech-like suction on the skin, blurring the boundaries of the body and confusing the categories of subject and object – seemed to trespass the limits of inert matter. The new relational structure with the material universe engendered a perceptual crisis and defied comprehension, necessitating a return to the world of myth and monsters.

Jack Dillon's memories about the Passchendaele offensive are corroborated in the sound-archives by another broken voice: 'It was that deep – sucking mud – there's a memorial on the Menin Gate to 60,000 men . . . [who] were all sucked into the mud'.[38] The verb recurs obsessively: Owen's 'sucking clay', Sassoon 'clay-sucked', Read's 'sucking, clutching

Stevenage: Spa Books, 1987), 78. For a detailed discussion of tanks within war literature and culture, see Tate, *Modernism*, 120–46.

36 J. Dillon, Sound Archives, IWM, 4078/B/B.

37 Sartre, *Being and Nothingness*, 609.     38 W. Collins, Sound Archives, IWM, 9434/20.

death' and Jones's 'aquatic sucking'.[39] Is there a projection of infantile aggression onto the undifferentiated mud so that the soldier, in turn, becomes a powerless nipple before the polymorphous perversity of a monstrous child?[40] But the relationship is by no means stable: like mud's own anomalous nature, the soldiers' responses shift and slide, often in tortured and chaotic succession. In Remarque's *All Quiet*, as the soldier 'buries his face and his limbs in her [earth] from the fear of death by shell-fire, then she is his only friend, his brother, his mother'.[41] Gender categories and familial bonds break down. Remarque imagines that terrifying moment when the soldier, in order to escape from shell fire, buries himself in the mud: 'Our being, almost utterly carried away by the fury of the storm, streams back through our hands from thee, and we, thy redeemed ones, bury ourselves in thee, and through the long minutes in a mute agony of hope bite into thee with our lips!'[42] The soldier's charged sense of rejuvenation, or redemption, born from his contact with the earth is reminiscent of Wilfred Owen's poem, 'The Wrestlers', where the young hero Antaeus could not be crushed as long as his arms or feet touched the ground for 'earth herself empowered him by her touch', a return to the old pastoral trope of 'mother earth'.[43]

But Remarque's account is more cynical for his soldier's sense of renewed life is fleeting and illusory: 'she [earth] shelters him and releases him for ten seconds to live, to run, ten seconds of life; receives him again and often for ever'.[44] The earth, for Remarque, both enwombs and entombs. If in the previous accounts of the 'sucking' mud, the soldier is figured implicitly as the nipple, here the earth in turn is imagined as the maternal breast ('bite into thee with our lips!'). The soldier attacks the maternal body with bombs and landmines. If the earth provides a moment-ary refuge from shell-fire, it also induces the opposite: a half-demented

---

39 Owen, *CL*, 427; Sassoon, 'The Redeemer', *Collected Poems*, 16; Read, 'Kneeshaw Goes to War', *Collected Poems* (London: Sinclair-Stevenson, 1966), 31; Jones, *In Parenthesis*, 88.

40 In 'Beyond the Pleasure Principle' (1920), while discussing the pleasures of the oral stage, Freud underlines the aggressive impulse: 'During the oral stage of organization of the libido, the act of obtaining mastery over an object coincides with that object's destruction' (Freud, *SE*, XVIII, 54).

41 *All Quiet*, 52.

42 *All Quiet*, 52–3.

43 Owen, 'The Wrestlers', *CP&F*, 521. Owen's poem is largely based on an essay published by his doctor at Craiglockhart, Arthur Brock. See Dominic Hibberd, 'A Sociological Cure for Shellshock: Dr Brock and Wilfred Owen', *Sociological Review*, 25, 2 (May 1977), 377–86.

44 *All Quiet*, 52. See also Tate, who speaks of earth's 'ambiguous nurturing' (*Modernism*, 88–9); for a different interpretation, see Klaus Theweleit, who portrays the earth as 'the giver of life': *Male Fantasies*, I, trans. Stephen Conway (Cambridge: Polity Press, 1987), 239.

soldier rushes out of the dug-out into the open. 'It is a case of claustro-phobia', the narrator remarks, and the other soldiers sigh in unison: 'We sit as if in our graves waiting only to be closed in'.[45] Temporary burial however can foster the sense of rebirth, as in Ford's tetralogy, *Parade's End* (1924–8). Towards the end of *A Man Could Stand Up* (1926), Christopher Tietjens, caught in a huge mudslide, tries to dig out his lance-corporal: 'His hands were under the slime and his forearms. He battled his hands down greasy cloth; under greasy cloth. *Slimy*, not greasy! He pushed outwards. The boy's hands and arms appeared.'[46] Tietjens's 'boy' is reborn in the place where Remarque's soldier died. Tietjens, Ford writes, 'felt tender, like a mother, and enormous'. But following the logic of the scene, the earth is giving birth and Tietjens almost acts as a midwife as he thrusts his hand into its slimy bowels. This is one of the few moments in First World War writings when the mud is figured in its regenerative, womb-like function. But trench mud is also the result of earth pulverised by industrial weaponry: to Rosenberg, she is being subjected to anal penetration or rape by the soldier as her 'bowel' is 'seared by jagged fire'.[47]

Life in the trenches may be said to lurch between an overwhelming urge to give order to experience and a daily assertion of its absurdity: the more human meanings were challenged, the more desperately a refuge was sought in superstition and legend.[48] War usually mobilises a set of deep convictions, beliefs and ideologies: in the final chapter of Barbusse's *Under Fire*, a soldier concludes: 'I shall know how to stick more suffering if I know it's *for* something'.[49] To continue life, and especially to continue to be prepared to die, a meaning or explanation must be sought or imposed. Modern mechanical warfare cancelled the logic of the all-important '*for*' and replaced it with luck. A soldier in Remarque's *All Quiet on the Western Front* (1929) remarks: 'Over us Chance hovers. If a shot comes, we can duck, that is all; we neither know nor can determine where it will fall'; similarly, Sassoon, in 'A Letter Home' writes: 'Everywhere men bang and

---

45 *All Quiet*, 97.
46 Ford Madox Ford, *Parade's End*, 638. The General finds the mud-splattered Tietjens 'disgustingly dirty' and, instead of rewarding his heroism, reprimands him: 'I shall send you back' (643).
47 Rosenberg, 'Dead Man's Dump', in *The Poems and Plays of Isaac Rosenberg* ed. Vivien Noakes (Oxford: Oxford University Press, 2004), 141.
48 Leed, *NML*, 115–23.
49 Henri Barbusse, *Under Fire*, trans. W. Fitzwater Wray (1919; London: Dent, 1965), 334; hereafter abbreviated Barbusse, *UF*.

blunder / Sweat and swear and worship Chance'.[50] David Trotter has argued that 'mess is what contingency's signature would look like, if contingency *had* a signature'.[51] When contingency becomes the ruling principle, as in the world of the trenches, and cancels human motive or meaning, life becomes absurd. Following this logic, the vast stretches of mud can be said to be the material trace of absurdity itself: the ooze traps and engulfs you without meaning or purpose. In Sassoon's poems such as 'The Redeemer' or 'Attack', chance is not only comprehended in a mental space but felt in the flesh as the soldier literally puts the wrong foot forward and 'flounders in mud'.[52] The image of the octopus may be said to be a pitiful attempt to bring incomprehensible, indifferent matter within the realm of signification: imagined as a monster or an octopus, mud made more sense, an intimate enemy that 'sucks'. What the similes try hard to hold at bay is the absurdity of being engulfed by matter.

### DISSOLVING BOUNDARIES

In his existentialist treatise *Being and Nothingness* (1943), Sartre proposes a rough correspondence between the following oppositions: the 'In-Itself' (*en-soi*) and the 'For-Itself' (*pour-soi*), matter and consciousness, passivity and activity. Slime, to him, poses the single most powerful threat to this distinction:

The slimy is *docile*. Only at the very moment when I believe that I possess it, behold by a curious reversal, *it* possesses me. . . . There exists a poisonous possession; there is a possibility that the In-Itself might absorb the For-Itself . . . into its foundationless existence. At this instant I suddenly understand the snare of the slimy: it is a fluidity which holds me and which compromises me.[53]

Slime thus endangers human subjectivity by blurring the boundaries of the body: 'to touch the slimy is to risk being dissolved in sliminess', giving an impression that 'the slimy is myself' (609). Sartre's exposition of slime is essentially a continuation of his fascination with the human body as evident in his novel *Nausea* (1938). Sartre's novel is deeply influenced by Céline's *Journey to the End of the Night* (1932) which, in turn, is shaped by the author's traumatic experience in the First World War trenches and obsessed with the theme of bodily abjection. Critics have noted the

---

50　*All Quiet*, 89. Sassoon, *Collected Poems*, 42–3.　　　51　Trotter, *Cooking With Mud*, 15.
52　Sassoon, 'Attack', *Collected Poems*, 71.
53　Sartre, *Being and Nothingness*, 608–9. See also Iris Murdoch, *Sartre: Romantic Rationalist* (1953;
　　London: Vintage, 1999), 39–51.

similarities between Céline's modern, estranged picaro Bardamu and Sartre's Roquentin, the isolated consciousness set adrift in a world to which he can only relate through disgust.[54]

In *Nausea*, if Roquentin is a 'pour-soi' enmeshed in the 'en-soi' of the world, mud figures prominently in the first two encounters. In the opening entry, Roquentin gingerly holds a pebble, 'wet and muddy' on one side, by its edges and he has another bout of 'sweet disgust' when he observes closely a paper partly 'hidden by a crust of mud' lying beside a puddle. 'Objects ought not to *touch*, since they are not alive. . . . But they touch me, it's unbearable.' Towards the end of the novel, he finds himself in a park where he feels that he is being sucked into a world of 'gelatinous' thingness, 'all soft, gumming everything up, all thick, a jelly'.[55] This fear receives its extended philosophical treatment in the passage on slime in *Being and Nothingness* (1943). Unlike *Nausea*, Sartre's treatise was written during another war, which inevitably brought back memories of, and analogies with, the previous war. While discussing the concept of freedom in the essay, he refers to *a* war (*une guerre*) rather than *the* war (*la guerre*), and, as opposed to his post-war essays such as 'What Is Literature?', he never names the Occupation as such. Philip Watts has suggested that, in parts of *Being and Nothingness*, Sartre 'seems to be drifting from 1943 back to 1914'.[56] This is most evident when, discussing the political responsibilities of the citizen during wartime, he quotes from none other than Jules Romains's First World War bestseller *Preface to Verdun* (1938), the fifteenth volume in his *Les hommes De Bonne Volonté*.

Romains did not see the war himself, serving in the auxiliary army in a Paris office, but his novel evokes the 'pulpy, fluid' trench landscape: 'Refuse-heap, house-wrecker's yard, cesspool, common-sewer . . . the place had something of all of them rolled together'. Industrial wreckage, rusty metalwork, military accoutrements and rotting bodies combine to form 'a sort of glutinous sauce' and 'to walk here was like walking through the dense thickness of a vast pudding concocted of corpses'.[57] *Preface to Verdun* was published in 1938, the same year as Sartre's *Nausea*. Clanricard

54 See Allen Thiher, 'Céline and Sartre', *Philological Quarterly*, 50, 2 (April 1971), 292–305. Sartre prefaced *Nausea* with a quotation from Céline and while dedicating the book to Simone de Beauvoir, he prefaced it with a line from Céline's little-known play, *L'Englise*.

55 Sartre, *Nausea* (1938), trans. Robert Baldick (Harmondsworth: Penguin, 2000), 10, 22, 192. The contact, in the last example, seems to have been with some 'yellow earth around me, out of which dead branches stuck up into the air' (193). See the introduction by James Wood, vii–xx.

56 Philip Watts, *Allegories of the Purge* (Stanford: Stanford University Press, 1998), 65.

57 Jules Romains, 'Preface to Verdun', in *Verdun*, trans. Gerard Hopkins (1938; London: Peter Davies, 1939), 89, 91.

was thus wading through trench sewage at a time when Roquentin was experiencing his dread of 'gelatinous subsidence'.[58] Sartre was familiar enough with Romains's book to quote from it in *Being and Nothingness*. His choice of the slimy as 'the ontological expression of the world' might have partly been guided by collective memory of the trenches, revived anew during the Occupation, and would have resonated deeply with a war-bereaved generation who knew, as the advertisement in one of the editions of *Verdun* mentioned, that 200,000 people disappeared into the mud of their country. While the rise of French existentialism is usually associated with the Second World War in the 1940s, it is important to remember that *Nausea* was written before this war. Sartrean existentialism was deeply influenced by German philosophy, but many of its central precepts – the emphasis on experience, the contingency and randomness of existence, and the uncanny pull of matter – seem close to some of the themes we have been exploring in the context of the First World War.[59]

There is a fundamental difference between Sartre's theorisation of slime and its horrid actualisation in the trenches. Yet, if we grasp in Sartre's project how the stubborn materiality of the object can compromise human autonomy, we can imagine its terrifying potential for the soldier in the trenches where men were being actually reduced to matter. War narrative is traumatised by the sheer *Thing*-ness of the human body: corpses are regularly referred to as 'sack', 'heap', 'tube'.[60] In *All Quiet on the Western Front*, Paul is haunted by the vision of his friend after his death: 'Under the nails is the dirt of the trenches, it shows through blue-black like poison. It strikes me that these nails will continue to grow like lean fantastic cellar-plants long after Kemmerich breathes no more. I see the picture before me. They twist themselves into corkscrews and grow and grow, and with them the hair on the decaying skull.'[61] Inorganic refuse – the *Schmutz* of the trenches – conspires with bodily parts to complete the

58 Sartre, *Nausea*, 192.

59 For a fresh exploration of the German roots of French existentialism, see Paul S. MacDonald (ed.), *The Existentialist Reader: An Anthology of Key Texts* (Edinburgh: Edinburgh University Press, 2000), 11–46. Gabriel Marcel, another prominent exponent of French existentialism, served during the First World War in the French Red Cross bureau which dealt with the families of those missing in action. The experience led him 'to consider the limits within which any inquiry at all is possible'. In his 'Autobiography', written in 1969, he closed his memoir with the observation: 'Never since [the First World War] have I ceased to feel, I can say in my flesh, the unutterable ordeal that our moral condition imposes on those who love' (Paul Schilpp ed., *The Philosophy of Gabriel Marcel*, Chicago: Open Court, 1969, 64).

60 Sassoon, *The Complete Memoirs of George Sherston* (1937; London: Faber, 1952), 274; Barbusse, *UF*, 147; Remarque, *All Quiet*, 240.

61 Remarque, *All Quiet*, 19.

revenge of matter over the human subject. This threat is explored by
Remarque's fellow poet and comrade-in-arms, August Stramm:

> Lumpish-mellow lulls to sleep the iron
> Bleedings filter oozing stains
> Rusts crumble
> Fleshes slime
> Sucking lusts around decay.[62]

Coming out of a specific artistic milieu – German Expressionism –
Stramm's poem not only establishes the ubiquity of 'slime' ('schleimen')
but evolves it into the dominant mode of consciousness. The
title 'Schlachtfeld' ('Battlefield') is undercut by the opening neologism,
'Schollenmürbe' (literally 'clods-crumbliness'), evoking the abiding image
of trench warfare: formlessness. Though the poem has powerful visual and
aural qualities, it calls for, stimulates, our sense of touch as we are sucked
into a world of varying substances: clay, iron, blood, rust, flesh are all
shown to lose their individual shape in the ooze. There is no human
player in this drama of deliquescence – only the materiality of objects and
human detritus, and the slow suction of time. The verb 'filzen' (translated
above as 'filter') in the second line is related to the noun 'felt'; the *Oxford
Duden German Dictionary* defines it as 'material made by beating and
pressing together wool or cotton'. Neither human nor matter, this coagu-
lated ooze resembles Kristeva's image of the 'wound with blood and
pus'.[63] In Stramm's poem, the abject seems to have usurped the place of
the subject. Yet, this festering wound might have a more specific historical
resonance, referring to gas gangrene. An eye-witness account notes: 'the
cut surface takes on a curious half-jellified, half-mummified look; then the

---

62 August Stramm, 'Battlefield', trans. Jeremy Adler, in Tim Cross, *The Lost Voices of World War I:
An International Anthology of Writers, Poets and Playwrights* (London: Bloomsbury, 1988), 139.
The original version of the poem follows:

> Schollenmürbe schläfert ein das Eisen
> Blute filzen Sickerflecke
> Roste krumen
> Fleische schleimen
> Saugen brünstet um Zerfallen.

Stramm's poems appeared in the Expressionist journal *Der Sturm* which had published key
modernist statements such as Marinetti's 'Futurist Manifesto' and Apollinaire's 'Modern
Painting' in 1913. Refer to Patrick Bridgwater, *The German Poets of the First World War* (London:
Croon, 1980), 38–61. I am grateful to Andreas Bücker for discussing the poem with me.
63 Kristeva, *Powers of Horror*, 3.

whole wounded limb begins to swell up and distend in the most extraordinary fashion'.[64] In the original German version, the phrase 'Fleische
schleimen' with its blurred linguistic boundaries hints at the confusion
between man and matter. The use of 'brüznsten' ('to lust', or more aptly,
'to rut', animal calls for mating) is ominous: it suggests even some
primitive blood lust on part of the earth in its incarnation as slime with
the by-now ritualistic phrase, 'suck' ('Saugen').

In everyday trench life, the boundaries of the body can no longer be
policed, as bodily fluids are perpetually on the brink of spillage. In *Blasting
and Bombardiering*, the officer breaks wind at the sound of shelling; men
vomit as they collect corpses in Graves's *Goodbye To All That* and Cloete's *A
Victorian Son*.[65] Winterbourne defecates in his trousers in *Death of a Hero*,
as does the young boy in Remarque's *All Quiet on the Western Front*.[66] Just
as bodily fluids leak out, similarly mud and slime seep in: Céline speaks of
'eating Flanders mud, my whole mouth full of it, fuller than full'; in 'A
Night of Horror', the narrator writes: 'The suffocating mud and slime /
Were trickling down my throat'. Remarque, towards the end of his novel,
observes: 'Our hands are earth, our bodies mud and our eyes puddles of
rain'.[67] Membranes have become permeable: the skin can no longer separate the inside and the outside, the self and the world.

Frederic Manning in *The Middle Parts of Fortune* notes, 'a man is dead
or not dead, and a man is just as dead by one means as by another; but it
is infinitely more horrible and revolting to see a man shattered and
eviscerated, than to see him shot'.[68] Manning points out one of the central
anxieties that trouble war narratives: the formlessness of the human body
caused a visceral trauma that cut deeper than the death of a comrade.
W. H. R. Rivers writes about the nervous breakdown of an officer who
had gone to look for a comrade, only to find his mangled body 'with head
and limbs lying separated from the trunk'. In the officer's subsequent
nightmares, his friend would appear, not always mutilated but rather 'in
the still more terrifying aspect of one whose limbs and features had been

64 Quoted in Ellis, *Eye-deep in Hell*, 113. See also Colonel Sir Almroth E. Wright, 'Conditions
   which Govern the Growth of the Bacillus of 'Gas Gangrene', *The Lancet*, 6 January 1917: 1, 9.
65 Lewis, *Blasting and Bombardiering*, 118; Robert Graves, *Goodbye to All That* (1929; London:
   Penguin, 1988), 137; Stuart Cloete, *Victorian Son: An Autobiography 1897–1922* (London: Collins,
   1972), 237.
66 Richard Aldington, *Death of a Hero* (London: Chatto and Windus, 1929), 335; Remarque, *All
   Quiet*, 43.
67 Céline, *Journey*, 24; Charles Walter Blackall, 'A Night of Horror' in A *Deep Cry*, ed. Anne
   Powell (Thrupp: Sutton, 1993), 347; Remarque, *All Quiet*, 202.
68 Frederic Manning, *The Middle Parts of Fortune* (1929; London: Peter Davies, 1977), 11.

eaten away by leprosy' and 'the mutilated or leprous officer of the dream would come nearer and nearer' until the dreamer woke up in terror.[69] Grief at the death of a friend is overtaken by horror at the sight or imagined touch of exposed flesh. Manning describes a corpse as 'festering, fly-blown corruption', Barbusse as 'larvae of pollution' and Leighton calls it a 'foetid heap of hideous putrescence'.[70]

### BARBUSSE AND THE REVENGE OF MATTER

Barbusse was forty-one-years old when the war broke out. A committed socialist and a pacifist, he nevertheless enlisted and went into line as a common soldier in the 55th Division, firmly believing that 'this war is a social war', directed against 'our old infamous time-honoured enemies: militarism and imperialism'.[71] Yet, disillusionment came soon and it was mud that brought home the ugliness of war, as evident in a letter written on New Year's Day 1915: 'What a life. Mud, earth, rain. We are saturated, dyed, kneaded. One finds dirt everywhere, in pockets, in handkerchiefs, in clothes, in food. It is a haunting memory, a nightmare of earth and mud.'[72] It is indeed this 'nightmare' of mud that oppresses *Le Feu* (1916). Barbusse served first as an infantryman and then as a stretcher-bearer, was awarded the Croix de Guerre for bravery in 1915 and was invalided out of the war in 1917. From October 1915, he kept a war diary which formed the basis of *Le Feu*, initially serialised in the left-wing journal *L'œuvre* and published as a book in December 1916. Written with an explicit pacifist aim, *Le Feu* was a phenomenal success, winning the Prix Goncourt in 1917, and, by the end of the war, it had sold 250,000 copies. Translated into English as *Under Fire* by Fitzwater Wray in 1917, the book was widely reviewed in England by prominent journals such as *The Egoist, New*

69 W. H. R. Rivers, *Instinct and the Unconscious: A Contribution to a Biological Theory of the Psycho-Neurosis* (1920; Cambridge: Cambridge University Press, 1922), 190. In another case discussed by F. W. Mott, a soldier had nightmares of being trapped in a mine passage with a leper approaching him. In analysis, he came up with memories of being disturbed years before by the sight of a leper when serving as an officer in South Africa. (F. W. Mott, *War Neuroses and Shell Shock*, London: Oxford University Press, 1919, 128.)

70 Manning, *Middle Parts*, 11; Barbusse, *UF*, 147; Leighton, letter to Vera Brittain in Powell (ed.), *A Deep Cry*, 43.

71 Henri Barbusse, *Paroles d'un combattant* (Paris: Flammarion, 1920), 7–8. For different approaches to *Under Fire*, see J. E. Flower, *Literature and the Left in France: Society, Politics and the Novel since the Late Nineteenth Century* (London: Methuen, 1983); Winter, *Sites of Memory*, 178–86; Tate, *Modernism*, 69–75.

72 Barbusse, *Lettres de Henri Barbusse à sa femme 1914–1917* (Paris: Flammarion, 1937), letter of 1 January 1915.

*Statesman* and *Times Literary Supplement* and was deeply admired by men such as Sassoon, Owen and Lenin.[73]

In a book titled *Under Fire*, the 'worst hell' is however not 'the flame of shells' or the 'suffocation of caverns' but what Wray translates as 'pillory of mud'. Soldiers, to him, are 'troglodytes' – a word taken up by Fussell to describe the world of the trenches – 'whom their caverns of mud but half reveal' (42). They are introduced as 'huge and misshapen lumps' extricating themselves from 'mud-masses', 'slime-beds' and 'puddles' where all is 'drenched, oozing, washed out and drowned'. Everything in Barbusse's narrative is in a state of 'liquid putrescence', dipped in 'Stygian immensity': the men are 'shapes', 'shadows' or 'silhouettes' who become visible only through their 'offensive cowl', 'infernal covering' and 'oozing coffin'. The term that Barbusse uses repeatedly to describe the coating of mud on human beings is *carapace*: the upper shell of a tortoise. Mud is an organic growth on the human form, dragging him down to his primitive state. The narrative culminates in the description of a massive landslide with echoes of the biblical flood:

Ah, the men! Where are the men? . . .

  Some distance away I can make out others, curled up and clinging like snails all along a rounded embankment, from which they have partly slipped back into the water. It is a motionless rank of clumsy lumps, of bundles placed side by side, dripping water and mud, and of the same colour as the soil with which they are blended. (320)

To Barbusse, it represents the 'end of all', the 'epic cessation': in Sartrean terms, a statement of pure 'antivalue'. Mud here becomes a powerful weapon to drive home the absurdity of war. Yet, the obsessive imagery points beyond the political investment into a general meditation on the limits between man and matter. While *Under Fire* is usually read as a political text, it can equally be read as an anti-evolutionary narrative, describing the regression of man into primordial slime.

  Shapelessness is a recurrent theme in war narratives. In *The Great Push*, Patrick MacGill observes, 'The shapelessness of Destruction reigned'; Blunden describes the trenches as 'terribly punished and shapeless';

---

73 Fitzwater Wray was born in 1867 and an entry for him in *Who Was Who* (1940) reads: 'W. Fitzwater Wray; of the literary staff of the *Daily Herald*, dealing exclusively with road travel, cycling etc; b. Hitchin, 3rd son of Rev. Samuel Wray, of Sancton, Yorks. . . . Began life as lithographic artist; then photoetcher and pen draughtsman, illustrating newspapers and other periodicals; began regular journalism, 1894.' Also see Jon Glover, 'Owen and Barbusse and Fitzwater Wray', *Stand*, 21, 2 (Spring 1980), 29.

Roland Leighton writes about 'shapeless earth'.[74] Similarly, in *Under Fire*, from the opening 'vision' of the cataclysm to the final landslide, the whole action unfolds within one vast stretch of slime: at various points in the narrative, he draws attention to the 'formless landscape' where 'there is no longer any shape' (150). Barbusse is often called the Zola of the trenches, and there are echoes of the pit disaster of *Germinal*, but the horrors of war make him push the limits of naturalism further.[75] What gives *Under Fire* its strange power is the way Barbusse combines the shapelessness of the landscape with the formlessness of the individual body: man and nature touch and blend in Barbusse's world not in Wordsworthian tranquillity but rather in a 'shapeless and sticky mass' (322). His evocative prose works through sensuous imagery with concentration on detail:

We drag ourselves to the spot. They are drowned men. Their arms and heads are submerged. On the surface of the plastery liquid appear their backs and the straps of their accoutrements. Their blue cloth trousers are inflated, with the feet attached askew upon the ballooning legs, like the black wooden feet on the shapeless legs of marionettes. From one sunken head the hair stands straight up like water-weeds. Here is a face which the water only lightly touches; the head is beached on the marge, and the body disappears in its turbid tomb. The face is lifted skyward. The eyes are two white holes; the mouth is a black hole. The mask's yellow and puffed-up skin appears soft and creased, like dough gone cold.[76]

This is characteristic of much of the material and style that *Under Fire* is famous for. The above passage can be said to be cinematic at a time when the medium was being freshly explored and exploited for the reverse kind of propaganda: *The Battle of the Somme* was released the same year as Barbusse's novel to unprecedented popularity and excitement. The camera lens, as it were, moves slowly through space, isolating, lingering on and bringing to life particular objects as they lie against the sticky flatness ('liquide plâtreux') of the water: the straps, the billowing blue trousers, the weed-like hair are all elevated to characters in this drama of dissolution as the scene builds up towards the upturned face. The above passage is a remarkably faithful translation from the original French with just one small difference which itself is illuminating. Barbusse writes, 'Voici une figure qui afleure';[77] Wray translates it as 'Here is a face which

74 MacGill, *The Great Push*, 159; Blunden, *Undertones of War* (1928; Harmondsworth: Penguin, 1982), 60; Leighton, letter quoted in Powell (ed.), *A Deep Cry*, 43.
75 See Catharine Savage Brosman, 'French Writing of the Great War' in *Cambridge Companion*, 170 (166–190).
76 Barbusse, *UF*, 320–1.
77 Barbusse, *Le Feu* (*Journal d'une Escouade*) (Paris: Ernest Flammarion, 1916), 352.

the water only lightly touches'. The slight amendment reveals how powerfully Barbusse's description was working on Wray. Like the word 'grazed' at the end of Rosenberg's 'Dead Man's Dump', Wray's embellishment 'lightly touches' not only suggests the onlooker's illusion that the face is still somewhat alive and vulnerable but also betrays the tactile quality underlying the gaze in Barbusse. Our vision is pulled into the holes from which the eyes have disappeared even as we try to resist the compulsion to look. The gaze climaxes on the organ of touch – the yellow and puffed-up skin ('La peau jaune, boursouflée'); texture and temperature are blended in the final simile of the 'dough gone cold' ('pâte refroidie') which can only be understood through physical contact. What fascinates Barbusse is not the body in pain, as with Owen, or even the moment of death, as with Remarque, but the gradual loss of human form.

The scene with 'shapeless legs' revisits the disturbing spectacle of the 'shapeless larvae of pollution' (147) that we meet halfway through Barbusse's narrative. Trudi Tate has drawn attention to the 'paradox of sameness and difference' among the corpses.[78] There is also a paradox of heightened realism and the grotesque. Norton Cru, in *Temoins* (1929), accused Barbusse of deforming the dead, and in *War Books* (1976) called his work a 'false *genre*, literature that claims to be testimony'.[79] Yet, the exaggerations and inventions that Cru deplores become a mode of exploring deeper anxieties which cannot be contained within a realistic mode: they become 'testimony' to psychic realities and threats. Consider, for example, the following scene, one of the most dramatic in the novel, as three friends come across 'a wet and bloodless head, with a heavy beard':

'I don't know him,' says Joseph . . .
'*I* recognise him,' replies Volpatte.
'That bearded man?' says Joseph.
'He has no beard. Look – 'Stooping, Volpatte passes the end of his stick under the chin of the corpse and breaks off a sort of slab of mud in which the head was set, a slab that looked like a beard. . . .
'Ah!' we all cried together, 'it's Cocon!'[80]

---

78 Tate, *Modernism*, 71.
79 Norton Cru, *War Books: A Study in Historical Criticism*, ed. and partially trans. Stanley J. Pincetl (San Diego: San Diego State UP, 1976), 42. Winter defends Barbusse, noting, 'But they [Norton Cru] missed the point. His tale was Biblical, not factual' (*Sites of Memory*, 184).
80 Barbusse, *UF*, 265.

The deliquescing body on the verge of organic/inorganic reassimilation is a common sight in war literature but why does the above scene disturb us so much? Here anomalous matter is shown *reconstructing* human identity after death through uncannily accurate bodily details – not merely a consumption but a perversion of Sartre's 'for-Itself' by the 'in-Itself'.

The tantalising process of identification exemplifies on an acutely physical level the anxiety informing Barbusse's text: the threat of trench mud to human identity, especially around margins. A daily growth around the mouth and yet something that can be easily cut away, beards, like nails, are examples of a bodily anomaly that 'disturbs identity, system'. Kristeva writes, 'My body extricates itself, as being alive, from that border. Such wastes drop so that I might live, until, from loss to loss, nothing remains in me and my entire body falls beyond the limit – *cadere*, cadaver.'[81] In Barbusse's description, the trench mud becomes humanoid, masquerading as bodily growth to complete the revenge of matter over human form. It is exactly this moment of 'in-betweenness' that Owen chooses in his first engagement with Barbusse in 'The Show'. The little clod of earth which had its first taste of human life through Cocon's beard grows in Owen's poetry into a grotesque, bearded old man – the metaphor for the trench: 'Across its beard, that horror of harsh wire / There moved thin caterpillars, slowly uncoiled'.[82]

The effect of *Under Fire* on the contemporary imagination can be seen in a painting by the German war artist, Otto Dix, titled *Flanders* (1934–6), conceived as a protest against Nazi Germany when his paintings were being banned. Dix had served in the trenches during the First World War, had come under mustard-gas attacks and his war experience was largely responsible for the bitter and savage tone of his work.[83] His *Flanders* was directly inspired by a passage from the concluding chapter of *Under Fire* describing the landslide.[84] Even twenty years after the war, it is the mud that obsesses Dix, and he draws on Barbusse's technique of excessive materiality. Dix's painting (Figure 1.3) evokes a sense of cosmic deluge: the sky, the stretches of water and the pockmarked land all merge

81 Kristeva, *Powers of Horror*, 4, 3.    82 Owen, 'The Show', *CP&F*, 155.

83 Linda F. McGreevy, *The Life and Works of Otto Dix: German Critical Realist* (Michigan: UMI Research Press, 1975), 17–30; Matthias Eberle, *World War I and the Weimar Artists: Dix, Grosz, Beckmann, Schlemmer* (New Haven: Yale University Press, 1985), 52.

84 Dix was particularly inspired by the following description: 'Out of the horror of the night, apparitions are issuing from this side and that who are clad in exactly the same uniform of misery and filth. It is the end of all' (Barbusse, *UF*, 322).

Figure 1.3. Otto Dix, *Flanders*, 1934–6. Courtesy of Nationalgalerie, Staatliche Museen zu Berlin. Photo: Jörg P. Anders.

into each other, providing a surreal space where clouds, corpses and tree stumps can float together. The strange brownish light, instead of highlighting the figures or the landscape, spreads like a dirty stain through the painting. The eye moves from the dense clouds to the encircling ooze to the rotting tree stumps to the barbed wire to human bodies: whatever the eye perceives is converted, for these objects to have effect, to the sense of touch. This process is almost inscribed within the painting in the strong sculptural quality of the three figures at the front where our eyes finally come to rest. Like Barbusse's 'misshapen lumps', they form one amorphous mass: the heavy folds of the paint make them seem like three figures in a half-finished state in an artist's workshop, struggling to come out of their clay moulds. This is macabre, for *Flanders* is a realistic painting rather than a piece of sculpture: the clay-like mantle passing over the head of the figure on the right and above the legs of the frontal figure is not the medium of representation trying to evoke an external world of texture but actuality itself. The three figures are human beings existing in historical time – soldiers of the First World War – encumbered by, and dissolving into, the mud that the painter's unflinching eye and hand have captured so faithfully. Around this huddled mass, the colours are dark, the surface ragged, scratchy: brown and crimson are layered thick on each other and then scraped back, like blood and mud battling for possession. The materiality of the paint draws attention to the suffocating excess of matter.

The skin, the dividing line between oneself and the surrounding world, is a site of anxiety in Barbusse:

> The skin of his fat cheeks is scored with the marks of the folds in the tent-cloth that has served him for nightcap. (6)

> His hand gropes within his greatcoat and his jacket till he finds the skin, and scratches. (7)

Skin is here imagined as something strangely external: like cloth, it can get crumpled, like a coat, it may go missing. Matter discolours and de-forms: Volpatte's face is 'yellow brown as though iodised', Breton's skin is grey, Foillade's skin 'the colour of violin', Blaire's 'horribly black'; Tir-loin's wrinkle looks like a muzzle, Lamuse scratches himself like a gorilla and Endore like a marmoset. *The Lancet* mentions the recurrence of skin diseases such as pediculosis, scabies and ringworm in the trenches.[85] Such skin diseases would no doubt have increased concerns about the status of the body as matter, the first step towards becoming *just* matter. Neither living nor dead, the yellow iodised skin and blackish patches of Barbusse's 'misshapen lumps' anticipate more disturbing descriptions: 'half-mouldy faces, the skin rusted, or yellow with dark spots. Of several, the faces are black as tar, the lips hugely distended – the heads of Negroes.' The racial anxiety may be partly because of the presence of African and Indian troops in France as well as the contemporary discourse on degeneration that was often conflated with racial impurity.[86] The sight of the skin changing colour disturbs the soldiers: in A. P. Herbert's *The Secret Battle*, the English officers are revolted by the sight of dead white bodies turning black in the heat; the bodies in Rosenberg's 'Dead Men's Dump' are 'burnt black by strange decay'; Manning, in *The Middle Parts of Fortune*, speaks of 'festering, fly-blown corruption . . . blackening in the heat'.[87]

---

85 H. G. Adamson, 'On the Treatment of Scabies and Some Other Common Skin Affections in Soldiers', *The Lancet*, 10 February 1917: 1, 221.

86 See Daniel Pick, *Faces Of Degeneration: A European Disorder* (Cambridge: Cambridge University Press, 1989).

87 A. P. Herbert, *The Secret Battle* (1919; London: Chatto and Windus, 1970), 105; Rosenberg, 'Dead Man's Dump', *Works*, 111; Frederic Manning, *The Middle Parts of Fortune* (1930; London: Peter Davies, 1977), 11.

All claims to realism are abandoned towards the end of *Under Fire* as the image of the landslide concludes with a pair of mud-caked corpses: 'Slowly we veer towards the mass formed by men curiously joined, leaning shoulder to shoulder and each with an arm round the neck of the other'.[88] Are they enemies engaged in a handfight or comrades holding on to each other to prevent drowning, the rescue team asks. No answer is given. Human meanings and emotions are cancelled as mud has the final say. If these two figures are static and indistinguishable, similarly the main characters – Lamuse, Volpatte, Cocon or Fouillade – do not grow and develop in course of the novel or engage our emotions. Our very frustration as readers becomes the index of Barbusse's success: the relentless reminder that the ultimate outcome of war is not the victory of one side but the dissolution of form. The 'two-dimensional' characterisation and rather chaotic structure for which the novel is criticised may not be a case of hastily converting a diary into a novel: it might more closely be integrated into a negative narrative of devolution where human beings are shown to be caught in a fatal entropic course as nations fight. While in Remarque's *All Quiet on the Western Front* or Blunden's *Undertones of War*, there is a clearly defined group of people with whom we can empathise or a set of events that mark time, in *Under Fire* there is almost no development in terms of plot or characterisation: the 'slimescape' that is evoked so powerfully impedes narrative progression.

The two men locked in eternal embrace throw off their mantle of 'trickling ochre' and resurface at the beginning of Céline's *Journey to the End of the Night* (1932) through a welter of bodily fluids: 'They were embracing each other for the moment and all eternity but the cavalryman's head was gone, all he had was an opening. . . . The colonel's belly was wide open. . . . All this tangled meat was bleeding furiously.'[89] The literary echo of Barbusse's 'double monument of woe', with blood replacing mud, is Céline's acknowledgement of his debt to one of his favourite novels and also a sign of his difference. Céline served in the '12 Cuir' and was attached to the 2nd Cavalry Squadron in 1914 and the novel is shaped by his traumatic trench experience.[90] The common idea of

---

88 Barbusse, *UF*, 323–4.          89 Céline, *Journey*, 22.
90 Catherine Savage Brosman notes, 'It could be argued that Céline's *Voyage au bout de la nuit*, 1932 (*Journey to the End of the Night*), derives principally from the Great War, although less than a fifth concerns the conflict itself' ('French Writing of the Great War', 184). See also John Sturrock, *Journey to the End of the Night* (Cambridge: Cambridge University Press, 1990), particularly the section on the body where he notes that, in Céline's imagination, 'human substance must dissolve unstoppably' (58).

'dust to dust' or 'ashes to ashes' is too dry for Céline: the human body must undergo a more sticky process of decomposition. The noun *pour-riture* ('rot', 'rottenness') and the verb *fondre* ('to melt') are recurring words in *Journey*. A soldier dies 'pissing blood'; as Henrouille dies, his heart, 'all juicy' and 'red' starts 'gushing'; the passengers on board the *Admiral Bragueton* begin to sweat and dissolve like 'squid at the bottom of a bathtub of unsavoury water'. The last image is reminiscent of the octopus simile in the trench newspaper. At one point in the text, Baryton, the asylum-keeper, screams, 'They're liquidating! They are liquidating', looking forward to *Nausea* which begins with an inscription from Céline. Indeed, one wonders how much of the slime seeps out of the trenches in *Under Fire* and coagulates into the 'yellow mud' of the park at the end of *Nausea* where Roquentin has his extended spell of existentialist crisis.

It is worth noting, given its widespread influence on contemporary thought, that Julia Kristeva's *Powers of Horror* (1982) is permeated by Céline's *Journey*. Kristeva's theory of abjection is rooted in her long-abiding interest in the mother.[91] At a time when the body was increasingly becoming a linguistic trace, Kristeva provided a powerful critical language to draw attention to its abject corporeality. What interests me here is the way Céline figures centrally in her analysis of the experience of reading and whether one can detect traces of First World War experience in the theory of abjection. Kristeva draws attention to Céline's 'mysterious, intimately nocturnal' style which draws us 'to the fragile spot of our subjectivity' revealing a 'flayed skin'. Six out of eleven chapters are devoted to Céline with a separate section on *Journey* which is quoted twenty-two times. As Leon S. Roudiez, her translator, points out, she not only 'plays with the titles of Céline's novels' but even borrows words such as 'petard'. She engages with him not merely at the critical but at a creative level. Céline, to her, is the most *abject* of writers, writing from within the horror, believing death and horror are what being is. Trying to understand his style, Kristeva finally focuses on his bodily wound: 'Aching in his head, his ear, his arm. Dizziness, noises, buzzings, vomitings.'[92]

The wound in Céline is a specific First World War injury, though controversy surrounds its exact site. Following heavy fighting from 15–25 October, he and six other men from his regiment were wounded on 27

---

91 There are also the voices of Freud, Lacan and Douglas in Kristeva's text. See Elizabeth Grosz, *Volatile Bodies: Towards a Corporeal Feminism* (Bloomington: Indiana University Press, 1994); John Lechte, *Julia Kristeva* (London: Routledge, 1990).
92 Kristeva, *Powers of Horror*, 133–5, viii, 134, 146.

October 1915. From 1930, he started complaining of persistent migraines and buzzing in his ears.[93] The wound he received in October, 1915 was however from a ricocheting bullet which hit his right arm, causing permanent damage. The 'suffering, horror, death' that Kristeva notes in *Journey* and that she abstracts into her theory of narrative ('Narrative as the recounting of suffering: fear, disgust and abjection crying out'[94]) is largely shaped by the writer's combat experience. 'The battle is fierce . . . I have never seen and will never see again so much horror', Céline writes to his parents from the trenches.[95] As Brosman notes, 'like his creator, Bardamu, the anti-heroic protagonist, is shaped forever by the Front'.[96] The trauma of bodily dissolution in the First World War trenches thus can be said to filter through Céline into the theory of abjection. As in Céline, so in Barbusse 'it is the human corpse that occasions the greatest concentration of abjection and fascination'(149). In recent years, the abject body has become something of a celebratory, emancipatory force, stretching the boundaries of the aesthetic, and endlessly represented in museums and art galleries.[97] It is important to remember, in this regard, that the horrors in the texts of Barbusse and Céline have a definite relation to actual experience: they cannot be wholly extrapolated from their historical contexts which give them a peculiar urgency, 'the touch of the real'.

MUDDY NARRATIVES: SASSOON, BLUNDEN, JONES

In the history of English First World War writings, one notes a curious phenomenon. The poetry can be said to have begun at the same time as the war. In August 1914, about a hundred poems a day arrived at *The Times*; three anthologies of war poetry appeared in September 1914, another in November, twelve in 1915, six more in 1916.[98] Some of the best-known war poets – Sorley, Rosenberg, Owen, Thomas – were dead by the time the war ended. Even the poets who survived wrote much of their verse during the war: Sassoon's satires were published in the *Cambridge Magazine*, Gurney's *Severn and Somme*, Robert Nichols's *Ardours*

---

93  Nicholas Hewitt, *The Life of Céline: A Critical Biography* (Oxford: Blackwell, 1999), 25–9.
94  Kristeva, *Powers of Horror*, 145.
95  Quoted in Hewitt, *Céline*, 25.
96  Brosman, 'French Writing of the Great War', 184.
97  See Martin Jay, 'Abjection Overruled', in *Cultural Semantics: Keywords of Our Time* (Amherst: University of Massachusetts Press, 1998), 144–56.
98  Hynes, *A War Imagined*, 25–33.

*and Endurances*, Robert Graves's *Fairies and Fusiliers* and Frederic Manning's *Eidolon* all came out in 1917. Yet, most of the prominent prose accounts started appearing almost a decade later: Ford Madox Ford's *Parade's End* from 1924–8, Blunden's *Undertones of War* in 1928, Robert Graves's *Goodbye To All That* in 1929, Frederic Manning's *The Middle Parts of Fortune* in 1929, Vera Brittain's *Testament of Youth* in 1933 and David Jones's *In Parenthesis* in 1937. While the trench lyric usually derives its power from its immediacy and contingent nature, it is as if more time was needed to heal the breach in time caused by the war and organise the war years into a coherent prose narrative. This section examines the ways mud affects English war writings, and how its literary life, in turn, is affected by generic considerations. I shall focus on three writers working at different points and in different genres: Siegfried Sassoon, Edmund Blunden and David Jones.

Sassoon called 'The Redeemer' 'my first frontline poem': it can be said to be the turning point in Sassoon's career from pre-war versifier to the representative First World War poet.[99] Published in *The Cambridge Magazine* (29 April 1916), it is in the depiction of 'mire' that one notes for the first time Sassoon's combination of realism and satire:

> Darkness: the rain sluiced down; the mire was deep;
> . . .
> We lugged our clay-sucked boots as best we might
> Along the trench; sometimes a bullet sang,
> And droning shells burst with a hollow bang;
> We were soaked, chilled and wretched, every one;
> Darkness; the distant wink of a huge gun.
>
> I turned in the black ditch, loathing the storm;
> A rocket fizzed and burnt with blanching flare,
> And lit the face of what had been a form
> Floundering in mirk. He stood before me there;
> I say that He was Christ;
> . . .
> Then the flame sank, and all grew black as pitch,
> While we began to struggle along the ditch;
> And someone flung his burden in the muck,
> Mumbling: 'O Christ Almighty, now I'm stuck!'[100]

99 Sassoon, *The War Poems*, ed. Sir Rupert Hart-Davis (London: Faber and Faber, 1983), 17.
100 Sassoon, 'The Redeemer', *Collected Poems*, 16–17. See Stallworthy, *Anthem for Doomed Youth*, for a comparison between 'The Redeemer' and 'Christ and the Soldier' (66).

The poem was written in Sassoon's first week in the trenches, 'inspired by working-parties at Festubert, Nov. 25 and 27 [1915]'.[101] In the diary entry for 27 November, he writes of 'dusky figures' in the moonlight, 'hobbling to avoid slipping, inhuman forms going to and from inhuman tasks' and subsequent diary entries record his nocturnal sojourn down the muddy trenches.[102] The disappearance of the visual horizon of one's body and the tactile nature of the experience are the defining trauma in Sassoon's narrative, introduced through the opening word, 'Darkness', kept up through 'Floundering in mirk' and reaching its conclusion through the shock of the colloquial rhyme, 'muck / stuck' with its trace of expletive. 'I say that He was Christ': in this refrain, one notes the process of 're-sacralization' that Winter has noted in First World War writings.[103] But this redemptive vision at the heart of the poem, of the 'English soldier, white and strong' carrying his cross, a common trope in the heroic tradition of Great War verse, suddenly turns 'black as pitch'. Faced with the ghastly prospect of burial, the soldier swears, 'O Christ Almighty'. Sassoon's satiric outburst is acute to phenomenological reality of the moment. Horror becomes the ground of blasphemy as slime threatens to trap and dissolve human form.

Mud becomes with Sassoon, as with Barbusse, a political tool to evoke the horrors of war: he uses a quotation from Barbusse's *Le Feu* to preface *Counter-Attack and Other Poems* (1918). In 'The Redeemer', the stressed monosyllables – mire, mirk, muck – combined with the set of 'sluiced', 'sucked' and 'soaked' stick in our consciousness in such a way that 'mercy' conjures up 'murky'. Or consider the following examples:

> Five miles of stodgy clay and freezing sludge,
> And everything but wretchedness forgotten.
> ('In the Pink')

> Stepping along barred trench-boards, often splashing
> Wretchedly where the sludge was ankle-deep.
> ('A Working Party')[104]

Drawing attention to the 'submerged lands' of poetic imagination, Virginia Woolf, reviewing *The Old Huntsman and Other Poems* for the *Times Literary Supplement* (31 May 1917), commended Sassoon's 'realism of the right, the poetic kind'.[105] But John Middleton Murry was not

101 Sassoon, *War Poems*, 17.        102 Sassoon, *Diaries, 1915–1918*, 20–1.
103 Winter, *Sites of Memory*, 221.
104 Sassoon, *The War Poems*, intro. Rupert Hart Davis (London: Faber, 1983), 22, 26.
105 Woolf, 'Mr Sassoon's Poems', *Times Literary Supplement*, May 31, 1917, 259.

impressed. On 13 July 1918, he wrote: 'Mr Sassoon's verses – they are not poetry – are such a cry. They touch not our imagination, but our sense . . . for these verses express nothing, save in so far as a cry expresses pain.' He did not approve of the rendering in poetry of the 'chaos of immediate sensation by a chaotic expression'.[106] The sharp disapproval shows how startlingly new and modern Sassoon's accommodation of messy physicality was to the contemporary poetic credo. Sassoon worked largely within the Victorian conventions of metre, syntax and rhyme and yet, in his use of colloquial diction and realism, he was one of the earliest of the First World War poets to forge a new literary language in order to assimilate contemporary history.

Murry would however have had sympathy for Herbert Read's more self-consciously modernist aesthetic in 'Kneeshaw Goes to War'. Read called 'Kneeshaw' his 'realistic war poem', distilling the world of the trenches into a single powerful image. In the poem, Kneeshaw's companion 'slowly sank, weighted down by equipment and arms':

> His terror grew –
> Grew visibly when the viscous ooze
> Reached his neck.
> And there he seemed to stick. . .[107]

Read's poem, like Sassoon's satires, subverts the Romantic pastoral and evolves the category of the horrifically sensuous. But, in the precision of the image and use of free verse, he follows the precepts of Imagism, only to mire the hard contours of Pound's 'granite' poetry or H. D.'s world of 'pure forms' in trench realism: there is a central tension between the avant-garde aesthetic and the terrifying formlessness of what it describes. In Read's poem, the witnessing soldier, unable to bear the sight any longer, shoots the man trapped in the mud: light soon appears on the horizon, as if dawn has so long been withheld in the poem because of this fundamental anomaly. One of the most powerful accounts, however, came from a woman writer – the American nurse Mary Borden who

106 John Middleton Murry, 'Mr Sassoon's War Verses', *Nation*, vol. 23 (13 July 1918), 398. When Sassoon published a collection of *War Poems* in 1919, the reviewing journals placed it in a special non-poetic category: 'a great pamphlet against war', the *Nation* commented, while according to the *London Mercury*, much of it 'can only be described as journalism' Robert Lynd, 'The Young Satirists', *The Nation*, vol. 26, Supplement (6 December 1919), 352; *London Mercury*, vol.1 (December 1919), 206.

107 Herbert Read, *Collected Poems* (London: Sinclair-Stevenson, 1966), 31–2.

served as a nurse in her mobile hospital unit near the battlefields of Ypres and the Somme – in 'The Song of the Mud':

The frothing, squirting, spurting, liquid mud that gurgles along the road belts;
The thick elastic mud that is kneaded and pounded and squeezed under the hoofs of the horses;
The invincible, inexhaustible mud of the war zone.
. . .
It has drowned our men.
Its monstrous distended belly reeks with the undigested dead.[108]

And so it continues for four pages, with the long irregular lines and the hammering beat of the word 'mud' which is repeated twenty-six times. The sheer length of the poem is almost a textual enactment of its theme. As in Barbusse, there is no sense of progression, as if the mud had literally impeded movement. The metaphor of the monster in the final quoted line connects it to the trench accounts of the soldiers.

Paul Fussell has drawn attention to the use of the pastoral in English war writings.[109] Trench mud is anti-pastoral: it is nature made unnatural. It serves Sassoon well in his war satires but how can it be contained within a pastoral narrative? Thus, ten years after the war, when Blunden chooses the pastoral form to represent what Wyndham Lewis refers to as 'an epic of mud', the choice seems curious.[110] The preface registers the anxiety: 'I must go over the ground again. A voice, perhaps not my own, answers within me. You will be going over the ground again.' Masefield's enormously popular line, 'I must down to the seas again' gets charged with grim irony. Much of the imaginative power of *Undertones of War* (1928) lies in the attempt to contain the horrors of war within the age-old and reassuring form of the pastoral. Blunden's narrative is called *Undertones of War*: what lies under never ceases to irritate and disrupt. Just as at 'some points in the trench, bones pierced through their shallow burial', similarly violent memories of the war would continually resurface in Blunden's imagination, stubbornly refusing to be repressed: 'Then the ground became torn and vile, the poisonous breath of fresh explosions skulked all about, and the mud which choked the narrow passages stank as one pulled through it' (48). Yet, there is a stubborn refusal to name the composition of the mud. That is implied through the euphemistic reference: 'Much lime was wanted in Cuinchy'. Later, Blunden refers to the

108 Borden, *FZ*, 179–82.        109 Fussell, *GWMM*, 231–69.
110 Lewis, *Blasting and Bombardiering*, 152.

'dead sea of mud'.[111] War experience is not so much repressed as concentrated into a single adjective. The grotesquery of Barbusse is replaced by the sinister use of commas in Blunden: 'mud, and death, and life'.

Towards the end of his life, Blunden noted, 'War dreams have been part of my life for forty years'; his widow said in 1981 that until his death in 1976, no day passed in which her husband did not refer to the war.[112] Building on Freud's work, Cathy Caruth has suggested that at the heart of trauma narratives, there is 'a kind of double telling, the oscillation between a crisis of death and the correlative crisis of life'.[113] Such crisis occurs when the battalion reaches Thiepval. The plight of comrades brings the survivors towards the edge of language and comprehension:

Schwaben Redoubt ahead was an almost obliterated cocoon of trenches in which mud, and death, and life were much the same thing – and there the deep dugouts, which faced the German guns, were cancerous with torn bodies, and to pass an entrance was to gulp poison; in one place a corpse had apparently been thrust in to stop up a doorway's dangerous displacement, and an arm swung stupidly. Men of the next battalion were found in mud up to the armpits, and their fate was not spoken of; those who found them could not get them out.[114]

The passage derives much of its impact from the literary quality of the framing narrative. The word 'cocoon' is innocuously inserted, a seemingly casual reminder of the original regenerative function of the mud; in the war context, it may also suggest a regression to the primal foetal posture, as in Remarque's account of the terrified soldier burying himself in the mud.[115] But the 'cocoon' has become 'cancerous', death threatening even unborn life. The voluminous alliterative phrase, 'door's dangerous displacement', a remnant from civilian times, sounds ludicrous in a world where corpses act as doorstops. The stupidly swinging arms, erasing the difference between inert matter and human limbs, verge on the grotesque. What is striking in the passage quoted is that even after these graphic horrors, Blunden is not direct about the common experience of trench warfare – drowning in the mud: 'their fate was not spoken of'. He can only speak about the silence of the survivors. The organic metaphor

---

111 Blunden, *Undertones of War*, 8, 25, 48, 221. Blunden took part in some of the worst fighting of the war, always carrying with him a copy of Julius Caesar's *De Bello Gallico*. After the war, he set down to write his memoir which he called *De Bello Germanico: A Fragment of Trench History*, but ten years later returned to the subject in *Undertones of War*. See also Barry Web, *Edmund Blunden: A Biography* (New Haven: Yale University Press, 1990).
112 *The Times*, 9 November 1981. Quoted in Hew Strachan, *First World War*, xix.
113 Caruth, *Unclaimed Experience*, 7.
114 Blunden, *Undertones*, 130–1.  115 *Remarque, All Quiet*, 41–2.

inherent in the word 'cancerous' is taken up and expanded, displacing images of mutilation to the landscape: 'The whole zone was a corpse, and the mud itself mortified'. No image can be more devastating to the pastoral vision: the very foundation of Blunden's narrative universe is imagined to be composed of human waste. What the silence ('not spoken of') does is not so much elide or repress history (men getting buried in the mud) as to resituate the crisis within the literary structure: trauma is acknowledged through the gap in telling while the metaphor of the 'corpse' undercuts the pastoral mode.

It would however be left to David Jones in *In Parenthesis* (1937) – one of the last works to come out of the war experience, and described by T. S. Eliot as 'a work of genius' – to evolve this threat into an acute literary self-consciousness, a profound meditation on the formlessness of war and literary form.[116] Jones's narrative covers the period between December 1915 and July 1916. Though concerned with war, he wanted his book 'to be about a good kind of peace'.[117] In this highly allusive narrative, human identity is powerfully asserted through the central, unifying consciousness of John Ball. In the context of Jones's work as a whole, it becomes clear that the 'peace' that *In Parenthesis* strives for is rooted in his belief in man's fundamental identity: *homo sapiens, homo faber* (man the knower, man the creator).[118] Despite all atrocities, the soldiers are portrayed as clinging onto things that make them human, trying to 'make order, for however brief a time and in whatever wilderness': whether through snatches of 'confused talking', ranging from discussing the poetry of Rupert Brooke to the characteristics of a Welshman, or through simple domestic gestures such as hanging up clothes and creating sleeping places. These are, to Jones, the marks of a 'sacramentalist', something his own writing powerfully performs. The poetic consciousness of the narrator gives value and meaning to the events that often do not make meaning by themselves. The song of Lance Corporal Aneirin, the prophet-figure, thus can save John Ball from sinking into the 'deep sludge'.[119] The power of art can create a new order of reality and prevent the descent of the cherished human race into slime.

---

116 Jones, *In Parenthesis*, vii.        117 Jones, *In Parenthesis*, xii–xiii.
118 Jones, *Epoch and Artist*, 184.
119 Jones, *In Parenthesis*, 45. Kathleen Henderson Staudt sees music-making as the central metaphor for poetic consciousness in the novel. For her, it is the single act that can counter the ravages of the war in Jones's understanding. (*At the Turn of a Civilisation*, Ann Arbor: University of Michigan Press, 1994, 51–65.)

In the preface, Jones writes, 'I have only tried to make a shape in words, using as data the complex of sights, sounds, fears, hopes, apprehensions'.[120] But midway through the text, Jones's narrative is suddenly intruded upon by a grotesque shapeless creature:

Thickly greaved with mud so that his boots and puttees and sandbag tie-ons were become one whole of trickling ochre. His minute pipe had its smoking bowl turned inversely. . . . He slipped back quickly, with a certain animal caution, into his hole; to almost immediately poke out his wool-work head, to ask if anyone had the time of day or could spare him some dark shag or a picture paper. Further, should they meet a white dog in the trench her name was Belle, and he would like to catch any bastard giving this Belle the boot.[121]

Characteristic of his intricate style, the threat of matter is suggested in Jones in a single word, 'greaved'. The *OED* defines 'greaved' as 'equipped with greaves', a greave being 'a piece of armour for the leg below the knee'. At the same time, in the above passage, mud is shown to be 'trickling' down the figure, and his 'great moustaches beaded with condensation under his nose'. Man and matter have become such an amorphous mass that it becomes impossible to distinguish between entrapment and porosity. More frighteningly, the blurring of physical boundaries here becomes coterminous with the disintegration of mental stability. This strange figure is first depicted through the animal imagery: 'slipped back', 'animal caution' or 'poke out his wool-work head'. But he continues to be defiantly human: time and tobacco and picture-paper get mixed up, fantasies of whiteness and femininity and masculine rivalry, relics of a bygone era, get displaced onto the trench-dog, Belle.

This strange presence in Jones's narrative, 'seemingly native to the place', is characterised by a terrifying in-betweenness. Neither man nor matter, neither wholly human nor bestial, he is a powerful example of the *abject* in English war writing. Kristeva notes, 'The abject confronts us . . . with those fragile states where man strays on the territories of *animal*'.[122] This ambiguous man-animal makes his appearance in Section 4, the central section in Jones's tightly structured narrative, and yet a section where the taut texture of Jones's narrative is constantly threatened with 'aquatic suckings', 'liquid action' and 'bleached forms'. In this section, right at the middle, as have been argued, we have Dai, 'the symbol of continuity': we have the 'most significant lyric digression', whose

120 Jones, *In Parenthesis*, x.
121 Jones, *In Parenthesis*, 89–90.    122 Kristeva, *Powers of Horror*, 12.

incantatory chants – 'I heard', 'I saw' or 'I was with' – connect present history to ancient heroic past, to myth and tradition.[123] Yet this 'amphibious man' is a presence the text cannot deny. If name signifies identity and lineage, he is nameless, belonging nowhere, literally *cast out*. Neither the vast store of Western culture nor Catholic theology nor Welsh mythology, through which Jones repeatedly orders his narrative, can contain him: cross-references or allusions are significantly absent; the structured verse of Dai's sermon breaks off into haphazard prose; Aneirin Lewis, the prophet, is conspicuously rendered 'motionless'; Corporal Quilter starts spitting. Instead, the 'trickling ochre' of his body resurfaces as description in the 'two unexploded yellow-ochre toffee-apples' and in the simile of the 'slime-beast' amidst the long list of industrial debris that marks the single-most difference of this war from previous wars. The product of modern industrial warfare, his act of asking time deals a fatal blow to the narrator's attempt to link the war with the past through allusions. He functions as human detritus, whose muddy boundaries disintegrate time and values and meaning in the semantic landscape of the text, and he profoundly troubles Jones's vision.

*In Parenthesis* transmutes historical experience into an acute aesthetic and linguistic self-consciousness. In its range of allusions and its playfulness with questions of time and genre, it takes its place alongside Eliot's *The Waste Land* as a quintessentially 'modernist' text. Literary modernism and its relation to the war remain a highly contested battleground.[124] In the note to the second edition of *The Penguin Book of First World War Poetry* (1981), Jon Silkin notes, 'With the exception of Jones, however, and, to a lesser extent Read and Rosenberg, these poets were not modernists'.[125] Written hurriedly in trenches, on leave or while recovering from shell-shock, the poetry of Sassoon, Blunden or Owen is not considered to have the same level of textual complexity or self-reflexivity that one associates with the writings of Eliot, Pound or Woolf. Yet, historically, at the heart of modernism lies the trauma of the trenches. Malcolm Bradbury notes, 'Many critics have seen the war as . . . the apocalypse

123　Staudt, *At the Turn*, 61.

124　Trudi Tate and Vincent Sherry have astutely explored the relation between literary modernism and the First World War. While Tate concentrates on prose narratives, Sherry focuses on high modernist writers such as Eliot, Pound and Woolf; interestingly, trench poetry does not figure in either account. See Tate *Modernism*, Sherry, *The Great War and the Language of Modernism* (New York: Oxford University Press, 2003).

125　Jon Silkin (ed.), *The Penguin Book of First World War Poetry* (1979; Harmondsworth: Penguin, 1996), 13.

that leads the way into Modernism as violation, intrusion, wound, the source of psychic anxiety'.[126] More recently, Edna Longley has argued that poetry of soldier-writers such as Owen, Thomas or Rosenberg is 'the point where poetry takes the full shock of the new' and that it grafts its 'own blood-dimmed iconography' on to 'a post-Christian and post-Romantic symbolic repertoire'.[127] Whether such poetry qualifies as 'modern' or not depends ultimately on what criteria we bring to define 'modernism' and in turn shows how diffuse the term continues to be.[128] With its complex negotiation between more traditional poetic and cultural traditions, local but powerful experimentations and historical specificity, the poetry of the trenches refuses to fit any strict literary label. What is undeniable however is that these muddy trench narratives arising out of immediate and sensuous experience unleash a strong current of formlessness within early twentieth-century verse.

In the pre-war years, both the Imagists and the Vorticists, in their different but related ways, rewrite the decadent male body of *fin-de-siècle* literature: it becomes 'hard', either imagined in terms of crystalline purity, as with Aldington and H. D., or abstracted into figures of mechanised energy, even violence, as in *Blast*. The poetry of Sassoon and Owen wrests the male body from the pure forms of Imagism or the aggressive muscularity of Vorticism into the abject corporeality of the physical world. The very sharpness of Middleton Murry's judgement of Sassoon's verse becomes an index of the novelty of such literature, recording, as he said, 'the chaos of immediate sensation'.[129] Words such as 'sploshed', 'muck', 'sludge', 'funk' or 'plastering slime' were not just new words in English poetry but introduced a new economy of bodily affect, new ways of experiencing and representing the male body with a strong historical resonance. And often these messy bodies migrate out of the trenches

126 Malcolm Bradbury, 'The Denuded Place: War and Form in *Parade's End* and *USA*', in *The First World War in Fiction*, ed. Holger Klein (London: Macmillan, 1976), 193–4.

127 Edna Longley, 'The Great War, History, and the English Lyric', in *Cambridge Companion*, 57–84. She argues for a broader and more nuanced understanding of what constitutes the 'modern', and shows how, in First World War verse, 'traditional forms internalize history as new complications of voice, syntax, diction, image, stanza, line, rhyme, assonance – ultimately, rhythm' (77).

128 In his introduction to *Modernist Sexualities*, ed. Hugh Stevens and Caroline Howlett (Manchester, Manchester University Press, 2000), Stevens asks: 'Is modernist writing defined by formal and stylistic features, such as a high degree of linguistic or aesthetic self-consciousness, or is it to be understood as writing emerging from a particular historical context? Who are the makers of modernism?' (1). These questions, though raised in a different context, are useful in thinking about war poetry's relation to literary modernism.

129 Murry, 'Mr Sassoon's War Verses', 399.

and plant themselves in the unsuspected civilian zones of more self-conscious modernist writings, such as Stetson's garden in Eliot's *The Waste Land* or the Piazza Vittorio Emmanuele at Florence in Lawrence's *Aaron's Rod*.

In this chapter, I have examined the threat of mud to the identity of the soldiers and how this impels, obstructs and even occasionally encrusts literary narratives. The next chapter explores further the geography of the trenches through ideas of darkness, claustrophobia and sound, and the relation between sense perception and literary narratives. While there has been much interest within contemporary critical thinking in the violated body or the 'shattering' of the subject, we have one of its most powerful examples in the First World War infantryman, suspended between the ravages of industrial weaponry on one hand and the glutinous chaos of matter on the other. And often it was the latter that caused the greater anxiety, as borne out by the popular trench-song: 'It wasn't the foe we feared / It wasn't the bullets that whined /. . .It was the MUD – MUD – MUD'.[130]

---

130 Song entitled 'Reminiscences of Rilken Ridge, August, 1917', in J. Bennett, 'Diary', IWM, 83/14/1.

# CHAPTER 2

# Geographies of sense

In his war memoir, *In Retreat* (1925), Herbert Read recalls seeking refuge with his men at a dug-out under a 'hellish bombardment'. The men squat on the floor around a few candles or cower on the 'mist-wet' earth as shell after shell continues to pound into the 'invisible foreground'.[1] This is a classic scenario in trench narratives, from Owen's letter describing being trapped in a dug-out under fire with '50 strong men trembling as with ague for 50 hours' to Hervey Allen's *Toward the Flame* (1934): 'we simply lay and trembled from sheer nervous tension'.[2] In Read's narrative, an offensive is taking place overhead, the bombardment carries on and yet nothing can be known. The men, 'dazed and quivering', reach the end of their tether and the anxiety mounts. Read continues: 'By ten o'clock or so, our hearts were like taut drum skins beaten reverberantly by every little incident. Then the skin smashed.' What exactly does he mean? There is a curious conflation of surface and depth, of sound and touch: the phrase seems to suggest, beyond its metaphoric dimension, a pulsing consciousness that hovers between the perceptual and the psychic, a state of nervous intensification when the world is experienced through the flesh rather than a single cognitive faculty. In 'The Raid', trying to describe the experience of fear, he writes: 'Their bodies broke in fear because the wild energy of the instinct was impingeing [*sic*] on a brittle red wall of physical being'.[3]

The present chapter examines the phenomenological geography of the trenches – a landscape not understood in terms of maps, places and names, but geography as processes of cognition, as subjective and sensuous states of experience, and its relation to literary narrative.[4] In *Sensuous*

---

1 Herbert Read, *In Retreat* (1925; London: Imperial War Museum, 1991), 12–13.
2 Owen, *CL*, 429; Allen, *Toward the Flame*, 53.
3 Read, *In Retreat*, 49.
4 For military geography, see Arthur Banks, *A Military Atlas of the First World War* (London: Leo Cooper, 1989). Eric Leed's *No Man's Land* (1979) remains the most insightful account of the sensory and psychological changes in the combatants engendered by 'war in the underground'

*Geography: Body, Sense and Space* (1994), Paul Rodaway argues for a return
to the experience of the senses for a fuller understanding of how we make
meaning of our surroundings: 'the senses both as a relationship to a world
and the senses as in themselves a kind of structuring of space and defining
of place'.[5] This sensuous awareness of the surrounding world marks the
experience of the trenches. 'Everything visible or audible or tangible to the
sense – to touch, smell and perception – is ugly beyond imagination',
wrote W. Beach Thomas after five months in the Somme.[6] If lines and
dots on the map defined the front line for the army commanders, the
soldiers often devised their own local geography. Consider the following
extract from the letter of Captain P. L. Sulman: 'There are two or three
trenches here very like one another except that a bosh [*sic*] has thought fit
to stick one foot out into the trench known as "one trench" because he has
only one foot out the other has two feet sticking into the trench so we call
that two trench'; similarly, Blunden remembers the sector around the
Schwaben Redoubt in terms of smell for 'to pass an entrance was to gulp
poison'.[7] In his evocation of 'ugliness', Beach Thomas underlines the role
of touch through repetition: can there be a geography of this intimate
sense as well? Rodaway notes that a visual ideology underpins geographical studies but he powerfully draws our attention to what he calls 'haptic
geography': the sense of touch not limited to the experience of fingers but
a more diffuse and active sense spread all over the body that helps in
the perception of space and includes locomotion and kinaesthesis.[8] Such a
notion, I shall argue, is particularly useful for understanding the world of

(138–50). Among recent works, see John Pegum's important study, 'Foreign Fields: Identity, and
  Location in Soldiers' Writings of the First World War' (Ph.D. thesis, Cambridge University,
  2005); Nuala C. Johnson, *Ireland, the Great War and the Geography of Remembrance*
  (Cambridge: Cambridge University Press, 2003). For a discussion of how ideas of space inform
  modernist literature, see Con Coroneos, *Space, Conrad, Modernity* (Oxford: Oxford University
  Press, 2002).

5 Paul Rodaway, *Sensuous Geographies: Body, Sense and Space* (London: Routledge, 1994), 4. There
  has been a strong phenomenological component in humanistic geography: J. D. Porteous,
  *Landscapes of the Mind: Worlds of Sense and Metaphor* (Toronto: Toronto University Press, 1990);
  Yi-Fi Tuan, *Passing Strange and Wonderful: Aesthetics, Nature and Culture* (Washington, DC:
  Island Press, 1993). See also Gillian Rose, *Feminism and Geography: The Limits of Geographical
  Knowledge* (Oxford: Polity Press, 1993); for an exemplary literary approach, see John Barrell,
  'Geographies of Hardy's Wessex', *Journal of Historical Geography*, 8, 4 (1982), 347–61.
6 W. Beach Thomas, *With the British on the Somme* (London: Methuen, 1917), 275.
7 Captain P. L. Sulman, letter of 19 January 1916 to 'Dear Tarawicks', IWM, 82/29/1; Blunden,
  *Undertones*, 130.
8 Rodaway notes: '"haptic geographies" refer to touch as an active sense which is integrally
  involved with the locomotive ability of the body and specifically focuses upon the role of touch
  in the perception of space and relationships to place' and that it covers both 'sensation-meaning
  (sense) and perception-presence (relation)' (*Sensuous Geographies*, 42, 47).

the trenches, drawing on a 'common' sense to translate the different kinds of sensory stimuli impinging on the consciousness. This chapter is divided into two sections: the first examines the 'haptic' geography of the trenches; the second analyses how such geography is represented in the work of the Jewish soldier-poet Isaac Rosenberg.

### HAPTIC GEOGRAPHIES

The absence of vision is a recurring theme in war writings, for night was the time of movement and action. A number of trench narratives – from Sassoon's 'The Redeemer', Owen's 'Strange Meeting' or Gurney's 'The Silent One' to novels such as Manning's *The Middle Parts of Fortune*, O'Flaherty's *Return of the Brute* or Céline's *Journey to the End of the Night* – begin with, or have as their setting, scenes of darkness. In fact, in *Clarté* (1919; translated as *Light* by Fitzwater Wray), Barbusse would choose darkness for his protagonist's first experience of the trenches:

We followed the trench along for three hours. For three hours we continued to immerse ourselves in distance and solitude, to immure ourselves in night, scraping its walls with our loads, and sometimes violently pulled up, where the defile shrunk into strangulation, by the sudden wedging of our pouches. It seemed as if the earth tried continually to clasp and choke us, that sometimes it roughly struck us. Above the unknown plains in which we were hiding, space was shot-riddled. A few star-shells were softly whitening some sections of the night, revealing the excavation's wet entrails and conjuring up a file of heavy shadows, borne down by lofty burdens, tramping in a black and black-bunged impasse, and jolting against the eddies. . . .

The trench came to a sudden end – to be resumed further on, it seemed. . . .

The men climbed the soft steps with bent heads, made their rush one by one, and ran hard into the belt whose only remaining defence was the dark. The thunder of shrapnel that shattered and dazzled the air here and there showed me too frightfully how fragile we all were. . . .

We began again to march one behind another, swaying about, hustled by the narrowness of this furrow they had scooped to the ancient depth of a grave, panting under the load, dragged towards the earth by the earth and pushed forward by will-power under a sky shrilling with the dizzy flight of bullets, tiger-striped with red, and in some seconds saturated with light. At forks in the way we turned sometimes right and sometimes left, all touching each other, the whole huge body of the company fleeing blindly toward its bourne.[9]

9 Henri Barbusse, *Light*, trans. Fitzwater Wray (London and Toronto: J. M. Dent & Sons, 1919), 111–12. Originally published as *Clarté* (Paris: Librarie Ernest Flammarion, 1919).

The dramatic, almost hallucinatory, power of the narrative lies in the way Barbusse suspends the first-person narrator – and the readers – between the two extreme experiences of space peculiar to trench life: the claustrophobia of the trenches and agoraphobia induced by the shot-riddled space overhead. The soldiers emerge out of the buried density of the trenches only to experience the terrors of the open night before disappearing back into the bowels of the earth. The geography of fear is thus registered and represented through a haptic mode of perception: the threat of enclosure and exposure alike produces a sense of space that is felt as volume surrounding the body rather than as surface or distance to be covered.

The night marches to and from the front along the communication lines were some of the most hated parts of trench life. The journey would last several miles but what made it particularly awful was the enormous load the private soldier had to carry. 'Our packs I cannot find words to describe. It's a cruel unnatural weight that no man should be called upon to carry', notes Roland Mountfort of 10th Battalion Fusiliers in a letter to his mother.[10] On average, the British private had to carry about sixty pounds of accoutrements which increased in winter to seventy-seven pounds. The weight of the German equipment was around seventy pounds while the French infantryman's load amounted to eighty-five pounds.[11] Robert Graves lists thirty items that would comprise the bare essentials of the British soldier's equipment. At the end of the journey, the soldier became a 'mere lifeless automaton': 'He is only conscious of the dead weight of his load, and the braces of his pack biting into his shoulders, of his thirst and the sweat of his body, and the longing to lie down and sleep'.[12] Sleep-walking is a common analogy. Private Macdonald notes that 'one would be kind of sleeping while marching', while Owen, in 'Dulce Et Decorum Est', writes 'Men marched asleep'.[13] In his description of the night journey quoted above, Barbusse juxtaposes the sense of exhaustion and overburdening with a sustained experience of claustrophobia. This sense of entrapment is a continuation of the 'nightmare of suffocation' that we first encounter in *Under Fire*: 'On all sides you bump and scrape yourself, you are clutched by the tightness of the passage, you are wedged and

---

10 R. D. Mountfort, 'Papers', IWM, Con Shelf.
11 Jon Ellis, *Eye-deep in Hell*, 33–4; also see Malcolm Brown, *Tommy Goes to War* (Charleston: Tempus, 1999), 30–9.
12 A. P. Herbert, *The Secret Battle* (1919; Oxford: Oxford University Press, 1982), 22.
13 T. Macdonald, 'Papers', IWM 76/213/1, 5; Owen, *CP&F*, 140.

stuck'.[14] As in *Under Fire*, Barbusse uses a rhetoric of exaggeration but it points precisely to the exaggerated fears and anxieties of the soldiers when the world is experienced as contact rather than through the eyes. David Jones speaks of 'perceptual knowledge' and as the fresh soldiers arrive, they experience 'at all their sense centres a perceiving of strange new things'.[15]

The constant buffeting of the body, as well as the discontinuity between the field of vision and the way the body inhabits and produces space, alter the structure of perception. In the above passage from *Light*, as the soldiers stumble through the sibilant dark, bowed under the weight of their packs, they have a heightened sense of their surroundings. The material universe seems to expand in mass, choking, vengeful, threateningly alive. Haptic geography is evoked through a careful modulation of verbs: plunge, follow, immerse, immure, scrape. In Wray's translation, if 'immerse' and 'immure' function at the level of literary language, the hint of the metaphoric 'wall' in 'immure' is suddenly literalised into a perceptual reality as the soldiers are depicted as 'scraping its walls with our loads'. What does, or can, 'it' refer to? The walls of the trench, surely, but at this point in the sentence, following the logic of the syntax, 'it' can only refer to 'night' whose darkness is conflated with the strangulating 'defile': the syntax captures the perceptual processes of the soldiers. This syntactic ambiguity is absent in the original French version where Barbusse directly underlines the materiality of the darkness: 'à se murer dans la nuit, râclant les parois de l'ombre avec le chargement'.[16] Here, the self-reflexive verb 'se murer' contains traces of 'mur' ('wall'), but instead of this usual noun, Barbusse employs a more poetic vocabulary in 'parois de l'ombre' ('wall of shadow'). In the soldiers' consciousness, time and space congeal to form a black mass through which they move. This impression is first conveyed through the spatial metaphor 'quartiers de nuit', and then in the phrase 'une impasse noire, bouchée de noir' which Fitzwater Wray acutely translates as 'black-bunged impasse': 'bouchée' is converted into the onomatopoeic 'bunged' ('bouché': adjective), as if darkness is a cork fitted into the mouth of the trench.

The dual terrors of entrapment and darkness recall Bachelard's exploration of the fears and fantasies associated with the cellar: 'The cellar dreamer knows that the walls of the cellar are buried walls, that they are walls with a single casing, walls that have the entire earth behind them. . . .

---

14 Barbusse, *UF*, 277.
15 Jones, *In Parenthesis*, 16, 18.
16 Barbusse, *Clarté*, 106.

The cellar then becomes buried madness, walled-in tragedy.'[17] 'In a mine, as in a cellar', notes Leed in his exploration of mining warfare, 'the essential feature of the environment disconnects a key element of perception: the distinction between inside and outside, figure and ground'.[18] Barbusse's description reveals that similar anxieties press upon the infantrymen as well, blurring the distinction between the literal and the figurative. While the analogy with the 'ancient depth of a grave' underlines the fear of burial – of 'walled-in tragedy' – the sudden image of 'excavation's wet entrails' brings in a primitive world, the fears of the night. The Verey lights are described as whitening 'some *sections* ['quartiers'] of the night', as if the night has assumed what he later calls 'the stillness of lifeless things' which light can now touch 'softly'. In the original French version, the senses of softness and wetness are linked together through sound ('mollement' and 'mouillées') and spill onto this shadowy world ('d'ombres massives'). Vignes Rouges, who was in a French sapper battalion, recalls, 'The darkness is a huge mass; you seem to be moving through a yielding substance; sight is a superfluous sense'.[19] Sassoon, in *Memoirs of an Infantry Officer*, writes about 'drowning in darkness', Ford about 'thick darkness', Blunden about the 'oily black night', Allen about 'inky' darkness while in 'August on the Somme' by 'Mark Vii', 'the darkness is pricked by lesser light'.[20] David Jones evokes this 'walled darkness' through the materiality of language:

Shuts down again the close dark; the stumbling dark of the blind, that Bruegel knew about – ditch circumscribed; this all depriving darkness split now by crazy flashing; marking hugely clear the spilled bowels of trees, splinter-spike, leper-ashen, sprawling the receding, unknowable, wall of night. . .

The ebb and flow of the sentence captures the processes of cognition: dark gets darker with each repetition, gathering texture through the pattern of alliteration (dark. . .ditch. . .depriving). The series of adjectives – close, stumbling, all depriving, receding – show how embodied the experience of darkness is; later in the description, he refers to the soldiers as 'thick-textured night cloaked'.[21] Darkness, as in the passage from Barbusse, seems to have acquired substance.

17  Gaston Bachelard, *The Poetics of Space*, trans. Maria Jolas (Boston: Beacon Press, 1969), 20.
18  Leed, *NML*, 145.
19  Vignes Rouges, 'Bourru', quoted in Leed, *NML*, 145.
20  Sassoon, *Memoirs of an Infantry Officer*, 21; Ford Madox Ford, *A Man Could Stand Up*, Part III of *Parade's End* (1924–8; Manchester: Carcanet, 1997), 563; Blunden, *Undertones*, 52; Allen, *Toward the Flame*, 57; 'Mark VII', 'August on the Somme', quoted in Brophy, *The Soldier's War*, 117.
21  Jones, *In Parenthesis*, 16, 31, 32.

If darkness takes on solidity in the subterranean world of the trenches, so does the sound of shelling, especially during a barrage. The First World War saw some of the most extensive uses of heavy artillery. The fourteen-inch gun of the British could fire a shell weighing 1,400 pounds while the 42 cm heavy howitzer of the Germans, nicknamed 'Dicke Bertha', could fire shells weighing over 2,000 pounds at the rate of ten rounds per hour. In the eight days commencing 24 June 1916 in the Somme, 1,732,873 shells were fired by the Allied Fourth Army; prior to the Messines assault, from 26 May to 6 June 1917, British artillery fired more than three and half million shells in support of the attack, something in the order of three and half shells per second for a twelve-day period.[22] These statistics are worth rehearsing to even begin to understand the level of noise. Graves once said in an interview, 'You couldn't; you can't communicate noise. Noise never stopped for one moment – ever.'[23] The noise frequently led to nervous breakdown; it also resulted in a strange sensory phenomenon – the experience of sound as something tangible. Lieutenant Chandos of the 2nd Grenadier Guards, comparing the sound of artillery shelling to the noise of an express train at sixty miles per hour running into a siding, noted that 'the sensation of this sort of artillery fire is not that of sound. You feel it in your ears more than hear it, unless it is only about one hundred yards away'; an NCO of the 22nd Manchester Rifles described the bombardment on the first day of the Somme not as 'a succession of explosions or a continuous roar' but rather a 'stationary panorama of sound' which 'hung over us'.[24] Sound waves, after a certain volume and intensity, literally touch the surface of the body, but consider the following two passages:

One's whole body seemed to be in a mad macabre dance. . .I felt that if I lifted a finger I should touch a solid ceiling of sound (it now had the attribute of solidity).[25]

22 The figures are taken from Philip J. Haythornthwaite, *The World War One Source Book* (London: Arms and Armour Press, 1994), 82–90. See also Peter Liddle, *The 1916 Battle of the Somme: A Reappraisal* (London: Leo Cooper, 1992); John Keegan, *The Face of Battle: A Study of Agincourt (France), Waterloo and Somme* (London: Jonathan Cape, 1976); Anthony Saunders, *Weapons of the Trench War 1914–1918* (Sutton: Stroud, 1999).
23 'The Great Years of Their Lives', *The Listener*, 15 July 1971, 74.
24 Both accounts have been quoted in Ellis, *Eye-deep in Hell*, 63.
25 A. McKee, *Vimy Ridge* (London: Souvenir Press, 1966), 91.

The forest of explosions gradually thickened into a solid whirling wall. We squatted together, every second expecting the annihilating hit that would blow us and our concrete blocks away, and leave our strongpoint level with the pitted desert all round.[26]

The first is from the account of a Canadian infantryman, describing the barrage at Vimy Ridge; the second is from a translation of Jünger's *Storm of Steel*. In both cases, sound seems to encase the body. The original German version is however slightly different: 'Der Wald von Einschlägen um uns verdichtete sich zu einer wirbelnden Wand.'[27] Jünger uses the acutely haptic noun *Einschlag* (related to the verb *einschlagen*: 1. to knock or hammer something into something; 2. smash in); it is translated into the more abstract 'explosions' which in turn is given a physical dimension through the extra word 'solid'. Similarly, the combination of sound and touch in the German 'schmetternden' (from verb *schmettern*: 1. hurl or crash into the ground; 2. to blare out or to bellow) is somewhat lost in the phrase 'annihilating hit'. In an article entitled 'Synaesthesia and Meaning', written in 1922, Wheeler and Cutsforth describe conducting experiments on a synaesthetic subject who had lost his eyesight at the age of eleven. In course of the experiment, his blurred tactual perception of points while recognising Braille letters was confirmed by visual imagery, by the colours that seemed to develop at his finger-tips. The authors concluded that 'it is the behaviour of attention with respect to the auditory, visual and kinaesthetic qualities which are present in the act of perceiving which constitutes the development of meaning'.[28] In the two accounts of haptic sound, which might be interpreted as an instance of momentary synaesthesia, something different happens. The anticipated effect – the terror of being buried underground by the 'solid' ceiling and walls of the dug-out – combined with the sense of claustrophobia (increased no doubt by the physical impact of noise) here determine the kinaesthetic perception of sound itself amidst the low-roofed, walled-in darkness.

The mechanised nature of the First World War severed the link between sight, space and danger, a connection that had traditionally been

---

26 Jünger, *Storm of Steel*. 1920. Trans. Michael Hofmann (London: Allen Lane, 2003), 161.
27 Jünger, Tagebücher I, *Der Erste Weltkrieg* (Stuttgart: Klett-Cotta, 1978), 170.
28 R. H. Wheeler and T. D. Cutsforth, 'Synaesthesia and Meaning', *The American Journal of Psychology*, 33 (July 1922), 370. For recent discussions of synaesthesia – particularly the current interest in transmodal or bi-modal perception – see Simon Baron-Cohen and John E. Harrison (eds.), *Synaesthesis: Classic and Contemporary Readings* (Oxford: Blackwell, 1997), particularly Part III 'Neuroscientific Perspectives', 109–207.

used to structure perception in wartime. This disjunction resulted in an exaggerated investment in sound, a process explored by Eric Leed in *No Man's Land*.[29] But no sound was as unbearable as that of shelling, and few writers describe it as acutely as Jünger:

It's an easier matter to describe these sounds than to endure them, because one cannot but associate every single sound of flying steel with the idea of death, and so I huddled in my hole in the ground with my hand in front of my face, imagining all the possible variants of being hit. I think I have found a comparison that captures the situation in which I and all the other soldiers who took part in this war so often found ourselves: you must imagine you are securely tied to a post, being menaced by a man swinging a heavy hammer. Now the hammer has been taken back over his head, ready to be swung, now it's cleaving the air towards you, on the point of touching your skull, then it's struck the post, and the splinters are flying – that's what it's like to experience heavy shelling in an exposed position.[30]

The passage provides insights into the phenomenology of the sound of shelling in an exposed position: the perception of every sound as physical collision and possible annihilation, *as a missed encounter with death*. The arc of the final sentence traces the swing of the hammer across space and time, looming larger and coming closer, infinitely stretching that moment of terror until the blow finally falls. Time then stands still as consciousness hovers between the crises of life and death. Indeed, the idea of a 'missed experience', is inherent in Freud's theory of war neurosis as set forth in *Beyond the Pleasure Principle* (1920): the mind fails to fully grasp the magnitude of the experience at the actual moment of occurrence and therefore is forever doomed to the compulsion to repeat.[31]

In a series of lectures entitled 'The Effects of High Explosives Upon the Central Nervous System' which were subsequently published in *The Lancet* (1916), F. W. Mott, while recognising the 'stress of prolonged active service', emphasised the role of 'physical forces' generated by high explosives in causing functional neuroses. In the first two lectures, he examines the pressures inflicted by high-velocity shell bursts on the

---

29 Leed, *NML*, 123–34. Leed writes about the 'roaring chaos of barrage', showing how it broke down sequential and rational structures of thought and marked a return to the world of myth and magic (126–31).

30 Jünger, *Storm*, 80–1.

31 Freud, 'Beyond the Pleasure Principle', *SE*, XVIII, 7–64. In her analysis of Freud's essays, Cathy Caruth notes: 'The shock of the mind's relation to the threat of death is thus not the direct experience of the threat, but precisely the *missing* of this experience' and that 'at the heart of Freud's rethinking of history' is the question: '*What does it mean to survive*' (*Unclaimed Experience*, 62, 60).

celebro-spinal fluid and the resultant dissociation of neurons, and the role of noxious gases.[32] Mott's view was typical of the early years of the war when the percussive effects of high explosives were thought to cause the variety of nervous disorders – mutism, partial paralysis, amnesia, nightmares – which were grouped under the common term 'shell-shock', pointing to its 'immediate exciting cause'.[33] By contrast, Freud underlined the psychological aspects. In *Beyond the Pleasure Principle* (1920), he writes, 'The latter [shock theory] regards the essence of the shock as being the direct damage to the molecular structure . . . whereas what *we* seek to understand are the effects produced on the organ of the mind by the breach in the shield against stimuli and by the problems that follow in its train.' Trying to explain trauma, Freud uses the curious image of the 'vesicle' (*Bläschen* in the original German, coming out of embryology) to describe the psychical system and the 'ceaseless impact of external stimuli' on its surface: 'This little fragment of living substance is suspended in the middle of an external world charged with the most powerful energies; and it would be killed by the stimulation emanating from these if it were not provided with a protective shield against stimuli.' Written immediately after the war, the description is also richly resonant with the actual physical condition of the infantryman in his little dug-out ('protective shield') which is being constantly bombarded, the fragile human organism suspended in the middle of a world charged with destructive energies. The idea of defence seems to have been foremost in Freud's mind: '*Protection against* stimuli is an almost more important function for the living organism than *reception of* stimuli'.[34] In a way, the shock theorists would have been largely right if they had listened more carefully to an approaching shell, paying heed not just to its percussive force but to the 'breach' it caused in the psychic sheath, or what Read calls the 'skin drum' of the heart.

32  F. W. Mott, 'The Effects of High Explosives Upon the Central Nervous System', published in three instalments (12 and 26 February, and 11 March), *The Lancet* (1916), 331–8, 441–9, 545–53.

33  'Neurasthenia and Shell Shock', *The Lancet* (18 March 1916), 627. See also Mott, *War Neuroses and Shell Shock* (London: Hodder and Stoughton, 1919); Rivers, *Instinct and the Unconscious*; Norman Fenton, *Shell Shock and its Aftermath* (London: Henry Kimpton, 1926). For recent discussions, see *Journal of Contemporary History*, 35(1) (January 2000), special issue on 'shell-shock', and Ben Shephard, *A War of Nerves* (London: Jonathan Cape, 2000).

34  Freud, 'Beyond the Pleasure Principle', 31, 26–7, 27. Freud uses the image of *Bläschen* (meaning 'amniotic sac', or 'vesicle' as Strachey translates it) to present the 'living organism in its most simplified possible form' (26). The image underlines the notion of fragility and looks forward to the subsequent metaphor of 'envelope or membrane' that Freud uses. (27)

The extended analogy of the sledge-hammer highlights what was so traumatically modern about the present conflict: the war of materials over men, the triumph of chance over agency, the sense of impotence. On 20 September 1916, Arthur Graeme West wrote in his diary about soldiers sitting in their funk-holes like 'animals for the market, like hens in cages . . . shivering a little as a shell draws near'.[35] Some soldiers, in their diaries or memoirs, point to the development of 'shell sense', a new cognitive category that seems to combine perception of sound, danger and space. 'My ear had somehow become attuned, so that as soon as the first sound was heard I knew approximately where the shell would burst.'[36] Shell sense could potentially prevent shell shock. The ability to judge the direction of a coming shell prevented the psyche from being battered repeatedly with the possibility of death. But not all soldiers acquired this 'valuable instinct'. Charles Carrington is more typical of the frontline soldier when he writes that he got into a 'thoroughly neurotic state' during shelling, thinking of 'absurd omens and fetishes to ward off the shell you hear coming'.[37]

Faced with an absurd universe and the terror of death, the precarious subject often tries to rediscover human worth, indeed warmth. Jünger notes how once, during heavy shelling, '[I] pressed myself unconsciously against a man lying beside me on the pallet'; similarly, Gus Sivertz recalled how, during a bombardment, 'it's terrible to be alone. . .one feels that all the enemy guns are pointed at one. . .and naked. You want to touch someone.'[38] Physical intimacy becomes the shield against the impersonal onslaught of the machine. Jünger recalls huddling up with 'my hand in front of my face'. This reflex action underlines at once the vulnerability and the self-protective instinct of men under bombarment. 'Clothing and its part in the psychology of war', notes Wyndham Lewis, who served as a gunner in the Western Front, 'is a neglected subject': 'I would have braved an eleven-inch shell in my trenchboots, but would have declined an encounter with a pipsqueak in my bare feet'.[39] Heavy

---

35  *The Diary of A Dead Officer: Being the Posthumous Papers of Arthur Graeme West* (London: George Allen and Unwin, 1919), 67.
36  Stephen Foot, *Three Lives* (London: W. Heinemann, 1934), quoted in Andy Simpson, *Hot Blood and Cold Steel: Life and Death in the Trenches of the First World War* (London: Tom Donovan, 1993), 81. Foot notes: 'The possession of this "shell sense" must have been a great relief to one's nervous system and it is possible that some of the worst cases of nervous breakdown occurred in men who never acquired this valuable instinct'; Simpson, *Hot Blood* (81).
37  Charles Carrington, *A Subaltern's War* (London: Peter Davies, 1929), 161–2.
38  Jünger, *Storm*, 160; McKee, *Vimy Ridge*, 126.
39  Lewis, *Blasting and Bombardiering*, 121.

shelling induced neurotic states amongst the soldiers whereby the anxiety would be centred on particular zones of the body. For Jünger, it was the face that needed to be covered; to Lewis, '*the whole* of his feet are man's 'Achilles heel''. The moment the first shell would come, Lewis would roll out of his flea-bag and get into his boots. In the absurd world of the trenches, anything that could cover the 'naked' body during a bombardment – a hand, a piece of fabric or a pair of boots – assumed the dimensions of an impenetrable fortress.

If the sound of shelling is associated with terror, there is another response that regularly marks trench narratives: the sense of disgust, usually associated with smell. Trench narratives often describe smell as one of the most 'disintegrative' principles and yet it is not much discussed because of the '*lack* of an appropriate semantic field'.[40] Private Alfred Griffin recalls: 'Ooohh, a horrible smell. There's nothing like a dead body's smell. It's a putrid, decaying smell, makes you stop breathing, you think of disease. It's a smell you can't describe unless you've smelt rotten meat.'[41] The opening exclamation rather than formal language seems to capture best its essence, producing the paradoxical urge towards amplification. The four-fold address to the reader is not fortuitous: for Griffin's words to have meaning, we readers have to relive sensuously the experience, either by association or through memory. Blunden writes about the 'heavy and clothy' smell of German dug-outs, while a careful examination of Jünger's *Storm of Steel* reveals a whole olfactory geography: 'a horribly penetrating smell' alerts a newly arrived platoon to the recent history of a sector, even though there was 'always the sweetish smell' of death.[42] In Jules Romains's *Verdun*, as Clanricard lifts an old tarpaulin covering the entrance to a dug-out, he feels 'as though he had run his head against a wall':

Impossible to find words strong enough to describe the atmosphere down there. It stood up like something solid through which he'd got to force a way: 'thick enough to cut with a knife'. Every kind of foul vapour, everything least acceptable to nose and lungs, seemed to have been rolled and churned into a substance just not heavy enough to clutch with his hands, yet impossible to designate as air. There was something of every kind in it – bad breath, wind, the smell of wet dog; reminders of a policeman's boots, of stale tobacco; even of the kind of fried-fish shop one comes across in the slums, and traces of suicide by charcoal fumes.[43]

40  Trotter, 'The British Novel and the War', in *Cambridge Companion*, 39.
41  A. Griffin, Sound Archive, IWM, AC 9101.
42  Blunden, *Undertones*, 133; Jünger, *Storm*, 96–7.
43  Jules Romains, *Verdun* (vol. VIII of *Men of Good Will*), trans. Gerard Hopkins (1938; London: Peter Davies, 1939), 88.

The sense of smell, unlike vision, touch or taste, is severed from its object and is a stimulus to the powers of both memory and fantasy. The long list of possible items is suggestive of a particular consciousness rather than simply the nature of the smell (musty, stale, putrid). There is also a representational crisis. Like the shadows in Barbusse's *Light*, the various odours here have congealed into a 'wall', a 'solid' mass thick enough to cut with a knife and yet not solid enough to clutch with the hands – we are left with the impression of something hovering between a wreath and a rind, a world of texture without substance. Yet, what it reveals, like the passages on sound, is the strong impulse towards materiality.

One of the situations where the different sensory formations I have been suggesting – the kinaesthetic, the auditory and the olfactory – come together is during the night patrol. Night patrol was a daily routine of the trenches where soldiers would slip in through cut wire into no man's land to gather information or for reconnaissance purposes: it was a mission at once dangerous and purposive. War narratives from Jünger's *Storm of Steel* to Blunden's *Undertones of War* or Sassoon's *Memoirs of An Infantry Officer* all have a section on night-patrol, a momentary throwback to the notion of war as an adventure. However, I would like to focus on a less well-known text, Arthur Graeme West's 'Night Patrol'. The poem brings together the different sensuous geographies I have been exploring, and, while so far I have been discussing prose accounts written at a slightly later date, it might be useful to examine a poetic testimony, written only a month after the actual event.

Arthur Graeme West has now been forgotten even within the First World War canon. Educated at Blundells School and then Balliol College, Oxford, he joined as a Private because of poor eyesight: shy, reclusive and virulently anti-war, his diary – published posthumously as *The Diary of A Dead Officer* (1918) – remains one of the most vivid accounts of daily life in the trenches. 'Night Patrol' is based on an actual experience that West recounted to a friend in a letter of 12 February 1916. 'I had rather an exciting time myself with two other men on a patrol in the "no man's land" between the lines. A dangerous business, and most repulsive on account of the smells and appearance of the heaps of dead men that lie unburied there as they fell, on some attack or other, about four months ago.' A month later, in March 1916, West wrote 'The Night Patrol':

                                                          And we placed
          Our hands on the top most sand-bags, leapt, and stood
          A second with curved backs, then crept to the wire,
          Wormed ourselves tinkling through, glanced back, and dropped.
          . . .
          Half-seen, as rose and sank the flares, were strewn
          With the wrecks of our attack: the bandoliers,
          Packs, rifles, bayonets, belts, and haversacks,
          Shell fragments, and the huge whole forms of shells
          Shot fruitlessly – and everywhere the dead.
          Only the dead were always present – present
          As a vile sickly smell of rottenness; . . .

          We crawled on belly and elbows . . .
          We lay in shelter of the last dead man,
          Ourselves as dead, and heard their shovels ring
          Turning the earth, then talk and cough at times.
          A sentry fired and a machine-gun spat;
          They shot a flare above us, when it fell
          And spluttered out in the pools of No Man's Land,
          We turned and crawled past the remembered dead:
          Past him and him, and them and him, until,
          For he lay some way apart, we caught the scent
          Of the Crusader and slid past his legs,
          And through the wire and home, and got our rum.[44]

In *Phenomenology of Perception* (1962), Merleau-Ponty notes that visual perception 'pushes objectification further than does tactile experience'. While a spectacle, appearing at a distance, helps us to flatter ourselves that we constitute the world, in the case of touch, 'it is through my body that I go to the world, and tactile experience occurs "ahead" of me.'[45] The world in West's poem is no longer spread out before the eyes but suddenly contracts and adheres to the skin – as barbed wire or unburied bodies – while the body feels its way forward in the dark, scraping, colliding, uncertain. West underwrites the spatial disorientation, both conceptually and rhythmically. In the first three and half lines of the quoted passage, the enjambment and the caesura, the irregular metre and the rhythm, see-sawing between the iambic and the trochaic, alert us to the breathless and angled movements within and across the lines. But the sentence tips from an account of daring to a

44 West, 'The Night Patrol', in *The Diary of a Dead Officer*, 82–3.
45 Merleau-Ponty, *Phenomenology*, 369.

sense of the subhuman with the word 'wormed', which is carried into the final line through a set of phonemes: 'wire', 'home' and 'rum'. Head first, the rest of the body dragging behind on the soil, the verb ('wormed') suggests a tactile and horizontal mode of movement without any vision. On the other hand, 'tinkling', resonant with the sheep-bells of English pastoral verse, is grimly ironic: the sound records processes of touch as the tingling flesh cuts through the tangled wire, hoary with frost.

As momentary flares light up no man's land, familiar objects usually strapped around the body – 'Packs, rifles, bayonets, belts, and haver-sacks' – appear uncanny when seen as the only residues of their former owners and now part of the forbidden landscape. Existing without purpose or function, they retain a certain obdurate presence, contrasting with the passage of matter into waste. The sudden ubiquity of the dead – 'everywhere', 'always', the repetition of 'dead' and 'present' – alerts us to the fact that the visual landscape has been interrupted by a more immediate perceptual field: the 'vile sickly smell of rottenness'. Like Jünger in *Storm of Steel*, West leads us into this world through its scent: the movements of the men are charted through the way the smell changes from 'vile sickly' to 'pungent and sharp' to 'that vague foetor'. But a more discontinuous geography opens up with human voices and the clink of shovels. The sense of space, evoked through 'vague foetor', shrinks into a relation between places and people. Unlike the visual or the olfactory, every sound is a point of action and movement and, in this context, danger. As the three night patrollers crawl back, the official map gives way to an intimately recognised geography: 'Past him and him, and them and him'. Similarly, in Jünger's *Storm of Steel*, the narrator notes 'a strangely constellated group of corpses serving as a landmark': 'One of the dead lay there as if crucified on the chalk slope'.[46] In West's narrative, he earns a name ('the Crusader') and disgust is turned into a positive force, as the 'vile sickly smell' becomes a sign of homecoming. Yet, the penultimate verb in the poem is 'slid'. West adopts the Sas-soonesque mode and evokes no man's land through, to quote Murry, the 'chaos of immediate sensation'. It was, however, left to poets such as Rosenberg to assimilate such objective description into a complex literary subjectivity.

---

46 Jünger, *Storm*, 96.

ROSENBERG: SENSUOUS POLITICS

In the foreword to the *Collected Works* (1937) of Isaac Rosenberg, Sassoon writes: 'Behind all his poetry there is a racial quality – biblical and prophetic. Scriptural and sculptural are the epithets I would apply to him.' He continues, 'his imagination had a sinewy and muscular aliveness; often he saw things in terms of sculpture, but he did not carve or chisel; he *modelled* words with fierce energy and aspiration.'[47] 'Scriptural and sculptural': the near-repetition brings together the racial politics and aesthetic practice of this Jewish poet-painter from the East End of London in more intimate ways than Sassoon had perhaps envisaged. While Rosenberg is usually regarded as a visual poet – particularly given his training as an artist at the Slade and his own dilemma whether to regard himself primarily as a poet or a painter – the tactile metaphor used by Sassoon may hold new possibilities of meaning. Moments of touch underlie some of his most successful war verse. In poems such as 'Break of Day in the Trenches', 'Louse Hunting' or 'Dead Man's Dump', the world of the trenches is brought alive through a moment of contact: the hand being touched by a rat, the ritual of delousing, or lurching over the unburied dead. These poems are widely admired for their trench realism but at the same time, there is also a complex Jewish subjectivity at work. The haptic geography of the trenches is used in the poems to explore certain political, social and personal questions, but without sacrificing the immediacy of the surroundings; there is also a shrewd, ironic humour which creates a frisson with the seriousness of the subjects, and never allows us to rest comfortably with one particular line of interpretation.

Rosenberg was one of the few 'soldier-poets' who served as a private, enlisting for financial rather than patriotic reasons: 'I would be doing the most criminal thing a man can do'.[48] At the time of enlisting, he wrote,

---

47 Sassoon, 'Foreword', reprinted in *The Collected Works of Isaac Rosenberg*, ed. Ian Parsons (London: Chatto and Windus, 1984), ix; hereafter abbreviated Rosenberg, *CW*. See also *The Poetry and Plays of Isaac Rosenberg*, ed. Vivien Noakes (Oxford: Oxford University Press, 2004), xviii. Noakes prints all of Rosenberg's surviving poetry and plays and presents the full variants and useful notes on individual poems. Hereafter abbreviated *PP* and all references to his poems and plays are from this authoritative edition. The biographies are Jean Liddiard, *Isaac Rosenberg: The Half-Used Life* (London: Victor Gollancz, 1975) and Jean Moorcroft Wilson, *Isaac Rosenberg: Poet and Painter* (London: Cecil Woolf, 1975). Also see Wilson's article 'Visions from the Trenches', *The Guardian Review*, 8 November 2003, 4–6; D. W. Harding, *Experience Into Words: Essays on Poetry* (Cambridge: Cambridge University Press, 1963), 91–103; Dennis Silk, 'Isaac Rosenberg (1890–1918)', *Judaism*, 14 (Fall 1965), 462–74; Jon Silkin, *Out of Battle: The Poetry of The Great War* (Oxford: Oxford University Press, 1972), 249–314.

48 *CW*, 216. He later claimed that he joined so that his mother could receive the statutory Separation Allowance, but by the end of the year she had not received anything. See *PP*, xliii–xliv.

'I despise war and hate war, and hope that the Kaiser William will have his bottom smacked'.[49] He had one of the longest stretches in France, serving for twenty-one months from June 1916 till his death during a wiring patrol on 1 April 1918 (except a ten-day leave and a couple of months in 1917 when he was hospitalised with influenza). He had his share of the war horrors that we find in Sassoon, Blunden or Owen; there were additional problems specific to being a Jewish private in a regiment marked out by physical difference:

I could not get the work I thought I might so I have joined this Bantam Battalion (as I was too short for any other) which seems to be the most rascally affair in the world. I have to eat out of a basin together with some horribly smelling scavenger who spits and sneezes into it etc. . . . . Besides my being a Jew makes it bad amongst these wretches.[50]

We get to discover aspects of war experience we do not come across in the records of the officer-writers: the pathetic plea for a pound to buy a pair of good boots and some cakes; the absence of any private time (particularly when we compare it to Sassoon reading Hardy's *Jude the Obscure* or Blunden reading Butler's *Erewhon*); a poem written on lavatory paper or a letter cut short because of the lack of candle; sleeping on damp floors and the long hours of manual labour in the trenches, 'coal fatigueing all day (a most inhuman job)'.[51] All these meant that the body of the private soldier went through a different regime of discipline and discomfort. When we combine these facts with his racial and cultural difference, we realise that the war writings of this sensitive and immensely gifted young man would be very different from that of the middle-class English officer-poets.

In the pre-war years, Sassoon and Rosenberg, though united through Jewish ancestry, may be said to represent the two poles of the English social spectrum. Sassoon's fox-hunting background and Cambridge training were more typical of the officer-poet; the upbringing of Rosenberg, the private soldier, was rather different. The son of educated but poor Lithuanian Jewish immigrants, Rosenberg grew up amidst poverty around the East End of London. 'You mustn't forget', he wrote, 'the circumstances I have been brought up in, the little education I have had. Nobody ever told me what to read, or ever put poetry in my way.'[52]

---

49 *CW*, 205.       50 *CW*, 219.
51 Isaac Rosenberg, *Selected Poems and Letters*, ed. and intro, Jean Liddard (London: Enitharmon, 2003), 150.
52 *CW*, 181.

However, in London, he met other young Jewish writers and artists such as Stephen Winsten, Joseph Leftwich and John Rodker. He was extremely lucky to find patrons to send him to the Slade School of Art and to be acquainted with a number of influential literary figures: Edward Marsh, Lascelles Abercrombie, Gordon Bottomley and Laurence Binyon. He was also part of the literary milieu surrounding the Café Royal, where Mark Gertler introduced him to T. E. Hulme and Edward Marsh, then private secretary to Winston Churchill. This constant wavering between two worlds – the Jewish community with its radical politics and the English authoritarian structures as embodied in Edward Marsh – fractured further Rosenberg's Anglo-Jewish identity.[53] The Jewish aspect became increasingly important to him in the trenches: he tried for a transfer to the Jewish Battalion in Mesopotamia; some of his last poems – 'The Burning of the Temple', 'The Destruction of Jerusalem by the Babylonian Hordes' and 'Through these Pale Cold Days' – dwell on Old Testament themes; in his last letter, he mentions the 'J. B.' (Jewish Battalion) and that he 'wanted to write a battle song for the Judaens'. While the Judaic component is usually discussed in relation to his religious and mythical narratives, the way it informs his shorter and more well-known trench poems has not received much attention. This is partly because of the consummate artistry of the poems themselves. 'Simple *poetry*' Rosenberg wrote in a letter to Bottomley, 'is where an interesting complexity of thought is kept in tone and right value to the dominating idea so that it is understandable and still ungraspable'.[54]

The materiality of the creative process that Sassoon notes is underlined by Rosenberg himself in a letter to Edward Marsh on 4 August 1916: 'You know how earnestly one must wait on ideas, (you cannot coax real ones to you) and let as it were, a skin grow naturally round and through them.' When the ideas come 'hot', the artist must 'seize them with the skin in tatters raw, crude, in some parts beautiful in others monstrous'. While some poets show a tactile, almost erotic, relation to words – most notably Keats, and more immediately, Owen – Rosenberg presents us with the viscera, as it were, of the creative process. The image of the skin growing

---

53  Featherstone, *War Poetry*, 73. Featherstone is one of the few critics to explore the 'radical intellectual and political culture' of the immigrant Jewish community in the East End where Rosenberg grew up. He examines the influence of the Jewish writer Israel Zangwill who mediated between the Jewish ghetto and English literary establishment and places Rosenberg 'at the centre of the movement from a radical, deracinated culture . . . to a more anglicised version of Jewishness' (72–5).

54  *CW*, 272, 238.

'round and through' ideas points to the rare quality of sensuous thought that marks his verse. Language is used as an affective medium to explore and even organise ideas rather than as a sheath or embellishment. Analogies about the poetic process change but the physical element is maintained: 'I've freshly written this thing – red from the anvil'. The image is not simply a 'metaphor': it is part of the social and economic world of this poet who, at the age of fourteen, was apprenticed to a firm of art publishers to learn engraving and plate-making. It was a job he loathed, 'chained' and 'bound', he felt, for the best years of his life to 'this fiendish mangling machine'.[55] Yet, the language of the smithy and hard physical labour permeate his works: 'Moses', a protest against pre-war social conditions through a biblical framework, is punctuated with verbs such as *torn, broken, prick, crack, boil, grip, break*.[56]

The materiality of the body is an abiding theme in Rosenberg's art. In one of his self-portraits (1912), the hand is suggestively thrust towards the audience, eager to establish contact. For a poet who was to write hauntingly about isolation, the hand is a recurring trope, in poems such as 'The World Rumbles by me', 'Aspiration' or 'Wedded'. He begins his essay titled 'Art' by saying 'We all, more or less, feel a work of art' and goes on to note that 'the roots of a dead universe are torn up by hands, feverish and consuming with an exuberant vitality'.[57] Whether it is in the context of religion, love or war, the body is palpably present. Images of eyes, ears, brow, necks, hands, backs, limbs appear in his trench poetry but they do not have the angry sensuality of Sassoon or the erotic pathos of Owen, the two modes of bodily representation we usually associate with war poetry. With Rosenberg, the body is more unobtrusive, represented in its quotidian routine, as in 'Marching (As Seen from the Left File)' or, more strikingly, in 'The Troop Ship'. The latter survives in a remarkable document he sent his friend Trevelyan from the trenches: a single sheet of paper which, for want of space, combines letter, poem and sketch.[58] (Figure 2.1) The general theme, not surprisingly, is crampedness – 'the contortions we get into to try and wriggle ourselves into a little sleep' – the geography of the page, every tiny inch filled with his scrawl, being the

---

55  *CW*, 239, 238, 180.
56  See Patrick Quinn (ed.), *British Poets of the Great War: Brooke, Rosenberg, Thomas, A Documentary Volume* (Farmington: Gale, 2000), 191.
57  *CW*, 289, 294.
58  Rosenberg, Manuscripts, IWM, PP/MCR/C38, IR/I/232 (a)(b).

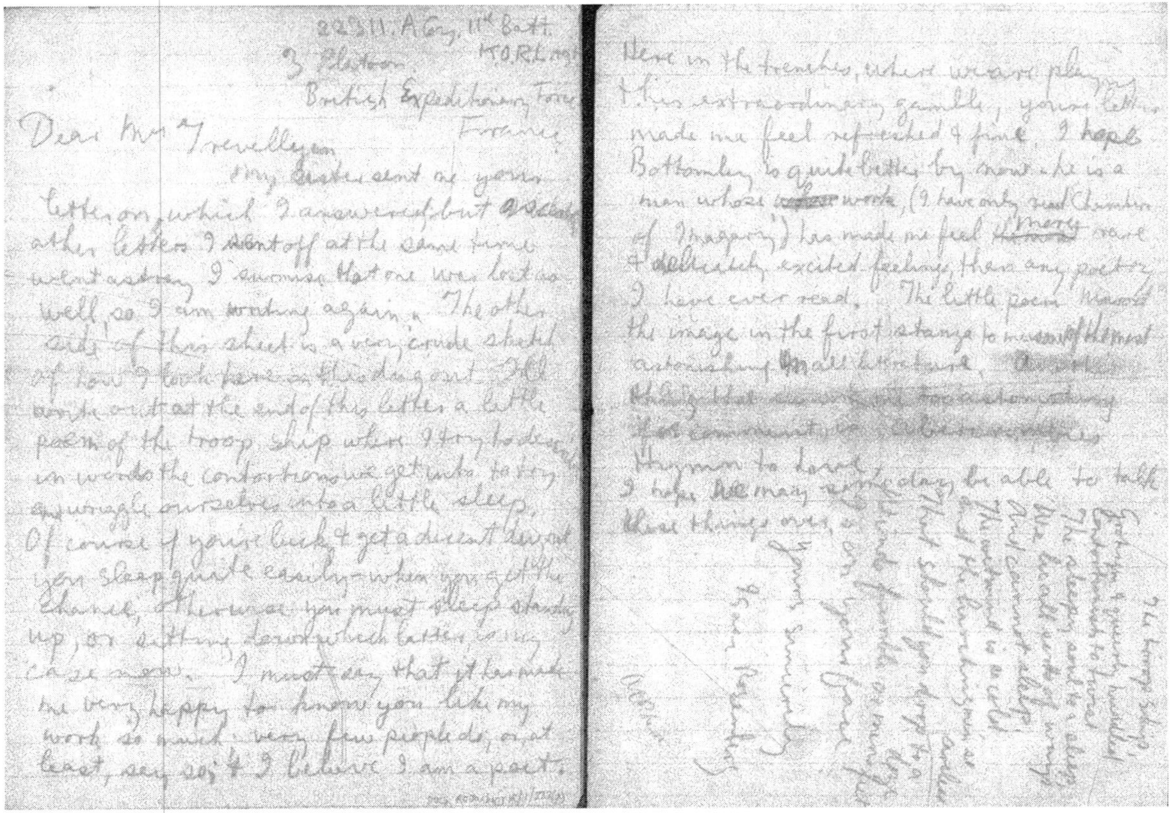
22311. A Coy, 11th Batt.
3 Platoon. KORL
British Expeditionary Force
France

Dear Mr Trevellyan
My sister sent me your letter on, which I answered, but as all other letters I sent off at the same time went astray I assume that one was lost as well, so I am writing again. The other side of this sheet is a very crude sketch of how I look here in this dug out. I'll work out at the end of this letter a little poem of the troop ship where I try to describe in words the contortions we get into to try and wriggle ourselves into a little sleep. Of course if you're lucky & get a decent berth you sleep quite easily – when you get the chance, otherwise you must sleep standing up, or sitting down which latter is my case now. I must say that it has made me very happy to know you like my work so much. very few people do, or at least, say so; & I believe I am a poet.

Here in the trenches, where we are playing this extraordinary gamble, your letter made me feel refreshed & fine. I hope Bottomley is quite better by now. he is a man whose work (I have only read 'Chambers of Imagery') has made me feel more rare & delicately excited feelings than any poetry I have ever read. The little poem 'Avarice' the image in the first stanza to me is one of the most astonishing in all literature. [illegible] Hymn to Love. I hope we may some day be able to talk these things over,

The troop ship.
Grotesque & queerly huddled
Contortionists to twist
The sleepy soul to a sleep,
We lie all sorts of ways
And cannot sleep.
The wet wind is so cold
And the lurching men so careless
That should you drop to a doze
Winds' fumble or men's feet
Is on your face

Yours sincerely
Isaac Rosenberg

Figure 2.1. (a) Letter of Rosenberg to R. C. Trevelyan, 'The Papers of Isaac Rosenberg', PP/MCR/C38 (IR/I/232), IWM (DOC).

Figure 2.1. (b) Rosenberg's sketch of himself in the dug-out on the reverse side of the letter to Trevelyan, 'The Papers of Isaac Rosenberg', PP/MCR/C38 (IR/I/232), IWM (DOC).

strongest illustration of the theme. Scribbled horizontally in the right-hand corner of the paper is the poem:

> Grotesque and queerly huddled
> Contortionists to twist
> The sleepy soul to a sleep,
> We lie all sorts of ways
> But cannot sleep.
> The wet wind is so cold,
> And the lurching men so careless,
> That, should you drop to a doze,
> Wind's fumble or men's feet
> Is on your face.[59]

If we compare the poem to Brooke's 'Fragment' – another troop-ship poem, describing the narrator standing concealed at the doorway and fondly gazing at his men ('link'd beauty of bodies') – we realise how the voyeuristic spectacle of an upper-middle-class officer is replaced here by the haptic perception of a private soldier who actually inhabits the crowded space of the troop-ship.[60] Desmond Graham has noted about the poem that 'always there is human contact, the sense of touch so strong that even when bodies are out of immediate contact, they live in palpable relationship'.[61] This kind of contact however does not have any of the homoerotic dalliance of Brooke or Owen; instead, it shows Rosenberg's acute awareness of the body and its discontents.

The syntactic contortion and the queer, jerky rhythm powerfully convey the restricted movement of the body: adjective, adverb and analogy withhold the subject and the active verb ('We lie') till the fourth line, draining the bodies of both agency and individuality. The sketch (Figure 2.1b) on the reverse side similarly shows a limp, contorted figure, hemmed in by the left-hand margin of the page. A thick pencil-line running vertically down the page confines the subject to the left-hand side: the diagonal beam overhead and the shading increase the sense of claustrophobia. The queer triangle formed by the four limbs – the outline of the left leg partly coincides with the margin of the page and the hands are locked fast – shows the narrowest possible space into which the human figure can be compressed. West, another private soldier, notes in his diary:

---

59 *PP*, 127. Also see *PP*, 358.
60 Brooke, 'Fragment', *The Collected Poems* (1929; London: Papermac, 1987), 318.
61 Desmond Graham, *The Truth of War: Owen, Blunden, Rosenberg* (Manchester: Carcanet Press, 1984), 140. Graham's study is keenly sensitive to Rosenberg's treatment of the body and the nuances of language (135–57).

'five or six funk-holes . . . take the body of a man in a very huddled and uncomfortable position, with no room to move'.[62] Rosenberg's sketch can also be read as a metaphor for trench life in general: in a letter, he complains, 'one is so cramped intellectually'.[63] The congestion of bodies in narrow spaces may have been part of childhood memory, of a rather big family packed into a small house in the East End.[64] At the bottom of the figure, there is a little rat near a tin of marmalade, next to a sort of trench map marked 'Fleas headquarter', 'Fleasreserves', 'rats headquarters' and 'blackbeetles /'cocroaches' [*sic*].

The attention to vermin is wholly realistic within the world of the trenches and they figure powerfully in his poems. But the imagery gains a new dimension when placed within the anti-Semitic discourse of the day, especially in the European context. 'The great reservoir of Semiticism', wrote Edouard Drumont in *La France juive* (1886), 'pour[s] forth incessantly their stinking hordes . . . who let fall vermin wherever they pass'; in Daudet's *Le Voyage de Shakespeare* (1896), the Jew is 'like a little insect', a 'termite'.[65] Wilson in *Ideology and Experience* (1987) shows how, at the turn-of-the-century France, the Jew is identified with 'dirt, filth and vermin' while Wertheimer, studying the immigration of East European Jews in imperial Germany between 1871 and 1914, finds exactly the same tropes.[66] In England, anti-Semitism was far less vicious or widespread: it however appeared in the wake of a financial scandal in 1912 – the Marconi affair – in which two high-ranking Jewish officials were implicated, and during the war years, following the sinking of the *Lusitania* when some newspapers identified the whole community with the Germans.[67] More locally – but with particular relevance for Rosenberg – there was prejudice against the 100,000-strong community of Jews who came, like Rosenberg's parents, from Eastern Europe and settled in the Whitechapel and Stepney areas in London. Rosenberg grew up at 58 Jubilee Street, Stepney, and in 1907, when he was seventeen, the family moved to Oxford Street,

---

62 West, *Diary of a Dead Officer*, 67.      63 *CW*, 249.

64 Jean Moorcroft Wilson notes, 'Isaac would certainly have had to share a room with his brother, perhaps even with some of his sisters' (Wilson, *Rosenberg*, 20–1).

65 Edouard Drumont, *La France juive* (Paris, 1886), I, 451–2; Leon Daudet, *Le Voyage de Shakespeare* (Paris, 1896), 187. Both are quoted in Stephen Wilson, *Ideology and Experience: Antisemitism in France at the Time of the Dreyfus Affair* (London: Fairleigh Dickinson University Press, 1982), 491, 490.

66 Stephen Wilson, *Ideology and Experience*, 491; Jack Wertheimer, *Unwelcome Strangers* (New York: Oxford University Press, 1987), 25–6. See also Bryan Cheyette and Laura Marcus (eds.), *Modernity, Culture and 'the Jew'* (Oxford: Polity Press, 1998).

67 See Leon Poliakov, *The History of Anti-Semitism: Suicidal Europe, 1870–1913*, vol. IV, trans. George Klin (Oxford: Oxford University Press, 1985), 188–93.

London East. In 1902 – in the same year that Rosenberg began classes in
Stepney Green Art School – the bishop of Stepney compared the immigrant community to a conquering army 'that eats the Christians out of
house and home'; on the eve of the war, the *Times* published, under the
title 'London Ghettos', an article in which it accused foreign Jews of
forming a state within a state.[68] Rosenberg's acute consciousness of, and
indignation at, the resentment towards his race is evident in a poem like
'The Jew' which concludes with the smarting line, 'Then why do they
sneer at me?'[69]

Once in the trenches, he writes, 'I will not leave a corner of my
consciousness covered up, but saturate myself with the strange and
extraordinary conditions of this life'.[70] Rosenberg wrote almost all his
war poetry, as Vivien Noakes points out, 'in, or close to, the front line':
'the immediacy of the trench experience in his writing could be seen not
only in the condition of many of the manuscripts, but also in the dustings
of mud which fell from some of the creases as the papers were unfolded'.[71]
While his longer poems such as 'Daughters of War' or his ambitious verse
play 'The Unicorn' are locked in a private mythological world, his shorter
– and often more successful – trench poems inhabit the local geography,
as does 'Break of Day in the Trenches':

> The darkness crumbles away.
> It is the same old Druid Time as ever.
> Only a live thing leaps my hand,
> A queer sardonic rat,
> . . .
> Droll rat, they would shoot you if they knew
> Your cosmopolitan sympathies.
> Now you have touched this English hand
> You will do the same to a German
> Soon, no doubt, if it be your pleasure
> To cross the sleeping green between.[72]

The power of the poem lies in the sheer lightness of touch with which the
situation is presented: contrary impulses – irony and wishfulfilment,
impertinence and pathos, personal history and trench realism – are held
and released in the poem with as much play and pleasure as suits this
'queer sardonic' creature. Rats were the most loathed animals in the
trenches, though David Jones was moved to sketch them and William

---

68 Both passages are quoted in Poliakov, *Anti-Semitism*, 189.        69 *PP*, 126.
70 *CW*, 248.        71 *PP*, xviii.        72 *PP*, 128.

Berridge addressed a mawkish sonnet to one caught on a piece of wire.[73] But the account of Stuart Dolden is more typical: 'they [the rats] were bloated and loathsome to look on. We were filled with an instinctive hatred of them. . .one could not help feeling that they fed on the dead.' He continues: 'One night a rat ran across my face. Unfortunately my mouth happened to be open and the hind legs of the filthy beast went right in.'[74] Rosenberg's rat would have shuddered at such disgusting behaviour from its fellow creature: sophisticated, debonair and wholly irreverent about the whole 'stupid' business of war, it works instead as a prestigious ambassador, joining the German and English hand in a phantasmatic handshake. Intimate contact replaces impersonal combat.

While the rat is a wonderful piece of trench realism, it also comes with a whole history of racial prejudice. A few years later, we have T. S. Eliot's notorious lines: 'The rats are underneath the piles / The Jew is underneath the lot'.[75] Many of the images in Rosenberg's poem including the rat and the poppies are brought in from the verse-play *Moses*; there are also echoes of 'The Flea' where the 'droll shape' of the rat is like a 'torch to light my wit'.[76] But the rat in 'Break of Day' is not only 'queer, sardonic' but also 'cosmopolitan': if the link between the migratory rat and the immigrant Jew can no longer be denied, the anti-Semitic trope here gets subverted through brilliant irony. Amidst the narrow patriotism and hatred engendered by war, the rat is the only creature that is enlightened and guiltless. Moreover, if the English and German soldiers – the 'haughty athletes' – are confined to their narrow dug-outs, the rat exults in its freedom, no longer restricted to a particular nation but touching whoever it wants to. As Featherstone notes, the image of the rat 'is both an acknowledgement of his predicament and an imaginative escape'.[77] The rat is also a marginalized creature and there may be more personal points of identification with the poet. Rosenberg's sense of racial discrimination is evident in 'The Jew'; as an adolescent, he was forced by poverty into a job which he hated;

---

73 William Berridge, 'To a Rat (Caught on a piece of wire in a communication trench 4:45 a.m. April 1916)', in Powell (ed.), *A Deep Cry*, 122.

74 A. Stuart Dolden, *Cannon Fodder: An Infantryman's Life on the Western Front 1914–18* (Poole: Blandford Press, 1980 but based on his wartime diaries), 110–11.

75 'Burbank with a Baedeker: Bleistein with a Cigar', in *The Complete Poems and Plays of T. S. Eliot* (London: Faber, 1969), 41. See also Anthony Julius, *T. S. Eliot: Anti-Semitism and Literary Form* (Cambridge: Cambridge University Press, 1995), 22; and Maud Ellman, 'Writing Like a Rat', *Critical Quarterly*, 46, 4 (2004), 59–76, for an exploration of the figure of the rat in modernism.

76 *PP*, 95.

77 Featherstone, *War Poetry*, 78.

as a soldier, he was found to be physically wanting. Racially, socially, even physically marginalised throughout his life, the poet is led to identify himself with the rat; the adjective 'live' emphasises at once the living bond as well as the instinct for survival. Instead of any kind of self-hatred or moral earnestness, there is ironic humour as the 'cosmopolitan' poet – educated at the Slade, just returned from South Africa and consorting with Edward Marsh – turns the wretched animal of the trenches into the most debonair of literary creatures.

Underneath the emphatically differentiated hands – on which the effectiveness of the polemic lies – it is perhaps possible to detect a common trace: the hand of the Jewish soldier who, like the rat, could be found on either side of no man's land. For if '*this* English hand' – i.e. the poet's – is Jewish, it is equally possible that the German hand also has Jewish blood. In some lines later excised from the poem, he writes, 'A shell's haphazard fury / What rootless poppies dropping?'[78] Rosenberg would have been aware that thousands of Jewish soldiers were fighting for the German empire and killing their kin on the French, English and Russian side, making this European war a horrible fratricide for the 'rootless' Jew. In Germany, when war was declared, around 96,000 Jews volunteered to fight for the country: 12 per cent of these were volunteers, 77 per cent served at the Front and casualty rates ran at 12 per cent.[79] In France, by August 1914, 8,500 out of 30,000 Jewish immigrants, many of whom did not even have French passports, had joined the French army.[80] The image of 'rootless poppies' gathers added poignancy when we realise that the German war poet Franz Janowitz came, like Rosenberg, from a Jewish family: he too hated the war and died of wounds on 4 November 1917.[81]

---

78  *PP*, 128. The image of the 'root' is complex and multivalent in Rosenberg's poetry, recurring in 'First Fruit', 'Chagrin', 'At Night', 'Moses' and 'The Unicorn'. For a detailed examination, see Silkin, *Out of Battle*, 262–5, and Quinn (ed.), *British Poets*, 105–6. While discussing how 'Chagrin' ends with an image of rootlessness, Silkin comments: '"The secret roots of the sun" are those nurturing, life-giving organs without which all human life would die. The Jews, and other groups similarly subsisting, enjoy this nurturing only in patches' (265).

79  The statistics are taken from Ulrich Sieg, 'Judenzählung', in *Enzyklopädie Erster Weltkrieg* ed. Gerhard Hirschfeld, Gerd Krumeich and Irina Renz (Munich: Ferdinand Schöningh, 2004), 600. See also George L. Mosse, *The Jews and the German War Experience, 1914–1918* (New York: Leo Baeck Institute, 1977).

80  'Exhibition honours Jewish soldiers in First World War' by Emmanuel Le Roux, *Le Monde* (reprinted in *The Guardian*), 24 October 2002.

81  Franz Janowitz (1892–1917) was born into a middle-class, artistic family in the Bohemian town of Elbe. His collection of poems *Auf der Erde* (*On the Earth*), consisting of fifty-one poems, was published in 1919 under the auspices of Karl Kraus. Largely forgotten now, he employed a neo-romanticist style with a mystical vein. See *The Lost Voices of World War I*, ed. Tim Cross (London: Bloomsbury, 1988), 109–11.

In 'Louse Hunting', Rosenberg focuses on the other equally loathed vermin. In a letter to Bottomley (February 1917), he mentions sending 'a very slight sketch of a louse-hunt' but the drawing does not seem to have survived.[82] His first poetic attempt on the subject is 'Immortals' where the analogy between delousing and carnage is laboured: 'I killed and killed with slaughter mad'.[83] But 'Louse Hunting' is more ambivalent: 'Nudes – stark aglisten/Yelling in lurid glee'. A regular feature of trench life is defamiliarised into a phantasmagoria of movement and action. Yet, the focus of the poem is not the action itself but its projection on the walls of the dug-out. Touching is converted into seeing in a way that makes touch more threatening, more oppressively real:

> Then we all sprung up and stript
> To hunt the vermin brood.
> Soon like a demons' pantomime
> The place was raging.
> See the silhouettes agape,
> See the gibbering shadows
> Mixed with the battled arms on the wall.
> See gargantuan hooked fingers
> Dug in supreme flesh
> To smutch the supreme littleness.[84]

Rosenberg assimilates into the chiaroscuro of the candle-lit dug-out what is essentially the art of the close-up: the shadow-world magnifies and distorts the figures, filling every inch of the dug-out screen with the immense materiality and hitherto unsuspected meanings of these acts of 'supreme littleness'.

Written in 1917 – around the same time when *The Battle of the Somme* (1916) was raising consciousness both about war and cinema among the masses – 'Louse Hunting' has more in common with its contemporary art-form than with a 'demons' pantomime', a phrase that better describes the obsessive harping on the shadow-world in Patrick MacGill's *The Great Push* (1917). Rosenberg deftly manoeuvres between the optic and haptic modes of representation, often used by early cinema-makers.[85] While the epanaphoric 'see', combining with 'silhouettes' and 'shadows', underlines the visual qualities, the proliferation of words to describe the

---

82  *CW*, 253.
83  'Immortals', *PP*, 134.
84  *PP*, 136. Noakes notes, 'It [the poem] exists only in a very rough draft, and is the most difficult of his works to transcribe' (*PP*, 363).
85  See Marks, *Touch: Sensuous Theory*, 7–9.

action – flesh, fingers, hooked, pluck, smutch – evokes the tangible body. The acuteness of such corporeal imagination is evident in the rough draft of the poem:

> See gargantuan hooked fingers
> <sup>pluck</sup>Dug in supreme flesh
> To smutch   supreme
> ~~For~~ the ~~mortifying~~ littleness.[86]

The precise nature of the touch here has been an editorial issue. While previous editors such as Bottomley and Parsons have gone for 'Pluck' which Rosenberg scrawled in the margin, Noakes replaces it with 'Dug' (which he did not cancel). Both verbs carry traces of the hooked finger-tips, reaching completion in 'smutch'. Yet the emotions of disgust or horror are held in check by the trochaic beat that injects life and motion into this kingdom of shadows while the deft manipulation of the varying sounds of the letter 'g' – raging, agape, gibbering, gargantuan, fingers – infects the grotesque with humour. Menace and comedy are precariously balanced in the poem, unsettling any single response from us. In a poem about projection and size, we note in the repetition of 'supreme' a sudden jolting of meaning and scale. 'Supreme', in the first instance, suggests visual immensity as well as the overriding reality of the body in the context of war. Yet, with repetition, the word suggests diminution and insignificance: the poem consequently lurches towards the mock-heroic, kept up in 'wizard vermin' and gradually fading into the gentle pathos of lost sleep. The elaborate imagery thus achieves something paradoxical: the soldiers become unsubstantial, locked in a shadow-fight, and yet, through magnification, invested with excessive physicality.

While discussing modernist visual technology – particularly the film – Walter Benjamin notes: 'With the close-up, space expands; with slow motion, movement is extended. The enlargement of a snapshot does not simply render more precise what in any case was visible, though unclear: it reveals entirely new structural formations . . . . The camera introduces us to unconscious optics as does psychoanalysis to unconscious impulses.'[87] Through enlargement, the daily ritual of delousing becomes an exposure of the aggressive, murderous impulses of the soldiers – a reading of war psychology that we come across in Freud's 'Thoughts for the Times on

---

86  Rosenberg, Manuscripts, IWM, PP/MCR/C38, IR/I/247.
87  Walter Benjamin, 'The Work of Art in the Age of Mechanical Reproduction', in *Illuminations: Essays and Reflections*, trans. Harry Zohn and ed. Hannah Arendt (New York: Schocken Books, 1968), 236.

War and Death' (1915): 'If we are to be judged by our unconscious wishful impulses, we ourselves are, like primaeval man, a gang of murderers. . . . [War] strips us of the later accretions of civilisation and lays bare the primal man in each of us.'[88] This view of the natural aggressiveness of man has been advanced in recent years by revisionist historians, particularly by Niall Ferguson in *The Pity of War* (1998).[89] Yet, the situation portrayed by Rosenberg is more ambivalent. Like the boss in Katherine Mansfield's short story, 'The Fly', the soldiers are at once the perpetrators and victims of violence. If the 'hooked fingers' suggest the grasp of the impersonal war machine, they belong at a literal level to the soldiers: their implication in the carnage is powerfully acknowledged, a sentiment reiterated in 'Dead Man's Dump' in the image of man's 'blind fingers' loosening a chain of destruction.[90]

The imagery of delousing was widespread within the anti-Semitic discourse of the time. In 1882, German regulations were introduced, requiring the delousing of Eastern Jews before they entered the country; train carriages bringing them had to be steamed after every journey.[91] In October 1915 – at a time when German Jewish soldiers were giving up their lives for the nation – Germany's field medical commander decreed that all persons entering the country from the east via rail should be deloused to maintain the 'purity' of the Reich. In France, *Le Rappel*, the organ of the radical Left, noted in November 1920: 'We must, as we have said, prohibit barracks where twenty Jews spread their lice and their blemishes'.[92] We do not know how familiar Rosenberg was with this specific trope and how consciously he was using it in 'Louse Hunting'. However, given his Eastern European background, his general education and 'cosmopolitan' exposure and his acute consciousness of racial discrimination (as evident in 'The Jew'), it is unlikely that the symbolic undertones of 'louse hunting' would be lost on him. To push this line of enquiry further, one might even say that the 'gargantuan' hooked fingers ready to 'smutch' (OED meanings: 1. to blacken, make dirty, smut, smudge; 2. To stain, sully, besmirch etc., morally or otherwise) or image of the 'shirt verminously busy. . . aflare / Over the candle' suggest the menace of a progrom. Yet the symbolic intensification is never allowed to

---

88 Freud, *SE*, XIV, 297, 299.
89 Niall Ferguson, *The Pity of War* (London: Allen Lane, 1998), especially the controversial section, 'The Joy of War', 357–66.
90 *CW*, 112.
91 Wertheimer, *Unwelcome Strangers*, 25–6.
92 Quoted in Poliakov, *Anti-Semitism*, 289.

intrude into or override the matter-of-factness of the description. More-over, unlike 'Break of Day', the poem carries no special bond or identification with the 'vermin brood'. In fact, the exaggerated theatricality pushes it to the brink of comedy, almost endangering our relation to the gravity of the theme.

The torture of the small ('supreme littleness') by the great dramatised through the act may have a personal significance for Rosenberg, the diminutive private: it may suggest the ritual of bullying in the army. In a letter to Marsh, he writes that he does not mind 'actual duties' of the private as much as 'the brutal militaristic bullying meanness of the way they're served out to us. You're always being threatened with "clink".'[93] This is an aspect of war life that gets ignored in the letters or memoirs of the officer-soldiers. At the same time, it is important to remember that Rosenberg was particularly unfortunate with respect to the regiment to which he was assigned.[94] Poor, vulnerable and having always been dependent on patrons, he was particularly sensitive to the intricacies of power. Yet, the playful tone defies any particular interpretation. In spite of the aggressive potential, there is also a marked release of energy which seems to bind the soldiers together into a single, over-excited body. Group identity – a feeling so rare in Rosenberg – is achieved in an act that combines both self-preservation and destruction.

The ambiguity that marks 'Break of Day in the Trenches' and 'Louse Hunting' is absent in 'Dead Man's Dump'. Here, Rosenberg pushes towards the inadvertent contact between the living and the dead that recurs in trench narratives. Tate has argued that, in the trenches, 'corpses are a spectacle, uncanny and fascinating, that the men keep returning to see'.[95] But what happens when there is actual physical contact? In his disturbing chapter, 'As Touching the Dead' in *A Private in the Guards* (1928), Stephen Graham gives examples of 'extraordinary callousness' of the soldiers towards the dead. He draws our attention to one of the most unpleasant aspects of trench life: stripping the dead for possession, 'leaving them even more bare'. And yet, on occasions, there is a curious bond of empathy: in the same chapter, the corpses are described as crouching 'unnaturally', as if 'one had evidently been saying to the other, "Keep your

---

93  *CW*, 226. In another letter, he notes, 'We have pups for officers – at least one – who seems to dislike me – and you know his position gives him power to make me feel it without being able of resist'; he calls the army doctor 'a ridiculous bullying brute' whom he had marked for 'special treatment when I come to write about the army' (224).

94  See his letter to Marsh, *CW*, 228–9.

95  Tate, *Modernism*, 77.

head down"'.[96] In *Undertones of War*, Blunden rationalises: 'Nearly corpses ourselves . . . how should we find the strange and the remote in these corpses?'[97] The physical intimacy between the dead and the living is the subject of the Italian poet Giuseppe Ungaretti's haunting lyric 'Vigil' where he writes of spending a night with the body of one of his men: 'with the congestion /of his hands / thrust right / into my silence'. The narrator has never been so 'coupled', he feels, 'to life'.[98] In Rosenberg's poem, the gap between the worlds of life and death could not have been wider.

In 'Dead Man's Dump', phenomenological unease becomes the point of departure for a profound questioning of the relation between the two worlds. In a letter to Marsh dated 8 May 1917, Rosenberg observed, 'I've written some lines suggested by going out wiring, or rather carrying wire up the line on limbers and running over dead bodies lying about'.[99] In a poem that explores the absoluteness of the gap between the living and the dead, the only moment of contact, when it occurs, is through the wheels of the limber: 'The wheels lurched over sprawled dead / But pained them not, though their bones crunched'.[100] Silkin has called 'lurched' 'the painful exact word'.[101] It is important to note that there is little ooze here, only the dry crunching of bones: what to West and Sassoon would have afforded the ideal moment of disgust is here deftly turned into an acute sense of guilt, a problem of consciousness. For, like Owen's 'still warm' boy, these bodies, no longer sentient subjects and not yet wholly objects, seem particularly vulnerable when they are seen and not felt; or felt indirectly. Metaphysical and moral unrest replaces responses such as disgust or horror, and the whole poem lurches into a new register as much under the renewed pressure of the cart-wheels as under the narrator's sudden change of perspective:

> Here is one not long dead;
> His dark hearing caught our far wheels,
> And the choked soul stretched weak hands
> To reach the living word the far wheels said,
> The blood-dazed intelligence beating for light,
> Crying through the suspense of the far torturing wheels
> . . .

---

96  Stephen Graham, *A Private in the Guards* (London: William Heinemann, 1928), 212, 210, 211.
97  Blunden, *Undertones*, 56.
98  Ungaretti, 'Vigil', *The Penguin Book of First World War Poetry*, 264.
99  *CW*, 254.
100  *PP*, 139.
101  Silkin, *Out of Battle*, 282.

> We heard his weak scream,
> We heard his very last sound,
> And our wheels grazed his dead face.[102]

In *A Private in the Guards*, Graham, looking at the faces of the dead, thinks that 'the open mouth and white teeth seemed to betoken calls to their comrades as they ran'.[103] In this poem, the 'sprawled dead' after all are not 'long dead', not even wholly dead as Rosenberg delves into the consciousness of the dying man: sights and sounds graze the borders of perception as delicately as do the wheels his face which, though 'dead', guides our angle of vision. The 'plunging', 'racketed', limber, with its rickety din, recedes into a 'far' sound, the three-fold repetition emphasising the growing distance. Spirit and body join in one last struggle as 'the choked soul stretched weak hands': the image gathers up the eager hands stretched across his earlier poems into a final impression of spiritual and physical desolation rather than death.

The theme of desolation is particularly poignant within the Jewish context. The racial aspect is evident in the powerful description of soldier's ambivalent relation to earth in the third and fourth stanzas; the mythological bias of these two stanzas has led scholars to connect them with 'Daughters of War'.[104] The phrase, 'God-ancestralled essences' – introduced later in the margin – looks back to 'The Jew' where the anxious subject claims Mosaic ancestry through a moment of physical intimacy: 'Moses, from whose loins I sprung'. The image of the empty sack figures the dead soldier as inert matter and no more, undercutting Brooke's vision of the soul as 'a pulse in the eternal mind'.[105] Later in the poem, the phrase 'great sunk silences' evokes the submerged landscape of the Western Front as well as the utter spiritual desolation – sunkenness as opposed to resurrection – of muddy death ('what is worse – where their soul sinks', as in the opening letter in the previous chapter). The threat of becoming one with 'coloured clay' lends urgency to the spiritual enquiry: 'Who hurled them out? Who hurled?' The sense of being *hurled out* – of being despised and rejected – is acute, and personal. Rosenberg, the isolated Jewish infantryman, re-enacts the condition of his race in being hurled out as were his ancestors repeatedly in European history. The sense of war community that we find in Sassoon and Owen is absent in

---

102 *PP*, 141–2. For the complex textual history of the poem, see *PP*, 367–9.
103 Graham, *Private*, 210.
104 See Silkin, *Out of Battle*, 283.
105 Brooke, 'The Soldier', *Collected Poems*, 148.

Rosenberg. If in 'Moses', the prophet's aim is to put the Jews back into contact with 'the roots' hid secrecy', in 'Dead Man's Dump', the 'loosed' earth of the Western Front evokes the rootlessness of the Jewish diaspora and echoes biblical narratives of exile. Yet, in his last poem 'Through These Pale Cold Days', the spirits of this ancient race ('Out of three thousand years') are seen to 'grope' for the 'pools of Hebron again – / For Lebanon's summer slope'.[106]

The nature poet Edward Thomas, who like Rosenberg fought and died in the war, was once asked whether he knew what he was fighting for. He 'stopped, and picked up a pinch of earth. "Literally, for this." He crumbled it between finger and thumb, and let it fall.'[107] In spite of his Welsh parentage, for Thomas, educated at Oxford and steeped in English literary and cultural traditions, there is a continuous relationship between soil and the nation which is also true of English poets such as Sassoon and Owen. By contrast, for the Anglo-Jewish soldier of immigrant parents and brought up in the Jewish ghetto in the East End of London, the relation between homeland and the nation is necessarily fractured. If the war for Thomas brings inevitable comparisons with the countryside, Rosenberg goes back in his final poem to the ancient historical city of Hebron where Abraham built his first home (Genesis 13:18), pointing us to the 'pools' where his creative self sought sustenance. This wandering between different worlds in turn affects his relation to the world of the trenches: the quirky details which catch his eye and spur his creativity show how intimately the perception of the trench landscape is bound up with his personal history of alienation. Yet, the originality of his verse resists easy assimilation: Rosenberg does not 'fit' as easily as Owen or Sassoon into the First World War canon which has largely been formed by public-school officer-poets and a middle-class readership. Moreover, the ironic humour and the playful imagination do not easily accord with the piety and pathos that are commonly associated with trench poetry. Unlike Sassoon or West, horrific sensuousness is never the whole point with this complex and enormously talented poet: the geography of the trenches is evoked in all its immediacy and yet always 'touched', as he wrote in an essay on art, 'with the adumbrations of some subtly felt idea'.[108]

---

106 *PP*, 148.
107 Quoted in Silkin, *Out of Battle*, 87–8.
108 *CW*, 292.

# PART II

## *Intimacies*

Men of the Duke of Wellington's Regiment after the capture of Marfaux on 23 July 1918, during the battles of the Marne. Q6867. Photograph courtesy of Imperial War Museum.

CHAPTER 3

# 'Kiss me, Hardy': the dying kiss in the First World War trenches

January 12, 1916 saw a peculiar drama enacted in the trenches – two men, who had left their girlfriends back in England, were exchanging a ritual of kisses:

As we arrived at the barn-door he said, 'Just a moment, Frank, before we go in I've something else to give you – put that light out.' I put the lamp out and into my pocket, wondering what was coming. Then I felt an arm round my neck, and the dear lad kissed me once – 'that's from Evelyn' [Cocker's fiancée] he said; then he kissed me again and said, 'that's from your Mother.' I returned his tender salute and said, 'that's from me.' There we were, two men, like a couple of girls, – but then, there was no one about, and the matter was a sacred one between us, – and you.[1]

This is Lieutenant Frank Cocker's letter to his girlfriend Evelyn, written from the trenches. The exchange of this 'tender salute' is a climactic episode in the charged friendship between Cocker and his 'dear Charlie', a relationship that can be pieced together from the letters Cocker wrote to Evelyn and to his sister, Minnie. What is striking is not so much the nascent homoeroticism but how this kiss between the two men is snugly contained within a heterosexual framework through the trope of the girlfriend and the mother. With its detailed stage management, the narrative transmits some of the excitement of the actual moment, as does Cocker's ready reciprocity with the frank acknowledgement, 'that's from me'. Physical demonstrations of such ardour could perhaps just be contained within the parameters of the 'romantic friendship' that characterised late

---

1 Lieutenant Frank Cocker, 'Papers', IWM, 82/11/1. In the letters, Charlie is often the object of adoration: 'I have watched Charlie's face intently under all manner of circumstances'; 'I gazed at him and loved him'; 'We suddenly caught each other's glance and both his eyes and mine were hot with tears'. But the letters also express the most tender feelings towards Evelyn as well as elation at Charlie's engagement to a 'dear Christian girl in Doncaster'. After the war, Cocker married Evelyn.

Victorian culture and intensified during wartime.[2] Anxieties about sexuality
– or, at least awareness of the surreptitious nature of the act ('there was no
one about') – are filtered through a mock violation of gender categories
and their tactile norms with the slightly pejorative simile ('two men, like a
couple of girls'), intended to point up silliness rather than deviance. Yet
the moment cannot so easily be dismissed. Following the logic of the
sentence, if 'sacred' is taken to be a Freudian slip for 'secret', the moment
hovers curiously between the sacrosanct and the furtive. On the other
hand, if 'sacred' is a deliberately chosen word, it might betray an under-
standably overzealous attempt to ward off 'profanity', while at the same
time, perhaps unconsciously, echoing the marriage vow. Situated between
a radical innocence and a transgressive thrill, the exchange mirrors a
moment of epistemological crisis in the interlocked histories of sexuality,
gender and gesture at a crucial moment in modernist history and culture.

The kiss had just started to be theorised in the realm of sexology,
which, in turn, was beginning to be conceptualised by men such as
Havelock Ellis and Sigmund Freud. Both would write pioneering essays
on homosexuality, resulting in the epoch-making conclusion that 'the
sexual instinct and the sexual object are merely soldered together'.[3] It was
also the time of what Alan Sinfield calls 'the consolidation of the queer
image' through a nexus of effeminacy, aestheticism and decadence.[4] The
war hero, and wartime bonding, informed by 'manly' sentiments and
noble ends, were honourably exempt from such charges and yet, as
Cocker's letter demonstrates, not without a trace of anxiety. Insofar as
historical constructions shape desire, this epistemological uncertainty might
well have engendered a greater emotional fluidity: maternal empathy,

2  For a literary-historical elucidation of the Victorian cult of 'romantic friendship' between young
   men, see Peter Parker, *The Old Lie: The Great War and the Public School Ethos* (London:
   Constable, 1987); Jeffrey Richards, '"Passing the Love of Women": Manly Love and Victorian
   Society', in *Manliness and Morality: Middle-Class Masculinity in Britain and America, 1800–1940*,
   ed. J. A. Mangan and James Walvin (Manchester: Manchester University Press, 1987), 108–24.
3  Sigmund Freud, 'Three Essays on the Theory of Sexuality', *SE*, VII, 148. Given the fluidity of
   Cocker's gesture, one might be tempted to place the kiss on a bisexual continuum. But the kiss in
   Cocker's narrative wavers not only between sexual categories but between varyingly nuanced
   emotional registers which are historically contingent; furthermore, to read the kiss as a bisexual
   gesture compromises the quirkiness and complexity of the act. For the recent interest in and
   celebration of bisexuality as 'sexually postmodern', see Joseph Bristow and Angelia R. Wilson
   (eds.), *Activating Theory: Lesbian, Gay and Bisexual Politics* (London: Lawrence and Wishart,
   1993).
4  Alan Sinfield, *The Wilde Century: Effeminacy, Oscar Wilde and the Queer Moment* (London:
   Cassell, 1994), 84–108. See Jeffrey Weeks, *Sex, Politics and Society: The Regulation of Sexuality since
   1800* (London: Longman, 1989), 96–121.

heterosexual romance and homoerotic frisson merge in the kiss, defying the familiar categories of gender and sexuality.

In the trenches of World War I, the norms of tactile contact between men changed profoundly. Mutilation and mortality, loneliness and boredom, the strain of constant bombardment, the breakdown of language and the sense of alienation from home led to a new level of intimacy and intensity under which the carefully constructed mores of civilian society broke down. As the historian Joanna Bourke has documented, men nursed and fed their friends when ill; they bathed together (Figures 3.1 and 3.2); they held each other as they danced, and during the long winter months, wrapped blankets around each other.[5] More recently it has been observed that instead of celebrating 'long-lasting bonds and commitments', First World War writings often privilege 'moments of generosity, mutuality and commonalty'.[6] It is important to note in this context that these moments were usually grounded in experiential reality, the nature of these encounters – men on the verge of death, under fire, or being ill – giving them an emotional and physical intensity that outlive their contingent nature and continue to grow in significance. C. H. Cox remembers how his comrade 'laid back in my arms and his last words were for his mother as he died in my arms'.[7] The soldiers are often haunted by the *feel* of their comrades' bodies as life ebbed out and the warm mutuality of the embrace was lost forever. While it is important to be alerted to the limits of 'mateship' in the trenches – particularly across class, race and military ranks to which recent historians have drawn our attention[8] – the numerous letters, diary entries, memoirs and trench narratives show an undeniable intensification and quickening of male bonds. David Jones speaks of 'the intimate, continuing, domestic life of small contingents of men' in

5 Joanna Bourke, *Dismembering the Male: Men's Bodies, Britain and the Great War* (London: Reaktion Books, 1996), 133–6 (124–70). She provides many stirring accounts of comradeship and recovers important archival material from the time which are not touched by the retrospective nostalgia revisionist historians have suspected in memoirs.

6 Sarah Cole, *Modernism, Male Friendship, and the First World War* (Cambridge: Cambridge University Press, 2003), 152. Cole highlights the war's potential to destroy, through death, the possibility of long-term friendship, giving rise to a sense of alienation. However, the war creates the scope for male intimacy in the first place: the war thus generates a powerful double bind and Cole explores the complex relation between what she calls the 'importance and vulnerability of friendship' (140–73) with reference to a range of modernist writers including Forster, Conrad and some of the war poets.

7 C. H. Cox, 'A Few Experiences of the First World War', IWM, 88/11/1.

8 See Bourke, *Dismembering the Male*, 144–53; Audoin-Rouzeau in 'Brotherhood in the Trenches?' in *Men At War 1914–1918*, 46–56, questions the extension of 'brotherhood' to all soldiers but, at the same time, he notes that 'bonds of astonishing strength developed' and that faced with mutilation and mortality, 'soldiers felt themselves swept up on extraordinary surges of friendship' (47).

Figure 3.1. Interior of Undressing Room, IWM, Q 58122. Photograph courtesy of Imperial War Museum.

Figure 3.2. Soldiers bathing in the pond of a farm near St Eloi, 19 June 1917, Q 5500. Photograph Courtesy of Imperial War Museum.

the early years of the war 'within whose structure Roland could find, and, for a reasonable while, enjoy, his Oliver'.[9] One of the most poignant examples of comradeship is the discovery in 2001 of the bodies of twenty British soldiers buried arm-in-arm in a grave near Arras. They were identified as the 'Grimsby Chums', the nickname for the 10th Battalion Lincolnshire Regiment. Alain Jacques, the leader of the French archaeological team, observed, 'Can you imagine the friendship and dedication of those who went about laying down the remains in this way. To go out and get a leg and position it in line – what a remarkable act. They must have died within hours of each other.'[10]

It is debatable whether the bonds were those of 'comradeship' or 'friendship' or trench 'brotherhood': each had its particular nuance and value, but they all fed into the continuum of male relationships under extreme conditions. Many returned soldiers carried with them photographs of or small items that belonged to their dead comrades; men such as Ivor Gurney remembered the voices of the men in his company – the

9 Jones, *In Parenthesis*, ix.      10 'The Grimsby Chums', *The Times*, 20 June 2001, 5.

'roguish words by Welsh pit boys'.[11] And yet, the most intimate moments were those of actual body contact, often with relative strangers: the trench journal *Poil et Plume* (October 1916) records an incident where a severely wounded man fell on a stretcher-bearer and said, 'Embrace me. I want to die with you.'[12] On the other hand, W. A. Quinton recalls how one night, as he lay shivering, 'old Petch put his overcoat in addition to my own over me, taking care to tuck me in as a mother would a child'.[13] A. F. B. notes, in *The Third Battalion Magazine,* that Smalley was the great favourite of the 3rd Battalion for 'his heart was as big as his body – his strength like a lion's – his touch to the wounded as a woman's.'[14] Another soldier, Jack, must close his letter to Miss Williams as 'my *wife* is in bed & wants me to keep her warm but it is only a Palestine wife. another Sussex boy . . . it is very chilly at night right now. [*sic*] & it is nice to have someone to keep each other warm.'[15] A new world of largely non-genital tactile tenderness was opening up in which pity, thrill, affection and eroticism are fused and confused depending on the circumstances, degrees of knowledge, normative practices and sexual orientations, as well as the available models of male–male relationships.

The most immediate and evanescent of human senses, touch could only be preserved in memory and through language. Consequently, there is the urgent need within war writings to remember and re-present these moments: 'I clasp his hand', 'I had clasped warm, last night' and 'he dies in your arms'.[16] Remarque in *All Quiet on the Western Front* distils all the poignancy of *Freundschaft* into a single, silent gesture: 'Kat's hands are warm, I pass my hand under his shoulders in order to rub his temples with some tea. I feel my fingers becoming moist.'[17] Sherriff's *Journey's End,* one of the most popular war plays, culminates in a similarly intense scene of tactile tenderness: '*Stanhope . . . lightly runs his fingers over Raleigh's tousled hair.*'[18] War literature is haunted by the sense of touch, from Rupert Brooke's 'linked beauty of bodies' to the 'full-nerved, still warm' limbs of Wilfred Owen's dying boy and from Siegfried Sassoon's

11 Ivor Gurney, 'First Time In', in *Lads: Love Poetry of the Trenches,* ed. Martin Taylor (London: Duckworth, 1998), 78.
12 Quoted in Audoin-Rouzeau, *Men At War 1914–1918,* 47.
13 W. A. Quinton, Unpublished memoirs, IWM, 79/35/1.
14 A. F. B., 'Smalley', in *The Third Battalion Magazine* (August 1918), 8.
15 Miss D. Williams, 'Papers', IWM, 85/4/1.
16 Heywood, 'My Pal', Choyce, 'A May Morning', quoted in Taylor, (ed.), *Lads,* 95, 96; Jones, *In Parenthesis,* 174.
17 Remarque, *All Quiet,* 245.
18 Robert Cedric Sherriff, *Journey's End: A Play* (London: Samuel French, 1929), 82–3.

'my fingers touch his face' to Robert Nichols's more sentimental 'My comrade, that you could rest / Your tired body on mine'.[19]

If shell-shock, as Elaine Showalter has argued, was the language of masculine complaint, the poetic efflorescence of the 1920s could be said to be the celebration of what the Lawrentian hero Mellors famously describes as the 'courage of physical tenderness' forged among men in the trenches: 'I knew it with the men. I had to be in touch with them, physically and not go back on it. I had to be bodily aware of them and a bit tender to them.'[20] Whether or not there is any conscious or unconscious erotic investment in these moments, they indicate a new level of intensity and intimacy in male–male relationships. I focus on these moments of charged physical contact because they raise questions about the relation between the experiential reality of the body under physical extremity and the social constructions of gender and sexuality. They highlight the continuity and overlap between different emotions and impulses in the response of men to other men during wartime, and show how these historical specificities shape desire. Above all, these moments of physical bonding and tactile tenderness during trench warfare require us to reconceptualise masculinity, conventional gender roles, and notions of same-sex intimacy in post-war England in more nuanced ways than have been acknowledged in the criticism of war culture, studies of gender and sexuality, or the more general histories of the body, emotion and gesture.[21]

### EMOTION, EXTREMITY, EROTICISM

Magnus Hirschfeld in *The Sexual History of the First World War* (1930) alerts us to that ambiguous zone between male bonding, war camaraderie and eroticism:

The comradeship which developed between the soldiers who shared all the trials and dangers of war, this splendid fruit of war so much praised by Remarque, must have been especially pleasing to the homosexuals for obvious reasons. . . .

19 Brooke, 'Fragment', in *The Collected Poems* (1929; London: Papermac, 1987), 318; Owen, 'Futility', in *CP&F*, 158; Sassoon, 'The Last Meeting', typescript, Cambridge University Library, Add MS 7973 S/75; Nichols, 'Casualty', in *Aurelia and Other Poems* (London: Chatto & Windus, 1920), 75.
20 Elaine Showalter, 'Rivers and Sassoon: The Inscription of Male Gender Anxieties', in *Behind the Lines*, 64 (61–9). D. H. Lawrence, *Lady Chatterley's Lover* (Harmondsworth: Penguin, 1961), 290.
21 Most studies on gender and World War I focus on the relation between the sexes, as in Sandra Gilbert and Susan Gubar, *No Man's Land, The War of Words*, vol. II (New Haven: Yale University Press, 1989), or, following Fussell, on a general idealised notion of the 'homoerotic sensuousness' of First World War verse (*GWMM*, 286). More recent critics such as Caesar and Cole have however alerted us to the more tortured nature of some of these relationships.

Very frequently, even among normal people, it penetrated beyond the outer limits of the homoerotic and was thus, to speak the language of psychoanalysis, characterized by libidinous components.[22]

In spite of severe laws against same-sex practices, a certain amount of homosexual activity went on in the trenches: in the course of the war and the year following, twenty-two officers and 270 other ranks were court-martialled for indecency.[23] However, this was a negligible fraction in context of the millions of soldiers who fought. The issue of World War I homoeroticism largely centres on Hirschfeld's latter category of 'normal', or rather straight-identified, men who formed strong attachments, often with a romantic slant – relationships that Hirschfeld regards as 'unconsciously erotic'. By the time of the Great War, Ellis and Freud had already written their essays on homosexuality, John Addington Symonds and Hirschfeld were advocating reforms, and Walt Whitman and Edward Carpenter had introduced a language of masculine desire into English poetry. But older cultural models prevailed over the scientific and literary discourses: people had yet to recover from the Oscar Wilde trials and in the public perception, homosexuality was associated with the effeminate dandy. In a culture that demonised homosexuality, wartime relationships were often honourably exempt, as in the following loud disclaimer from Richard Aldington: 'Let me at once disabuse the eager-eyed Sodomites among my readers by stating emphatically once and for all that there was nothing sodomitical in these friendships'.[24] But other men were more sensitive to the finer shades of eroticism. Thus, J. R. Ackerley reminiscences that '[my] personal runners and servants were usually chosen for their looks'[25] while a character in Robert Graves's play, *But It Still Goes On*, asks, 'Do you know how a platoon of men will

22 Magnus Hirschfeld, 'Homosexuality and Transvestism in the Trenches', in *The Sexual History of the World War* (1930; New York: Cadillac, 1946), 116–17 (110–22). Also see Fussell, *GWMM*, 270–309; Taylor (ed.), *Lads*, 1–58. Jeffrey Weeks, in *Between the Acts: Lives of Homosexual Men, 1885–1967* (London: Routledge, 1991), interviews a World War I soldier who met his partner in the trenches (7). Hirschfeld documents similar cases, but agrees that such examples are few (*Sexual History*, 115). Taylor notes, 'Given the physical conditions of the front line, the filth, the lice and the lack of privacy, and the probable sexual orientation of most soldiers, it is unlikely that any sexual contact was possible or even desirable' (*Lads*, 27). Raymond Asquith writes to Lady Diana Manners in September 1916, 'I had two terribly strenuous days – 10 hours each before a court martial defending a fellow officer upon 5 charges of "homosexualism" – unsuccessfully' (*Raymond Asquith: Life and Letters*, ed. John Joliffe, London: Collins, 1980, 292).

23 Hynes, *A War Imagined*, 225. While 'any act of gross indecency with another male person' was punishable with two years' imprisonment, sodomy incurred a sentence for ten years (224–5).

24 Richard Aldington, *Death of a Hero* (London: Chatto and Windus, 1929), 26.

25 J. R. Ackerley, *My Father and Myself* (London: Bodley Head, 1968), 119.

absolutely worship a good-looking gallant officer? . . . Of course, they don't realise exactly what's happening, neither does he; but it's a very, very strong romantic link.'[26] Discussion of wartime homoeroticism must consider such 'very, very strong romantic links', although they often were as 'sentimental' and 'chaste' as Graves's Charterhouse friendships.[27]

In so far as World War I has become a literary-historical phenomenon, it is perhaps possible to 'queer' it. Its three major poets, Brooke, Owen and Sassoon, had homoerotic encounters, inclination or relationships.[28] Three of its major prose works, *Goodbye to all That, The Middle Parts of Fortune* and *Seven Pillars of Wisdom* were written by men who had similar experiences. Three of the major plays, *Journey's End, Prisoners of War* and *But It Still Goes On* have homoerotic themes. But any hasty claim for conscious and explicit sexual dissidence will encounter problems, both circumstantial and epistemological.[29] Central to the construction of sexuality is the idea of the male-as-subject-of-desire, a tenet that led Michel Foucault to reformulate his enquiry in *The History of Sexuality*:

In order to understand how the modern individual could experience himself as the subject of a 'sexuality', it was essential first to determine how, for centuries, Western man had been brought to recognise himself as a subject of desire.[30]

The application of this model, highly influential in the discussion of same-sex eroticism from classical Greece to nineteenth-century England, is deeply problematic in relation to the war scenario. In the trenches, the male body became an instrument of pain rather than of desire. World War I lasted over four years and claimed over nine million lives; an average of 6,046 men were killed every day. From the British army alone, 41,000

26  Robert Graves, *But It Still Goes On* (London: Jonathon Cape, 1930), 245.
27  Graves, *Goodbye to All That* (1929; Harmondsworth: Penguin, 1988), 23. 'Romantic friendship' (or even 'love') is the term used by many critics in their discussions of such same-sex intimacy where the erotic element is confused, unknown or unconscious. Sinfield, in *The Wilde Century*, notes, ' "Same-sex passion" is the best term I have been able to find for the period up to 1900' (11).
28  While in Brooke's case there is documented evidence of at least one encounter, Sassoon was a self-confessed homosexual. Owen's letters and poems evince a strong homoerotic impulse but provide little evidence of any actual sexual encounter or relationship. For a discussion of the sexuality of these three poets through a focus on suffering, see Adrian Caesar, *Taking It Like a Man*; for a useful introduction to First World War gender politics, see Featherstone, *War Poetry*, 95–115, and Taylor, *Lads*, 1–58.
29  A good example of the dialogue between past and present is David M. Halperin's *One Hundred Years of Homosexuality and Other Essays on Greek Love* (New York: Routledge, 1990). The pioneering work on queer theory is Eve Kosofsky Sedgwick, *Between Men: English Literature and Male Homosocial Desire* (New York: Columbia University Press, 1985). Also see Paul Hammond, *Love Between Men in English Literature* (London: Macmillan, 1996); Stevens and Howlett (eds.), *Modernist Sexualities*.
30  Michel Foucault, *The Use of Pleasure, History of Sexuality*, vol. II, trans. Robert Hurley (Harmondsworth: Penguin, 1992), 5–6.

servicemen had limbs amputated and 65,000 continued to suffer from shell-shock.[31] Given this context, homoeroticism has to be understood within new conceptual parameters and a different economy of emotions.

In the military, bodily contact is often the primary means of fostering loyalty, trust and unity within an army unit. In the trenches of the Western Front, where life expectancy could be as short as a couple of weeks, same-sex ardour, bodily contact and (in some cases) eroticism should not be understood solely in contrast to heterosexuality, nor viewed only through the lenses of gender and sexuality. Such intimacy must also be understood *in opposition to and as a triumph over death*: it must be seen as a celebration of life, of young men huddled against long winter nights, rotting corpses and falling shells. Thus, A. J. Abraham, in his private memoirs, recalls how, one winter morning, he saw men sleeping in the open 'wrapped in their greatcoats and groundsheets, white with frost': 'They had spent the night thus, mostly in couples to share a little warmth'.[32] Physical contact was the transmission of the wonderful assurance of being alive, and more sex-specific eroticism, though concomitant, was subsidiary. In a world of visual squalor, little gestures – closing a dead comrade's eyes, wiping his brow, or holding him in one's arms – were felt as acts of supreme beauty that made life worth living. Although these acts may overlap with eroticism, such experiences should not simply be conflated with it – or, for that matter, with the repression or sublimation of sexual drives.

While discussing homosexual writers such as Sassoon, Ackerley or Manning, it is important to remember that they were a sexual minority, writing within a masculinist, heterosexual field. Their conception of same-sex 'love' and its relation to sexual identity was very different from ours, verging precariously between the Victorian cult of 'manly love' and the 'unspeakable bestiality' of the Greeks.[33] Moreover, they were mostly young men in extreme circumstances whose sexuality was not yet strongly formed, either in relation to erotic experiences or an intellectual tradition of sexual dissidence, as was the case for Wilde, Symonds or Carpenter. Above all, sexual orientation should not be highlighted at the cost of other nuances of feeling. Sassoon, in *Memoirs of An Infantry Officer*, recalls coming across a dead German soldier: 'As I stepped over one of the Germans an impulse made me lift him up from the miserable ditch. Propped against the bank, his blond face was undisfigured, except by the

---

31 Niall Ferguson, *The Pity of War* (Harmondsworth: Penguin, 1998), 436–7.
32 A. J. Abraham, 'Memoirs of a Non-Hero, 1914–18', IWM, P191, 14–15.
33 See Richards, 'Passing the Love of Women'; Taylor (ed.), *Lads*, and Parker, *Old Lie*.

mud which I wiped from his eyes and mouth with my coat sleeve.'[34] It is reductive to interpret this gesture solely, as Fussell does, in terms of Sassoon's fascination with young blond Germans.[35] The moment of tactile tenderness is equally informed by a recognition of human dignity and waste, a deep feeling of *caritas* that overcomes political hostility. In a poem written on the following day (6 July 1916), Sassoon recounts the episode: 'Wiped mud from mouth and eyes, and beardless cheek, . . . / Till he looked tidy for a hostile corpse!'[36] The mud is an affront to the boy's dignity as well as to his beauty, making 'death' ugly – 'a shameless thing'. Wiping away the mud becomes a pitiful attempt to save the human form from the absurdity of a world where, as discussed in the previous chapter, men were becoming 'things'. Even when there are more consciously erotic experiences, they have to be aligned with a whole range of emotional needs such as succour, sympathy, assurance and security as well as states of bodily extremity. Consequently, in order to discuss same-sex relations during war, we must introduce a different and less distinctly sexualised array of emotional intensities and bodily sensations, a fresh category of *nongenital tactile tenderness* that goes beyond strict gender divisions and sexual binaries.[37] We will explore this terrain through the representation of the dying kiss.

THE DYING KISS

A notoriously unstable signifier, often slipping from a sign to a sensation, the kiss was increasingly discussed in fin-de-siècle culture: 'The Curiosities

---

34  Siegfried Sassoon, *Memoirs of An Infantry Officer* (1930; London: Faber, 1997), 57.

35  Fussell, *GWMM*, 276.

36  These lines, written on 6 July 1916 (the day after the incident), appear underneath the date in the manuscript of the poem, 'The Night Attack', now in the Harry Ransom Humanities Research Centre, University of Texas at Austin. These lines were excised from the poem 'A Night Attack' when it was published in the *Stand* in 1970–1, and it is this excised version that Rupert Hart-Davis reprints in *The War Poems*, 42–3. See Jean Moorcroft Wilson, *Siegfried Sassoon: The Making of a War Poet, A Biography, 1886–1918* (London: Duckworth, 1998), 270–1.

37  Due to the peculiarity of war circumstances, the continuum of non-genital tactile tenderness seems to combine elements of Sedgwick's 'homosocial desire' with certain features of Rich's paradigm of the lesbian continuum of 'resignation, despair, effacement, self-denial'. See Adrienne Rich, 'Compulsory Heterosexuality and Lesbian Existence', in *Blood, Bread and Poetry, Selected Prose, 1979–1985* (London: Virago, 1986), 53–4. The bonds I examine are not based on triangulated desire and are more bodily than in Sedgwick. They are not usually consciously erotic, nor are they associated with structures of power. See Sedgwick, *Between Men: English Literature and Male Homosocial Desire*, and Richard Dellamora, *Masculine Desire: The Sexual Politics of Victorian Aestheticism* (Chapel Hill: University of North Carolina Press, 1990).

of Kissing' in *Galaxy*, 16 (July–December 1873), 'The History of Kissing' in *Belgravia: An Illustrated London Magazine*, 47 (July–October 1882), 'An Epidemic of Kisses in America' in *Pall Mall Magazine*, 18 (May–August 1899), 'The Kiss Poetical' in *The Fortnightly Review*, 82 (August 1904), 'Kiss' in *Catholic Encyclopaedia* (New York, 1910), and finally Havelock Ellis's 'The Origins of the Kiss', in the fourth volume of his monumental *Studies in the Psychology of Sex* (1923).[38] But how would the specifically same-sex kiss be perceived at a moment when English culture was precariously poised between the Victorian cult of 'manly love' and the 'sodomical' deeds of Oscar Wilde? In *The Kiss and its History* (1901), Christopher Nyrop remembers 'former times' when 'the friendly kiss was very common with us between man and man', but notes that in recent times 'the friendly kiss usually occurs only between ladies'.[39] But wartime extremity suspends normal tactile codes: soldier and sailor brothers were seen to kiss each other in greeting (Figure 3.3), and the male-to-male kiss was doing its round in the trenches, mostly in close proximity to danger and death. 'Kissing was never out of favour' in the trenches, Evelyn muses in Lawrence's 'England, My England', while a world-weary Stanhope in Sheriff's *Journey's End* (1929) pleads with Osborne: 'Kiss me, Uncle'; in Ernest Hemingway's *A Farewell to Arms* (1929), Rinaldi's interactions with Frederic largely revolve around Frederic agreeing to a kiss which is denied throughout the novel.[40] But the dying kiss had very different connotations. The most obvious association would perhaps have been with the kiss by which grace is bestowed, varying from the *New Testament* kiss of peace and brotherhood (1 Corinthians 16:20, 2 Corinthians 13:2) to the transmission of the Holy Spirit. However, in 1924, when most of the war lyrics were appearing in print, Stephen Gaselee in an article, 'The Soul in the Kiss', traced the classical concept of a mingling and migration of souls through the kiss after death.[41] For an Englishman, the religious and classical

---

38  For a detailed study of the kiss, see Nicolas James Perella, *The Kiss Sacred and Profane: An Interpretative History of Kiss Symbolism & Related Religio-Erotic Themes* (Berkeley: University of California Press, 1969); Willem Frijhoft, 'The Kiss Sacred and Profane: Reflections on a Cross-Cultural Confrontation', in *A Cultural History of Gesture: From Antiquity to the Present Day*, ed. Jan Bremmer and Herman Roodenburg (Malden, Mass.: Polity Press, 1991), 210–36.

39  Christopher Nyrop, *The Kiss and its History*, trans. William Frederick Harvey (London: Sands, 1901), 141–2.

40  Lawrence, 'England, My England' (1915 version), in *England, My England and Other Stories*, ed. Bruce Steele (Cambridge: Cambridge University Press, 1990), 227; R. C. Sherriff, *Journey's End* (London: Samuel French, 1929), 25; Ernest Hemingway, *A Farewell to Arms* (London, Vintage, 1999), 151.

41  Stephen Gaselee, 'The Soul in the Kiss', *Criterion*, 2 (April 1924), 349–59.

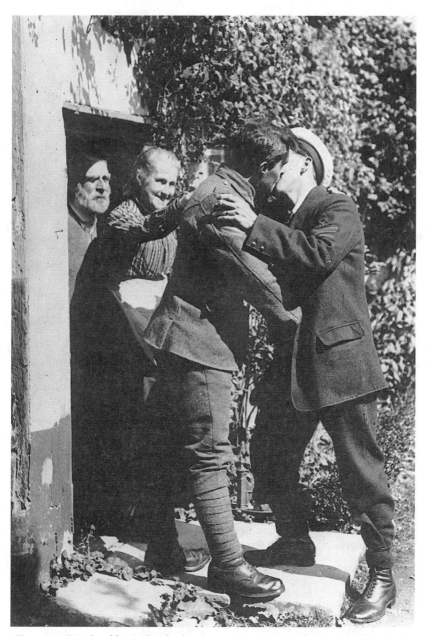

Figure 3.3. British soldier and sailor brothers greeting one another outside their home while on leave, Q 31046. Photograph courtesy of Imperial War Museum.

connotations might be overshadowed by a more flesh-and-blood incident from national history: Admiral Nelson's dying words: 'Kiss me, Hardy', an image of heroic martyrdom and camaraderie.[42] But what do the trench letters tell us?

The Reverend Carl Parry Okeden writes to his wife: 'One dear lad very badly wounded . . . said, "Hello Padre old sport" and then "Come and kiss me Padre" and he put his arms round me and kissed me'.[43] The Reverend Connor writes on 22 December 1914: 'I prayed to God for the dear lad – I said, "I'll give you your mother's kiss" – "Let me do it to you", & the dear lad kissed me'.[44] Similarly, when his close friend Jim dies, a grief-stricken Lance-Corporal D. H. Fenton writes to his mother, Mrs Noone:

I suddenly saw Jim reel to the left and fall with a choking sob. I did what I could for him, but his stout heart had already almost ceased to beat and death must have been mercifully instantaneous. I held him in my arms to the end, and when his soul had departed I kissed him twice where I knew you would have kissed him – on the brow – once for his mother and once for myself.[45]

The recurring, almost ritualistic phrase, 'mother's kiss', suggests a powerful reconceptualisation of both masculinity and male–male bonds through an assumed maternal impulse of security and tenderness. Strangely, the dying kiss is seldom associated with the father. Though there is often a paternalistic discourse in the discussion of the officer's relationship to his men, tenderness and support, even when extended by the padre (as with the Reverend Connor), remain anchored to the trope of the mother.[46] In Fenton's letter to Mrs Noone, the phrase 'I held him in my arms', with the subsequent connection to maternity, is almost an unconscious reworking of the *Pietà*, showing how deeply Christian imagery informs experiential reality within shared Western culture. If a grieving Saint Veronica wipes Christ's brows, Fenton goes a step further, planting the kiss of life. And yet there is a fleeting hesitancy to specify the bodily part, as

---

42  Christopher Hibbert, *Nelson: A Personal History* (New York: Viking, 1994), 376. Hardy kisses Nelson not once but twice, the first time on Nelson's bidding, 'Then, as though he thought Nelson might think he had kissed him only because he had been asked to do so, he knelt down again and kissed his forehead' (376).

43  Reverend Carl Parry Okeden to May Okeden, IWM, 90/7/1.

44  Reverend Connor, 'Diary', IWM, 87/10/1. See also Bourke, *Dismembering the Male*, where she notes that 'the omnipresence of death enabled emotion' (137).

45  Lance-Corporal D. H. Fenton, 'Papers', IWM, 87/13/1, 26.

46  Mike Roper discusses the importance of the figure of the mother in First World War trench writing, and kindly sent me his paper 'Beyond Containing: Middle-class Sons and the Maternal Relations in First World War' where he develops a psychoanalytic approach, drawing on the work of Alfred Bion.

if deflecting it to a maternal prerogative were a subconscious avoidance of the merest hint of misinterpretation. Yet, it is anachronistic to mark in the kiss an actively transgressive eros: it is a response based on the perception of the male body as a seat of pain and transience rather than of fulfilment. Sublimated eroticism, if present, does not exist at the level of deliberate personal intention, but results from a deep structural overlap with sentimentalism, tenderness and aestheticism, centring on the death of a youth, as in the various representations of the Deposition of Christ. But how can a literary language be built around such moments? Can imaginative reconstructions by soldier-writers help us to understand the emotional history of the First World War? I shall examine the motif of the dying kiss in fiction, poetry and the short story in order to show the interaction between gender, psychosexual complexities and literary modes.

## WAR CAMARADERIE AND THE PUBLIC SCHOOL ROMANCE

The dying kiss appears in war literature perhaps for the first time in *Wooden Crosses* (1920) by Roland Dorgelès.[47] But few war novels dwell on the dying kiss as passionately and in such detail as Arthur Newberry Choyce's *Lips at the Brim* (1920). Choyce was commissioned in December 1916 as a Second Lieutenant in the 9th Battalion, Leicestershire Regiment and served in France, 1917–18. He produced many books of war poetry such as *Crimson Stains* (1918), *Memory* (1920) and *Not Until Gilboa* (1931) which are marked by a lush romantic vocabulary. In *Lips at the Brim*, Peter and Raymond, close friends at school, enlist in the war as officer and soldier respectively and Choyce shows school friendship as flowering and fusing into officer-soldier romance in the battlefields at the moment of death:

'Lift me higher, Peter – higher up . . . thank God! . . . you're back! I want . . . to look at you . . . old man.'

Dumbly Peter raised his head higher, holding him against his rough tunic, and wiping his lips with his own numbed fingers.

Raymond looked into his eyes, and though Peter was half-dazed with the tragedy of these last hours, his heart was stirred by the adoration of friendship that he saw. It was the reallest thing he had known in his life.

---

47 Raymond Dorgeles, *Wooden Crosses* (London: William Heinemann, 1920), 264–6.

'Passing the love of women.'

'Pete,' he said, and the words were fainter and more faint, 'together till the end
. . . together . . . end. Come one day. Peter . . . Joyce . . . Pete, old man . . . Pete
. . .' and then no more.

Five minutes, ten minutes, the officer held him there, staring hard at the half-
closed eyes, without thinking, without moving.

. . .

Afterwards he drew a deep sobbing breath and bent lower and lower, pressing his
fevered mouth against the damp hair, and the cold, hard forehead, and the pitiful
blood-flecked lips.[48]

The maternal empathy that one notes in the letters of Fenton or Connor
is here supplanted by a language of desire – fevered mouth, half-closed
eyes, blood-flecked lips – that breaks through the rhetoric of Christianity,
patriotism or war camaraderie. The theatricality of the scene is permeated
with sentimentalism and sensationalism but there is also a physical frisson
that extends well beyond the limits of school friendship or official duty.
The blood-smeared kiss is the climactic episode in a narrative where plot
and character developments are structured around a series of abortive
heterosexual kisses.[49] While sexual innocence on the part of Peter and
Raymond, both straight-identified males, does not prevent the kiss from
being distinctly homoerotic, eroticism informing the above scene has to be
understood in terms of idealisation, affection and ardour rather than as a
straightforward case of repression or sublimation of the sexual drives.

Parker, speaking of the Victorian creed of Romantic friendship, notes
that 'the lush unfolding of a chaste romance between two boys was clearly
considered charming', having 'all the agreeable elements of a clandestine
yet carefree affair without the complication of sex'.[50] Contemporary forms
of knowledge, types of normativity, and ideological pressures play a part
not only in the interpretation of sexual experience, but often underlie the
structure of desire.[51] Phrases such as 'self-appointed task of devotion',

---

48 Arthur Newberry Choyce, *Lips at the Brim: A Novel* (London: John Bale, Sons & Danielsson,
  1920), 165–6.
49 In the first flush of adolescent passion, as Peter tries to follow 'the impulse of his lips', Tess throws
  some forget-me-nots at his face and runs away. At the end of the narrative, when Peter is about to
  kiss Claire, she says, 'God help me! I am Claude Paler's wife' (*Lips at the Brim*, 197). Similarly, the
  battle between religious ardour and sexual passion is fought at a moment when Peter is going to
  kiss the chalice: Tess pretends to faint, Peter gets distracted and the chalice drops on the floor.
50 Parker, *Old Lie*, 114.
51 Dollimore notes, 'What is less often conceded or, if conceded, considered – Bersani being a
  significant exception – is that if gender is socially constituted, *so too is desire*. Desire is informed by

'adoration of friendship', 'a straight young god with a clean young body', or the biblical echo, 'Passing the love of women' show that, instead of being a simple conflict between physical passion and homophobic structures, eroticism is paradoxically a function of ideological investments in contemporary discourses: the Victorian cult of manly love, the Christian rhetoric of service, the wartime duty of an officer. Love, respect, grief for a friend, a soldier, a martyr: all contribute to that mood of extravagant emotionalism of which the kiss is the token. The dominant Victorian ideology of religiosity, purity and manliness, which interlocks with each of these discourses and claims a moral high ground over heterosexual conjugality, fosters the classic 'homosocial bond' Eve Kosofsky Sedgwick speaks of in her analysis of nineteenth-century male friendships.[52] Joyce becomes the mediating agent in this triangulated desire, epitomised in Peter's penultimate gesture of taking off Joyce's love token and hanging it round Raymond's neck. Given the physicality and sentimentalism inherent in the theatre of war and death, the kiss indeed serves as a faultline in the contemporary construction of both masculinity and male bonding. While, in the aggrieved letter of Fenton, the kiss is more of an act of spontaneity and beauty, in Choyce's studied fictional treatment, it becomes the fine point where homosociability and homoeroticism – the polarities in the Victorian ideological spectrum of male relationships – intersect at the levels of both experiential reality and hermeneutic interpretation.

Yet the 'blood-flecked' kiss may also characterise the genre of public school romance Choyce draws on. The public school novels are marked by a tortured dialectic between earnest homoeroticism and homophobic paranoia. Friendship is celebrated through a language of high romance in novels such as J. E. C. Welldon's *Gerald Eversley's Friendship* (1896), H. A. Vachell's *The Hill* (1905) or E. F. Benson's *David Blaize* (1916). A typical example is the following passage from Sturgis's *Tim* (1891): '[Tim] felt his love for his friend almost a religion to him. . . . "What woman could ever love him as I do?" thought Tim . . . As Tim's hungry eyes rested on the face of his friend, he turned towards him and smiled.'[53] When asked about such fraught relationships, G. H. Rendall, Headmaster of Charterhouse from 1897 to 1911, said, 'My boys are amorous but seldom erotic'.[54] 'Yet I agree with Rendall's distinction', Graves writes. Stating that 'in English

the same oppressive constructions of gender that we would willingly dispense with. Desire is of its 'nature' saturated by the social.' See Jonathan Dollimore, *Sexual Dissidence: Augustine to Wilde, Freud to Foucault* (Oxford: Oxford University Press, 1991), 325.
52 Sedgwick, *Between Men*.
53 H. O. Sturgis, *Tim* (London: Macmillan, 1891), 158–9.     54 Graves, *Goodbye*, 39.

preparatory and public schools romance is necessarily homosexual',
Graves however notes that 'nine of these ten are as honourably chaste
and sentimental as I was'.[55] In many of the novels, such as Welldon's
*Gerald Eversley's Friendship* (1895) or Raymond's *Tell England* (1922),
there is either an episode of 'attempted beastliness' or a figure of the
'degenerate', as if the sanctity of the central relationship could be defined
only in relation to such tropes.[56] In an atmosphere 'always heavy with
romance of a conventional early-Victorian type', it was important to have
a strict embargo on the ambiguous world of physical contact.[57] Even in
the pre-Wildean England of Farrar's *Eric* (1857–8), a scene in which Eric
'stooping down kissed fondly the pale white forehead of his friend' drew
negative critical responses.[58] The *Saturday Review* complained, 'to the
infinite indignation of all English readers, [the boys] occasionally kiss each
other, exchanging moreover such endearments as "dear fellow" and the
like'.[59] In Hughes's *Tom Brown at Oxford* (1889), after Tom gives up the
barmaid and is reconciled with Hardy, 'Tom rushed across to his friend,
dearer to him now, and threw his arm round his neck; and if the un-
English truth must out, had three parts of a mind to kiss the rough face.'[60]

The male-to-male kiss is 'un-English' but, in 1889, just four years after
the Labouchère Amendment, the source of anxiety is not difficult to
guess. Added to the Criminal Law Amendment Act (1885), this amendment criminalised homosexuality – or, as it was termed, gross indecency
between males – with a penalty of up to three years' imprisonment. The
climactic kiss in Choyce's narrative needs to be considered in this context
of paranoia. Choyce exploits the contemporary historical catastrophe
not only to relegitimise the kiss but to display it proudly in his narrative
framework. He does not merely suffuse the kiss with all the suppressed
romance of the genre but gives it a decadent slant as well. The physical
intimacy between Peter and Raymond collapses the fine distinction
between the amorous and the erotic; moreover, Raymond being dead,
the mutuality of the gesture will never be known nor will it cast its shadow
over the relationship. The ardour of the dying kiss could safely be
contained within the physicality and the sentimentality inherent in the

---

55 Graves, *Goodbye*, 23.          56 Richards, 'Passing the Love of Women', 113–17.
57 Graves, *Goodbye*, 39.
58 F. W. Farrar, *Eric or Little by Little* (1857; London: Ward Lock, n.d.), 139–40.
59 H. Montgomery Hyde, *The Other Love* (London: Mayflower, 1972), 131.
60 Thomas Hughes, *Tom Brown at Oxford* (London: Macmillan, 1889), 193–4.

theatre of war and death and Choyce knew that a post-war mourning public would translate it into a narrative of sacrifice and comradeship.

## TRENCH POETRY AND THE LANGUAGE OF SENSATIONS

Amorousness was perhaps permissible among boys but not between men in Victorian England. The love and grief Alfred Tennyson felt at the death of his friend, Arthur Henry Hallam, finds statement in the image of a dying kiss at the centre of 'In Memoriam' (1850).[61] Whitman, in the first edition of *Leaves of Grass* (1855), employs a more overtly erotic vocabulary to describe same-sex affection – 'comrade's long dwelling kiss' – but carefully harnesses it into a democratic vision, or a rhetoric of sacrifice, as in 'The Wound Dresser': 'Many a soldier's kiss dwells on these bearded lips'.[62] Herbert Read turns to this literary tradition in 'My Company', first published in *Naked Warriors* (1919). In Read's poem, the dying kiss is set exactly in the central section: 'It is not thus I would have him kiss'd / but with the warm passionate lips / of his comrade here'.[63] In Read's modernist poetics, Whitman is invoked both for sexual and political reasons: erotic charge is made the basis of military bonding. Army relationships are here reconceptualised as personal romance: 'O beautiful men, O men I loved / O whither are you gone, my company?' Fussell notes that the above stanza 'seems to recover the world of Whitman's *Calamus* and *Drumtaps*'.[64] But there is an essential difference between the Whitmanesque model the central section posits and the rest of the poem:

> I cannot tell
> what time your life became mine:
> perhaps when one summer night
> we halted on the roadside
> in the starlight only
> and you sang your sad home-songs
> dirges which I standing outside you
> coldly condemned.
> Perhaps, one night, descending cold
> when rum was mighty acceptable,
> and my doling gave birth to sensual gratitude.

61 Alfred Tennyson, 'In Memoriam', in *The Poems of Alfred Tennyson*, ed. Christopher Ricks (Essex: Longman, 1987), II, 337 (Section XVIII).
62 Walt Whitman, 'The Wound-Dresser', in *The Portable Walt Whitman*, ed. Mark Van Doren (New York: Penguin, 1977), 229.
63 Herbert Read, 'My Company', in *Collected Poems 1913–25* (London: Faber and Gwyer, 1926), 88.
64 Fussell, *GWMM*, 280.

And then our fights: we've fought together
compact, unanimous
and I have felt the pride of leadership.[65]

This is the language of the amorous subject, but it draws on the rhetorics of heterosexual romance, laddish indulgences, and officer–soldier camaraderie. The shifts in register suggest that these realms, kept separate in ordinary life through the varying discourses of desire, friendship and duty have come together. Here the catalyst is clearly not physical charge but rather constant companionship, growth, mutual dependence and support. Manning, in *The Middle Parts of Fortune* (1929), speaks of war camaraderie as having 'an intensity of feeling which friendship never touches', remembering how 'When young Evans heard the Colonel had been left on the wire, he ran back into hell to do what he could for him'.[66] What the eroticisation of the kiss in Read's poem suggests is not an actively transgressive politics of sexual difference as it often does in Whitman, but rather two different, although related, concepts. First, eroticism is primarily on the side of life, meaning and beauty; it stands in opposition to the Baudelairian grotesquery of rotting lips, and subsequent categories of homo/hetero are strictly secondary. Secondly, Read's poem asks, for a sensitive heterosexual male, can emotional intensity accommodate the physical? Or, conversely, is heterosexual desire the necessary structuring principle of social units?

If a questioning of heterosexual norms is implicit in Read's model, Robert Nichols openly employs the motif of the dying kiss to challenge civilian domestic structures. Nichols's *Ardours and Endurances* (1917) was one of the most popular wartime collections of poems, rapturously reviewed in the *Times Literary Supplement* (12 July 1917). 'The Secret', though appearing in his second book, *Aurelia* (1920), sums up the main thrust of *Ardours*: before the war the poet was both in 'love' and 'passion,' but in a post-war life, he could find solace in romantically mourning two friends, Richard Pinsent, killed at Loos (1915), and Harold Stuart Gough, killed at Ypres (1916). Initially, 'The Secret' seems to reproduce the age-old asymmetrical opposition between male camaraderie and heterosexual romance, but in the last stanza, there is a subtle shift. The difference between male–male and male–female relationship is predicated not on an absence/presence of the body but on a *distinction* between processes of

---

65 'My Company', 85.
66 Manning, *The Middle Parts of Fortune*, 79–80.

touch. Different kinds of physicalities and masculinities are at work in the poem:

> I, that have held strong hands which palter,
> Borne the full weight of limbs that falter,
> Bound live flesh on the surgeon's altar,
> What need have I of woman's hand?
> I, that have felt the dead's embrace;
> I, whose arms were his resting-place;
> I, that have kissed a dead man's face;
> Ah, but how should you understand
> *Now I can only turn away.*[67]

Heterosexual investment is contrasted with the noble, altruistic love of comrades but the process of remembrance and representation is astonishing. The gruesome memories of bandaging wounds are fondly cherished, nightmarish experiences are transformed through language into a fantasy of romance. The overarching Christian framework of suffering and service comes up against an almost desirable relish heard in the wording, sound-pattern, rhythm and rhyme. This effect is produced not merely through the labials and sibilants ('live flesh', 'limbs', 'strong hands'), but in the way the falling cadence of the feminine rhyme ('palter' / 'falter' / 'altar') is gathered up by a strong masculine subjectivity grounded in the anaphoric 'I' and the alliterative beat of the stressed syllables of the trochee and the spondee: 'Borne' and 'Bound'. In this romance of language between two kinds of masculinity, sympathy flows into empathy, and the 'woman's hand', receiving the stress at the wrong end of the line, grates harshly. The kiss is the climactic point in the poem: if the rhetorical dismissal of the 'woman's hand' is a repudiation of marriage, is kissing the comrade meant to show that the symbol of heterosexual romance has also lost its meaning in post-war England?

The aestheticisation of the male body and eroticisation of male experience that one notes in Read and Nicols – writers who, unlike Sassoon or Ackerley, were not overtly concerned with homosexuality – might result from the effort to find a suitable poetic language to articulate the specificity of war experiences. In journals, diaries and letters that are not self-consciously literary or written by public school officers, one finds a slightly different statement of experience, as in the unpublished memoirs of W. A. Quinton:

67 Robert Nichols, 'The Secret', in *Aurelia*, 77.

Sharing everything, down to the last cigarette end, the last army biscuit, the last bit of cover under an enemy bombardment, can you wonder when I say we almost loved each other. Facing hardships & death together day after day, brings out that something in a man that lies dormant in the monotonous round of everyday civilian life. I well remember on one occasion when I was sickly, how old Petch tried to nurse me . . . taking care to tuck me in as a mother would a child.[68]

Tactile tenderness, figured through the maternal embrace, defines the final moment in Quinton's reconceptualisation of male–male bonds premised on a language of mutual dependence. The bodily intimacy he suggests is of a different order from desire. The physical continuum – touching, nursing, reassuring – was central to these relationships, which did not fit either the classical or the Christian models of 'manly love', both of which largely ignored the body. Without a language to describe this physicality, most poets fell back on a model of Whitmanesque passion or Georgian aestheticism. At the same time, these soldier-writers developed a troubled relationship to these modes as they tried to evoke a different order of experience. This is evident in the conflict that lies at the heart of Read's and Nichols's poems: the central disjunction between an experiential reality and ideology of 'greater love', and an inherited poetic language of exquisite sensations. Having challenged the centrality of desire as the structuring principle of heterosexual civilian society, most poets would nonetheless draw on a rhetoric of desire – yet the constant effort to evoke another experience is perceptible in their language and suggests a different kind of relationship.

Perhaps retreat into older poetic modes was the inevitable result of a conjunction of class politics, literary history, and the culture of mourning. Jon Silkin's *The Penguin Book of First World War Poetry* (1979) shows that what has come to be regarded as the World War I literary canon was largely built on the works of public school officer-poets. Many of them had 'sentimental and chaste' but distinctly 'homosexual' crushes, as Graves writes, at school; for many of them, the army, with its network of male relationships, was basically an extension of the public school and they transposed the language of school romance with a rhetoric of mourning.[69] Moreover, from the aestheticism of Walter Pater to the

---

68 W. A. Quinton, 'Memoirs', IWM, 79/35/1, 56.

69 Graves, *Goodbye*, 40–1. Ackerley notes, 'the army with its male relationships was simply an extension of my public school'. J. R. Ackerley, *My Father and Myself* (London: Bodley Head, 1968), 117. For a different point of view, see Priestley: 'I never hailed with relief, as men in the opposing class did, a wholly masculine way of life uncomplicated by women'. J. B. Priestley, *Margin Released: A Writer's Reminiscences and Reflections* (London: Heinemann, 1962), 89.

pastoral poignancy of A. E. Housman's *A Shropshire Lad* to the Uranian poetry of William Johnson Cory, English poetry was suffused with what Fussell calls a tradition of 'warm homoeroticism' through which the youthful male body was endlessly aestheticised, idealised and eulogised. Sensuousness mixed with pathos as the wistfulness of *l'amour impossible* was deflected onto the early death of the boy.[70] Most of the war poets eagerly tapped into this tradition. If in 1869 a slightly perturbed father of Arthur Hallam, after reading Shakespeare's *Sonnets*, had detected 'weakness and folly in all excessive and mis-placed affection', in the case of war poetry, such excesses were 'redeemed by the touches of nobler sentiments'.[71] Moreover, at a time when a whole generation had been destroyed by unimaginable forms of violence, homophobia was checked through the sheer intensity of grief. The threat of homoeroticism was arrested by the absence of the desired object and the conception of the body as a seat of pain. This explains the appeal of the dying kiss: the strength and sweetness of a whole tradition of 'warm homoeroticism' could be gathered into the 'warm, passionate' kiss but any direct homoerotic threat would be halted by the image of the dead body. It would always be a one-sided narrative; the life–death boundary would overpower transgressive eros and the kiss could be written into a language of greater love.

And yet for many homosexuals, it was the source of much anxiety. Sassoon, tormented by his homosexuality (although he may not have been active at the time) could not celebrate the 'warm, passionate' kiss of comrades in the context of war with the ease and fluency of Read or Nichols. Sassoon mentions the dying kiss only once, but it has a painful history. By August 1915, Sassoon was deeply in love with David Cuthbert Thomas, the young Sandhurst subaltern, ten years his junior, whom he calls 'Dick Tiltwood' in *Memoirs of a Fox Hunting Man*.[72] By 18 March 1916, David was dead, hit by a stray bullet in the throat. The entry in Sassoon's diary for the following day reads:

70 Fussell, *GWMM*, 270–86. See also Timothy D'Arch Smith, *Love in Ernest: Some Notes on the Lives and Writings of English Uranian Poets* (London: Routledge, 1970).

71 Alan Sinfield, *Alfred Tennyson* (Malden, Mass.: Blackwell, 1986), 127.

72 See Jean Moorcroft Wilson's detailed acount in *Sassoon*, 237–41. She observes, 'Without exaggeration, Sassoon found the loss almost unbearable' (239).

But they came afterwards and told me that my little Tommy had been hit by a stray bullet and died last night. When last I saw him, two nights ago, he had his notebook in his hand, reading my last poem. And I said good night to him, in the moonlit trenches. Had I but known! – the old, human-weak cry. Now he comes back to me in memories, like an angel, with the light in his yellow hair, and I think of him at Cambridge late August when we lived together four weeks in Pembroke College in rooms where the previous occupant's name, Paradise, was written above the door.[73]

In May 1916, Sassoon wrote 'The Last Meeting', a pastoral elegy mourning the death of David. In a letter to Edward Dent on 18 May 1918 – roughly the time which many critics think marks the end of Sassoon's most creative period – Sassoon wrote that he thought all his poems were 'tosh' except the 'Last Meeting' and 'The Working Party'.[74] In a poem where the male body is consistently woven into a fantasy of space, purity and disembodiedness, Sassoon concludes with a surprisingly intimate gesture: 'And lips that touched me once in Paradise'.[75] By framing the kiss, happy with warmly personal details, at the climactic point of the pastoral elegy, the poet places his love on a continuum of intense male love and loss. If the church, the state, and modern sexology had reduced homosexuality to a sin, a crime, or an aberration, he falls back on an 'honourable' genre that not only has the weight of classical antiquity but is incorporated within the tradition of 'Englishness' from Milton to Shelley to Arnold. But in a sad example of how gay history is erased through homosexual panic, either personal or institutional, these lines are found only in the original draft sent to Edward Dent, now housed in Cambridge University Library. The 1919 collection of *War Poems* (and all subsequent editions) changes the paradisal kiss into a dying one: 'And youth, that dying, touched my lips to song'.[76]

### CONTEMPORARY SEXOLOGY AND TÜGEL'S 'OVER THE TOP'

But do First World War writers ever directly address the anxieties over gender and sexual identity that seem to hover around the dying kiss? A unique example is Ludwig Tügel's short story, 'Over the Top', originally written in German and translated in the popular anthology, *Great War*

---

73 Sassoon, *Diaries, 1915–16*, 44–5.        74 Quoted in Wilson, *Sassoon*, 557.
75 Siegfried Sassoon, 'The Last Meeting', E. J. Dent Collection, Cambridge University Library, Add. MS 7973, S/75. Typescript of the poem sent to E. J. Dent.
76 Sassoon, 'The Last Meeting', *Collected Poems*, 40.

*Short Stories* (1930), introduced by Edmund Blunden. The story is set in a tiny dug-out on the eve of a fatal offensive. The first-person narrator reads a letter written by his close friend Paul to his girlfriend, while Paul lies asleep. When a barrage starts outside the dug-out, Paul wakes up in absolute terror:

'You've been reading it, haven't you? You've been reading it?'

'Yes,' I managed to gasp, and I saw him pull the trigger. The bullet flew past my ear; we struggled and rolled over together. Chest to chest, head to head, we were lying locked against each other.

I don't know what happened. We were trying to bite each other's throats like savage beasts, and our lips met harshly, then relaxed and remained together. We murmured brokenly, incomprehensibly, as we wept and kissed and clung. Outside in front of the dug-out they were shouting: 'Take cover! Take cover!'[77]

The scene begins as one of male hysteria. What should have been an hour of need and mutual support turns instead into one of homosocial rivalry and physical violence. A moment of silence marks the slide into eroticism in the otherwise detailed narrative – 'I don't know what happened' – as Tügel shows aggression flowering into desire without a break or mediating pause. The adjective 'harshly' is a curious one: while, through the logic of the narrative, it follows from the language of physical aggression ('savage beasts'), it also suggests something very masculine, with the hint of a stubble. Ironically, in the literary theatre of the First World War, Brooke's vision of 'the rough male kiss of blankets' reaches its apotheosis on the other side of no man's land.

The kiss is the pivot on which the story turns, the site of complex psychosexual mediation. In Tügel's narrative, the kiss is situated between two other kisses. The first is the romantic kiss of Paul's girlfriend, his 'dearest memory'. But for the first-person narrator, the kiss takes him back to the 'earliest memory' of his mother:

I remember you, my own earthly mother. . . . I am again a boy of three, and you have just given birth to my brother. . . . you were lying pale in your bed. I could not help crying as I looked at you, and I threw myself on the bed and kissed you, understanding nothing, but perhaps realising unconsciously that life gives love and only love can give life.[78]

---

77 Ludwig Tügel, 'Over the Top' (293–301) in *Great First World War Stories* (London: Chancellor, 1994), 296–7. Originally published as *Great Short Stories of the War* (London: Eyre and Spottiswood, 1930).
78 Tügel, 'Over the Top', 298–9.

In *Three Essays on the Theory of Sexuality* (1905), Freud notes the significance of the fact that the individual's first and most formative relationship to the world is an oral one. To Freud, 'sucking at his mother's breast has become the prototype of every relation of love' and that 'the satisfaction of the erotogenic zone is associated, in the first instance, with the satisfaction of the need for nourishment'.[79] But with the growth of the child, there is a split between the sensual enjoyment and the need for nourishment. There is a gradual journey from sucking to kissing as the adolescent resumes, with newfound intensity of appetite and inhibition, his 'oral education', now connected with an emerging capacity for genital sexuality.[80] In a sentence added in 1915, Freud suggests that the instinct of self-preservation lingers on, and that sexual activity 'does not become independent of them until later'.[81] The kiss in Tügel's narrative, exchanged before imminent death, is almost a regression to the childhood world of 'love' and 'life' contained in the infantile *Lutscherli*. If we, following Adam Phillips, take Freud's ideas to their extreme, interpreting the kiss to harbour a 'narcissistic intent' (the child unsatisfactorily substituting the 'corresponding part of another's body'),[82] then the dying kiss suggests an important link between narcissism and homoeroticism. 'It's a pity I can't kiss myself', Freud's child parenthetically exclaims.[83] If this disappointment is the grudge at the root of sexuality, making the kiss, as Phillips suggests, the mouth's elegy to itself, Tügel presents us with a grim literalisation as the two men go over the top, the kiss being their last – and lasting – memory. While it transports the narrator to his own childhood world of comfort and security, here he also plays the protective role. However, the framing vocabulary oscillates between heterosexual romance and homosocial camaraderie:

Paul pressed closely against me, and I sheltered him in my arms as once I might have sheltered a woman whom I loved. 'All right, old man. All right.' We said no more.[84]

Self-preservation, protection, romance, camaraderie, eroticism: different emotions and instincts slip through 'lips at the brim' in Tügel's narrative universe.

The revolutionary potential of Tügel's story can fully be appreciated when placed in the context of contemporary debates about homosexuality, especially in Germany. The earliest theories of sexual inversion came from

---

79 Freud, *SE*, vol. VII, 181–2.
80 See Adam Phillips, *On Kissing, Tickling and Being Bored* (London: Faber, 1993), 103–7, where he both explores and extends Freud's ideas.
81 Freud, *SE*, VII, 182.          82 Phillips, *On Kissing, Tickling and Being Bored*, 106–7.
83 Freud, *SE*, VII, 182.          84 Tügel, 'Over the Top', 297.

German sexologists – Karl Heinrich Ulrichs and Richard von Krafft-Ebing – who sought a medical explanation, thus starting the debate about congenital versus acquired sexuality. Having universally acknowledged homosexuality to be an abnormality and yet failing to establish any specific 'abnormal' link, these scrupulous and enlightened thinkers raided the diverse fields of gender, genetics and neurology, inadvertently infecting homosexuality with the terror of each. Ulrichs advanced the theory of *anima muliebris virile corpore inclusa*, a female soul in a male body while Krafft-Ebing, in the twelfth edition of *Psychopathia Sexualis* (1892), attributed same-sex desire to neurasthenia.[85] Ellis's *Sexual Inversion* (1897), though far more enlightened and sympathetic, nevertheless terms homosexuality as 'a congenital abnormality, to be classed with the other congenital abnormalities which have psychic concomitants'.[86] Freud broke new ground in 1903 by separating the sexual object and the sexual instinct, thus separating gender from sexuality and claiming the polymorphous perversity of human desire. By placing the kiss in the overtly masculine atmosphere evoked by wrestling and death on the battlefield, Tügel subtly discredits both Ulrichs's model of a female soul in a male body and the social construction of the effeminate dandy associated with Wilde; his story is more suggestive of Freud's argument that the sexual object and sexual aim are merely soldered together. Tügel's story thus differs from the Victorian tendency to read sexual preference through the trope of gender transgression.

While the whole debate concerning congenital or acquired homosexuality often revolved around the question of intentionality, Tügel does away with this debate by selecting a genre that focuses on contingent moments. In his narrative, the moment of arousal is based on accidental and arbitrary processes of touch. More importantly, Tügel places sexuality on a continuum of emotions such as vulnerability, helplessness, fear and the universal need to be loved and cared for: in the meeting of 'lips', the erotics of greed are overwhelmed by the reassurances of affection. Rather than celebrating Tügel's story as the gay love song of the trenches, it should be read in the context of imminent mutilation and mortality. As one of the most intimate modes of adult communication, sex becomes the

85 For a detailed discussion of sexological debates at the time, see Jeffrey Weeks, *Coming Out: Homosexual Politics in Britain from the Nineteenth Century to the Present* (London: Quartet Books, 1977); Frank Mort, *Dangerous Sexualities: Medico-moral Politics in England since 1830* (New York: Routledge, 1987); and Lesley A. Hall, *Hidden Anxieties: Male Sexuality, 1900–1950* (Malden, Mass.: Polity Press, 1991).

86 Havelock Ellis, *Sexual Inversion: Studies in the Psychology of Sex* (London: University Press, 1897), I, 137.

most readily available language. Words such as 'pressed', 'wept', 'hand in hand' or the twice repeated 'clung' and 'sheltered' show the overpowering need of bodily reassurance rather than erotic gratification. The kiss – or as Freud defined it, 'the particular contact . . . between the mucous membrane of the lips of the two people concerned', held in 'high sexual esteem' – becomes a language of support, succour and solace.[87]

What the dying kiss suggests is a sense of nakedness between men in the trenches: 'naked' in the sense of how physical extremity can lead to a bodily intimacy and immediacy that are perhaps inimical to linguistic representation. Language had been temporarily suspended – or rendered irrelevant – as the mouth, the organ of speech, reverted back to a more primal mode of communication: 'Come and kiss me, Padre', the boy had asked the Reverend Carl Parry Okeden as he lay dying.[88] To borrow a phrase from Roland Barthes, these are moments of 'frightful intimacy'.[89] If First World War writing is seen as a resurrection of the dead, these soldier-writers seem to be evoking moments they had known with the searing immediacy of their bodies. In the letter to his girlfriend in Tügel's story, Paul mentions a curious episode: 'Yesterday Frohlich the bombardier had an attack of madness, and my friend had to tie him down in the dugout. He called me up to show me . . . and then he said quite calmly: "I'm just telling you in case you've to do it to me".'[90] It is a great irony that the world's first industrial war, which brutalised the male body on such an enormous scale, also nurtured the most intense of male bonds. The myth of heroic masculinity fostered through the works of Rider Haggard and Rudyard Kipling and encouraged through the public school sporting system exploded in the mud and blood of the Western Front. A very different order of male experience, one that accommodated fear, vulnerability, support and physical tenderness, sprang up in its place. What challenged heterosexuality in post-war England was not sexual dissidence but memories of such relationships. These were neither of romantic love nor blokish bonding nor homoerotic frisson: with each of these elements, there is a distinct overlap and, yet always, a distinct difference. Eroticism might occasionally have played a part, but it was not the founding impulse. Sexuality had not yet hijacked an intimate history of human emotions. 'Frightful intimacy' is as far as language can go: the dying kiss was perhaps its true sign, the mouth filling the gap left by language.

87  Freud, *SE*, VII, 150.          88  Okeden, IWM, 90/7/1.
89  Roland Barthes, *A Lover's Discourse*, 189.          90  Tügel, 'Over the Top', 294.

CHAPTER 4

# Wilfred Owen and the sense of touch

A month before his death on 4 November, 1918, Wilfred Owen, in a letter marked 'strictly private', wrote to his mother about his 'excellent little servant Jones': 'Of whose blood lies yet crimson on my shoulder where his head was – and where so lately yours was'. The moment is however recalled differently to Sassoon: 'the boy by my side, shot through the head, lay on top of me, soaking my shoulder, for half an hour'.[1] Owen evokes the juddering of the self through 'half an hour' of tactile contact; it is also a peculiarly intimate scene. The invocation of the maternal in the first letter is particularly resonant in the context of the 'mother's kiss' in the letters of Connor and Fenton.[2] The whole range of emotional and physical intensities between men in the trenches that we have been exploring in the previous chapter finds in the poetry of Wilfred Owen one of its most powerful and complex testimonies.

The sense of touch, this chapter argues, was particularly acute in the case of England's most famous war poet and is fundamental to understanding his art. Owen's relationship with his mother, the main love in his life, was summed up in terms of a 'tangible caress': 'Oh how I stand (yes and sit, lie, kneel and walk, too,) in need of some tangible caress from you [mother] . . . my affections are physical as well as abstract – intensely so'. Owen's first letter, written when he was only five – inscribed in pencil by Susan Owen, 'Wilfie's first letter 1898' and discovered in her jewel-box – has a border of kisses.[3] On his nineteenth birthday, he composed verses about kissing his mother's portrait and her

---

1 *Wilfred Owen: Collected Letters*, ed. Harold Owen and John Bell (London: Oxford University Press, 1967), 580, 581; hereafter abbreviated *CL*.

2 Connor, 'Diary', IWM, 87/10/1; Fenton, 'Papers', IWM, 87/13/1. I discuss these letters in Chapter 3, pp. 122–123.

3 *CL*, 137, 21; also see Jon Stallworthy, *Wilfred Owen* (London: Oxford University Press, 1973), 14; hereafter abbreviated Stallworthy, *WO*.

letter 'as if it were thy hand'.[4] Much of the sexual confusion that marked
his adolescent years as the vicar's assistant at Dunsden (1911–12) seemed
to centre on a moment of some intimate hand contact. He left Dunsden
for France as the tutor for two young boys, only to be 'slobbered' by the
French Decadent poet, Laurent Tailhade.[5] He drops occasional hints to
his mother: 'If you knew what hands have been laid on my arm, in the
night, along the Bordeaux streets'.[6] The hand was to become a recurring
trope in his poetry, connecting the war poems with his pre-war adolescent verse. Combat experience and the famous meeting with Sassoon at
Craiglockhart undoubtedly provided a powerful impetus to his literary
creativity, but it is important to read the war poems in the light of his
pre-war juvenilia.[7] Indeed, many of the war poems can be seen as a
continuation, adaptation and fruition of earlier themes and concerns: it
is only through close attention to his pre-war writings and experiences as
well as the war years that we can have access to the full complexity of his
art. As early as 'Lines written on My Nineteenth Birthday' (March 1912),
one notes the integral relation between poetic subjectivity and tactile
aesthetics that, as I shall show, marks his mature verse, with its curious
mingling of pain and pleasure.

To Owen, both reading and writing were intensely physical processes.
While studying some of Keats's letters and poems in the British Museum
on 17 September 1917, Owen was struck by his sketch of an ivy leaf on the
manuscript of 'St. Mark's Eve' and noted, '[Keats's] writing is rather large
and slopes like mine – <u>not at all</u> old fashioned and sloping as Shelley's is.
He also has my trick of not joining letters in a word.'[8] The manuscript,
unlike the printed book, bears the weight of the living hand as it rests,
sketches or scratches, even before imagination or memory is fully active:
the ivy leaf, the false start record the moment of hesitation and doubt.
Educated at the local Birkenhead Institute, Owen feels an instinctive
affinity with Keats's untrained letters – unlike Shelley's public school

---

4 *Wilfred Owen: Complete Poems and Fragments*, ed. Jon Stallworthy, 2 vols. (London: Chatto,
   Hogarth and Oxford University Press, 1983), 12; hereafter abbreviated *CP&F*. This is a
   monumental edition, providing detailed draft versions of the poems and fragments. All my
   references to Owen's poetry are to this edition unless otherwise specified. In addition, I have
   consulted and at times referred to the original manuscripts, now housed in the British Library,
   London, and the English Faculty Library, Oxford.
5 *CL*, 282.
6 *CL*, 234.
7 See James Fenton, 'Wilfred Owen's Juvenilia', in *The Strength of Poetry* (Oxford: Oxford
   University Press, 2001), 23–43, where he asks us 'not to see the experience of combat as utterly
   decisive in the poetry' (26–7).
8 *CL*, 82. See also Beer, 'Four Bodies on the Beagle', for a reading of Keats's 'hand'.

perfected hand – as if the slope of the writing held the essence of his mentor's being and mirrored his own. Now housed in the British Library, Owen's manuscripts – poems written often on Craiglockhart notepaper in thick-nibbed blue ink, sometimes with Sassoon's suggestions pencilled on the margins – tease us with their combination of meaning and materiality. Harold Owen remembers his brother's hand as 'blue-veined, white and delicate'.[9] After reading W. M. Rossetti's *Life and Writings of John Keats*, Owen felt that 'Rossetti guided my groping hand right into the wound, and I touched, for one moment the incandescent Heart of Keats'. Beyond the hints of a strong Evangelical upbringing and the influence of the *fin-de-siècle* writers such as Wilde and Swinburne, one can discern a peculiarly tactile sensibility. Romantic agony becomes for the adolescent poet a bodily organ where red blood might flow again: the heart of the beloved, like his hand, is warm and capable of grasping. After a visit to Keats's house at Teignmouth, he told his mother, 'To be in love with a youth and a dead un' is perhaps sillier than with a real, live maid'.[10] While the act of reading is figured as an act of touching, in 'A Poet In Pain', he under-scores the physicality of writing, of its onslaught on the senses: 'to proof-test upon my flesh / The thoughts I think, and in words bleeding-fresh'.[11]

The *Collected Letters* (1967) as well as Jon Stallworthy's groundbreaking biography *Wilfred Owen* (1973) provide a richly evocative account of the artist as a young man. In his new biography, Dominic Hibberd, who has done a series of important studies of Owen, remarks that it is 'undoubt-edly true' that the poet was 'gay' and speculates that he might have been 'up secret stairs' in London and Edinburgh.[12] While Owen's poems and letters suggest a strong homoerotic inclination, there is no historical evidence as yet to show that he ever actually had any sexual encounters

---

9 Harold Owen, *Journey From Obscurity*, 3 vols. (London: Oxford University Press, 1963–5), I, 85.
10 *CL*, 161, 187.
11 'The Poet in Pain', *CP&F*, III.
12 Dominic Hibberd, *Wilfred Owen: A New Biography* (London: Weidenfeld & Nicolson, 2002), xix, 301–2; hereafter abbreviated Hibberd, *WONB*. In this biography, Hibberd gives an exhaustive account, particularly of Owen's war years including maps of battles, and draws our attention to how passages from Owen's letters were excised by his brother Harold (xviii). Hibberd's speculation about Owen's encounters with rent boys in London and Edinburgh is based on a group of poems involving secrecy and ghosts, including 'Who is the God of Canongate?'. He however immediately qualifies his statement, adding that 'or perhaps he had just heard stories at Half Moon Street and from Bainbrigge' (302). It is possible that Scott Moncrieff managed to seduce Owen under the influence of alcohol but again this is largely a matter of conjecture. Hibberd's other works include *Wilfred Owen: War Poems and Others* (London: Chatto, 1973) and *Owen The Poet* (Basingstoke: Macmillan, 1986) (hereafter abbreviated *OTP*), and *Wilfred Owen: The Last Year, 1917–1918* (London: Constable, 1992). See also Dennis Welland, *Wilfred Owen: A Critical Study* (London: Chatto, 1960); Fussell, *GWMM*, 286–99; Silkin, *Out of Battle*, 197–248; Sven Backman, *Tradition*

(unlike in the case of Rupert Brooke or Siegfried Sassoon). We thus do not know, one way or the other, but given his strict Evangelical upbringing and his indoctrination in the cult of 'cleanliness', it is doubtful whether Owen would have 'lain' with the anonymous 'ghosts' in Canongate or Covent Garden. If the erotic at times overwhelms the political in his poetry, if the pleasure principle gets strangely, boldly, out of hand, eros in Owen is perhaps not best found in the darkness of the Shadwell stairs or even amidst the decadent splendour of 50 Half-Moon Street, London (the residence of Robert Ross). In the pre-war years, his homoeroticism was sublimated into ardent, pedagogical relationships with young male pupils while in the trenches it at once fed into and conflicted with the credo of 'greater love'. Sexual repression rather than consummation seems to give his poetry its erotic pulse. Even when there might have been an erotic possibility – a loving glance stolen at the young, handsome lad who figures in the tantalising 'Lines to a Beauty seen in Limehouse' – it is ultimately language that becomes the skin through which the male body is touched, against which the poet's passion 'rubs and sidles'.[13]

One of the obstacles to an understanding of Owen's poetry is his own Preface, written at Ripon probably in 1918: 'Above all I am not concerned with Poetry. My subject is War, and the pity of War. The Poetry is in the pity.'[14] It is often forgotten that Owen's manifesto is the first explicit statement of poetry as testimony in the twentieth century: poetry is refashioned as missives from the trenches. Yet, for a poet so avowedly political, music and eros can pose problems. In lines such as 'Your slender attitude / Trembles not exquisite like limbs knife-skewed' from his early decadent war poem 'Greater Love', the labials, assonance and the swinging metre speed us on with an exultant thoughtlessness, blinding us to the combination of eros and violence with its touch of misogyny. What can be the connection between mutilated male flesh and the aroused female body, except in a context of erotic fantasy on one hand and erotic resentment on the other? The perverse aestheticisation of violence, present even in later poems such as 'The Kind Ghosts' or 'Disabled', is not much talked about because it compromises his status as the quintessential

*Transformed: Studies in the Poetry of Wilfred Owen* (Lund: Gleerup, 1979). Recent works include Desmond Graham, *The Truth of War: Owen, Blunden and Rosenberg*, Douglas Kerr, *Wilfred Owen's Voices: Language and Community* (Oxford: Oxford University Press, 1993); Adrian Caesar, *Taking It Like a Man: Suffering, Sexuality and the War Poets: Brooke, Sassoon, Owen and Graves* (Manchester: Manchester University Press, 1993); and Jahan Ramazani, *Poetry of Mourning: The Modern Elegy from Hardy to Heaney* (Chicago: Chicago University Press, 1994).
13  *CP&F*, 482.        14  *CP&F*, 535.

pacifist poet;[15] secondly, it implicates the reader as well for the seductive quality of his verse works precisely on this heady combination. Consider the opening lines from a poem as late and explicitly political as 'Disabled' which was meant to be the title poem of his intended collection, *Disabled & Other Poems*:

> He sat in a wheeled chair, waiting for dark,
> And shivered in his ghastly suit of grey,
> Legless, sewn short at elbow.[16]

In spite of a leaner use of language than 'Greater Love', the hiss of sibilance draws us into the moment through an intrusion of what Kristeva calls the 'semiotic': it makes us wince and tighten. In spite of the comma after 'legless', the alliteration ('legless sewn') drives us forward, and we stop only after 'short'. But as we complete reading the whole line, freshly urged by the 'w' and 'o' sounds ('sewn. . .short. . .elbow'), we realise that it is not only at the knees, as the sibilance and caesura have deluded us to believe, but at the elbows that the soldier has been cut short. The man has, in effect, lost all four limbs. Physical mutilation is the stuff this poetry is made of. Irony and realism chafe uneasily against aesthetic surprise as 'sewn' is pulled in different directions, visually and aurally. This is not to be confused with the perverse homoerotic aesthetic of 'Greater Love', nor is the poetry solely in pity (which however informs Owen's poetry in abundant measure).

Owen, through a strange manipulation of sound-effects, draws us into moments we would otherwise flinch from: moments when limbs are sliced off ('limbs knife-skewed', 'shaved us with his scythe'), the flesh is ripped apart ('shatter of flying muscles', 'Ripped from my own back / In scarlet shreds', 'limped on, blood-shod') or the mouth starts bleeding ('I saw his round mouth's crimson deepen as it fell').[17] A visceral thrill as well as an acute physical empathy constitute the body in pain in Owen's poetry, hovering around moments when we no longer know where the *is* ends and the *was* begins. In 'Asleep', the 'aborted life' is still 'quaking' while in 'Futility', the limbs are 'still warm'. It is often overlooked that, unlike in Barbusse's *Under Fire* or Sassoon's *Counter-Attack And Other*

---

15 Caesar, in *Taking it like a Man*, has however explored the 'sado-masochistic' elements in the war verse of Brooke, Sassoon, Owen and Graves. 'What is troubling in Owen's work', he notes, 'is that the celebration of love between men takes place in a context of massive violence' (154). See also Hibberd, *OTP*, 112–15.

16 'Disabled', *CP&F*, 175.

17 *CP&F*, 166, 165, 169, 178, 140, 123.

*Poems* (the two war books that Owen most admired), the corpse is almost absent in Owen's poetry, reduced to metonymies ('hopes lay strewn') and synecdoches ('piteous mouths that coughed').[18] The boy who described the sound of violin as, quoting Keats, 'yearning like a God in pain' would later become the soldier-poet to write of drums pulsing 'fearfully-voluptuously, as great hearts in death'.[19]

### 'TOUCH ME NOT': ILLNESS, PAIN AND EROS

Born with 'nerves exquisitely sensitive to painful sensation', often exposed to things that 'offend and lacerate' them, Owen in his pre-war letters obsessively refers to disease and bodily pain.[20] Letter after letter informs Susan Owen about the latest physical discomfort with painful articulateness: the parting stab of a headache, swollen gum, sore neck, gnawing toothache, granulated pharynx, vertigo, and nerves 'weak as water'.[21] Hypochondria was a secret bond between the mother and her eldest son, to the point of telepathic empathy ('unconfinable sympathy'). It was a remarkable bodily knowledge and intimacy developed in childhood and adolescence through repeated visits to the doctor, and continued to the very last lines of his last letter to his mother: 'I think of you always in bed'. Consider the following letter, suggesting not only a pre-verbal bond between the mother and the son, but also a deep link between bodily discomfort and writing:

Even while licking-up the envelope of the last Missive, on Wednesday, I noticed that my saliva-glands were a trifle addled, so to speak, and sure enough on Thursday morning I was down with a sore throat (sore neck, rather than throat) and a head sore all over: – Influenza – a dry, grim, sardonic form, born of the devilish winds that prevailed in the early part of the week, glacial, stabbing, filing the eyeballs, as a dentist files the teeth.[22]

Melodrama, with a distinct Romantic accent, becomes a way of responding to and communicating pain and illness. The image of 'filing the eyeballs' – Owen would have remembered the dentist filing his teeth[23] – reveals a sensibility that later would re-figure Keats's image of

---

18  *CP&F*, 124, 166. A notable exception is 'The Show' which was written under the immediate influence of Barbusse's *Under Fire*.
19  *CL*, 102, 388.
20  *CL*, 167. See Stallworthy, *WO*, 48, 95; Hibberd, *OTP*, 17; *WONB*, 75, 113.
21  *CL*, 81, 83, 85, 124, 127,169,171, 181, 183, 212, 225, 379, 172.
22  *CL*, 204, 591, 327.        23  *CL*, 81, 182.

'palsy' shaking a 'few, sad, last grey hairs' as 'the twitching agonies of men among its brambles'.[24] Elaine Scarry in *The Body In Pain* (1985) – a work I shall engage with more fully in my next chapter – speaks of bodily pain as the only condition that cannot be shared and argues that pain resists 'objectification in language'.[25] As a young boy, with his mother, Owen had learnt curiously to overcome this deadlock. Pain not only led to linguistic innovations ('the gum, and my nose, which is, like Bardolph's, 'all barbukles and whelks, and knobs and flames of fire' or 'It was the Enter: I̲-tis I̲ that killed it')[26] but spilled onto the page through sketches of coiled spiral to represent a headache, or a spinning room to portray a 'dervishy vertigo'.[27] The body in pain in Owen's mature verse was essentially the body he had lived in first as a child.

In 'Narcissism: An Introduction' (1914), Freud starts the essay by discussing illness and hypochondria, exploring them as states of bodily experience that reveal strong links with narcissism. Hypochondria, to Freud, 'like organic disease, manifests itself in distressing and painful bodily sensations, and it has the same effect as organic disease on the distribution of libido': libido is withdrawn from external objects and lavished on the (supposed) site of pain.[28] Freud continues: 'Now the familiar prototype of an organ that is painfully tender . . . is the genital organ in its states of excitation'.[29] Nine years later, in *The Ego and the Id* (1923), he states more directly that bodily pain is a way of bodily discovery and suggests that to figure sexuality as illness is indicative of a moralistic framework of guilt, a 'moral' factor: 'as far as the patient is concerned this sense of guilt is dumb; it does not tell him he is guilty; he does not feel guilty, he feels ill'.[30] Owen's strong homoerotic impulses, matched by his equally strong Evangelical training, might partly explain what Harold Owen called his brother's 'morbid absorption' in his own health in his youth.[31] In 1911–12, Owen took up the post of an assistant-cum-pupil at the Evangelical vicarage in Dunsden under the offices of the Reverend Herbert Wigan. But the repressive regime of the vicarage soon began to

24 *CP&F*, 185.
25 Elaine Scarry, *The Body In Pain: The Making and Unmaking of the World* (Oxford: Oxford University Press, 1985), 5.
26 *CL*, 83, 212.
27 *CL*, 137, 169.
28 Freud, 'Narcissism: An Introduction', *SE*, xiv, 83 (73–102).
29 'Narcissism', 84. Also see Butler, *Bodies that Matter*, 58.
30 Freud, 'The Ego and the Id', *SE*, xix, 49–50.
31 Harold Owen, *Journey From Obscurity*, I, 161.

stifle the adolescent. Owen at once felt excited and tormented by male beauty and companionship, evident in his charged relationship with the twelve-year-old Vivian Rampton. The letters written from Dunsden are often a list of physical malaises: his nerves are in a 'shocking state', his chest is 'continually "too full"', his head reels with 'dervishy vertigo'.[32] Freud would argue that eros, stricken with guilt, afflicted the adolescent Owen as illness. At the same time, there were other causes: religious disagreement with the 'strong Conservatism' of the vicar, academic frustration and exposure to poverty in Dunsden. Insomnia, indigestion, giddy fits, palpitations: these were not just symptoms but the first *protests* written by the young Owen on his own body against the narrow-minded Evangelicalism practised at Dunsden. His fevered body at the vicarage thus becomes the bearer of a terrible knowledge: of the wrongs within Evangelical Christianity as well as of a love that dare not express itself.

In 'The Economic Problem of Masochism' (1924), Freud pushes his conclusions further, linking illness and hypochondria resulting from unconscious guilt to what he calls 'moral masochism'. What is involved is 'a need which is satisfied by punishment and suffering'.[33] Suffering and punishment were both on Owen's mind on the morning of his nineteenth birthday. In 'Lines written on my Nineteenth Birthday', the 'unrelenting gnawing [of indigestion] within' makes him fantasise that his 'frail body' is being strangled and twisted by the 'tightening hand of Pain':

> 'No joy is comparable
> Unto the *Melting* – soft and gradual –
> *Of Torture's needles in the flesh.* . . .'[34]

Narcissism, repressed homoeroticism and a morbid religious imagination convert a bout of indigestion into a religious aesthetic of suffering and martyrdom: in the process, as Freud would note, 'morality becomes sexualised'.[35] The poems written around this time show a repeated staging of masochistic desire: in 'Supposed Confessions of a Secondrate Sensitive Mind in Dejection', despair drags the poet, corpse-like, into a 'sucking, slimy fen'; in 'The Dread of Falling into Naught', he is tortured by cold winds from the 'icy cavern of the dead'; in 'The time was aeon', the religious connotations become more evident in the cry,

---

32 *CL*, 171, 169.          33 Freud, 'The Economic Problem of Masochism', *SE*, XIX, 165, 169.
34 *CP&F*, 12.              35 Freud, 'The Economic Problem of Masochism', 169.

'Crucify him!'[36] Suppressed eroticism is thus converted into a language of 'secret sin', wounds and scars. On returning from Dunsden, Owen increasingly began to see himself as 'a Chattertonian figure, consumptive and impecunious in an attic'.[37] What interests me – an aspect that, though hitherto overlooked in studies of Owen, is crucial to an understanding of Owen's poetry – is the intimate link between bodily illness and the writing of verse. Are there parts of the body where pain and pleasure are particularly concentrated and does their recurrence point to a more personal history that goes beyond the immediate war context?

The throat – site of Romantic excess and of the skylark and the nightingale – was the site of recurrent pain for Owen. Childhood letters had referred to sore throat, diptheric throat and granulated pharynx. One of his earliest pieces was inspired by Harold's tonsillitis: 'He [the village doctor] lets them take hot iodine / And burn out half his throat'.[38] In the post-Dunsden convalescent phase, he wrote to his mother: 'I mentioned that phlegm still collected in the throat. This was due to adenoid tissue, which he there and then proceeded to extirpate by touching with "silver". I touch them daily with an iodine paint.'[39] It is important to remember that this was an age before antibiotics and prolonged and painful infections were therefore a more common experience. Throat problems followed him to Bordeaux where he woke up with a 'painful throat' and, in a classic instance of transference, reported 'the most sepulchral-throated bells I ever heard'.[40] While training as a cadet in the spring of 1916, Owen had to go to London twice to have some harmless lumps cauterised from the throat.[41] As late as 27 February 1917 – by which time he had joined the 2nd Manchesters on the Somme – he wrote to 'Mine own mother': 'I have been to the dentist here (Army) and also the Doctor. I have not much of a cough, but produce an <u>extra-ordinary amount</u> of phlegm, brown, black, and grey'.[42] A few months later, when he composed 'Cramped in that funnelled hole', was Owen coughing up the phlegm from what may be called the corporeal unconscious? Consider the following versions of a single line:

> And they ~~were~~ <sup>stuck</sup> in his ~~fetid~~ throat of fetid flem.
>
> . . .
>
> And they were sticking in his throat of phlegm.
>
> . . .
>
> Stuck in the bottom of his throat of phlegm[43]

36 *CP&F*, 13, 34, 73.   37 Stallworthy, *WO*, 95.   38 *CL*, 67.
39 *CL*, 182.   40 *CL*, 201, 205.   41 See Hibberd, *WONB*, 178.
42 *CL*, 438.   43 'Poems of Wilfred Owen', British Library Add. MS 43721. 30.

This 'dawn piece' is usually read (like 'The Show' composed in the same week) as an immediate response to Barbusse's *Under Fire*, Tennyson's 'six hundred' can be heard in the background.[44] In his reworking of Barbusse's images of claustrophobia, Owen changes the 'ragged jaws' into a personally sensitive body part: 'throat of phlegm'. In Owen's obsessively corporeal imagination, a universal threat ('soft mud') gets transformed into an all too familiar and remembered bodily fluid. In the poem, the muddy claustrophobic dug-out may be said to hideously replicate Owen's experience of his own earlier phlegmatic and tubercular body. His description of no man's land as disease-ridden shows continuity with his old preoccupations. In 'The Show', the trench landscape is described as 'pitted with great pocks and scabs of plagues' while in 'The Next War', it is heavy with 'the green thick odour' of death.[45]

Owen had lovely hands; Harold Owen remembers them as 'expressive and peculiarly indicative'.[46] Hands become a fraught image in Owen's poetry but to understand their broader significance at the time, it might be useful to place them briefly in a cultural context. In a poem to H. D. from the trenches in December 1916, Richard Aldington mourns: 'I am grieved for our hands, our hands that have caressed roses and women's flesh, old lovely books and marbles . . . I am grieved for our hands'.[47] There are echoes in Aldington's verse of Charles Bell's Bridgewater essay on *The Hand* which insists on the hand as more immediate than the eye,[48] but Aldington's paean has to be read also in the context of Victorian aestheticism and decadence. In 1905, Gordon Bottomley published 'A Hymn of Touch' where touch is the 'rule of all senses'.[49] The aesthetic credo was carried into the immediate pre-war years by Rupert Brooke through the nostalgic reminiscences of Georgian England where men 'Touched flowers and furs and cheeks'.[50] Around the same time, Owen was also writing a number of poems on the hand, but Brooke's class-specific contact would here be replaced by intimate and even painful

44 *CP&F*, 513.
45 *CP&F*, 155, 165. Stallworthy notes 'a marked sense of physical loathing' and 'this comes strangely, tragically, from a poet whose early poems are full of lyrical descriptions of beautiful bodies' (*Anthem for Doomed Youth: Twelve Soldier Poets of the First World War*, London: Constable, 2002, 103).
46 *Journey From Obscurity*, I, 85.
47 Aldington, *Images of War: A Book of Poems* (Westminster: C. W. Beaumont, 1919), 15.
48 Sir Charles Bell, *The Hand, its Mechanisms and Vital Endowments as Evincing Design* (Bridgewater Treatises, 4) (London, 1833).
49 Gordon Bottomley, *Poems and Plays* (London: The Bodley Head, 1953), 46–8.
50 Brooke, 'The Dead', *Collected Poems*, 147.

associations. In both England and France, Owen formed intense friend-ships with some young boys such as Vivian Rampton at Dunsden and Johnny de la Touche at Merignac. Affection, ease, a pastoral role and a diffuse eroticism seem to underlie these intense friendships though it is impossible to know whether or how far Owen was aware of the erotic component. A number of poems written around this time – 1913 to 1914, when Owen was teaching English in France – revolve round the image of the hand. The conflict between the world of 'warm Love' and that of the 'thin, and cold, and very dead' Christ is recorded in the closing couplet of 'Maundy Thursday': 'And yet I bowed, yea, kissed – my lips did cling. / (I kissed the warm live hand that held the thing.)'[51] In 'Impromptu': 'Now let me feel the feeling of thy hand – For it is softer than the breasts of girls'.[52] However, in 'To The Bitter-Sweet: A Dream', a poem dwelling centrally on hand-contact, the homoeroticism is anxious and nostalgic. The poem harks back to his 1914 poem, 'We two had known each other' where all the pain of the Dunsden years is gathered into a single moment of touch: 'Be better if I had not ~~touched my hand~~'.[53]

It is not known exactly what happened at Dunsden: a chunk of the crucial letter, describing 'the terrible bust-up', has been scissored out by Harold Owen.[54] A key to the Dunsden debacle may be found in a heavily cancelled and revised series of five fragments that have been grouped under the title 'Perseus'. In its hectic tone and images of sexual violence, 'Perseus' speaks of some intense personal crisis. Unsurprisingly, it is the image of the hand that is the connecting link between the five fragments. In the most tortured of these fragments beginning with the heavily inked out confession, '~~What have I done, O God, what have I done?~~', the crisis is played out through a repentant drama of self-mutilation:

> To my great friends I said 'Unhand ~~me~~
> For I has touched the godess, ~~and~~ touch me not."
> And to ~~my~~ all youth: Flee^far from me, I hate thee.[55]

Hibberd, regarding 'Perseus' as the central expression of Owen's poet-hood, asks suggestively in the biography: 'Was he [Owen] remembering

---

51 *CP&F*, 109.    52 *CP&F*, 76.    53 *CP&F*, 437.

54 *CL*, 174–5. The letter, as it exists now, reads, 'The furor [words missing] now abated in the Vicarage, thank Mnemosyne; but I hope that I, who discovered him something over a year ago, may [half page missing]'. According to Stallworthy, the Dunsden crisis might have to do with his friendship with Vivian Rampton (*WO*, 83–5); Hibberd suggests that there might have been some physical intimacy, referring to the image of the hand-contact (*OTP*, 21–3) but in the biography, he firmly asserts that 'there was certainly no sort of scandal' (*WONB*, 95–7).

55 'Poems of Wilfred Owen', British Library, Add. MS 43721.155.

touching a boy's hand [Vivian Rampton at Dunsden] during another spring idyll two years earlier? Had it really been Henriette who had excited him at Castelnau? Or had it been Raoul?'[56] What was in his mind would never be known. But what 'Perseus' does demonstrate is Owen at war with himself and it is a war staged against hands. Gender confusion – or rather rewriting – is central to the poem: it seems from the manuscript that he had written 'god' initially and then hastily changed it, evident not only in the misspelling ('godess') but more significantly in the position of the comma. Owen places the comma at some distance after the word (as after 'incandescence' or 'paused' earlier in the manuscript poem) as he would have done originally after 'god', and then having added 'ess', overwrites the comma. Having rejected the cold and very dead Christ, does Owen here reimagine the fair youth as a god through the prohibitive echoes of 'noli me tangere'? This crisis is carried forward into some of his later poetry through the image of the hand, invested with a new significance by the war.

The image of the hand appears in the central section of 'Apologia Pro Poema Meo' as he originally called it, before Sassoon corrected the faulty grammar and changed the title to 'Apologia Pro Poemate Meo'. The image of the hand is invoked through a potentially erotic framework, linked to 'lips' and 'eyes' in contrast with heterosexual romance. Owen's 'love is not the binding of fair lips' is not just a direct refutation of his poet-cousin, Leslie Gunston's 'Love is the binding of souls together, / The binding of lips' but engages more productively with Robert Graves's 'Two Fusiliers': 'By wire and wood and stake we're bound':

> For love is not the binding of fair lips
> With the soft silk of eyes that look and long,
>
> By Joy, whose ribbon slips, –
> But wound with war's hard wire whose stakes are strong;
> Bound with the bandage of the arm that drips;
> Knit in the webbing of the rifle-thong.[57]

The image of the 'arm that drips' is a convincing piece of trench realism and yet, for one familiar with his early verse, it is charged with special

---

56 Hibberd, *WONB*, 122.

57 'Apologia Pro Poemate Meo', *CP&F*, 124. The poem has elicited different responses. It evokes for Featherstone 'the terrible and absurd world of war' (*War Poetry*, 104) while Caesar has called it a 'sado-masochistic hymn' (*Taking it Like a Man*, 150). The two responses are however not mutually exclusive.

meaning. As he sets out to sing the hymn of sacrificial love, the sensuous hands of Vivian Rampton and de la Touche boys, the 'groping hand' and 'beautiful fingers' of 'To Eros' and 'Impromptu' get mutilated. Homoerotic anxieties are thus deflected and displaced; true to the older masochistic imagination, painful sacrifice is celebrated. The innocuous 'ribbon', a seemingly casual remnant from the heterosexual paradigm, resurfaces with a macabre twist in the image of reddened, bruised flesh, implicit in the phrase 'Knit in the webbing of the rifle-thong'. Greater love is redefined not through the dying kiss but a bond of mutilated hands.

War and sexuality are similarly knotted in 'Exposure', see-sawing between irony and sensuousness as Owen refigures the Keatsian bower within the war landscape. A partly cancelled line from a related poem – 'Fastening of feeling fingers on my wrist' – connects the unknown hands that had been laid on Owen's arms 'in the night, along the Bordeaux streets' with the sensuous threat of the snow in this poem: 'Pale flakes with fingering stealth come feeling for our faces'.[58] In this poem, the assonance and half-rhymes ('snow-dazed' / 'sun-dozed') transform the brutality of trench life into a play of language and desire. The draft manuscript dwells tantalisingly on the moment of phantasmatic hand-shake or hand-grip as the fingers of the snow are now 'feeling' the hands of young soldiers:

> twist
> Before tonight their seize [?] their hands
> The frost shall stretch with into a strange,
>      is twisting        vain grasp.[59]
>
> See how t^Their are           in
> Their    hands already twisting now into a strange
>                     vain grasp.[60]
>
>    Something           stray vain
> The Stiffness    will stretch their hands into an empty grasp.[61]

In a piece of textual 'unhanding', the 'vain grasp' is deleted from the final version which simply states: 'Shrivelling many hands'. This poem, like 'Greater Love' or 'Apologia' raises disturbing questions about the relation

58 *CP&F*, 460; *CL*, 234; *CP&F*, 185. For the complex sources of the poem, see Hibberd, *OTP*, 78.
59 'Poems of Wilfred Owen' British Library, Add. MS 43721.27.
60 'Poems of Wilfred Owen', Add. MS 43721.28.
61 'Poems of Wilfred Owen', Add. MS 43721.29.

between Owen's political and poetic enterprise: between the responsibility of a war poet and a private masochistic imagination.

This conflict is powerfully evident in 'Disabled'. One of Owen's most politically ambitious poems, it reveals the hypocrisy of the War Office which often recruited under-age soldiers through the officials who 'smilingly' wrote 'his lie; aged nineteen years'; the final line is a parody of the 1914 recruiting poster, 'Will they never come?', equating fighting with football matches. In Owen's verse, though sounds of marching, charging or limping can occasionally be heard through the metre and rhyme (as in 'Dulce Et Decorum Est' or 'The Send-Off'), the image of feet is rather scarce, when compared to hands. In a letter from the trenches, he writes, 'My feet ached until they could ache no more, and so they temporarily died'.[62] In 'Dulce Et Decorum Est', the soldiers 'limped on, blood-shod'; in 'Mental Cases', they 'walk hell'.[63] In 'Disabled', the soldier is 'legless' but it is on the image of a leg-wound that the poem focuses, bringing together football and the war: 'And leap of purple spurted from his thigh / One time he liked a blood-smear down his leg'.[64] In spite of its Sassoon-like irony and satire, the language of decadent Romanticism ends up fetishising the wound: it undermines the political force of the juxtaposition and is particularly perverse in a context when the legs have been 'sewn short'. Moreover, the poem has private origins. A few months earlier, while recovering from shell-shock at Craiglockhart, Owen had written 'Lines to a Beauty Seen in Limehouse'. The 'Beauty' is a perverse fantasy about a handsome boy Owen might have seen in the East End, London, in 1915. The boy, possibly waiting for a girl, had been impervious to the poet's loving glances: in the poem, the boy becomes a 'god', the object of a masochistic religious ritual as the poet's gaze rests hungrily on the boy's knees:

> I saw the smooth, smooth nàked knees.
> . . .
>    For (So round
> Against thy knees so thy knees my passion rubs and sidles.
> . . .
> Thy knees are polished – with the rubbing of my thoughts[65]

---

62 *CL*, 430.        63 *CP&F*, 140, 169.        64 *CP&F*, 175.
65 'Disabled', *CP&F*, 481–2.

This homoerotic fantasy subsequently formed part of 'Disabled'. However, in the process of transformation, the knees of the handsome lad – the site of inaccessible pleasure – are thrown away bitterly through a piece of war realism: 'And girls glanced . . . before he threw away his knees'. Instead of a seamless blend of the private and the public, there is usually a conflict between the two, creating a powerful frisson in his mature verse. The erotic undertow complicates the political but also gives it a lyric intensity. The young male body that cannot be touched, legally or morally, is often mutilated in his verse.

### THE BODY OF SOUND

A useful entry-point for exploring the connections between a masochistic imagination and war testimony is a letter Owen wrote to his brother, Harold, after a visit to a war hospital in France. The letter is striking:[66]

First I saw a bullet, like this ▬▬▷ cut out of a Zouave's* leg. Then we did the round of the wards; and saw some fifty German wretches: all more seriously wounded than the French. The Doctor picked out those needing surgical attention; and these were brought on stretchers to the Operating Room; formerly a Class room; with the familiar ink-stains on floor, walls, and ceiling; now a chamber of horrors with blood where the ink was. Think of it: there were eight men in the room at once, Germans being treated without the slightest distinction from the French: one scarcely knew which was which. Considering the lack of

appliances – there was only one water-tap in the room – and the crowding – and the fact that the doctors were working for nothing – and on Germans too – really good work was done. Only there were no anaesthetics – no time – no money – no staff for that. So after that scene I need not fear to see the creepiest operations. One poor devil had his shin-bone crushed by a gun-carriage-wheel, and the doctor had to twist it about and push it like a piston to get out the pus. Another had a hole right through the knee; and the doctor passed a bandage thus:

66 *CL*, 284–5.

Another had a head into which a ball had entered and come out again.

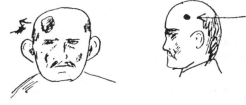

This is how the bullet lay in the Zouave. Sometimes the feet were covered with a brown, scaly, crust – dried blood.

I deliberately tell you all this to educate you to the actualities of the war.

The letter is undoubtedly informed by pity but it is not the only emotion present, nor is the stated objective – the education of Harold in the actualities of war – the whole truth. The spectacle of pain clearly engages the masochistic imagination. What is more disturbing is a certain morbid thrill in narration, evident in the sketches, with details like the twisting of the shinbone or the alliteration ('push it like a piston to get out the pus'). Critics such as Dominic Hibberd and Adrian Caesar have drawn attention to the 'sado-masochistic' element in Owen's poetry.[67] This is an important aspect of Owen's verse but the term 'sado-masochism' needs to be used with caution. The strange tactile thrill I have been discussing may be said to overlap with sado-masochism as a strictly aesthetic mode but cannot be conflated with it. The spectacle of pain excites his imagination through an acute bodily empathy rather than through personal agency or power. The distinction is crucial: he fantasises himself and other young men as being in the grip of pain but not about inflicting it on others. The sketches in the above letter are useful guides to how he conceptualised the body, trying to evoke the process or effect of painful touch – the wrenching of the shin-bone, the rope or the bullet cutting through flesh or the dried blood around the wound.

Pain and theatricality characterise the body in Owen's mature poetry. If, in Sassoon's 'The Redeemer' or Blunden's *Undertones of War*, soldiers are realised as tiny dots against the landscape, with Owen, it is this contorted body that defines space. Even as the poem begins, it is somehow ineluctably there, entering the poetic canvas in *medias res*. This is most

---

67 Hibberd, *WONB*, xix; Caesar, *Taking it Like a Man*, 150.

evident if we consider the first lines of some of his poems: 'Bent double, like old beggars under sacks' ('Dulce Et Decorum Est'), 'So neck to neck and obstinate knee to knee' ('The Wrestlers'), 'Head to limp head, the sunk-eyed wounded scanned' ('Smile, smile, smile'), 'His fingers wake, and flutter; up the bed' ('Conscious'), 'He sat in a wheeled chair' ('Disabled'), 'Patting goodbye, doubtless they told the lad' ('S.I.W'), 'Out there, we walked quite friendly up to Death' ('The Next War'). Many of the poems begin with verbs, or the verbs occur in the first line, propelling the body forward and establishing its relation to the phenomenal world: '*Move* him into the sun' ('Futility'), '*Cramped* in that funnelled hole' (fragment with the same title), 'So Abram *rose*, and *clave* the wood, and *went*' ('The Parable of the Old Man and the Young'), 'He *dropped*, – more sullenly than wearily' ('The Dead-Beat'), '*Sit* on the bed. I'm blind, and three parts shell' ('A Terre'), '*Halted* against the shade of a last hill' ('Spring Offensive').[68] Reading these opening lines is like observing the male body in slow motion – appropriately, the opening word of his final poem 'Spring Offensive' is 'Halted'. These verbs, implying movement, drama or contact, suggest an acute awareness of the embodiedness of the subject in a material universe: if lyric poetry is one of the most subjective of genres, Owen always manages to retain the status of the body as an object in the field of perception. In a letter written when he was nine years old – describing himself within a horse-carriage – he remarks: 'I can go down without anybody touching me, I can sit or stand which ever, I like'; and from the trenches, he reports, '[we] had to lie in the snow under the deadly wind. By day it was impossible to stand up or even crawl.'[69]

The insistent foregrounding of the body through movement and gesture has a Caravaggio-like quality. One is reminded of the painter's constant highlighting of the male body which enters the frame through a moment of high drama – about to be trampled by a horse, on the verge of decapitation or straining under the load of the Cross.[70] In spite of the difference in century, culture and religious outlook – and it is not known whether Owen ever saw any Caravaggio – there are similarities between the two in sensibility and treatment. Both share a morbid thrill in moments when the male body is bruised, wounded or racked by pain. In Owen's poetry, the body is so immediate that the traditional visual

68 The italics are mine.

69 *CL*, 21, 430.

70 The paintings referred to are *The Conversion of St Paul* (1601), *Judith and Holofernes* (1600) and *The Crucifixion of St Peter* (1601). Also see Leo Bersani, *Caravaggio's Secrets* (Cambridge, Mass.: MIT Press, 1998).

scheme of figure-horizon is often replaced by a physical horizon out of which individual features emerge: 'the chest and sleepy arms' in 'Asleep', the 'eyes, huge-bulged' in 'The Sentry', the face and forehead in 'Exposure', the 'drooping tongues' in 'Mental Cases'.[71] In his illuminating study of war poetry, Desmond Graham observes that Owen repeatedly 'turns to facial expressions and bodily gestures' to reveal to us 'the truths he found in war' and that 'such expressions are beyond words'.[72] Indeed, through the strange use of light and sound respectively, it is the sense of touch that both artists seem to evoke. Caravaggio does this through chiaroscuro – the most remarkable feature of his paintings – as the light illuminates the firm yet tender skin in *St John the Baptist* (1600) and *The Entombment of Christ* (1602–4), the wrinkled forehead in *Ecce Homo* (1605) or the trickle of blood on Christ's forehead in *The Crowning with Thorns* (1600). The best-known example is *The Doubting of St Thomas* where he plays on the relation between the surface of the paint and the skin: the light creates a *trompe l'œil* effect in the painting, suggesting a touch that seems to penetrate 'the reality of representation itself'.[73] But how can sound – which is central to lyric poetry – evoke the processes of touch and how can they be conceptualised and evolved through the formal structure of a poem? I shall focus closely on three of his best-known poems – 'Dulce Et Decorum Est', 'Futility' and 'Spring Offensive' – and examine the fraught relation between sound and sense.

Consider 'Dulce Et Decorum Est':

> Bent double, like old beggars under sacks,
> Knock-kneed, coughing like hags, we cursed through sludge,
> Till on the haunting flares we turned our backs
> And towards our distant rest began to trudge.
> Men marched asleep. Many had lost their boots
> But limped on, blood-shod. All went lame; all blind;
> [. . .]
> Gas! Gas! Quick, boys! – An ecstasy of fumbling,
> Fitting the clumsy helmets just in time;
> But someone still was yelling out and stumbling,
> And flound'ring like a man in fire or lime. . .
> Dim, through the misty panes and thick green light,
> As under a green sea, I saw him drowning.

---

71 Similarly, in Caravaggio, parts of the anatomy are illuminated: the right arm and eyes in *Judith and Holofernes*, the veined arm and muscular torso of the dead Christ in *The Entombment of Christ*, the right thigh and leg of the young boy in *The Calling of St Matthew*.
72 Graham, *The Truth of War*, 69, 70.
73 See Stewart, *Poetry and the Fate of the Senses*, 159.

In all my dreams, before my helpless sight,
He plunges at me, guttering, choking, drowning.
[. . .]
If you could hear, at every jolt, the blood
Come gargling from the froth-corrupted lungs,
Obscene as cancer, bitter as the cud
Of vile, incurable sores on innocent tongues, –
My friend, you would not tell with such high zest
To children ardent for some desperate glory,
The old Lie: Dulce et decorum est
Pro patria mori.[74]

This is a typical example of Owen's poetry of protest where the first person experience of the soldier is set against the abstract language of heroism. In a letter to his mother, he writes, 'Here is a gas poem, done yesterday, (which is not private, but not final)'.[75] Though the gas attack is at the centre of the poem, Owen here combines and plays three separate experiences – a night march, a gas attack and traumatic neurosis – along almost a single bodily Gestalt for maximum effect. It is the pulse of pain that he traces, discovering and charting the body and its parts as it moves from the exposed feet onto the exposed nerves. At the thematic level, the poem thus bears out the theme of 'passive suffering' that led Yeats to object to war poetry, but any simple notion of passivity is countered by the intersubjectivity of the lyric voice which oscillates between the victim, the witness and the reader. The dramatic imagination is evident from the way the focus shifts from the wrought muscular tension of the figures in the opening stanza through the 'ecstasy of fumbling' onto the psychic conflict. Time is held in suspense as one nightmarish experience follows, and blurs into, another until the final part of the poem is literally about a nightmare: the repetitive rhythm of the march gives way to the traumatic compulsion to repeat a particular moment.

The opening lines, through their alliterative and visual force, situate the bodies in our field of perception: bent-double, knock-kneed, they continue to limp on with their bloodied feet as iambs and trochees straggle within the pentameter in order to keep up with the somnambulist rhythm of the march. In a letter, he describes the terrain: 'It is pock-marked like a body of foulest disease and its odour is the breath of cancer'.[76] Cancer spreads into the poem as taste rather than as smell but the external world, as in sculpture, is registered only in so far as it touches and bruises the

74 *CP&F*, 140.          75 *CP&F*, 140.          76 *CL*, 429.

flesh: the crushing weight overhead, the feet against the sludge or the flares 'clawing' (in a rough draft) on the back.[77] Instead of blocking out the visual horrors, as in 'Greater Love', the sound here acts out the opening image in doubling back on itself ('Bent double, like old beggars'). Sound plays a particularly important role in a poem that climaxes on a savage contrast between tongues: the lacerated tongue of the soldier and the grand polysyllabic sound of the Latin phrase as he plays on the two meanings of 'lingua' (in Latin, it means both tongue and language).[78] If the heavy, monosyllabic rhymes of the first stanza and the insistent 'd' and 'g' are reminiscent of Sassoon's war realism, there is a more intimate sound-pattern that his mentor never manages to achieve. This is the wail of vowels where language breaks down – the 'e', 'o' and 'u' sounds (knock-kneed, coughing, cursed, sludge, our, trudge, lost, blood-shod, even, outstripped) in the opening stanza – which culminates in the noises of the retching body in the final lines. The sounds of the similes ('beggars', 'hags') soon metamorphose into the central reality ('gargling'). Mustard gas corrodes the body from within. The testimony of the gas attack accordingly moves from visual impressions to guttural processes; from sounds produced between the body and the world – fumbling, stumbling, flound'ring, drowning – to sounds within the body: guttering, choking, writhing, gargling. While war protest is habitually written through a language of wounds, Owen's visceral imagination takes it a step further, a movement horrifically apt for our own times of biological and chemical warfare. The hypochondriac adolescent who coughed up phlegm not only recognises his past self in the troops 'coughing like hags', but is now forever haunted by the spectre of a man coughing up his lungs. If 'Exposure' writes the horrors on the surface of the body through the 'fingering stealth' of adverse elements, 'Dulce Est Decorum Est' is a poem obsessed with the insides of the body.

Siegfried Sassoon did not like the use of the word 'ecstasy': he under-lined it in the manuscript and put a question mark beside it.[79] But Owen, gaining in confidence, seems to have ignored this demurral. The word remains a challenge to the transparency and realism of the poem, and to critical interpretation, striking that note of 'mystery' that the murdered

---

77 'Poems of Wilfred Owen', British Library, Add. MS 43721.41.

78 Douglas Kerr, in *Wilfred Owen's Voices*, notes that the soldiers in Owen's later poetry are usually mute.

79 'Dulce Et Decorum Est', 'Poems of Wilfred Owen', British Library, Add. MS 43721.41.

poet claims in 'Strange Meeting'. The curious word may point to Owen's awareness of the problems of metaphor, of the gap between the event and its representation. A psychological explanation hinting at a state where ecstasy and horror meet through extremity may be sought in Owen's letter where he describes the 'exhilaration' of going over the top, a point I shall explore later in connection to 'Spring Offensive'. Jon Silkin, while discussing the poem in *Out of Battle*, suggests 'the fevered sense of the terrified fumbling itself, which appears akin to that of joy, but is in fact so opposite to it'.[80] On the other hand, Freud in one of his essays on sexuality, notes that 'feelings of apprehension, fright or horror' have a 'sexually exciting effect' and that 'all comparatively intense affective processes, including even terrifying ones, trench upon sexuality'.[81] Yet, in a poem that explores the complicity of language in violence – the dangers of Horace's 'sweet' phrase[82] – 'ecstasy' seems to suggest, almost inadvertently, the perverse narrative impulse itself: poetic language, asked to describe violence, touches itself instead through alliteration and echo (ecstasy/clumsy/misty) and experiences exhilaration, replacing real-life horror with linguistic pleasure. Owen, thus criticising the 'sweetness' of a particular poetic tradition, seems to be trapped insidiously in the 'sweet-ness' of the lyric form itself: in the use of 'ecstasy', is there a glimmering of the central problem of 'poetic' testimony – as opposed to other forms of writing – that stretches from 'Greater Love' through 'Disabled' to 'The Kind Ghosts'?

The second stanza – almost functioning as a sestet for the poem is structured like two sonnets, bound through the fatal temporal logic of trauma – is marked by one of the most unsettling uses of sound. The excessive music of the rhyme, conspiring with sibilance and labials – as verbs are stretched beyond their bounds and an extra foot is left 'hanging' at the end of the lines (fumbling/stumbling/drowning) – creates a sonic realm that obscenely mimes, if not aestheticises, the spectral space created around the floundering body through its own jerky, erratic movements. But at the same time, the compulsive rhyme of the gerundive '-ing' is intensely affective: it suggests the eternal now of the trauma victim who, as Freud noted in *Beyond the Pleasure Principle* (1920), is forced to relive the past experience as a perpetual present. The image of eyes connects the

80 Silkin, *Out of Battle*, 220.　　　81 Sigmund Freud, 'Infantile Sexuality', in *SE*, VII. 203.

82 In the letter describing the poem to his mother, he writes, 'The famous Latin tag [from Horace, *Odes*, III.ii.13] means of course *It is sweet and meet to die for one's country. Sweet!* And *decorous!*', *CL*, 499–500.

poem to the traumatic encounter with 'eyes huge-bulged' in 'The Sentry', while the accusatory gesture ('He plunges at me') looks forward to the 'pawing' men in 'Mental Cases', showing how certain images were bound up in Owen's experience and representation of war neurosis.

The surreal landscape of the Western Front with which the poem opens ultimately narrows down to the insides of the mouth. Owen has a troubled relation to mouths, especially when they belong to young men. In his pre-war years, we have several poems lingering on lips: 'Better my lips should bruise you so'; 'you loosed away my lips' in 'To Eros'; or, 'Thy mouth has kisses all too rich for me' in the 'Perseus' fragment.[83] The last two poems have been linked to the Dunsden crisis, and, therefore, to Vivian Rampton. In his war verse, this fantasised mouth-contact or the dying kiss seems to be absent. Yet, there is an obsessive concern with lips: 'Red lips are not so red / As the stained stones kissed by the English dead' ('Greater Love'); 'As out of mouths, or deep wounds deepening' ('The Show'); 'Nor what red mouths were torn to make their blooms' ('The Kind Ghosts'); 'I saw his round mouth's crimson deepen as it fell' (the opening line of an untitled poem); and finally, in a rough draft of 'Dulce', 'small[?] kissed tongues', a phrase subsequently crossed out.[84] The decadent vocabulary, going back to Wilde and Swinburne, complicates the status of these images as testimony to real-life violence. Yet, one may note here a psychological knot: a rigorous Protestant ethic and suppressed eroticism, combined with a hatred of war, produce these tortured images. Lips that cannot be kissed are habitually torn in his poetry. In 'Dulce' – a poem where there is a surfeit of music – the focus shrinks to the organ of speech where lyric poetry has its origin; war protest is articulated by ultimately drawing attention to the physicality of the tongue which, now pitted with scabs and sores, literally cannot utter the lie. While 'realistic' in the best tradition of war verse, it also marks Owen's coming of age and war poetry's complex negotiation with Romanticism as 'the vile, incurable sores on innocent tongues' is a masterly rewriting of Keats's 'palate fine'. The 'froth-corrupted lungs' would have particular poignancy for one who was haunted by Keats and believed himself to have suffered from tuberculosis. Within the sensory field of the poem, the war horrors tip over from vision and touch through sound to taste which in fact is an extension, or a more intimate form, of touch.

83 'To – ', 'Poems of Wilfred Owen', British Library, Add. MS 43,721.38 (verso); 'To Eros' and 'Perseus' (*CP&F*, 115, 470).

84 'Poems of Wilfred Owen', British Library, Add. MS 43720.22.

Touch is closely related to emotion and affect. Elegies often have as their emotive core this elusive sense as death takes away the mutuality of the embrace. The spirit of Keats, in Shelley's 'Adonais', is 'a presence to be felt and known / In darkness and in light'; Tennyson, in 'In Memoriam' dramatises the spiritual encounter through physical contact: 'The dead man touched me from the past'.[85] It is also Owen's point of entry into the tradition:

> Move him into the sun –
> Gently its touch awoke him once,
> At home, whispering of fields half-sown,
> Always it woke him, even in France,
> Until this morning and this snow,
> If anything might rouse him now
> The kind old sun will know.
>
> Think how it wakes the seeds –
> Woke once the clays of a cold star.
> Are limbs, so dear achieved, are sides
> Full-nerved, still warm, too hard to stir?
> Was it for this the clay grew tall?
> – O what made fatuous sunbeams toil
> To break earth's sleep at all?[86]

In what is one of the gentlest of his poems, the 'futility' arises out of Owen choosing the most caressive of lyric voices to portray a moment of unyielding touch. It is a moment that expands spectacularly in scope within the poem from actual physical contact to accommodate and ultimately challenge the whole process of creation. Yet the development is wholly natural, almost organic. Two key words – 'sun' and 'wake' – provide the central situation and image as well as a pattern of repetition and echo, driving the poem towards to its inexorable logic. 'Futility' is closely related to 'Asleep' which also invokes the idea of sleep and waking – a poem he was revising around the same time (May 1918). But 'Futility' moves away from the descriptive realism of 'Asleep' to explore the idea of contact itself: between bodies, words and worlds. The meshing of the literal and the metaphoric aspects of the sun's 'touch' enables him to traverse a remarkable range of emotions and references within fourteen lines: nature and nostalgia, eros and geology, elegy and protest.

85 Percy Bysshe Shelley, 'Adonais' in *Shelley: Poetical Works*, ed. Thomas Hutchinson (Oxford: Oxford University Press, 1970), 441; Alfred Tennyson, 'In Memoriam' in *The Poems of Tennyson*, ed. Christopher Ricks, vol. ii (Harlow:, Longman, 1987), 413.
86 'Futility', *CP&F*, 158.

The opening trochee brings not just the addressed soldier but also the reader into immediate touch with the prostrate body, a body that will reject the reciprocity of the gesture. It is the terrible force of this rejection that provides the impetus for the poem as Owen would now stroke the male body with the lightest of materials – light, playing on the vestigial relation between light and heat, vision and touch. A month before his death, he writes to his mother about how 'the warmth came like the rising of the May-day sun'.[87] The interpenetration of these two aspects of the sun – light and temperature – is crucial in the poem for the word 'woke' to accrete significance, for, by the second stanza, the sun has whirled the poem into another place, another time. We note in the varying uses of 'wake' and its cognates one of Owen's favourite techniques: repetition. But this is not actually repetition, for to repeat is not to repeat but to change. Thus, in the oft-quoted line 'The pallor of girls' brows shall be their pall' from 'Anthem for Doomed Youth', the linguistic reiteration underscores the semantic difference. In 'Futility', 'woke' changes through panels of time, growing in scope from contact and consciousness to germination and genesis. At the level of sound, it combines with the 'sun', weaving itself into the rhyme scheme to produce new patterns: para-rhymes (sun/sown), assonance (sown/snow), alliteration (snow/now), full-rhyme (snow/know). This intermeshing is the auditory equivalent of the mutuality of the embrace whose denial forms the core of the poem; these sensuous folds of sound only highlight by contrast the unresponsive body they contain. The repetitive sound in this intricate rhyme-scheme of the first stanza is 'o', moaning through 'cold' worlds and culminating in a cry ('O') in the penultimate line.

The repetition of words also helps to distinguish the words that are not repeated. Thus, 'touch', occurring between sun and waking, is mentioned just once, as if over-use would take away its meaning. In Owen's poems, memories and even ideas are often etched on the skin. In 'Disabled', the mutilated war hero remembers 'how slim / Girls' waists are, or how warm their subtle hands'.[88] Sexual excitement is swiftly converted, through bitterness, into misogyny: 'All of them touch him like some queer disease'. 'A Terre' continues the theme of mutilation. In order to enter the world of 'A Terre' and to empathise with the hero, we have to close our eyes for the lyric subject is blind. Lines such as 'This bandage feels like pennies on my eyes' depend directly on our wincing for their effect. The

87  *CL*, 584.          88  *CP&F*, 175.

mutilated war veteran evokes touch to join time: 'Soft rains will touch me, – as they could touch once'.[89] In 'Futility', the sun not only connects 'this morning and this snow' with the geological past, showing how different worlds were integrally related in his mind, but reaches out, beyond the half-sown field and the half-used life, to a literary landscape in order to rouse dead poets and writers. For there lies behind the poem's soldier another young 'boy' – the androgynous Fidele in Shakespeare's *Cymbeline* – who in fact will be woken up by the 'heat o' the Sun'. But the image of 'old sun' points, beyond Shakespeare, and Donne's 'Busy old fool, unruly sun', to another source: the 'maturing sun' of Keats's 'To Autumn' that helps to mature the season's plenty but itself matures and dies. Similarly, the 'old' sun here is at once all-powerful and impotent: once it had moved whole worlds to consciousness, but now cannot touch the young boy to life. Since the entire world is contained, for Owen and for us, in that single body, the whole narrative of creation is rendered absurd. 'Was it for this the clay grew tall?': the question, gathering depth through the biblical allusion, has, within its lyric parameters, the dramatic force and poignancy of Lear's 'Is this the promised end?'[90]

The cessation of world and time because the beloved is dead is a stock motif in verse, stretching from classical elegies to Auden's 'Stop all the clocks'.[91] 'Nothing now', Auden mourns, 'can ever come to any good'. Yet, the immediacy with which 'Futility' manages to convey this sense is remarkable. This is partly achieved through the two lines that caused Owen much trouble; he circled them in his manuscript and revised them repeatedly:

> Are    ~~almost~~
> ~~Yet~~ Are limbs, perfect ~~at last~~, and sides
> ~~And heart still warm it cannot~~
> ~~Almost~~ life-warm ~~too hard to~~ stir ?[92]
> Full-nerved, still warm too hard

Both 'heart' and 'warm' in the rough draft bear traces of Keats's 'this living hand' but Owen would transmute the language of emotion ('heart')

89 *CP&F*, 179.
90 'As, in your vision, the feet and toes were part potter's clay and part iron, it shall be a divided kingdom. Its core shall be partly of iron just as you saw iron mixed with the common clay' (Daniel 2:42).
91 W. H. Auden, 'XXXIV', in *Poems, Essays and Dramatic Writings 1927–1939*, ed. Edward Mendelson (London: Faber, 1997), 163.
92 'Poems of Wilfred Owen', British Library, Add. MS 43720.53 (verso).

to that of sense. The male body that has so long been ignored is brought into the poem and back to life for a fleeting moment through the lightest of touches. The contact established through 'move' is pressed towards tactual perception, and evocation of body texture and temperature, through acute details (nerves, warm, hard) and linguistic energy. The opening spondees ('full-nerved, still warm'), labials, sibilance and long vowels are all marshalled in a single line in a final attempt at resuscitation, only to come up against the awkward caesura and the hardness of 'd' and 'r'. The word 'still' combines the dual sense of 'yet' and 'motionless', and pushes the homoerotic aesthetic towards a recognition of the contiguity of life and death on the battlefield. The moment of attempted resurrection is also informed by certain age-old narratives such as Christ restoring eyesight through touch or Pygmalion ('clay' brings in this reference) making the statue to move. In Owen's 'The Sleeping Beauty', the princess is kissed 'to the world of Consciousness', showing how certain ideas persisted and were brought to fruition within the context of war.[93] The appeal of these stories and the poignancy of the poem lie in the irreducible fact of our bodily existence, and in the realisation that we need touch in order to develop and enter into meaningful relationship with each other. The mention of 'sleep' in the final line is reminiscent of the concluding lines of both 'Asleep' and 'Strange Meeting', showing how death and lyric closure were linked in his mind. But pathos here is coupled with anger, evident in the final question as well as the change from 'kind' to 'fatuous', a word that leaps out of the monosyllabic base of the poem, suggesting that the sun now fails to touch the poet as well.

The sun would appear once more in his last poem, 'Spring Offensive', if only to be 'spurned' by the soldiers as they prepare for the fatal offensive. Here, the sun is a benign though powerless presence, 'a friend with whom their love is done'. Yet, unlike the elegiac tone of 'Futility', 'Spring Offensive' has an exhilarating force as Owen sets his spirit 'surging light and clear'. Two letters frame, though do not determine, our reading of the poem. The first is written to his mother, 'I can find no word to qualify my experiences except the word SHEER. . . . I lost all my earthly faculties, and fought like an angel.'[94] The second letter, written to his brother Colin, describes the assault at Savy Wood in April 1917 on which 'Spring Offensive' is loosely based:

---

93  *CP&F*, 104. For an exploration of some of the myths of creation, their literary lives and underlying meanings, see Stewart, *Poetry and the Fate of the Senses*, 160–78.
94  *CL*, 580. The letter, presumably written after the poem, is nonetheless illuminating.

There was an extraordinary exultation in the act of slowly walking forward, showing ourselves openly. . . .

Then we were caught in a Tornado of Shells. The various 'waves' were all broken up. . . . When I looked back and saw the ground all crawling and wormy with wounded bodies, I felt no horror at all but only immense exultation at having got through the Barrage.[95]

In this final poem, rooted in an actual offensive, Owen reconceptualises poetry as testimony to the senses as the body, going over the top, faces the 'SHEER' and chasms into 'infinite space'. The apocalyptic end-rhymes – 'last hill', 'beyond the ridge', 'end of the world', 'last high place', 'world's verge', 'existence's brink' – show not just traumatic repetition but the figuration of survival as chance in its purest form, the body 'up / On the hot blast' waiting to pause or to fall. Such testimony in effect becomes the principle of poetic insight in 'Spring Offensive' that makes sound and the senses race ahead of knowledge or thought:

> ~~Glorious Lightly~~
> **So, soon**
> ~~Proudly~~          *    *    *          ~~went~~ raced
> ~~Splendid,~~  ~~Bright-faced~~              ~~ran~~
> ~~Turning~~, they topped the hill, and ~~walked~~ together
> **Down**    stretch    ~~green~~ ^herbs^
> Over an open ~~plain~~ of ~~wind~~ and heather
> Exposed. And instantly the whole sky burned
>                          set sudden cups
>                   ~~and c [ ? ]~~ and
>                     set [ ? ] and
> With ~~fl~~ fury against them; ~~and that easy slope~~
>                     earth ~~hell~~
> ~~Opened To catch their blood~~ In thousands for their blood; and the
>                          green slope. . .[96]

The heavily cancelled, revised and often illegible manuscript version shows that a poem rooted in unthinkable horror was conceived as a poem not about killing or being killed but about exhilaration. The cancelled words, 'splendid', 'bright faced', or 'Glorious Lightly' turn a suicidal offensive into an hour of 'seraphic' ecstasy, an unbearable lightness of being. Alcohol, as before the offensive in Sherriff's *Journey's End*, may partly explain the recklessness, the release into drunken jouissance. At an

95 *CL*, 458.
96 'Spring Offensive', 'Poems of Wilfred Owen', British Library Add. MS 43720.28.

immediate level, both the letters and the poem bear witness to the incomprehensibility and exultation of survival, of having come alive through the barrage. But this may point to something more disturbing, something that Freud placed at the very heart of *Civilization and Its Discontents* (1929): 'in the blindest fury of destructiveness, we cannot fail to recognize that the satisfaction of the instinct is accompanied by an extraordinarily high degree of narcissistic enjoyment'.[97]

The true poets must be truthful, Owen famously remarked. Truth to bodily sensations is as urgent as political protest and morality, he seems to be saying in this poem. It is a world perceived through the skin, in so much as the sky is perceived as 'glass' hanging 'sharp' on 'souls'. 'Spring Offensive' marks a new music in Owen's oeuvre:

>        hung                  ~~crest~~^line
> Sharp on their souls ~~loomed~~ the imminent ~~ridge~~ of grass,
> Fearfully flashed the sky's mysterious glass.

The half-rhyme and sibilance no longer aestheticise: they introduce into the cascade of sound the 'imminent' terror through details such as the 'ridge of grass', 'flashed' or the 'mysterious glass'. 'Hung' captures the vertiginous motion and swinging angles of the body as it faces the ridge and the sky, and hints at the fates of the soldiers hanging in balance. Both are *felt* on the 'souls', as Owen, like Keats, finally abandons the hierarchies of body and mind. The buttercups, a childhood memory going back to Shropshire, are imagined as chalices hungry for blood in a final dismissal of religious consolation ('Some say God caught them'). This image may also be a reworking of Keats's 'Fast fading violets covered up in leaves' from 'To a Nightingale' where the leaves are imagined as a potential grave for the dying poet. Only the tactile continuum – and consolation – of army life ('leaning on the nearest chest or knees') is offered in way of Owen's final vision of community as the male body is wrested from the 'sorrowing arms' of nature and 'carelessly' flung into the 'fury of hell's upsurge'. Dante, whose *Purgatorio* the young Owen assiduously read and underlined, is acknowledged in the final stanza in the abandonment of all hope – and youth.

---

97 Freud, 'Civilisation and Its Discontents', *SE*, XXI, 121. Freud's observations are congruent with some of the experiences and emotions Ernst Jünger recalls in *Storm of Steel*, and, more recently, in some revisionist accounts of war, as in Ferguson's *The Pity of War* (1998) which has a section on 'The Joy of War', 357–66.

### DREAMS AND POEMS

In *Health and Conduct* (1923), Arthur J. Brock – the doctor who treated Wilfred Owen for shell-shock at Craiglockhart with his method of 'ergotherapy' – physical and mental labour in contrast to Rivers's talking cure – remembers his famous patient: 'In the powerful war-poems of Wilfred Owen we read the heroic testimony of one who having in the most literal sense "faced the phantoms of the mind" had *all but* laid them ere the last call came; they still appear in his poetry but he fears them no longer'.[98] Even before his first call to the front, phantoms of the mind haunted Owen. His letters from Bordeaux refer to 'phantasies', 'horrors' and 'phantasms'.[99] A letter written on 25 February 1914 dates their onset – 'today a YEAR ago the pneumonia definitely appeared. It was "to-night" I had the first phantasms'[100] – locating them in the nervous illness following the Dunsden crisis. At Dunsden, Owen had hinted in verse at 'long night steep / In bloodiness and stains of shadowy crime', reiterated in the 'furor' [*sic*] letter: 'Dreading the Dark thou know'st not how to illume'.[101] As early as June 1911, Owen mentioned 'guilty mystery' hanging upon the 'forbidden Night incestuously' but it is only in 'Supposed Confessions' that we confront the 'phantasm': 'But, face to face, she fixed on me her stare: / Woe, woe, my blood has never moved since then'.[102] Some of these pre-war images might have come back and joined the 'bellicose dreams' that troubled him at Craiglockhart.

On May 1917, a trembling and stammering Owen was admitted to Craiglockhart under the care of Arthur Brock. Both Stallworthy and Hibberd have documented vividly Owen's ordeal in the trenches, but a few incidents are worth repeating. Immediately after joining the Regular Army 2nd Battalion of the Manchester Regiment on 1 January 1917, Owen fought in several fierce but comparatively minor battles along the Beaumont Hamel section of the Western Front. He was almost buried alive thrice. On 12 January 1917, he and his platoon were trapped for 'fifty hours' under 'terrific bombardment' in a dug-out. On 14 March 1917, he accidentally fell into a well or a cellar and suffered concussion. The worst near-burial was, however, during a bombardment in April, when he was blown up in the air by a shell, and on regaining consciousness,

---

98 Arthur J. Brock, *Health and Conduct* (London: Williams and Norgate, 1923), 171–2.

99 *CL*, 206, 212, 235. In a letter to Susan Owen, he writes of 'a sad, sad dream the other night' (*CL*, 212).

100 *CL*, 235.

101 *CP&F*, 14; *CL*, 175.     102 *CP&F*, 426, 13. See Hibberd, *Owen*, 67.

found himself 'in a railway Cutting, in a hole just big enough to lie in, and covered with corrugated iron'. Ten days later, he was diagnosed with 'neurasthenia' and was sent to 13th Casualty Clearing Station where Dr William Brown treated him. In a letter to his mother, he wrote, 'Do not for a moment suppose I have had a 'breakdown'. I am simply <u>avoiding</u> one.' Two days later, he however confided in her, '<u>Some</u> of us have been sent down here as a little mad. Possibly I am among them.'[103]

The hospital at Craiglockhart has been described by Sassoon as the 'underworld of dreams' where every night, 'each man was back in his doomed sector of a horror-stricken Front Line'. To W. H. R. Rivers, who ran the hospital and became Sassoon's father-figure, dream was the primal clue to repressed material and, by working through these materials, it marked the way to recovery. Sassoon remembers how Rivers would note down the 'significant' dreams and 'try to remove repressions'.[104] As early as February 1917, Owen was suffering from acute insomnia but the first mention of 'bellicose dreams of late' comes in a letter from Craiglockhart written on 15 August 1917. Subsequent letters show that Owen was having war-dreams for quite some time. However, on 22 August, he writes, 'The Barrage'd Nights are quite the exception' and in early September, he occasionally had 'disastrous dreams, but they are taking on a more civilian character, motor accidents and so on'.[105] Rivers would have nodded approvingly. One of the first signs of improvement, Rivers noted in *Conflict and Dream* (1923), was 'some amount of transformation' where war experience was replaced by 'incidents of other kinds'.[106] Later, Owen wrote: 'I confess I *bring on* what few war dreams I now have, entirely by *willingly* considering war of an evening. I do so because I have my duty to perform towards War.'[107] What does Owen mean here? The recent biography gives a detailed account of Owen's activities at Craiglockhart, and his relationship with Brock and Sassoon. What is less closely examined is the relationship between war trauma and writing, between shell-shock, nightmares and poetic production.

Two of Owen's poems directly mention – or rather spring from – war dreams:

103  *CL*, 428, 452, 453, 454.
104  Sassoon, *The Complete Memoirs of George Sherston*, 556–7.
105  *CL*, 438, 484, 488, 490.
106  W. H. R. Rivers, *Conflict and Dream* (London: Kegan Paul, 1923), 67.
107  *CL*, 533–4.

We dredged it up, for dead, until he whined,
'O Sir – my eyes, – I'm blind, – I'm blind, – I'm blind.'
Coaxing, I held a flame against his lids
And said if he could see the least blurred light
He was not blind; in time they'd get all right.
'I can't,' he sobbed. Eyeballs, huge-bulged like squids',
Watch my dreams still, – yet I forgot him there

('The Sentry')

Dim, through the misty panes and thick green light,
As under a green sea, I saw him drowning.

In all my dreams, before my helpless sight,
He plunges at me, guttering, choking, drowning.

If in some smothering dreams you too could pace
Behind the wagon that we flung him in,
And watch the white eyes writhing in his face,
His hanging face, like a devil's sick of sin;

('Dulce Et Decorum Est')[108]

Both the passages are fixated on the image of the eyes that, as noted earlier, goes back to Owen's pre-war experience. 'The Sentry' refers to being trapped in a dug-out under 'terrific bombardment' when he 'nearly broke down and let myself drown in the water': 'In the Platoon on my left the sentries over the dug-out were blown to nothing. . . . one lad was blown down and, I am afraid, blinded.'[109] This incident may also lie behind the imagery of eyes in 'Dulce Et Decorum Est' which is primarily about a gas attack.

The two poems bear witness to the process by which a dream-image is transformed into the most powerful and poignant testimony: the image of the eyes writhing in the face results from not only what has been witnessed but what has been begotten by the unconscious testimony of the dream. In the first poem, the original trauma of encountering – or discovering – blindness by the candle flare gives rise to, but is subsumed by, the affective overload of the dream-image. In the second poem, the reader-spectator is asked to bear witness not to actuality but to images spawned out of the dream: 'If in some smothering dream you too could pace'. The horrors of the war are located not in objective trench reality or even in the process of cognition but in memory and dreams, in a super-sensitised subjective consciousness. 'I'm blind, – I'm blind, – I'm blind' resonates with the

108 *CP&F*, 188, 140.
109 *CL*, 428; see Stallworthy, *WO*, 274.

same pathos and cadence as Lear's 'Never', only to cancel the possibility of both catharsis and death. The repetition points not only to the irretrievability of vision but also its traumatic impact on the senses of the witness, the repetitive nightmares ('watch my dreams still') that Freud noticed among the shell-shock victims in *Beyond the Pleasure Principle* (1920). Owen's verse suggests what contemporary trauma theory holds as survivor guilt ('He plunges at me') manifesting itself through 'night terrors' ('smothering dreams').[110] 'Eyeballs, huge-bulged': in Owen's poetry, war trauma is evoked through reflexes of sound in the way 'bulged' can be said to be linguistically 'writhing' out of 'huge', gathering within it all the previous phonemes ('blind', 'lids', 'blurred', 'sobbed') and carrying forward the aquamarine imagery of the first stanza through the image of 'squids'. The trauma in 'The Sentry' is rooted in an act of seeming forgetfulness: the helplessness of the officer coming back as a forgetting of his duty towards his wounded subordinate ('I forgot him there') as well as forgetting – or psychically failing – to react adequately to the moment. Elaborating on Freud's ideas, Caruth, in *Unclaimed Experience*, argues that, at the heart of a traumatic encounter, there is the inability of the mind to know the event fully, and that 'the way it was precisely not known in the first instance – returns to haunt the survivor later on'.[111] Trauma thus results from the failure of the mind to either understand, or react adequately, to the original moment of crisis (the blinding or the gas attack) which then haunts the survivor later through repetitive re-enactments: a lifelong race, as it were, to catch up with the wagon where the body was originally, carelessly, 'flung in'.

The image of the eyes relates to the Dunsden 'phantasms' and the Medusa-like gaze of 'Despondency'. Dr William Brown, who initially treated Owen for shell-shock at the 13th Casualty Clearing Station, believed in relating the symptoms of war-neurosis to conflicts in the patient's earlier life.[112] Brown's views were echoed by Rivers, who held that war dreams were accompanied by regression, of 'throwing back in sleep to modes of mental activity and expression characteristic of earlier periods of life'. The war image, to Rivers, was the first stage of war trauma where 'the dream follows the grim reality faithfully' accompanied by 'an affect of a peculiarly intense kind'. In *Conflict and Dream* – published in

---

110 See also Deidre Barrett (ed.), *Trauma and Dreams* (Cambridge, Mass.: Harvard University Press, 1996).
111 Caruth, *Unclaimed Experience*, 4.
112 William Brown, 'The Treatment of Cases of Shell Shock in an Advanced Neurological Centre', *The Lancet*, 17 August 1918: ii, 197–200.

the same year as Brock's *Health and Conduct* (1923) – he notes: 'I prefer, therefore, to regard the dream as the expression of a conflict, and as an attempt to solve the conflict by such means as are available during sleep'.[113] 'Strange Meeting', I would suggest, provides the staging of the conflict which is shuttered behind the blinded eyes in 'The Sentry' and 'Dulce Et Decorum Est'.

Drafted at Scarborough or Ripon between January and March 1918, 'Strange Meeting' was written at a later date than either 'The Sentry' or 'Dulce Et Decorum Est', incorporating two previously composed fragments.[114] At Craiglockhart, Owen's own doctor Arthur Brock encouraged Owen's artistic talents as a means of therapy. Owen's 'The Wrestlers' and the 'Outlook Tower' essay were written under the immediate influence of Brock who also made him the editor of the Craiglockhart journal, *Hydra*. 'Strange Meeting' might be regarded as a further process in therapeutic healing, accosting the 'phantoms of the mind' through a dream framework. In *Health and Conduct*, Brock refers to the Roman poet Lucretius as a 'psycho-therapist' and discusses the 'psycho-therapeutic role' of *De Rerum Natura* through which Lucretius practises his 'democratic gospel of thought-control'.[115]

If to Arthur Brock, Lucretius is the arch psychotherapist, Owen in 'Strange Meeting' seeks the 'psycho-therapeutic' help of Dante, Shelley, Wordsworth and Blake. The poem's title acknowledges the influence of Shelley ('now strange meeting did befall / In a strange land'). However, the political philosophy of the poem, rather than according with Shelleyan views of human perfectibility, echoes in its 'trek from progress' Russell's essay on 'The Danger to Civilization' in *Justice in War-Time* (1916). The poem is given a dramatic urgency through the reconfiguration of the murdered enemy as a poet, the poet as another romantic youth. The use of doubles in this poem enacts the flow between the friend and the enemy, crucial to the poem's staging of the conflict, gathering it into a general vision of apocalypse. The poem resurrects the gazes of 'The Sentry' and 'Dulce'. If helplessness at the blinding of the sentry had been transformed into the guilty reproach of 'eyes huge-bulged' in these two

113 Rivers, *Conflict and Dream*, 75, 67, 66, 17.

114 According to Stallworthy, the poem may be a development of the fragment 'With those that are become' (*CP&F*, 492) and 'Earth's wheels run oiled with blood' (*CP&F*, 514). For the various literary and religious echoes in the poem, see Backman, *Tradition Transformed*, 96–117; for a discussion of the complex intertextuality of Owen's poetry and how they often take place 'on a cosmic stage', see Longley, 'The Great War, History, and the English Lyric', 67–72.

115 Brock, *Health and Conduct*, 197.

poems, in 'Strange Meeting' the gaze is no longer 'smothering': the 'eyes', now fixed with 'piteous recognition', are at once those of the enemy-friend ('German conscript') and of the poet. In this poem Owen would address not just survivor guilt but actual political responsibility through a final invocation of his old trope.

Two moments of action stand out in this drama of male intimacy and intensity, speaking to and accosting each other – a moment of benediction and a moment of murder:

> Then, as I probed them, one sprang up, and stared
> With piteous recognition in fixed eyes,
> Lifting distressful hands, as if to bless.
> . . .
> 'I am the enemy you killed, my friend.
> I knew you in this dark: for so you frowned
> Yesterday through me as you jabbed and killed.
> I parried; but my hands were loath and cold.
> Let us sleep now. . . .'[116]

The poem has been connected by critics to the fragment, 'With those that are become' through the similar lines: 'I loved ~~him~~ the more ~~close~~ near than brotherly / 'For each man slays the one he loves [']'.[117] In this fragment, violence is centred on the hand whose erotic undertone is evident in the allusion to Wilde's 'The Ballad of Reading Gaol'. Erotic guilt is conflated with political responsibility in the rough draft of 'Strange Meeting' in the line ('But I ~~am dead was wounded. And~~ by your hand, ~~my~~ poor friend')[118] that directly looks forward to 'I am the enemy you killed, my friend'. Is the discarded line from the rough draft another piece of textual unhanding, as in 'Perseus' or 'Exposure'? But the image reappears in the penultimate lines of 'Strange Meeting' in a bold acceptance of individual political responsibility: 'Yesterday through me as you jabbed and killed'. This central 'truth' of warfare, like pity, is finally acknowledged through the tortured trope of hands, in a knotting of war and sexuality. There is a fleeting trace of the old decadent imagination as the moment of murder – the thrust of 'jabbed and killed' – is also a moment of frightful intimacy. But the poem is also an acknowledgement of war reality that is unique in the corpus of First World War literature: the role of the pacifist poet as a political murderer. The English war poet maims and murders other war poets, idealists and youths.

---

116 'Strange Meeting', *CP&F*, 148–9.        117 *CP&F*, 492.
118 *CP&F*, 309.

In an article in 1919, Middleton Murry, pointing out the influence of Keats's 'The Fall of Hyperion' behind 'Strange Meeting', wrote: 'the sombre imagination, the sombre rhythm is that of the dying Keats . . . this poem by a boy with the certainty of death in his heart, like his great forerunner, is the most magnificent expression of the emotional significance of the war that has yet been achieved by English poetry'.[119] If Moneta's 'bright-blanch'd' face lies behind the 'fixed eyes' in 'Strange Meeting', so does the 'warm scribe my hand' that records the 'dream' in Keats's poem. It is only appropriate that the phantasmatic hand of Keats that induced Owen to his poethood with its uncommon slant would figure in this final manifesto of Owen, the poet, 'held peer by Georgians'. The hand of the poet now wrestles not only with the 'coldness' of the grave, as in Keats, but with the 'loathing' of murder: loath to kill and the loathing of having killed are expressed simultaneously in the blurring of the two voices. The use of doppelgänger or alter ego retains our empathy even while portraying unpalatable political reality, imbuing the dramatic monologue with lyric intensity. Two gestures of the enemy-friend at the opening and the closing of the monologue – the 'distressful' hands ready to bless and loath to kill – converge and gather up the violence and the guilt of the hand contact or combat ('jabbed and killed'), reconfiguring that terrible moment into an act of forgiveness – and futility.

On 14 August 1912, a nineteen-year-old Owen, while still at the Dunsden vicarage, had a cycling accident. He described the incident, as usual, to his mother:

I was washing some of the dirt out of the wound, & had applied some of my Carbolic Ointment, when sudden twilight seemed to fall upon the world, an horror of great darkness closed around me – strange noises and a sensation of swimming under water overtooked [sic] me, and in fact I fell into a regular syncope.[120]

Even for a reader now acquainted with Owen's sensibility, the description is striking. Pain excites the imagination and bodies forth images that will be reworked in a war context: the sensation 'under water', reiterated in another pre-war letter ('sinking feeling . . . up to the neck in quicksand')[121] looks forward to 'Dulce Et Decorum Est' ('As under a green sea, I saw him drowning') or the underground darkness that

119 John Middleton Murry, 'The Condition of English Poetry', *Athenaeum* (5 December 1919), 1284 (1283–5).
120 *CL*, 153.     121 *CL*, 183.

encumbers the 'sleepers' in the 'sullen hall' in 'Strange Meeting'.[122] The morbid, adolescent imagination not only leads to war poetry but will also be grotesquely realised in the trenches. In the same year as the cycling accident, 1912, Owen had fantasised, 'Since my dread Ghost has once a finger laid / Upon my flesh, and left a burning mark'.[123] If, in conclusion, we briefly go back to the letter to Sassoon with which we started the chapter – the missive describing 'excellent little servant Jones' whose blood soaked Owen's shoulder for 'half an hour' – we realise the ways in which a metaphor becomes a reality. Owen had asked Sassoon: 'Can you photograph the crimson-hot iron as it cools from the smelting? That is what Jones's blood looked like, and felt like.'[124] The 'crimson-hot iron' is no longer visualised but *felt*. Owen's conception of poetry as a mark, a scalding, is now soldered onto trench reality: what had been a decadent fantasy now becomes actual experience. The senses are 'charred', and yet the moment is associated with the creative stimulus ('I shall feel again as soon as I dare'). A single moment of touch gathers up the central paradox in the very term 'war poet': the war kills, maims and yet creates unique moments of intensity. These, in turn, are connected with the concept of romantic agony, creativity and selfhood, with representation as re-presentation. Writing about modern subjectivity, Roland Barthes notes:

. . . for us the 'subject' (since Christianity) is *the one who suffers*: where is a wound, there is a subject: *die Wunde! die Wunde!* says Parsifal, thereby becoming 'himself'; and deeper the wound, at the body's centre (at the 'heart'), the more the subject becomes a subject: for the subject is *intimacy* ('The wound. . .is of a frightful intimacy').[125]

The hand that touched, or thought it had touched, the burning heart of Keats and in the trenches had cradled 'little' Jones, finally probes into the mental wounds – 'the body's centre' – and *writes*.

---

122 Important, in this context, is his letter to his mother recalling his experience of being trapped in the London underground with a vivid evocation of claustrophobia (*CL*, 377). For an exploration of the underground imagery in Owen's poetry, see Hibberd, *OTP*, 92–3, and Stallworthy, *Anthem for Doomed Youth*, 98.
123 *CP&F*, 15.
124 *CL*, 581.          125 Roland Barthes, *A Lover's Discourse*, 189.

# PART III

# *Wounds*

The entry for 4 February 1917 from the diary of M. A. Brown. 88/7/1 IWM (DOC).

CHAPTER 5

# 'The impotence of sympathy': service and suffering in the nurses' memoirs

Mary Ann Brown, who served wounded Turkish soldiers in a hospital ship, recorded in her diary on 4 February 1917:

Heard to-day that Miss Rait is leaving us in ten days time.

Very busy. Amp. of rt arm. (Turk died a few hrs later) Amp left leg. Spinal Anaesthetic. Amp. rt leg. Spinal Anaesthetic. Turk quite happy, smoked a cig. all the time they were sawing off his leg. one amp of finger. one amp of thumb one secondary haemorrhage. one incision of leg 7 altogether, no off duty finished 6:30.[1]

Written under the exacting compulsion of the moment, Brown's account reads like a relentless catalogue of facts without any emotional outlet. Individuals become a series of body parts on the operation table, jumbled as much into abbreviated syntax as into abbreviated time. The mention of the 'happy' Turk is like the intrusion of macabre humour into the narrative. The emotionless tone is perhaps because of the pressures of time and extreme physical exhaustion; it is also the voice of one who is inside the moment of horror, as if efficient nursing service – the amputation of body parts in this case – had resulted in, or even demanded, the amputation of one's own intimate nerves.

Brown's account is characteristic of the experience of thousands of young women who left home to serve the war-wounded. Brown's more articulate and illustrious colleague Vera Brittain would write about the 'self-protective callousness' required by the young female nurse to cope with the 'general atmosphere of inhumanness' prevailing in the war hospitals. As she dresses for the first time a 'gangrenous leg wound, slimy and green and scarlet', she feels 'sick and faint'; with time and experience, she learns to 'dress unaided and without emotion, the quivering stump of a newly amputated limb'.[2] Yet, the language itself quivers with the raw

---

1 M. A. Brown, 'Diary', IWM, 88/7/1.
2 Vera Brittain, *Testament of Youth* (1933; London: Virago, 1978), 176, 211, 216.

precision of the detail, hinting at what Freud in *Beyond the Pleasure Principle* (1920) calls a 'breach' in the protective psychic sheath:[3] the repressed emotion surfaces in the form of nightmares as Brittain, like some of her male patients, starts dreaming about mutilated bodies. In her memoir, *Testament of Youth* (1933), she dwells on moments when the young, sheltered, female body comes in actual physical contact with male wounds. Such moments occur obsessively in the nurses' writings, as if the hand was doomed to a compulsion to repeat the experiences from which it most shuddered.

In 'Greater Love' (originally dedicated 'To Any Woman'), when Owen issues his caveat to women, 'for you may touch them not', he at once invokes and throws away the religious allusion – erotic resentment being a powerful undertow – to suggest an integral relation between male experience and the body of knowledge during wartime. Yet, by January 1916, as conscription was enforced in England, it was predominantly women who were entrusted with the repair of the war-ravaged bodies of men. They volunteered in thousands to serve the wounded in France, Belgium, Serbia and Mesopotamia. The experience of women is not comparable, in kind or degree, to the scale of devastation undergone by the soldiers. But at the same time, it is important to remember that these nurses worked amidst horrific conditions and occasionally even came under shelling. Moreover, the Voluntary Aid Detachment or V.A.D. nurses were often genteel Edwardian ladies, and not trained, like the doctors and the medical staff, to be de-sensitized to the sight, smell or touch of exposed flesh. In recent years, there has been a revival of interest in women's war writings, resulting in fresh anthologies and new editions of their memoirs.[4] Feminist critics such as Margaret Higonnet, Jane Marcus and Claire Tylee have brought important gender concerns to the cultural and literary history of the war.[5] While there has been extensive

---

3 Freud, 'Beyond the Pleasure Principle', in *SE*, XVIII, 29.
4 See Catherine Reilly, *The Virago Book of Women's War Poetry and Verse* (London: Virago, 1998); Joyce Marlowe, *The Virago Book of Women and the Great War* (London: Virago, 1998); Agnes Cardinal, Dorothy Goldman and Judith Hattaway, *Women's Writing on the First World War* (Oxford: Oxford University Press, 1999); Margaret Higonnet (ed.), *Lines Of Fire: Women Writers of World War I* (Harmondsworth: Penguin, 1999) and *Nurses at the Front: Writing the Wounds of the Great War* (Boston: Northeastern University Press, 2001); Claire Tylee, Elaine Turner and Agnes Cardinal (eds.), *War Plays by Women: An International Anthology* (London: Routledge, 1999) and Angela Smith, *Women's Writing of the First World War* (Manchester: Manchester University Press, 2000).
5 Jane Marcus, 'Corpus/Corps/Corpse: Writing the Body in/at War', Afterword, Helen Zenna Smith, *Not So Quiet . . . Stepdaughters of War* (New York: The Feminist Press, 1989), 241–300; Claire M. Tylee, *The Great War and Women's Consciousness: Images of Militarism and Womanhood*

work on shell-shock and the soldiers, the plight of women as witnesses to violence – particularly of the nurses who were exposed to gruesome wounds – has just begun to be recognised. This chapter examines the relation between testimony, touch and trauma through the writings of the women Owen so uncharitably left out: more specifically, the Voluntary Aid Detachment nurses. While much of recent criticism has fruitfully, if exclusively, employed the category of gender to explore women's relation to the war, I would suggest that the anguish in the nurses' memoirs lies not only in gender difference but in its fraught relation to traumatic witnessing and the limits of empathy: *in the awareness of the incommensurability and absoluteness of physical pain.*

The present chapter and the next examine the experience of the First World War women nurses – the process and the problems of understanding and representing it – through moments of physical intimacy with the male body. These accounts often hint at a hierarchy of horrors: the smell of gas gangrene, for example, causes more distress than the sight of wounds. But it is the shock of actual body contact that forms the tortured core of these nursing memoirs. Brittain writes to her fiancé Roland Leighton in the trenches: 'I don't mind the general butcher's shop appearance, or holes in various parts of people that you could put your fist into, half so much as having to hold a head or a leg for the sister to dress it while the man moans & tries to squirm about'; while another British nurse Irene Rathbone remembers that, while sorting little bones from a raw wound, it was 'sickening' to watch a metallic instrument boring into 'lacerated muscles' but 'to *feel* it [was] almost unendurable'.[6] Beyond the sight and stench of festering wounds lies the horror of inspecting, washing, bandaging or operating on smashed body parts. E. B. Pemberton observes, 'you turn down the blanket to wash an arm

*in Women's Writings, 1914–64* (Basingstoke: Macmillan, 1990); Margaret Higonnet, *et al.* (eds.), *Behind the Lines: Gender and the Two World Wars* (New Haven: Yale University Press, 1987); Higonnet, 'Women in the Forbidden Zone: War, Women and Death', in *Death and Representation* ed. Sarah W. Goodwin and Elisabeth Bronfen (Baltimore: Johns Hopkins University Press, 1993), 192–209, and 'Authenticity and Art in Trauma Narratives of World War I', *Modernism/Modernity*, 9, 1 (January 2002) 91–107. See also Sharon Ouditt, *Fighting Forces, Writing Women: Identity and Ideology in the First World War* (London: Routledge, 1994); Trudi Tate and Suzanne Raitt (eds.), *Women's Fiction and the Great War* (Oxford: Oxford University Press, 1997) and Angela Smith, *The Second Battlefield: Women, Modernism and the First World War* (Manchester: Manchester University Press, 2000).

6 Alan Bishop and Mark Bostridge (eds.), *Letters from a Lost Generation: First World War Letters of Vera Brittain and Four Friends* (London: Little, Brown and Company, 1998), 179–80; Irene Rathbone, *We That Were Young* (1932; New York: The Feminist Press, 1989), 197. Hereafter abbreviated *WTWY.*

and find no arm only a soaking bandage that was once white'.[7] Katherine Hodges North recalls how, during particularly painful operations conducted without anaesthesia, '[I used to] give him my hands to hold' and that 'my hands and arms were sometimes black and blue with bruises from the frenzied grips'.[8] Neither fully assimilated into consciousness nor properly articulated, these moments of physical contact often define the subjectivity of the women, marking their transformation both as witnesses and participants.

The nurses in France and in England recorded their experiences in a variety of ways. As we go through the Women's Work Collection in the Imperial War Museum archives, we come across their letters, diaries, journals, memoirs, short sketches as well as letters and Christmas cards from the soldiers. In one of the letters, Sybil Harry, a nurse, sketches an '**O**' to describe a bullet wound, concluding, 'I never knew they [wounded soldiers] suffered so horribly'.[9] Particularly poignant are the autograph books signed by different wounded soldiers on the eve of their departure: these books form a unique genre where the narrative continuity lies not in the author but in the figure of the addressee. They provide a vivid map of personal networks as well as a formal language that legitimises the articulation of intimacy: the entries vary from sentimental farewells and messages to rather risqué poems and even sketches (Figures 5.1–5.3).[10] Though these autograph books are fascinating in the sheer variety of entries, for a more comprehensive account of the life that produced them as well as for a record of female subjectivity, we have to go back to the writings by the women nurses.

The shattered male body is a central concern during and after the war years. What differing claims do the women make upon this body and how do they write it – with their own bodies responding, recoiling or rarefied – in their texts?[11] I shall argue for the importance of the tremulous, private body of the young female nurse as a way of knowing and representing

7 E. B. Pemberton, Papers, IWM, 83/33/1, 9.
8 Katherine Hodges North, 'Diary: A Driver at the Front', IWM, 92/22/1, 86.
9 Sybil Harry, letter dated 22 October 1914, IWM, 88/41/1.
10 There are scores of these autograph books in the IWM. They contain a range of responses from maudlin sentiments, common quotations such as 'In your golden chain of friendship / Regard me as a link' and jokes to watercolours, cartoons and original verse. Particularly interesting are autograph album of Nurse E. Campbell (IWM Misc. 93 [1386]) and the Nurses' Autograph Book, Malta, 1915–1916 (IWM Misc. 154 Item 2396).
11 For a compelling literary exploration of the bodily degradation the women nurses and ambulance-drivers had to go through – lice, long hours of driving, lack of sleep – see Marcus, 'Corpus/Corps/ Corpses', 241–300.

The longer the War continues the shorter the skirt becomes

Pte E Benstead
1st East York reg[t]
Wounded at Fricourt
on the Somme July 1st
1916

Figure 5.1. A poem and a sketch, 'Two Autograph Albums', Misc. 31, Item 573, IWM (DOC).

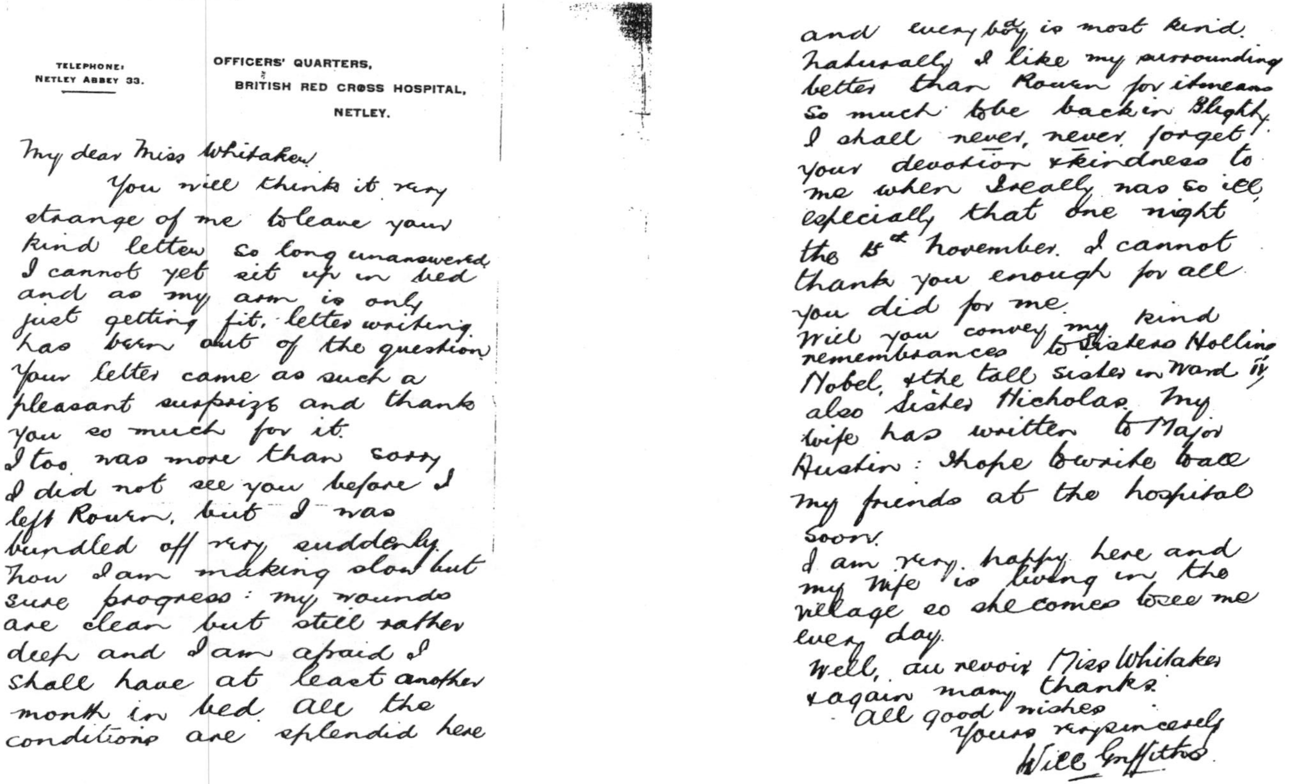

TELEPHONE:
NETLEY ABBEY 33.

OFFICERS' QUARTERS,
BRITISH RED CROSS HOSPITAL,
NETLEY.

My dear Miss Whitaker

You will think it very strange of me to leave your kind letter so long unanswered I cannot yet sit up in bed and as my arm is only just getting fit, letter writing has been out of the question. Your letter came as such a pleasant surprise and thanks you so much for it. I too was more than sorry I did not see you before I left Rouen, but I was bundled off very suddenly but how I am milling about but sure progress: my wounds are clean but still rather deep and I am afraid I shall have at least another month in bed. All the conditions are splendid here and everybody is most kind. Naturally I like my surrounding better than Rouen for I mean so much better back in Blighty. I shall never never forget your devotion + kindness to me when laying so ill especially that one night the 15th of November. I cannot thank you enough for all you did for me. Will you convey to Sister Nellie my remembrance to Sister Nobel, + tell Sister Nicholas. My wife has also written to Major Austin; hope beside the men my friends at the hospital soon. I am very happy here and my wife is living in the village so she comes to see me every day. Well, au revoir [Miss Whitaker] again many thanks. All good wishes Yours sincerely

Figure 5.2. A letter from a soldier-patient to Nurse Ruth Whitaker, Papers, 76/123/1, IWM (DOC).

Last year he lit you cigarette
And as our lips caressing.met
Your smoke was powerless.to disguise
The lovelight in his lingering eyes.
Now he has gone your magic fails
And I, since anxious fear assails
Know. that your power is on the wane
Till he shall light you once again.

Figure 5.3. An entry in an autograph album, 'Two Autograph Albums',
Misc. 31 Item 573, IWM (DOC).

historical trauma. At the same time, these issues raise specific problems
about language and therefore, in the next chapter, I do close readings of
three 'operating scenes' by three women nurses to analyse the relation
between trauma and literary form. In the present chapter, I shall examine
a range of writings – from unpublished letters and diaries written under
the pressure of the moment to memoirs and fictionalised accounts composed at a later date. The aim is two-fold: first, to understand more fully
the hectic tenor of lives, as lived in casualty stations and hospitals; second,
to investigate what the experience of the nurses means for the conceptualisation of trauma and its narratives, particularly at a time when Freud and
Ferenczi were writing on the subject. I start by looking at V.A.D. nursing
during the war.

ACQUAINTANCE WITH GRIEF

If there was a visceral core of secret knowledge about the war, it was *not exclusively* masculine. Consider the preface to *The Forbidden Zone* (1929), a collection of 'fragments' by Mary Borden, an American nurse, who set up her mobile hospital behind the lines in the Western Front:

> I have dared to dedicate these pages to the Poilus who *passed through our hands* during the war, because I believe they would recognize the dimmed reality reflected in these pictures. But the book is not meant for them. They know, not only everything that is contained in it, but all the rest that can never be written.[12]

The terrible knowledge has already 'passed' between fingers: though femininity is partly the hurdle to be 'dared', the gap here is between experience and representation, between touching and seeing, the warm bodies becoming unsubstantial spectres – 'reflected . . . pictures' – as the body is translated into cold print. Borden points to the limits of under-standing, memory and representation ('all the rest that can never be written'), showing an acute awareness of the problems that the trauma theorists have alerted us to in recent years. But the 'hands', engaged in the text and yet locked into the past, also help to bridge the gap as we turn the pages of the book meant for us. Midway through the text, Borden muses: 'How many men had passed through my hands during the last thirty-six hours'?[13] Earlier, she notes, 'You are continually doing things with your hands': cutting off clothes stiffened with blood, washing the edges of festering wounds, amputating gangrenous limbs.[14] The hands are the actual points of contact between war wounds and the female body. And yet the phrase 'passed through our hands' also has a bureaucratic feel: intimacy of gesture is balanced by the professionalisation of service as the patients gradually fade out of the memory of the nurses, often causing feelings of guilt. Almost sixty years after the war, while interviewing octogenarians who served as nurses in the war, the historian Lyn Macdonald writes, 'What comes through most strongly is their remarkable resili-ence . . . "Oh dear, I'm sorry to be so clumsy. It's these stupid stiff fingers of mine." It was an apology I heard literally scores of times as a photo-graph slipped to the floor, or two drops of tea into a saucer.' Macdonald continues, 'The "stupid stiff fingers" were most scarred when they were

---

12 Mary Borden, *The Forbidden Zone* (London: William Heinemann, 1929), Preface, my italics; hereafter abbreviated Borden, *FZ*. *Poilu* refers to the French infantryman. The term, meaning 'hairy', derives from the customary thick whiskers of the soldier.
13 Borden, *FZ*, 168.          14 Borden, *FZ*, 124.

lanced to release the pus from a septic hand.'[15] Gladys Stanford, a First World War nurse, remembers how she got 'a very bad septic hand doing that [dressing], because V.A.D.s [Voluntary Aid Detachment] didn't wear rubber gloves. Only the Sister wore gloves, and if you got the slightest prick it always went septic.'[16] In one of her early diary entries after joining the hospital at Buxton, Vera Brittain comments on the sad state of her fingers, while the nurse-narrator in Irene Rathbone's *We That Were Young* (1932) falls ill from a septic infection in the hand which swells to twice its original size.

The 'our' in Mary Borden's preface is also a footnote to history, stressing female presence and communality within the forbidden zone. Many of the hospital units were close to the actual trenches. The two extraordinary 'Women of Pervyse', Baroness de T'Serclaes and Mairi Chisholm, drove the wounded to the hospitals and tended to soldiers 'laid out on the floors'; the American nurse, Ellen N. La Motte, served in the mobile surgical hospital which was assembled by Borden and was 'situated ten kilometers behind the lines, in Belgium'; Evadne Price (Helen Zenna Smith), in her novel, lays claim to what was usually seen as men's experience when she writes about 'blood and mud and vermin'.[17] Nor did all women escape violence. Mabel Lethbridge was seriously wounded in a munitions factory explosion that killed seventy-one women; Edith Cavell, the Red Cross Nurse who helped Allied soldiers to escape, was court-martialled by Germans and hastily executed in 1915; on 27 June 1918, the hospital ship, Llandovery, was shot at and destroyed, killing fourteen Canadian nurses.[18] A look at the names listed under just the first two letters of the alphabet in the Roll of Honour of British nurses gives one some idea of the considerable death toll among the female nursing community as well.[19]

Though my study focuses on the memoirs of the nurses, it is important to pause and reflect briefly on the experience of civilian women and their written responses. The war records of women, as Tylee notes, often 'tend to be much wider and more subtle in scope than battle-tales'.[20] The war

15 Lyn Macdonald, *Roses on No Man's Land* (Basingstoke: Papermac, 1980), 12.
16 Macdonald, *Roses*, 169.
17 Baroness de T'Serclaes, *Flanders and Other Fields* (London: George G. Harrap, 1964), 46; Ellen N. La Motte, *The Backwash of War: The Human Wreckage of the Battlefield as Witnessed by an American Hospital Nurse* (London: Putnam, 1919), v; Smith, *Not So Quiet*, 59.
18 Women's Work Collection, IWM, BRCS 25.8
19 'British Women's Work During the Great War 1914–1918', IWM 13924.
20 Tylee, *Women's Consciousness*, 13.

becomes a consciousness rather than an event, so central that often it does not need to be mentioned at all. Thus Cynthia Asquith, wife of the Prime Minister and glamorous socialite, writes about taking back 'a hat which made a trench in my forehead . . . hellish morning in pursuit of my summer tweeds . . . sharp skirmish with Harrods'.[21] Or consider the following diary entry of Virginia Woolf for 18 February 1921:

> The most significant sign of peace this year is the sales; just over; the shops have been flooded with cheap clothes. . . . And I have found a street market in Soho where I buy stockings at 1/a pair: silk ones (flawed slightly) at 1/10. . . . Milk is high, 11d a quart. Butter fallen to 3/- but this is Danish butter. Eggs – I don't know what eggs are . . . I think it true to say that during the past 2 months we have perceptibly moved towards cheapness – *just* perceptibly. It is just perceptible too that there are very few wounded soldiers abroad in blue, though stiff legs, single legs, sticks shod with rubber, & empty sleeves are common enough. Also at Waterloo I sometimes see dreadful looking spiders propelling themselves along the platform – men all body – legs trimmed off close to the body. There are few soldiers about.[22]

The transition from silk stockings with the wonderful aside, '(flawed slightly)' – unnecessarily meticulous but yet so essential to the writing of history for Woolf – to 'empty sleeves' uncovers a body of hurt, and of knowledge, as scarred as Borden's. But 'old Virginia' with characteristic appetite takes in everything – even observing that the butter is Danish – exposing history as it impacts the intimate self with its contingent and quirky materiality. Taste, texture, travel all mesh in with Woolf robustly engaging with each: not only an 'empty chatterbox' or a bourgeois consciousness but rather stubbornly resisting prioritisation, the appetite for life and the threnody of loss yoked fiercely at the experiential and linguistic threshold – '*just* perceptibly'. She brings her own body – and the readers' – so close to the surface of her writing through clothes and food that the sudden intrusion of 'single legs, sticks shod with rubber' grates. Pathos is compacted with repulsion – in ways the reader at once empathises and flinches – as the image of the man-spider slowly moves across the fragmented syntax and fixes itself on 'trimmed', a residue in language from the world of clothing evoked a few sentences earlier. Bodies of soldiers become the swathes of cheap clothing sewn up hastily for consumption: the fabric of Woolf's prose becomes her critique. The combination of pathos with repulsion, the involuntary flinching of young

21 Asquith, *Diaries 1915–18* (London: Hutchinson, 1968), 5.
22 Woolf, *The Diary of Virginia Woolf*, II, *1920–24*, ed. Anne Olivier Bell (London: Hogarth, 1978), 92–3.

female bodies before what Brittain calls the 'jarringness' of even healed mutilation becomes very much part of the women's consciousness.[23] This is particularly true in the post-war years, as men such as Clifford Chatterley are sent back to their young wives in 'bits'. In *Bid Me To Live*, Julia complains of the smell of battlefields as she sleeps with her oversexed husband-officer just returned from the trenches; in Mary Borden's 'The Beach', a beautiful young woman is 'tied' to her mutilated husband who 'could never touch her again'.[24]

During the war years, nursing was considered to be woman's best chance to make up for the missed encounter with history that many, like Freud's little Hans, believed had happened only at 'the fwont'.[25] Brittain, on beginning probation work in the local Buxton Hospital, writes in her diary, 'I shall hate it, but I will be all the more ready to do it on that account. *He* has to face far worse things than any sight or act I could come across; he can bear it – & so can I'; in her memoir, she notes, 'I wanted to do the next best thing'.[26] The Voluntary Aid Detachment or V.A.D. Organization was created on 16 August 1909 but it was the First World War that changed its function and public role.[27] On 14 September 1914, two remarkable women doctors, Dr Flora Murray and Dr Louisa Garrett Anderson, left England for France, having assembled Women's Hospital Corps to turn the newly built, luxurious Hotel Claridge into a hospital for the Allied troops. On 1 August 1914, there were 47,196 female Voluntary Aid Detachment nurses and by 1 April 1920, this had swelled to 82,857; in August 1918, the number of women working with the British Expeditionary Force, France was 7,123 while Queen Mary's Army Auxiliary Corps employed 7,808 women.[28] The V.A.D. recruitment campaign conflated class prejudices with the idea of service: it worked on the assumption that upper- and middle-class women, by dint of their 'character' and 'breeding', were more fit to serve and represent the country than working-class women. In fact, there was often tension, even antagonism, between these

---

23 *Testament*, 220.
24 Hilda Doolittle, *Bid Me to Live* (1960; London: Virago, 1984), 39; Mary Borden, 'The Beach' in *FZ*, 48.
25 Freud, 'Beyond the Pleasure Principle', *SE*, XVIII, 16.
26 Vera Brittain, *Chronicle of Youth: Great War Diary 1913–17*, ed. Alan Bishop (1970; London: Phoenix, 2000), 186 (hereafter abbreviated *Chronicle*); *Testament*, 213–14.
27 See Sharon Ouditt, *Fighting Forces, Writing Women: Identity and Ideology in the First World War* (London: Routledge, 1994), 7–46 for an excellent account of V.A.D. nursing. For a more general history of army nursing, see Anne Summers, *Angels and Citizens: British Women as Military Nurses 1854–1914* (London: Routledge, 1988), 237–90.
28 Arthur Marwick, *Women at War 1914–1918* (London: Fontana, 1977), 168.

privileged but relatively untrained V.A.D.s and the professional nurses who worked for a living. In an attempt to erase visible tokens of class as well as to forge a sense of common identity, a rigid dress code was implemented (stiff white and 2⅜ inches deep collars, 3⅜ inches deep cuffs) which often engendered a sense of loss of individuality among the middle-class women, as evident in the writings of both Brittain and Bagnold.

The V.A.D. units drew women who would be identified as the first generation of 'feminists' and many of whom had participated in the suffragette movement. Yet, ideologically, the V.A.D. as an institution was circumscribed within a patriarchal and patriotic mould. 'The daughters are wanted by the Country as well as the sons' wrote Katharine Furse in 'The Ideals of the V.A.D.s'. Thekla Bowser, an Honorary Sister of the Order of St John, wrote:

The highest privilege goes to the man who may fight his country's battles, give his life for his King, risk living a maimed man to the end of his days; next comes the privilege of being of use to these men who are defending us and all we love.[29]

The V.A.D. nurses started their work in France in October 1914. Katharine Furse, the Commandant of the Paddington division, London, left for Boulogne with members from her division on 19 October. In January 1915, Furse came back to England to form the Central V.A.D. Head Quarters Office at Devonshire House, London.[30] Women trained to be genteel Edwardian ladies suddenly found themselves forming a 'curious community of suffering', especially after the Somme battles of July 1916 'in which one is glad to have been allowed to take one's part'. For many women, it signalled emancipation. Katherine Hodges North captures the mood of initial enthusiasm when she writes, 'We were young and to us it was going to be a wonderful adventure' and that it was 'the greatest adventure one could have'.[31] Statements such as these have led Sandra Gilbert to argue that the 'war's "topsy-turvy" role reversals did bring about a release of female libidinous energies' that women found 'exhilarating'.[32] Of course, there was excitement about breaking free from the shackles of the Edwardian home, of being in charge of hospitals and at the new-found sense of female

---

29 Katharine Furse, Women's Work Collection, IWM, BRCS 10/1; Thekla Bowser, *The Story of British V.A.D. Work in the Great War* (London: Andrew Melrose, 1917), 16.
30 These details can be found in Ouditt, *Fighting Forces*, 13.
31 E. M. Spearing, *From Cambridge to Camiers* (Cambridge: W. Heffer, 1917), 59; Katherine Hodges North, 'Diary: A Driver at the Front', IWM, 92/22/1, 3, 23.
32 Gilbert, 'Soldier's Heart: Literary Men, Literary Women, and the Great War', in *Behind the Lines*, ed. Higonnet, 197–226 (212).

communities and service in a man's world. But such exhilaration was usually laced, as North gradually realises, by a sense of horror and helplessness. Brittain likens the grief of a nurse at the death of a patient to the agony suffered by her fiancé, Roland, when losing a comrade in battle.[33]

Knowledge flows across genders not just in silent sympathy but through active service. Ruth Whitaker, a V.A.D. nurse, quotes one of her wounded soldiers, 'You know what I want before I do myself, Sister. What should I do without you?'[34] The vulnerability of the wounded soldiers, their child-like dependence on and attachment to the nurses, are particularly evident from the letters and cards they sent the nurses once they were transferred to other hospitals or were back home. In *The Forbidden Zone* (1929), Borden recasts the hospital as a 'second battle-field': this is where the 'real' battle is fought between the medical staff and their old enemies – death and pain. Boundaries break down: 'We are locked together, the old ones, and I, and the wounded men; we are bound together. We all feel it. We all know it. The same thing is throbbing in us, the single thing, the one life.'[35] And yet, the strident repetition of 'we' as 'one life', cancelling all distance between the soldier and the nurse, shows an over-eagerness to stake a claim on contemporary events whose under-side is moments of isolation and anxiety. After all, in the initial stages of the war, there had been scepticism about the role of women. Katherine Furse, when she arrived in Boulogne, was told: 'women were such a nuisance in war time and who were these odd women in uniform, anyway'; the British War Office told the suffragist Dr Elsie Inglis 'to go home and keep quiet' for the commanding officers 'did not want to be troubled with hysterical women'.[36]

Borden's sentiments are echoed by the male French doctor, Georges Duhamel: 'My fingers have groped in his flesh, his blood has flowed over them, and this creates strong ties between two men'.[37] Like Borden, Duhamel emphasises the bodily intimacy with the patient but there is also a fundamental difference. The strong tie, joining combatant and non-combatant, is here imagined as a homosocial bond to which the woman has no access. Moreover, Duhamel was a doctor, and this changes

33 *Testament*, 176.          34 Ruth Whitaker, 'Memoirs', TS, IWM, 76/123/1, 127.
35 Borden, *FZ*, 147, 155.
36 Katharine Furse, *Hearts and Pomegranates: The Story of Forty-five Years* (London: Peter Davies, 1940), 308; Margot Lawrence, *Shadow of Swords: A Biography of Elsie Inglis* (London: Michael Joseph, 1971), 98.
37 Georges Duhamel, *The New Book of Martyrs*, trans. Florence Simmonds (London: William Heinemann, 1918), 90.

the relationship with the patient's body. At the same time, for the male
medical staff – doctors, nurses and stretcher-bearers – the war experience
was closer to that of the women nurses, not only in relation to combat,
but in terms of the repeated exposure to wounds. Patrick MacGill, who
served as a stretcher-bearer on the Western Front, observes: 'The
stretcher-bearer sees all the horror of war written in blood and tears on
the shell-riven battlefield. The wounded man, thank heaven! Has only his
own pain to endure.'[38] Like the memoirs of the women nurses, the
narratives of the male doctors and nurses – such as Duhamel's *The New
Book of Martyrs* (1918) or Voigt's *Combed Out* (1920) – give graphic
descriptions of war wounds.

As the war progressed and the women proved their indispensability, the
sense of 'oddity' came back at moments not only through patriarchal
resentment or resistance but through an internal awareness of inhabiting
different worlds. The hospital, to Enid Bagnold, was 'alive'; she felt it 'like
a living being' and yet it made her acutely conscious of her status as a
woman and as a witness rather than as a participant: 'It is only I who
wonder – I, a woman, and therefore of the old, burnt-out world'.[39]
Gender that excluded women from battle also threatened to bar them
from a full understanding of the male ordeal. While the act of 'witnessing'
suggests a certain degree of exteriority and detachment, the idea of
'service' is of the order of action and participation. These two categories
are conflated in the nurses' 'testament': these memoirs become a covenant
between marginality and intimacy. These two senses – of at once being at
the periphery and at the centre – are the twin forces driving the nurses'
narratives. The sense of alienation that one detects in the extract from
Bagnold arises not merely from the feeling of being cast-out denizens of
an outmoded past – 'the old burnt-out world' – or through the asymmet-
ries of gender. Both the alienation and the agony spring also from
witnessing the actual debris of the male body at hand, from a realisation
of the gap between the witness and the body in pain.

THE IMPOTENCE OF SYMPATHY

In *The Body In Pain* (1985), Elaine Scarry powerfully argues for the inter-
iority and the absoluteness of physical pain. Having no referential object –
'It is not *of* or *for* anything'– and stubbornly resisting objectification in

38  MacGill, *The Great Push*, 96.
39  Enid Bagnold, *A Diary Without Dates* (1918; London: Virago, 1979), 39, 56.

language, pain is something that can neither be denied nor confirmed. Medical language is a courageous but often an inadequate attempt to coax the language of pain into clarity, and interpret it. Scarry continues:

> Whatever pain achieves, it achieves in part through its unsharability, and it ensures this unsharability through its resistance to language. . . . Physical pain does not simply resist language but actively destroys it, bringing about an immediate reversion to a state anterior to language, to the sounds and cries a human being makes before language is learned.[40]

Enid Bagnold seems to have come to the same conclusion in 1918 when, after nursing the war-wounded in the Royal Herbert Hospital, she writes: 'The pain of one creature cannot continue to have a meaning for another. It is almost impossible to nurse a man well whose pain you do not imagine. A deadlock.'[41] A deadlock in understanding results in a deadlock in representation. Flora Sandes writes about her early nursing experience, 'I used to ask the men where it hurt them, I had often been rather puzzled at the general reply of the new arrivals, 'Sve me boli' ('Everything hurts me')'. Similarly, C. E. Tisdall is haunted by the 'one English word' of her German patient, 'Pain'.[42]

Trench poetry was a rare genre where the body in pain was fluently translated into a lyric voice: the soldier-poet who wrote of 'vile incurable sores on innocent tongues' could and often did die the very next moment.[43] Wilfred Owen, as the previous chapter shows, had an uncanny ability to empathise with bodily pain and transmit it through reflexes of sound. Yet, the appeal of his verse is indissolubly bound up with our knowledge of his ordeal in the trenches, his ability to own the experience he describes. The unique phenomenon of soldier-writers and our aware-ness of their private hell – the weight of historical knowledge – succeed in surmounting an ontological impossibility: to participate in another's physical pain. In prose works such as Remarque's *All Quiet On the Western Front* or Manning's *The Middle Parts of Fortune*, the readers' empathy is largely contingent on the writer's effortless empathy, even identification, with the tragedy of the protagonist: we almost kiss the hand that smells of mortality. In women's writings, empathy becomes a yoke of conscience: we are made to feel the burden of the nurse-narrator,

40 Scarry, *The Body In Pain*, 5, 4.     41 Bagnold, *Diary*, 88.
42 Flora Sandes, *An English Woman-Sergeant in the Serbian Army* (London: Hodder and Stoughton, 1916), 161–2; C. E. Tisdall, 'Memoirs of the London Ambulance Column, 1914–18 by a V.A.D.', IWM, 92/22/1, 30.
43 Owen, 'Dulce Et Decorum Est', in *CP&F*, 117.

of bearing witness to another's pain. Called upon to serve the shattered remnants of the body, the subjectivity of the female nurse is doubly eroded – first, through the gap with the male trench experience and second, through the sheer magnitude of male suffering, an experience that can never be owned by them, either historically or ontologically. Young, healthy and mostly upper-middle class, these V.A.D. nurses experience embarrassment – a rite of shame – before male vulnerability, as in the cries of the men in Evadne Price's *Not So Quiet* or the sight of tears in Enid Bagnold's *A Diary Without Dates*. This is what makes women's war writings often far more depressing and painful than the men's memoirs: the helplessness of the nurse is translated into the haplessness of the witness – and in turn, the reader.

The personal and the subjective, which are so thoroughly denied in Brown's diary entry, later well up in memoirs and narratives:

The feeling of his bare body on my bare arms, his screams, his breath, the odour of blood and the sound of the knife softly passing through the flesh were too much for me. I managed to stand it until the operation was over and then went into the open air and was deathly sick.[44]

Responses in the nurses' narratives tend to be visceral, the body expelling what the mind cannot assimilate. Lesley Smith describes how she nearly fainted while replacing tubes in a pus-ridden shoulder.[45] Yet such moments are repeatedly dwelt on in women's writing, not only because of the acuteness of body memory but to establish some sort of bridge, a physical continuum with the male body and experience. At a deeper level, it is an attempt to redress what Robert Browning, though in a different context, called 'the gaping impotence of sympathy'.[46] This sense of powerlessness is a recurrent theme in the memoir *One Woman's Story* (1934) by Mary Britnieva who served at a hospital near Pilvishki, close to the German Frontier. After witnessing the agony of a dying man, she writes: 'I have never seen anyone dying before and the feeling of my utter helplessness was terrible'. But such experiences are eclipsed as she sees the victims of a gas attack stretched out on a field:

They lay on their backs mostly, their upturned faces terribly swollen and livid – some almost blue – choking and coughing, their bloodshot eyes protruding, unable to utter a word, yet fully conscious, only their eyes and their occasional

44 Ruth S. Farnam, *A Nation at Bay* (Indianapolis: Bobbs-Merrill Co., 1918), 18.
45 Leslie Smith, *Four Years Out Of Life* (London: Allan, 1931), 65.
46 Robert Browning, *The Ring and the Book*, ed. Richard D. Altick (Harmondsworth: Penguin, 1971), Book IX, 458.

spasmodic feeble movements proclaiming the supreme agony that they were enduring. . . . We felt utterly helpless, there was no remedy, we were powerless . . . .[47]

Nothing could be further from Sargent's depiction of the tall, blond heroes in *Gassed*. The account matches in horror, or even exceeds through its testimonial force and graphic details, Owen's description of the gas attack in 'Dulce Et Decorum Est'. In Britnieva's narrative, there is a crushing sense of 'helplessness' on part of the nurse-narrator with which the reader is partly led to identify. Traumatised by what she had witnessed, she is led to repeat her sense of inadequacy once more, as if only endless retelling would enable her to bear the burden of testimony: 'The realization of our helplessness was almost unbearable' (36).

Discussing the relation between pain and testimony, Susan Sontag in *Regarding the Pain of Others* (2003) passionately argues for a pacifist politics to be born out of our affective response to gruesome images of war. She observes, 'Photographs of the mutilated bodies certainly can be used the way Woolf does, to vivify the condemnation of war, and may bring home, for a spell, a portion of its reality to those who have no experience of war at all'.[48] The detailed description of wounds that we find in the nursing memoirs can be said to have a similar political aim: these nurse-narrators may be regarded as some of the first women to employ an affective mode to convince their anticipated audience about the futility of war and convert future generations of readers – 'who have no experience of war at all' – to pacifism. But there is also a fundamental difference. Sontag's aim is to rouse the masses to a political consciousness through photographs, television and journalism. She is thus primarily interested in the transmission of the horrors to people far away from the war zone rather than in first-hand experience; she is curiously silent about the feelings of the photographer or the photographed (she mentions photographs of facial injuries from the First World War). By contrast, it is the rawness of the first-hand encounter – the relationship between the witness and the victim of violence – that is fundamental to our understanding the experience of the nurses. The pain of others as mediated

---

47 Mary Britnieva, *One Woman's Story* (London: Arthur Barker, 1934), 18, 35–6.
48 Susan Sontag, *Regarding the Pain of Others* (Harmondsworth: Hamish Hamilton, 2003), 10. A critique of the United States governmental policy during its invasion of Iraq, Sontag's angry book is a plea for peace and justice, and the strident language overrides some of the ontological problems I have been hinting at, though she is aware of them: 'Let the atrocious images haunt us. Even if they are only tokens and cannot possibly encompass most of the reality to which they refer, they still perform a vital function' (102).

through representation and that encountered first hand are two different orders of experience. In *We That Were Young*, Joan mentions one of her patients, McIvor, whose face had been completely wrecked except the eyes. As she instinctively gaped at him in horror, 'she was always aware, too late, of having registered horror for those pathetic eyes to devour – no doubt wounding his spirit afresh'.[49] It is the perilous intimacy between the nurse and the patient – she watching the wounded men watch her watching their wounds – and her sense of powerlessness and even shame that are key to understanding her trauma.

For the First World War nurses, the fundamental unsharability of the ordeal, and yet the juddering of the senses by knowing and serving the wounded body so closely, leads to a crisis of experiencing: 'She [the nurse] is dead already just as I am – really dead, past resurrection. Her heart is dead. She killed it. She couldn't bear to feel it jumping in her side when Life, the sick animal, choked and rattled in her arms.'[50] If active service at the front was considered the supreme form of sacrifice, nursing – deemed the 'second best' – becomes a more insidious form: a constant emptying out of oneself before great need and greater pain, and yet somehow always falling short. Nausea – the literal flushing out of the body – only adds the shame of 'female fragility' to the torment of incomplete sympathy. In the nurses' accounts, the voice of the server is forever being choked before the absoluteness of physical pain; the youthful female flesh is constantly being made to witness the obscenity of male wounds. Mary Borden writes:

There are no men here, so why should I be a woman? There are heads and knees and mangled testicles. There are chests with holes as big as your fist, and pulpy thighs, shapeless; and stumps where legs once were fastened. There are eyes – eyes of sick dogs, sick cats, blind eyes, eyes of delirium; and mouths that cannot articulate; and parts of faces – the nose gone, or the jaw. There are these things, but no men; so how could I be a woman here and not die of it?[51]

Being woman, being young, becomes an unbearable burden. Female identity can only be salvaged through the bits and pieces of male flesh strewing no man's land. At the end of the war, Vera Brittain had lost all her male companions: her fiancé, her brother and her two closest male friends. Behind the debris of male bodies resonates the desolate cry of the woman: 'But there are years and years in which we shall still be young'.[52] Heads and legs and eyes are not just anatomical parts; they make sense

49 Rathbone, *WTWY*, 201.        50 Borden, *FZ*, 59.        51 Borden, *FZ*, 60.
52 Margaret Postgate Cole, 'Praematuri', in Reilly (ed.), *Women's War Poetry and Verse*, 22.

only in the embodied terrain of learning and hardihood and romance, all of which are destroyed now. The eyes become the twin concentrated points of pain and its inarticulateness. In *All Quiet*, Remarque writes, 'What great misery can be in two such small spots, no bigger than a man's thumb – in their eyes'. In Ellen N. La Motte's 'Alone', a story about the desolation of a dying man, the focus narrows down to the eyes: a red blind one and a dull white one.[53]

In the above extract from Borden, the terrible phrase 'mangled testicles' moves beyond the tightening, the violation and the waste to the absolute crushing of female subjectivity: these mangled 'things', neither human nor yet wholly objects, unmake the fundamental categories of gender and sexual difference that structure the human world: the woman is rendered irrelevant, unwanted. The process of de-individualisation that has started with the starched whiteness of V.A.D. uniforms culminates in the spectacle of the 'vile, incurable' debris of male bodies. As mouths gape open and horror usurps sympathy, the eyes of the witness – sick and delirious – seem almost to be scooped out in some absurd ritual of penance: 'the ghost of a woman – soulless, past redeeming'.[54] Though the nurses did not suffer from mutism or repetitive re-enactments that are usually associated with clinical definitions of First World War trauma, the experiences of the nurses can be said to have a traumatic component in the numbness of their senses at the time of nursing and a retrospective reckoning with what Cathy Caruth calls 'unclaimed experience'. Consider the following accounts from Mary Borden and Vera Brittain, both of whom served amidst horrific conditions and were haunted by their experiences for many years:

I think that woman, myself, must have been in a trance, or under some horrid spell. Her feet are lumps of fire, her face is clammy, her apron is splashed with blood; but she moves ceaselessly about with bright burning eyes and handles the dreadful wreckage of men as if in a dream.[55]

Having become, at last, the complete automaton, moving like a sleep-walker through the calm atmosphere of Millbank, I was no longer capable of either enthusiasm or fear. . . . with the ending of apprehension had come a deep, nullifying blankness, a sense of walking in a thick mist which hid all sights and muffled all sounds.[56]

53 *All Quiet*, 164; La Motte, *Backwash*, 58.     54 Borden, *FZ*, 60.
55 Borden, *FZ*, 151.          56 *Testament*, 458.

Both these accounts were, or perhaps could only be, written a decade after the war; at the time of occurrence, the experience is not fully understood and both writers invoke the trope of 'dream' or 'sleep'. Brittain suffered from repetitive nightmares for ten years after the war. The nursing memoirs provide us, as Higonnet suggests, with 'an alternate history of World War I traumas'.[57] The psychoanalyst Sandor Ferenczi in 'Trauma and Splitting of the Personality' (1932) – written three years after Borden's *The Forbidden Zone* (1929) and a year before Vera Brittain's *Testament of Youth* (1933) was published – notes with reference to one of his patients: 'The unbearable nature of a situation leads to a sleeplike state of mind, in which all that is possible can be altered as in dreams'.[58] This is not to establish any direct link between Ferenczi and the nurses' accounts but to suggest how theories and narratives of trauma resonate with each other at a particular historical juncture. The splintering of the self that Ferenczi writes about is echoed in the nurses' memoirs through fantasies of bodily transformation: Vera Brittain thinks that she is growing 'a beard, like a witch', and 'my hand began, at regular intervals, to steal towards my face'.[59] For both Borden and Brittain, the act of writing becomes a way of ordering experiences. The very titles of these works – *The Forbidden Zone* and *The Testament of Youth* – echo the act of reclaiming their previous selves which, having hovered too long in No Man's Land, have become 'No Women'.

### 'GERMAN SAUSAGE': TRAUMA AND GUILT

The word 'trauma', long in use in medicine and surgery, comes from Greek, meaning 'wound'. The notion of trauma has a primary somatic association but acquired a more psychological meaning when it was employed by J. M. Charcot, Pierre Janet, Alfred Binet, Josef Breuer and Sigmund Freud to describe the wounding of the mind due to sudden and unexpected emotional shock.[60] In an article in *The Lancet* (18 March

57 Higonnet, 'Authenticity and Art', 92.
58 Sandor Ferenczi, 'Trauma and Splitting of the Personality', in *The Clinical Diary of Sandor Ferenczi*, ed. Judith Dupont and trans. Michael Balint and Nicola Jackson (Cambridge, Mass.: Harvard University Press, 1988), 202.
59 *Testament*, 484.
60 See Ruth Leys, *Trauma: A Genealogy* (Chicago: University of Chicago Press, 2000); also see Shoshana Felman and Dori Laub, *Testimonies: Crises of Witnessing in Literature, Psychoanalysis, and History* (London: Routledge, 1992); Caruth, *Unclaimed Experience*; Caruth (ed.), *Trauma: Explorations in Memory* (Baltimore: Johns Hopkins University Press, 1994); Geoffrey Hartman, 'On Traumatic Knowledge and Literary Studies', *New Literary History*, 26, 3 (Summer, 1995),

1916) on 'Neurasthenia and Shell Shock', the writer, referring to its epidemic among soldiers, sadly notes: 'In medicine there is a neutral zone, a no-man's land, a regnum protisticum, which really defies definition. This nebulous zone shelters many among the sad examples of nervous trouble sent home from the front.'[61] The causes of such a state, a previous article reasoned, was not just the result of high explosives or participation in an offensive, but being a witness – often a passive witness – to 'the horrors of the battlefield', to 'the sight of blood, of suffering, and of death'.[62] The nurses, it is important to remember, were by no means exempt from such sights. War trauma or shell-shock can result from witnessing rather than direct participation; another article in *The Lancet* argues that it can affect civilians, even cows.[63] And yet, from both accounts, the figure of the nurse is strangely left out: neither a soldier nor a civilian, she is not granted a place even in this medical 'no man's land'. Entrusted with the repair of minds and bodies the war has ravaged, she is thought to be immune to war trauma. If the nurse falls prey to trauma herself while sifting through her cargo of mutilated flesh, hers is a shame that dare not speak its name.

Freud, in 'Beyond the Pleasure Principle' (1920), while discussing 'traumatic neurosis', attributes it to the 'condition' which occurs 'after severe mechanical concussions, railway disasters and other accidents involving a risk to life': 'The terrible war which has just ended gave rise to a great number of illnesses of this kind'. He continues, 'We describe as "traumatic" any excitations from outside which are powerful enough to break through the protective shield'. The traumatised subject is doomed to '*repeat* the repressed material as a contemporary experience instead of, as the physician would prefer to see, *remembering* it as something belonging to the past'.[64] To Sandor Ferenczi, 'repetition compulsion in the traumatized is a renewed attempt at a *better resolution*'.[65] Much of the recent theorisation of trauma centres upon this compulsion to repeat, but adds to Freud's thesis the problems of cognition, memory, knowledge and

536–63; Dominick LaCapra, *Writing History, Writing Trauma* (Baltimore: Johns Hopkins University Press, 2000); Mary Jacobus, *Psychoanalysis and the Scene of Reading* (Oxford: Oxford University Press, 1999), 124–62.
61 'Neurasthenia and Shell Shock', *The Lancet*, (18 March 1916), 627. Also see Frederick Walker Mott, *War Neuroses and Shell Shock* (London: Oxford, 1919) and Rivers, *Instinct and the Unconscious*.
62 *The Lancet* (4 September 1915), 553.
63 'War Shock in the Civilian', *The Lancet* (4 March 1916), 522; 'Shell Shock in Cows', *The Lancet* (2 February 1918), 187–8.
64 Freud, 'Beyond the Pleasure Principle', *SE*, XVIII, 12, 29, 18.
65 Ferenczi, 'What is "Trauma"?', in *Clinical Diary*, 182.

representation. While Dr Dori Laub goes as far as to say that 'massive trauma precludes its registration' creating a 'black hole' in the consciousness, Cathy Caruth holds that the flashback or re-enactment conveys both '*the truth of an event* and *the truth of its incomprehensibility*'.[66] Traumatic knowledge thus refuses to be assimilated into consciousness or ordinary memory, resisting understanding, figuration or transmission. Can these theories be extended to understand the experience of the nurses as witnesses to horror, or, to put the question differently, what does the experience of these nurses mean for the theorisation about the relationship between trauma and witnessing?

Consider the following two scenes. The first is from the memoir of Maria Luisa Perduca, who was awarded the Silver Medal of Merit of the Red Cross for her nursing service in the war zone and the second from the diary of Katherine Hodges North who served primarily as an ambulance driver:

He placed the tool between the torn limbs and began to saw.
A long crack, a blunt blow, it was over.
That instant penetrated us, our brains, our nerves, our flesh, our spirits, and did not abandon us for many days.
The leg fell by sheer force into the basin placed below, like an object that was dead, finished.
. . .
The stump resembled the trunk of a tree that had been sawn, within which we could see the nerves and the white circle of the marrow.[67]

I had never fainted in my life, but I came nearest to it one morning in the dressing room. I was working with B. on a patient and at the other end of the room a man who had a dreadful head wound was being dressed. The top of his head was split open and his brain was bulging out, suddenly he began to scream, a scream that I soon began to know only too well. I hope I may never have to hear it again. His voice went up into a high thin piercing shrill note, it was inhuman, it was frightful. One realized that it was the sound produced from a human being in a state of agony, which eliminated reason. It was so appallingly dreadful that for a minute or two the room was black and swaying in front of me.'[68]

In the first case, the description of the moment having 'penetrated' the witnessing subject is akin to Freud's notion of traumatic knowledge

---

66 Dori Laub, 'Bearing Witness or the Vicissitudes of Listening', in *Testimony*, 57, 64; Caruth (ed.), *Trauma*, 153–4.
67 Maria Luisa Perduca, 'An Amputation', trans. Sylvia Notini from *Un anno d'ospedale: giugno 1915–novembre 1916* (Milan: Fratelli Treves, 1917, 54–57) in Higonnet (ed.), *Lines of Fire*, 218.
68 Katherine Hodges North, 'Diary: A Driver at the Front', IWM, 92/22/1, 85.

breaking through the 'protective shield' and falling directly on the psyche, and hints at repetitive re-enactments ('did not abandon us for many days'). In the second case, the sudden 'blackness' with the 'swaying' suggests a momentary psychic 'disintegration' during an 'unbearable' encounter that, as Ferenczi noted, helps 'in a diminution of the pain'.[69] The first case involves sight, the second sound; but both seem to touch the body. What is common to both accounts is the remarkably acute corporeal memory: instead of a 'black hole' or a gap in consciousness that is usually associated with the experience of trauma, there is vivid power of recall. The recollection of these moments, set in linear narratives, does not fit either into the angry, fragmented textuality of Borden's *Not So Quiet* or the soothing anaesthetic of Rathbone's *We That Were Young*, the two modes of traumatic retelling that Marcus has uncovered in these respective texts. On the other hand, Higonnet has drawn our attention to the complex relation between an obstructed, specific consciousness of violence and a more philosophic knowledge in the experience and representation of such harrowing moments.[70] A fragmented, elliptical style, as exemplified by *Not So Quiet* or *The Forbidden Zone*, has become the favoured aesthetic form for such narratives. What interests me, in the context of the nurses, is not what is forgotten but what is *remembered*: the ways in which the astonishingly detailed description of wounds can help us to understand – or can even be interpreted as a function of – a particular relation between trauma and witnessing, and may point us to a different form of memory and narrative.

In his discussion of traumatic neurosis, Freud repeatedly stresses the 'factor of surprise, of fright' – he attributed the causation 'not to the effects of mechanical violence but to fright and the threat to life'.[71] He makes a careful semantic difference: '"Anxiety" ["Angst"] describes a particular state of expecting the danger or preparing for it, even though it may be an unknown one. "Fear" ["Furcht"] requires a definite object of which to be afraid. "Fright" ["Schreck"], however, is the name we give to the state a person gets into when he has run into danger without being prepared for it; it emphasizes the factor of surprise.'[72] *Schreck*, to Freud, is usually central to traumatic neurosis. The recent work on trauma has

69  Ferenczi, 'What is "Trauma"?', 181, 182.
70  Marcus, 'Afterword. The Nurse's Text: Acting Out an Anaesthetic Aesthetic' in Rathbone, *WTWY*, 477; Higonnet, 'Authenticity and Art', 101. According to Higonnet, 'The two kinds of consciousness cannot be separated but there is a movement from one to the other in the most creative and powerful of these World War I narratives'. (101).
71  Freud, 'Beyond the Pleasure Principle', *SE*, XVIII, 12, 31.        72  *SE*, XVIII, 12.

focused on its relation to testimony in the context of the Holocaust survivors who were kept in unbearable suspense about their fate. The case of the nurses was different, both from the First World World soldiers and the Holocaust survivors. Though some women ambulance drivers and nurses were exposed to shelling, or infections from the soldiers, and worked amidst horrific conditions, their lives were not usually actively endangered. Does the lack of surprise and the absence of direct threat to one's life modify the psychodynamic structure of traumatic witnessing and account for the detailed body memories of the nurses, set forth with such painful accuracy and articulacy, rather than a blank, a gap, a void? The ordeal of the nurses was usually one of witnessing and helplessness rather than of survival or of any direct 'threat to life'. While the narratives of the soldiers and the survivors are marked by an active 'fright' or *Schreck* – the memoirs of the nurses are marked more by 'anxiety' or 'Angst'. The nurses usually did not suffer from symptoms such as amnesia, mutism or partial paralysis that were widespread among the soldiers but they were also severely traumatised: the 'anxiety', as we have noted in the passages from Brittain, Borden or North, fails to 'protect' the witnessing subject from psychic wounding.[73] After describing some horribly 'smashed up' men she had driven to the hospital, North writes, 'It's difficult to realize how all this is affecting one's point of view. At present I am quite incoherent in my mind. I suppose it will adjust itself in time.'[74] Mrs M. A. A. Thomas mentions the case of 'Miss J' who, after having served the war-wounded in Mesopotamia, had 'taken to the bottle to blot out the memory of her horrible experiences'.[75]

I shall conclude the present chapter by examining an episode from Irene Rathbone's *We That Were Young* (1932) and observing how densely knotted are traumatic witnessing, service and gender in the experience of First World War nursing. Irene Rathbone's *We That Were Young* is a relatively happy text. Joan, the nurse-heroine, is the darling of the ward: she brings a sunny temperament and good cheer. Rathbone's novel is a traditional third-person narrative, beginning with a spring day at Hampstead in 1915 and moving beyond the war and post-war disillusionment to the dream of

---

73  Freud notes, 'In the case of quite a number of traumas, the difference between systems that are unprepared and systems that are well prepared through being hypercathected may be a decisive factor in determining the outcome' (*SE*, xviii, 31–2).

74  Katherine Hodges North, 'Diary', 24. Mary Jacobus notes how trauma narratives are bound to be belated 'both in telling and its meaning retrospective' (*Psychoanalysis and the Scene of Reading*, 134).

75  Mrs M. A. A. Thomas, IWM, 85/39/1.

a League of Nations. In her insightful analysis of the novel, Jane Marcus argues that the nurse in Rathbone's novel is a 'figurative painkiller', 'injecting the reader with a narrative aesthetic meant to function as a soothing anodyne to the reader's memories . . . *Rathbone's writing is an exact mimesis of nursing*'.[76] In spite of the attempt to repress the horrors, Rathbone's novel is nonetheless haunted by sensory memories of gruesome wounds. Every night during her first week in the hospital, Joan dreams about wounds, 'saw them floating before her eyes, almost had the stench of them in her nostrils'.[77] During the day, she would fortify herself with a 'safety-curtain' as she went about her duty; at night, 'the safety-curtain no longer functioning the horror rushed in on her in the shape of dreams'.[78] Joan is traumatised; her nightmares resemble those of the soldiers she nurses but after a week, the dreams cease. Meanwhile, the list of horror continues: with the Somme offensive in July, hideously wounded soldiers pour in. While Joan presents 'the face of gay endurance', the text cannot forget the sight, smell or touch of wounds. The accounts of the injuries are detailed and vivid. There is the description of McIvor, 'the jaw case' who, underneath his dressings, reveals 'flat holes plugged with gauze where a nose had been' and the wounds give off 'an acrid, putrefying' stench. McNeil writhes and screams as Joan sorts out loose bits of bone from his gangrenous limb; she peels the lint, piece by piece, off the body of Little O'Leary, aged nineteen, who has been burnt by liquid fire. And she continues, 'And the next, and the next, and the next. From bed to bed all morning. Lifting and holding mangled limbs.'[79] But Joan does not suffer from nightmares any more: she has triumphed. The safety-curtain has now been drawn even over the penumbra of dreams.

But there is a sudden tear. One evening, Joan is called upon to tend to a ruptured artery that seems fatal: 'She compressed with her two thumbs. . . . *Could* she hold on? Must. Mustn't relax pressure for an instant. Life and death. What did her silly wrist matter? That white face . . . .[80] The patient is saved but Joan develops a septic infection in her finger and runs a high temperature. The nightmares crowd back, but this time in a more personal guise:

---

76 Jane Marcus, 'Afterword. The Nurse's Text: Acting Out an Anaesthetic Aesthetic', in Rathbone, *WTWY*, 476 (467–98).
77 Rathbone, *WTWY*, 195.        78 Rathbone, *WTWY*, 195.
79 Rathbone, *WTWY*, 200, 201, 202.        80 Rathbone, *WTWY*, 235–6.

Her head was becoming worse, and her arm, now swollen to the dimensions of a nightmare German sausage, was causing her a lot of pain. She looked at it with stupid eyes as it lay crimson and tight-skinned on the counterpane. She didn't recognize it. She thought at moments that it must be her leg, which had somehow got outside the bedclothes.

. . .

In a detached way she wondered whether she would mind dying, and found that she wouldn't very much. Half of the youth of the world was dead already; she would be in good company.[81]

This is an intrusion of a traumatic moment into Rathbone's narrative, retelling a moment of physical and psychic wounding. The 'protective barrier' has been perforated as abruptly as the skin of Joan's finger, and with it, the 'anaesthesised' texture of Rathbone's narrative. If psychic disintegration is one of the characteristics of trauma, Joan, in her delirium, has fantasies of bodily fragmentation. As the gramophone from the officer's ward blares out the strains of the popular song of 1916, 'Broken Doll' which gets woven into her dreams, she herself becomes, as it were, the 'ghastly broken doll – half-waxen, half-human' whose arms and legs can be twisted, repaired and interchanged. The nurse as the 'broken doll' becomes an inversion of the image of the nurse in her Pietà-like posture in the popular recruiting poster, cradling her toy-like soldier. What essentially is a reversal of roles, facilitating a process of identification – the nurse in pain, like her patient – is intruded upon by a grotesque image: 'her arm, now swollen to the dimensions of a nightmare German sausage'. Where does this image come from, and what does it mean? Is it a metaphor employed by the narrator or is it spawned out of the fevered consciousness of Joan – or indeed, is it a moment of traumatic recollection that momentarily collapses the boundaries between autobiography and fiction?

Ferenczi, in 'Trauma and Splitting of the Personality' (1932) – written in the same year as Rathbone's text – argues that 'after a shock the emotions become severed from representations and thought processes and hidden away deep in the unconscious, indeed in the corporeal unconscious'.[82] In Joan's delirium, feelings of guilt and shame are dredged up from the 'corporeal unconscious' and grafted onto this all too solid flesh: the heavy, swollen, infected hand. In Joan's fevered consciousness, her fingers become enemy cartridges, digging holes into the soldier's

81 Rathbone, *WTWY*, 238–9.     82 Ferenczi, *Clinical Diary*, 203.

body, adding insult and pain, as in Borden, to injury. The bizarre image shows a tortured relation between the tropes of guilt, service and gender that has otherwise been repressed in the narrative. Abjection – the infected and swollen finger emitting pus – is presented through a food metaphor, the sausage hinting at cannibalism. Gender and political connotations are sharp with reproof. While the guilt, as Marcus has argued, is partly an internalisation 'of the guilt male writers also projected upon the disturbing figure of the nurse', repressing it into the hallucinatory image,[83] there is also the repression of a more immediate experience within the textual unconscious. The 'nightmare' happens after the sudden and painful dressing of Sergeant King. This brings in its wake not only the previous horrors for Joan but the pain she had inadvertently inflicted on the patients while dressing wounds. One of her patients, McNeil, had to shut his eyes and clutch Joan's arm as a little bodkin-shaped instrument started 'probing' into his lacerated muscles: 'to *feel* it [was] almost unendurable'.[84] In Joan's nightmare, acts such as probing, plunging, digging into men's bodies, that one comes across in nurses' memoirs, are not just phallic clichés ('sausage') or a shameful reversal of gender roles: the act is figured as unambiguously hostile, even predatory ('German').

Freud, while discussing the 'compulsion to repeat' even in 'normal' people, recounts two tragic narratives: a woman who nurses her three husbands but each of them dies, and the tragic story of Tancred who, twice by mistake, wounds and kills his beloved.[85] Freud's two examples, while explicating the temporal structure of trauma, also raise fascinating questions about the relationship between intention and inadvertency, witnessing and agency, the wound and the voice. What is common to both stories is an irrational and yet almost inevitable sense of guilt: with the woman, it is her misfortune; with Tancred, misfortune is further compounded with the problem of knowledge on one hand, and active agency on the other. In Rathbone's narrative, Joan does exactly the opposite: a nurse, she saves the life of the patient but her nightmare is infected with the anxious qualms of Freud's hapless woman as well as the remorse of Tancred at his unwitting act of aggression. Is a sense of guilt endemic to witnesses (and ineffectual participants) to trauma,

---

83 Marcus, 'Afterword', in Rathbone, *WTWY*, 492.
84 Rathbone, *WTWY*, 197.
85 Freud, 'Beyond the Pleasure Principle', *SE*, xviii, 22. The story of Tancred has become a site of critical controversy in trauma theory, especially between Caruth and Leys. See Caruth, *Unclaimed Experience*, 1–9; Leys, *Trauma*, 266–97.

and can such guilt be attributed to issues of empathy, survival and responsibility?

As Joan recovers, she realizes that 'there would always be a scar . . . Horrid it would look.'[86] The livid scar forms the basis of her war-ravaged identity. In its exacerbated sense of guilt, the image of the swollen hand as 'German sausage' strikes a discordant note in Rathbone's text and indeed, in the oeuvre of First World War nursing memoirs. The fetishisation of nurses as healers, as angels of mercy and compassion – a tool of state propaganda – was internalised by many nurses including women such as Rebecca West and Irene Rathbone. This feeling was compounded by a sense of satisfaction after a successful operation or after having saved a life. But there were also feelings of guilt and shame resulting from the involvement, voluntary or involuntary, in the nationalist and patriarchal war machine through the institution of nursing. La Motte and Borden openly attack the very ideology of V.A.D. nursing – the men are repaired and re-made only to be sent back to the trenches: 'we send our men to the war again and again, just as long as they will stand it; just until they are dead'.[87] La Motte, Bagnold and Borden debunk the fetishisation of women as healers and expose the complicity of V.A.D. nursing in the carnage. Elizabeth Haldene, a V.A.D. nurse, writes, 'that she who binds up the wounds that war has made has also helped that war to be carried on'.[88] Death becomes a saviour to this endless recycling, an end to pain: in Borden, the nurses become 'conspirators' against the right to die, pointing one towards La Motte's 'A Surgical Triumph' where a blinded and mutilated boy keeps jerking his four stumps and begs: 'Kill me, Papa'.[89] Bagnold writes, 'When one shoots at a man it makes a hole, and the doctor must make seven others'.[90] In Borden, hospitals become the 'second battlefield' so that towards the end of 'Conspiracy', the sound of cannon and the sound of ambulances are fused.

In Virginia Woolf's *The Years* (1937), Peggy and Eleanor pass the statue of the martyred war heroine, Nurse Edith Cavell, shot by the Germans. Eleanor thinks that the only sensible words uttered in the Great War were Edith Cavell's 'Patriotism is not enough'. To the tragedy of the execution, the government added the insult of propagandist commemoration. 'For King and Country' reads the banner at the top, overriding the opposite and original sentiment which is banished to the base of the statue in very

---

86 Rathbone, *WTWY*, 240.     87 Borden, *FZ*, 117.
88 Elizabeth Haldane, *The British Nurse in Peace and War* (London: John Murray, 1923), 3.
89 La Motte, *Backwash*, 155.     90 Bagnold, *Diary*, 90.

small letters.[91] The statue persists, speaking to future generations in this double voice. Similarly, the memoirs of the nurses speak to us in a double voice: the exhilaration of service – of taking part in a man's world and actively moulding the course of history through the remaking of the soldiers – often has as its underside the trauma of the helpless witness. If moments of actual physical contact help the nurses to stake their legitimate claim on history and establish a common ground with the soldiers, the recollection of the traumatic moments also serves as faultlines within the text, marking points of ideological rupture. While the appeal to Christian iconography – one of the most popular posters during the war years was that of the nurse depicted as the Madonna with her Christ-soldier – was a propagandist tool, many women internalised the notion of the nurse as the healer, investing the profession with a certain 'devotional glamour'. In the process, the hands of these devotees, having known the wounds too intimately, could also be marked with stigmata.

91 William Kent's *Encyclopedia of London* reports that 'Patriotism is not Enough' was added to the statue by the Labour Government in 1924 (524).

CHAPTER 6

# The operating theatre

The operating theatre was the place where soldiers were repaired, often broken first in order to be remade. If Borden powerfully recast the hospital as the 'second battlefield', the operating room was the actual venue of this battle: 'The battle now is going on over the helpless bodies of these men. It is we who are doing the fighting now, with their real enemies.'[1] My subject in this chapter is the 'helpless bodies' of both men and women in the operating room, as depicted in the nursing memoirs, in this battle between medical science and the ravages of industrial and chemical weaponry. If the female body was habitually a site of dissection and curiosity for men in late nineteenth-century culture and literature from the operations of Sir Thomas Spencer Well to their depiction in Hasselhorst's *J. C. G. Lucae and His Assistants*, there might seem to be a reversal of gender roles and structures of power in the First World War operating theatre. The mysteries and the workings of the male anatomy were finally disclosed to women who now had the ultimate control over them – except perhaps death. Yet in a world where morphine and anaesthesia were forever in short supply, the 'real' enemy was not death but pain, a 'monster bedfellow' which, as seen in the last chapter, often rendered the nurse 'helpless'.[2] The operating theatre could potentially be a place of excitement, achievement, even power: it was here that women participated most fully in the advance of medical science. Yet it is important to remember that professionally, the position of the women-nurses was subservient to that of the male doctors.[3] The V.A.D. nurses were the archetypal apprentices to medical history as they assisted the doctors, holding the

---

1 Borden, *FZ*, 147.    2 Borden, *FZ*, 61.
3 The number of women doctors and surgeons was low when compared to their male counterparts. A notable exception is the Women's Hospital Corps at Endell Street, run by Dr Flora Murray and Dr Louisa Garrett Anderson, which housed female doctors and surgeons such as Dr Amy Sheppard, Dr Helen Chambers, Dr Rosalie Jobson, Dr Gertrude Gazdar, etc. For details on this hospital, see Dr Flora Murray, *Women As Army Surgeons: Being the History of the Women's Hospital*

patient, removing the soiled dressings or disposing of an amputated limb. For women breaking out of the Victorian household, the operating theatre was the ultimate forbidden zone as the naked male body was laid on the table, ready to be remade in this human factory; it was also the place where young, healthy and educated women became 'the char-women of the battlefield, the cleaners of the worst possible human waste'.[4]

In Mary Borden's short story, 'In the Operating Room', the subjectivity of the nurse, caught between the shrieking patient and the overworked doctors, is thoroughly erased: she is reduced to a carrier of body parts, of knees and lungs and elbows. Flitting in and out of the operating room with her cargo of human organs, the nurse becomes a bodily vehicle catering to the needs of the doctors; she temporarily functions as a human strap or sling as she holds a gangrenous arm or leg while it is being sawed. Or worse:

> There was a man stretched on the table. His brain came off in my hands when I lifted the bandage from his head.
> When the dresser came back I said: 'His brain came off on the bandage.'
> 'Where have you put it?'
> 'I put it in the pail under the table.'[5]

How did the nurses feel, and how did they write their experience, or their seared senses into the experience? And whose bodies did they write about, and in what language, negotiating, as they were, with complex contemporary structures of female freedom and knowledge on one hand, and issues of social shame surrounding the naked male body? Moreover, such descriptions may also record a rupture between the professional ideology of nursing, as evident in the studied detachment of the above passage, and an individual affective response with the weight of personal history, as exemplified in Joan's nightmare in Rathbone's novel. While, in the previous chapter, I have raised some of these issues through a discussion of both archival and literary materials, here I shall explore them further by focusing closely on three 'operation scenes'. These scenes are from prose narratives, all written by women who served as nurses, each text

*Corps in Paris, Wimereux and Endell Street September 1914–October 1919* (London: Hodder and Stoughton Limited, 1920). Dr Murray mentions the prejudice against female doctors (129).
4 Marcus, 'Afterword: Corpus/Corps/Corpse', 245. In Borden's 'In The Operating Room', a short story structured like a play, a surgeon orders the female nurse: 'Take this dead man away, and bring the next abdomen. Wipe that table, mademoiselle, while I wash my hands. And you, there, mop up the floor a bit' (134–5).
5 Borden, *FZ*, 142–3.

belonging to a different genre and written at a different point in time: Vera Brittain's *Chronicle of Youth: Great War Diary 1913–1917* (but published only in 1981), Enid Bagnold's *A Diary Without Dates* (1918) and Mary Borden's *The Forbidden Zone* (1929). In particular, I shall be examining the sensory structure of witnessing, and its relation to female subjectivity and modes of representation.

### BRITTAIN: SERVING ROLAND

On 27 June 1915, an idealistic Vera Brittain – eager to serve – joined the Devonshire Hospital with the acute memory of two kisses. Earlier that year, in January, after a thrilling rendezvous, as Brittain, about to get off the train, extended her hand to say goodbye, her boyfriend Roland 'took it quite collectedly & then suddenly raised it to his lips & kissed it'.[6] A couple of months later, on 18 March 1915, as Roland, now bound for the trenches, mentioned marriage, 'He took my hand and kissed it again as he did in the train once before – but this time there was no glove upon it'.[7] The patriotic idealism of the public school officers in the initial stages of the war could perhaps only be matched by the sexual naivety of their Edwardian ladies: to quote Larkin, 'Never such innocence again'.[8] If the gloves were the sign of the 'mental flannel' that bound women of a particular class to their Edwardian homes, as Tylee has argued,[9] the new gloves this sixteen-year-old girl who had just secured a place at Oxford was called upon to wear were the 'self-protective callousness' of the nursing profession.[10] And yet initially, as with fighting itself, there was enthusiasm. 'Behold, a new experience beginneth' starts the diary entry for Sunday, 27 June, as Brittain starts working at the Devonshire Hospital. Listing the patients attended to and the duties performed, the entry concludes with a sudden rush of emotion: 'Oh! I love the British Tommy! I shall get so fond of these men, I know. And when I look after any one of them, it is like nursing Roland by proxy. Oh! if only one of them could be the Beloved One!'[11]

---

6 Brittain, *Chronicle*, 148. In *Testament* (1933), the incident is remembered somewhat differently: 'With sudden vehemence he pressed it [hand] against his lips, and kept it there until the train stopped' (123).
7 *Chronicle*, 160.
8 Philip Larkin, 'M C M X I V', in Michael Schmidt (ed.), *The Harvill Book of Twentieth-Century Poetry* (London: The Harvill Press, 1999), 395.
9 Tylee, *Women's Consciousness*, 47–74. See also Paul Berry and Mark Bostridge, *Vera Brittain: A Life* (London: Chatto & Windus, 1995).
10 *Testament*, 176.
11 *Chronicle*, 215.

Eighteen years later, the patriotic and religious ardour is tempered as the emotions are revisited and examined with maturity and hindsight:

In the early days of the War the majority of soldier-patients belonged to a first-rate physical type which neither wounds nor sickness, unless mortal, could permanently impair, and from the constant handling of their lean, muscular bodies, I came to understand the essential cleanliness, the innate nobility, of sexual love on its physical side. Although there was much to shock in Army hospital service, much to terrify, much, even, to disgust, this day-by-day contact with male anatomy was never part of the shame. Since it was always Roland whom I was nursing by proxy, my attitude towards him imperceptibly changed; it became less romantic and more realistic, and thus a new depth was added to my love.[12]

There is a complex entanglement of the tropes of sexual knowledge, patriotic service and personal history. In 'Patriarchal Thought and the Drive for Knowledge' Toril Moi, following one of James Strachey's translations of Freud's term *Wisstrieb* (literally 'know-drive'), powerfully puts forward the concept of 'epistemophilia'.[13] The body within the field of vision and touch is *par excellence* the object both of knowing and desire, knowing as desire, desire as knowing. For a woman of Vera Brittain's class and generation – educated, curious but sheltered, having 'never looked upon the nude body of an adult male' – nursing becomes an exercise in the demystification of the male body: 'I still have reason to be thankful for the knowledge of masculine functioning which the care of them gave me, and for my early release from the sex-inhibitions'.[14] The candour is disarming.

In *Girls Growing up in Late Victorian and Edwardian England* (1981), Carol Dyhouse notes how young middle-class women were usually kept ignorant about sexual matters. Often educated at home and segregated from men, they were brought up on a regime of purity and virtue where the body and its functions were causes of shame: menstruation was a secret pollution and sex was considered to be degrading.[15] G. Stanley Hall, an influential writer on female adolescence, suggested in his enormously popular *Youth: Its Regimen and Hygiene* (1906) that young girls should

---

12 *Testament*, 166.
13 Toril Moi, 'Patriarchal Thought and the Drive for Knowledge', in *Between Psychoanalysis and Feminism*, ed. Teresa Brennan (London: Routledge, 1989), 198–9.
14 *Testament*, 166.
15 Carol Dyhouse, *Girls Growing Up in Late Victorian and Edwardian England* (Routledge: London, 1981), esp. the chapter titled 'Adolescent Girlhood: Autonomy Versus Dependence', 115–38.

ideally be sent to institutions 'in the country in the midst of hills', away from the male sex, 'the callow, unripe youths' of their own age.[16] They needed to be protected all the more, Hall contended, once they have crossed the 'Rubicon of Menstruation'.[17] Coming from a sequestered upper-middle-class background, Brittain however shows little alarm, shock or shame. Nursing, for her, becomes a ritual in reclaiming the male body and its parts: phrases such as 'essential cleanliness' and 'innate nobility' resituate the male body within the same discourse of purity and cleanliness which had been used against it, revealing at once her investment in and modification of contemporary ideology. There is an anxious attempt to separate physicality from sexuality, the aesthetic from the erotic. On one hand, there is an unabashed appreciation of the 'first-rate physical type', reminding one of her frank admiration of the 'dark & good-looking' patient on her very first day at the hospital.[18] But any suggestion of inward 'impropriety' or outward 'shame' is countered by an appeal to what she later calls the 'sacred glamour' of nursing, which she embraces with 'the fervour of a religious devotee'.[19] And yet, the very conceptualisation of service – nursing Roland 'by proxy', the only phrase that survives from the diary into the memoir, revealing its enduring value for Brittain – goes precisely against the ethic of impersonal appreciation and selfless sacrifice that such an innocent aside is meant to exemplify. If the wounded soldiers bring home the vulnerability of Roland, how does such vicarious enjoyment of Roland's body in turn affect the daily 'handling' of the 'lean, muscular bodies'?

Vera Brittain's war diary (1913–17) which she twice contemplated publishing under the title, 'A Chronicle of Youth', first in 1922 and then again in 1938–9 – and which was published only after her death in 1981 – forms the basis of her autobiography, *Testament of Youth*. The war diary is usually read as a growth of the soul through a vale of tears but it is also an intimate account of a young woman discovering her body as it encounters love and war and desolation. The middle section covers the period between the pre-war literary idyll and the post-Roland benumbment. The horrors of war wounds to which Brittain was exposed during these months – as her letters and autobiography tell us – are usually repressed in

---

16  Stanley Hall, *Youth: Its Regimen and Hygiene* (New York: Appleton, 1906), 309, 295.
17  Stanley Hall, *Educational Problems* (New York: Appleton, 1911), 11, 33.
18  *Chronicle*, 214. The language Brittain uses about the male body would now be perceived as disturbing if used by a male nurse or doctor about a female patient, compromising, as it does, the status of the nurse as the 'chaste servant'.
19  *Testament*, 210, 174.

the diary, pared down to minimal comments: 'Another strenuous day' or 'The same as usual – even in its disappointments'.[20] Instead, lovingly enclasped in the central section, lies the lingering entry – the longest in the diary, stretching to over ten pages – for Sunday, 22 August 1915, as a tumultuous Brittain takes an after-dinner walk with Roland, on leave from the trenches. The moonlit sea, the darkness, the heather and the gorse – all crossed by the shadow of the war – induce a rare moment of tenderness. Roland takes Brittain in his arms – 'closer than I have ever been before' – playing with her hair and finally kissing her on the mouth. She recalls, 'There, on that dark heather-covered cliff beside the sea, I realised the depth & strength of my own passion – realised it & was afraid'.[21] The phrase, 'heather-covered cliff', with its echo of Heathcliff in *Wuthering Heights,* reveals how close the literary and the intimate were intertwined for the young Brittain and hints at the emotional turbulence of the encounter. The war revealed and legitimated this brave new world, only to reduce the object of desire to fits of remoteness – an occasional letter from the trenches – and instead leaving her, now a V.A.D. nurse, with a daily crop of mangled flesh. Roland, as he goes back to the trenches, becomes a phantom of the mind: 'Do I seem very much of a phantom in the void to you?'[22] Yet, at other moments, he is an over-whelming physical presence: 'Often I have to press my fingers tight into my hand when I recall the feel of his arm around me' or 'each time I recall anything it means a sharp pain – like a knife-stab . . . I have to clench my hand tight so as to bear it'.[23] The months of October and November 1915, when the diary entries are 'nearly mad with longing for him, I wanted him so',[24] are also incidentally the months of her exposure to the most ghastly wounds. Even after fifteen years, she vividly remembers dressing a gangrenous leg wound, 'slimy and green and scarlet, with the bone laid bare'.[25]

Horrific accounts of war wounds that dot the letters and autobiography are comparatively scarce in the war diary. Instead, her diary is a lover's discourse amidst the war, a private, nocturnal space where she remembers, reimagines and resurrects the warm body she had known amidst the heather-covered cliff: 'the silkiness of his fair moustache', 'the recollection of his kisses, his touch', 'the merest remembrance of his touch', 'Roland in the flesh', 'to hold & kiss & worship him once more' or 'a desperate

20 *Chronicle,* 222, 216.    21 *Chronicle,* 256.    22 *Testament,* 216.
23 *Chronicle,* 269, 275.    24 *Chronicle,* 290.    25 *Testament,* 211.

longing to see and touch him'. Privileging touch over the other senses as the most archaic and subtle mode of perception, the French feminist, Luce Irigaray, links the gesture of the caress to the regeneration and fecundity of life, to a love given over to the night 'where things have not yet taken their places but remain possible'.[26] Touch, to Irigaray, is a perpetual reaffirmation of palpable flesh as well as a participation in its transmutability:

Before orality comes to be, touch is already in existence. No nourishment can compensate for the grace or work of touching. Touch makes it possible to wait, to gather strength, so that the other will return to caress and reshape, from within and from without, a flesh that is given back to itself in the gesture of love. The most subtly necessary guardian of my life is the other's flesh.[27]

Is Brittain's obsessive harping on the desire to *touch* Roland the yearning of the amorous subject – the need 'to wait, to gather strength' – or is it related in complex ways to the daily 'handling' of mutilated flesh? During the day, she would often dress unaided a 'newly amputated limb' and at night, she would dream of Roland 'holding my hands to warm them as you did on the cliff that evening'.[28] Can longing so effortlessly translate itself to dream-thoughts completely unscathed by the harrowing residues of the day? Or, does physical revulsion induce a reciprocal need for physical union, even erotic contact, as if only the coming together of healthy bodies in a context of wholeness and pleasure could soothe the daily assault on the most intimate of human senses? In a festering atmosphere of physicality, the imagined touch of Roland becomes a reclaiming of her own body, subjectivity and youth, 'the most subtly necessary guardian of my life'.

In *No So Quiet*, the ambulance driver 'Nell' sleeps with the young, healthy Robin to stave off the procession of maimed soldiers across her mind just as the four comrades in Smith's Ur-text, Remarque's *All Quiet on the Western Front* visit prostitutes not so much for erotic gratification as for bodily reassurance: 'And if I press ever deeper into the arms that embrace me, perhaps a miracle may happen. . .'.[29] In Brittain's case, every fresh wound she nurses injects her own distress with fear about Roland's safety. In the initial entries of the diary, she prays that Roland should get a 'desirable' wound that would transport him back to her; but as the war

---

26　Luce Irigaray, *An Ethics of Sexual Difference*, trans. Carolyn Burke and Gillian C. Gill (London: The Athlone Press, 1993), 197.

27　Irigaray, *Ethics*, 187.　　　28　*Testament*, 216, 222.　　　29　Remarque, *All Quiet*, 131.

continues and the wounded flood in, an increasingly anxious Brittain hopes that Roland goes through the war 'unscathed'.[30] The repeated fondling of Roland through language, infusing him with the warmth she had known among the heather and the gorse, seems a desperate attempt not just to safeguard her own emotional well-being, as with Remarque's soldier or Smith's driver, but rather to serve as an amulet against Roland's injury or death, the guardian of *his* life as well.

This vertiginous movement between abjection and desire, the shattered ruins of the battlefields and the longing for that one perfect body, becomes evident in a grief-crazed entry after the death of Roland:

I got back just in time for a small operation in the ward – the cutting of an abscess in Holland's thigh. It was an extremely minor operation but rather messy. I had never seen even anything so small before, but such things never seem to affect me physically at all. All I had to do was to hold the hand lamp, as someone had to hold it, & was thus saved from the embarrassment of handling instruments etc. But all the time my mind was with that operation at Louvencourt; it was Roland I saw struggling under the anaesthetic with His beautiful eyes closed and his sturdy limbs all helpless; it was from Roland's wound that I saw the blood pour out in a scarlet stream. . . . So I was glad it was soon over.[31]

The social 'embarrassment' of touching the naked male body – of 'handling instruments etc.' (does 'etc.' mean the male organ?) – is acknowledged but soon subsumed within a transformative vision. What we note instead is an extraordinary process of transfiguration where the public body of service and the private body of longing – so carefully kept separate – suddenly come together. Holland and Roland, the names chiming so closely, are united under the numbing anaesthesia of a religious aesthetic: Christ pouring out 'the red, sweet wine of youth', a line endlessly exchanged between Vera and Roland. The wrought prose blurs the distinction between the literal and the figurative; for that fleeting moment there is a hallucinatory intensity about her vision brought out through the anaphoric structure ('It was Roland . . . it was from Roland's wound'), though she is almost immediately aware of the fact that it had been in her mind's eye, a daydream.

In *Testament of Youth*, Brittain speaks of a dream that would recur for ten years where Roland would be without an arm or leg or horribly disfigured – 'But always he was alive, and within range of sight and touch'.[32]

---

30 *Testament*, 220.  31 *Chronicle*, 322.  32 *Testament*, 273.

'We are helped in these difficult matters', writes the psychoanalyst, Winnicott, 'by remembering that hallucinations are dream phenomena that have come forward into the waking life and that hallucinating is no more an illness in itself than the corresponding fact that the day's events and the memories of real happenings are drawn across the barrier into sleep and into dream formation.'[33] Horror, in her dream, acts as a protective screen as images of mutilation are culled from the nurse's world to deny the reality of the beloved's death, the complete vanishing of his body. As the dream-thoughts – themselves the day's residues – pass back into the light of the common day, they are harnessed to the contingency of the waking, indeed working, moment: Brittain's fantasy is one of substitution rather than of vision, built on the simultaneous acknowledgement and denial of death. The minute nature of the wound and the physical proximity of Brittain to the body being operated on make the experience acutely haptic. The diary entry moves through the wavering capitalisation of His/his where Holland-Roland is at once the dead soldier/Christ and a patient etherised upon the table, struggling under chloroform. If wish-fulfilment was one of the chief forces behind dreams and hallucinations, her fantasy, though obsessive, is by no means perverse: it shows the need of the amorous subject to create *meaning* in order to survive. For at its core lies not just loss but the precipice of non-meaning.

Roland, the brilliant schoolboy, did not die leading a glorious charge but was sniped at in the dark while mending barbed wire: shot in the abdomen, the death was painful and messy in a clearing station where he had to be dosed with morphine. Even in 1933, at the time of writing *Testament of Youth*, after the absurdity of the war had sunk in, Brittain could not still get over the essential ignominy of the moment: 'Oh, my love! – so proud, so confident, so contemptuous of humiliation, you who were meant to lead a forlorn hope, to fall in a great fight – just to be shot like a rat in the dark! . . . Dearest, why did you, why did you?'[34] The visionary moment in the above operation scene is a desperate attempt to grasp and transform a moment of humiliation that would never be fully known and yet would forever haunt: for Vera to survive, Roland must still be adored, and for Roland to be adored, the moment must be redeemed. The war, at this stage at least, must still be believed in: Roland had died

33 D. W. Winnicott, 'Creativity and its Origins', *Playing and Reality* (1971; Harmondsworth: Penguin, 1974), 78.
34 *Testament*, 243.

for it, her brother Edward was still fighting and she had disrupted her studies at Oxford to serve the 'British Tommies'.

When so much was at stake and the mind still incredulous – and there was a young soldier on the operation table bleeding just as Roland must have done – could the grief-crazed young mind not perform a perceptual sleight of hand, a mere substitution of bodies? If reality told a different story, fantasy must be summoned to fashion the Madonna-Pietà image and assimilate loss into a transcendent, religious aesthetic of service and sacrifice. The professional and the personal are inextricably interlocked as the amorous subject – now in her nurse's role – is called upon to serve the adored object at its most vulnerable moment: this is the supreme fantasy of *service*. The wound on which this fantasy culminates is love's wound as well as war's but the affective source remains firmly embedded within a strong religious tradition of images and affect. At the centre of this tradition is the young male body on the Cross, the wound in that body, the pain in that wound: the mark of reality and redemption. Religion, love and war are fused and confused in Brittain's fantasy which, like that one drop of Christ's blood at the end of Marlowe's play, can redeem 'the horror! the horror!' of so dreadful a death. It is also a curiously *intimate* scene: the lover can only be known fully when he is not conscious, the wound is fetishised. Brittain's letters are obsessed with the essential un-knowability of Roland, 'a brilliant, incomprehensible & elusive person' whose reality is forever in question. In the last few months in the trenches, Roland had stopped communicating with Brittain; in his last few hours, he had not even mentioned her name, something she could not come to terms with: 'I had learnt all that there was to know, and that in his last hour I had been quite forgotten'.[35] Roland Barthes, as I noted in Chapter 4, writes of modern subjectivity in relation to the wound within a shared Christian tradition: 'where there is a wound, there is a subject: *die Wunde! die Wunde!* says Parsifal, thereby becoming 'himself'; . . . ('The wound. . . is of a frightful intimacy').'[36] A fantasised glimpse into Roland's wound ('it was Roland I saw. . .it was from Roland's wound') becomes a pitiful attempt to gain an insight into the ineluctable mystery of the beloved and to reclaim their love, not just cruelly cut short but almost denied in the final hour, through a moment of 'frightful intimacy'.

Brittain's diary is remarkable in the way it constructs woman as the tragic subject of the war: instead of a 'chronicle', it is an intimate account

---

35 *Testament*, 287, 244.     36 Barthes, *A Lover's Discourse*, 189.

of the self, drawing the reader into its inner world as fully as the war memoirs of Robert Graves or Siegfried Sassoon. The operation scene remains a classic example of how Brittain, through the intensity and weight of personal history, would powerfully relocate the tragedy of the war. Away from the battlefields, the war is placed not even in the wounds of the male body but in the bereaved, hallucinatory consciousness of the woman. The patient is thoroughly subsumed into the nurse's fevered consciousness that causes a breach in the very ethics of nursing as well as in the genre of chronicle-writing and yet the reader suspends judgement, completely engrossed by the nurse's story. This is indeed a unique moment in nurses' memoirs and its peculiarity stands out if we compare it with another 'operation scene' – from Enid Bagnold's *A Diary Without Dates* (1918), a book that caused a furore on its publication. If Brittain's account privileges the subjectivity of the nurse almost at the cost of the materiality of the body at hand – like the nurse, the reader also tends to forget Holland – Bagnold's diary records the reverse process.

### BAGNOLD: THROUGH GLASS DOORS

In January 1918, Virginia Woolf wrote to Vanessa Bell, 'Did you ever meet a woman called Enid Bagnold – would be clever, and also smart? . . . She has written a book, called, as you can imagine, 'A Diary Without Dates', all to prove that she's the most attractive, and popular and exquisite of creatures.'[37] Woolf's refusal to review *A Diary Without Dates* did not lessen its impact on publication. Fifteen thousand copies were produced. Bagnold worked as a nurse at the Royal Herbert Hospital at the foot of Shooters Hill, a 700-bed mid-Victorian institution. The Herbert had been built in the wake of Florence Nightingale's experiences in the Crimea and named after her staunch friend and supporter, Lord Herbert of Lea. On the publication of *Diary*, Bagnold was immediately dismissed from the hospital for breaching military discipline. However, Lady Cynthia Asquith wrote in her diary on 28 March 1918, 'I read *A Diary Without Dates* – wonderfully gripping, pitiless and true, and so vividly written. [Robert] Nichols says it is the only good English thing of the war – bar Siegfried Sassoon.'[38]

---

37 Virginia Woolf, quoted in Anne Sebba, *Enid Bagnold: The Authorised Biography* (London: Weidenfeld & Nicolson, 1986), 61.
38 Cynthia Asquith, *Diaries 1915–18*, 425.

The personal history that freights every sentence in Brittain is conspicuous by its absence in Bagnold's work and yet, it is the central impetus behind the book. If Brittain's *Chronicle Of Youth* is, in some ways, a tribute to the memory of Roland, Bagnold's *A Diary Without Dates* was originally written for the handsome Romanian-French aristocrat, Prince Antoine Bibesco, with whom Bagnold was in love. Bagnold's memoir was culled from letters written to the Prince when she was working as a V.A.D. nurse at Woolwich. 'To that friend of mine', the dedication reads, 'who, when I wrote him endless letters, said coldly, "Why not keep something for yourself!"'[39] In the pre-war years, Enid Bagnold – young, beautiful and sophisticated – was a London socialite, part of the artistic bohemian circles of W. R. Sickert, Frank Harris and Henri Gaudier-Brszeska. The meeting with Prince Bibesco was a turning point in her life: rechristened by Antoine as 'Virgilia' for her talent in verse, she was at once strongly drawn towards and distressed by the 'detached elusiveness' of this French aristocrat who had known Proust and Liszt. Antoine had made the terms of his affection very clear: 'Don't care for me too much; it's no use. Besides does it not stop you from getting married?'[40] While Bagnold wanted love, Antoine saw his role in her life as a literary instigator: 'Your letters are brilliant', he told her. 'But really, don't scatter yourself. Believe me, either passion or love . . . There is only one way – steady continuous work.'[41] Passion, thwarted in real life, flows into art: literary success, Bagnold believed, could help her win back the errant prince. Inscribed on the first page of her *Reflections of a V.A.D.*, specially illustrated and bound for Bibesco, are the words: 'These are letters I might have written you'. Yet these personal letters are sharp with political overtones.

Bagnold called the first two sections of her diary 'Inside Glass Doors': glass doors expose what lies behind and yet always create distance, at once revealing and sealing off adjacent worlds. Strangely clinical, laying bare and resisting contact at the same time, they convert private places to public spaces. What comes across powerfully in the text is a sense of isolation, and a deep frustration at the professional bar on intimacy between soldiers and nurses. This lack of personal interaction is inscribed through Bagnold's prose into the relationship between the reader and the narrator: the disjointed narrative and objective tone, in sharp contrast to Brittain or Rathbone's war memoirs, actively resist the readers'

---

39 Bagnold, *Diary*, dedication page.  40 Sebba, *Bagnold*, 53, 58.
41 Sebba, *Bagnold*, 58.

empathetic involvement in the activities of the hospital. Her detached narrative becomes her critique of the impersonal ethic of nursing. The very short paragraphs, with their temporal shifts and flitting from subject to subject, mimic the distraction of this young nurse as she walks down the long corridors, looking at the patient-filled wards on either side through glass doors. To her, the hospital is a place where 'a patient may be washed, fed, dressed but not talked to':[42] they come and go, an endless succession of bodies behind glass doors. In Borden's account, sympathy is habitually checked rather than enlarged in the actual practice of nursing:

But we forgot to talk of it to Corrigan. The needle was into his shoulder before he knew why his shirt was held up.

His wrath came like an avalanche; . . . Sister shrugged her shoulders and laughed; I listened to him as I cleaned the syringe.

I gathered that it was the indignity that had shocked his sense of individual pride. 'Treating me like a cow. . .' I heard him say to Smiff [. . .][43]

Given her range of sympathy for the patients and the way the scene unfolds, what comes across is in fact resentment at the 'indignity' meted out to a human subject: 'Treating me like a cow'. It is the ruthless professionalisation of the trained nurses that is exposed by Bagnold through the ritual desecration of the male body: 'there are no individual-ists now; his "system" belongs to us'.[44] The dehumanisation of the male body that had begun in the trenches culminates in the hospital wards. What she finds so difficult to accept is that an institution that is founded on the vulnerability and service of the body should be so wholly closed to the worlds of hurt it contains as well as to individual dignity or need. Resentment wells up against the emptiness of words, emotions and gestures. 'There you are, Sonnie, it's almost finished. . .' parrots the sister-in-charge as a seventeen-year-old boy groans in agony, while the narrator is asked to 'Run along and do the sympathetic V.A.D. touch!'[45] Bagnold's critique of the institution of nursing culminates in the description of an operation, in the exactness of its details:

Waker is not everything a man should be: he isn't clever. But he is so very brave.

After his tenth operation two days ago there was a question as to whether he should have his pluggings changed under gas or not. The discussion went on between the doctors over his bed.

42 Bagnold, *Diary*, 74.    43 Bagnold, *Diary*, 86–7.
44 Bagnold, *Diary*, 87.    45 Bagnold, *Diary*, 82.

But the anaesthetist couldn't be found. . . .

It was all very fine for the theatre people to fill his shoulder chockful of pluggings while he lay unconscious on the table; they had packed it as you might stuff linen into a bag: it was another matter to get it out.

I did not dare touch his hand with that too-easy compassion which I have noticed here, or whisper to him, 'It's nearly over. . .' as the forceps pulled at the stiffened gauze. It wasn't nearly over.

Six inches deep the gauze stuck, crackling under the pull of the forceps, blood and pus leaping forward from the cavities as the steady hand of the doctor pulled inch after inch of the gauze to the light. And when one hole was emptied there was another, five in all.

Sometimes, when your mind has a grip like iron, your stomach will undo you; sometimes, when you could say 'To-day is Tuesday, the fifth of August,' you faint. There are so many parts of the body to look after, one of the flock may slip your control while you are holding the other by the neck. But Waker had his whole being in his hands, without so much as clenching them.

When we had finished and Sister told me to wipe the sweat on his forehead, I did so reluctantly, as though one were being too exacting in drawing attention to so small a sign.[46]

What makes the above passage so very difficult – almost impossible – to read is the relentless precision of facts without any emotional outlet. We emerge from the passage, harrowed. Whether due to the huge number of the war-wounded resulting in severe under-staffing or medical callousness, a single sentence, 'The anesthetist couldn't be found', changes Bagnold's operation scene from that of Brittain more fundamentally than the burden of the latter's personal history. Holland was unconscious; Waker is writhing, defiantly alone in a world of pain. If Brittain's account shows the self-absorption of the mourning subject where the personal completely takes over, the absoluteness of Waker's pain defies any subjective response.

Written and published during the war, Bagnold's *A Diary Without Dates* was more actively political than most of the other nurses' memoirs. The abstract heroism of the war is here being weighed against the reality of physical pain; the impersonality of death statistics is tested against the suffering individual body; the image of the nurse as the bedside Madonna is exploded through shocking examples of medical callousness. The above passage continues to haunt writings on the war: it is quoted by David

---

46 Bagnold, *Diary*, 122–3.

Mitchell in *Women on the Warpath: The Story of the Women of the First World War* (1966), by Claire Tylee in *The Great War and Women's Consciousness* (1990) as well in the two recent anthologies: Agnes Cardinal's *Women's Writing on the First World War* (2000) and Angela Smith's *Women's Writing of the First World War: An Anthology* (2000). Always quoted, it is hardly ever commented on, as if the scene resists an articulated response: the critical silence strangely mirrors that of the witness. Even a critic as sensitive and alert as Tylee is curiously reticent about the passage: 'Her admiration is typical of the tribute paid by women to the men they helped'.[47] Waker's pain seems to confront us with one of the central problems of both frightful witnessing and representation: the limits of sympathy and language.

The wound makes external what is ineluctably internal and private: to see the wound is to feel the pain. Elaine Scarry writes, 'Physical pain is not identical with either agency or damage but these things are referential . . . the nail [is not] identical with the sentient experience of pain; and yet because it has shape, length, and colour, because it either exists (in the first case) or can be pictured as existing (in the second case) at the external boundary of the body, it begins to externalize, objectify, and make sharable what is originally an interior and unsharable experience.'[48] The detailed, often gruesome, description of wounds that one finds in nurses' memoirs is not only prompted by the weight of memory but is also an attempt to transmit the pain. In the short sketch, 'Alone', Ellen N. La Motte describes how 'into the deep, yawning wound, they put many compresses of gauze, soaked in carbolic acid, which acid burned deep' while Irene Rathbone writes about 'two pieces of rubber tubing' jabbed into 'a large area of raw flesh' for drainage purposes.[49] Bagnold similarly uses a structure of bodily damage and agency to break through the representational crisis and convey Waker's pain: the verb 'crackling' combines both sound and texture, especially when produced 'six inches deep'. The witnessing body registers the horror through haptic vision as forceps 'pull' out 'stiffened' gauze from the six-inch-deep wounds, five in all. Penetration into Waker's body becomes a penetration into the readers' consciousness, only to leave us, like the nurse, with 'the gaping impotence of sympathy' that we have noticed in the previous chapter. Bagnold quietly grounds language in the graphic materiality of the

---

47 Tylee, *Women's Consciousness*, 192.          48 Scarry, *The Body in Pain*, 16.
49 La Motte, *Backwash*, 52; Rathbone, *WTWY*, 197.

injured body: the five gaping wounds, six inches deep, create a gap in comprehension as the mouth can only silently articulate horror – the opposite of empathy. And yet horror – of both the nurse and the reader – is checked by the sheer endurance of Waker who never lets out as much as a scream: human will and fortitude triumph, preventing the scene from tipping into abjection and instead continuing to demand empathy.

The scene creates an emotional vertigo in the act of witnessing, lurching between the twin acts of reaching out and looking away: there is at once a connection and a cut in the imagining. Physical pain obliterates the consciousness of everything apart from its own absolute reality: what about the witness, the young nurse who writes now and whose voice was so thoroughly choked then? As the measured shock of clinical language passes to the hollow depth of Biblical echoes – the five wounds of Christ or Saint Veronica wiping His brow – the two tiny gestures inscribing the self – 'I did not dare' and 'I did so reluctantly' – reveal the terrible predicament of the witnessing subject. The remarkable and unexpected metaphor of the 'flock' foregrounds this by an appeal to the reader: 'Sometimes, when your mind has a grip like iron, your stomach will undo you;. . .There are so many parts of the body to look after, one of the flock may slip your control while you are holding the other by the neck.' This extraordinary metaphor alerts us to the trauma of witnessing, the steeling of nerves required by these young women suddenly transported from comfortable bourgeois settings into the operating theatre. Is the nurse here about to faint, as Lesley Smith does while the Medical Officer replaces tubes in a pus-ridden shoulder?[50] However, as we finish the paragraph, the body is reclaimed by Waker, his open fists eluding our grasp: the incommensurability of the body in pain, the unmaking of the world. The nurse, as well as the reader, is left with a crippling sense of inadequacy. Yet for that moment in the text, the three bodies – Waker's, the narrator's and the reader's – are compacted through an act of visceral tightening.

## BORDEN: SHAME AND ITS SISTERS

The operating room in Mary Borden is no longer the impersonal theatre of Bagnold's hospital: it is the 'second battlefield' where the 'real' battle is being fought. Borden was a millionaire from Chicago who, when the war

---

50 Lesley Smith, *Four Years Out of Life* (London: Allan, 1931), 65.

broke out, travelled to the front to nurse the wounded and created a surgical hospital of her own, staffing it with British and American nurses. In course of the war, her mobile unit moved from the war zone near Ypres in Belgium to the Somme in France and, for her war service, she won the French Croix de Guerre and was conferred the membership of the French Legion of Honour.[51] Borden composed her reminiscences both during and after the war, publishing *The Forbidden Zone* in 1929, a year that also saw the publication of Remarque's *All Quiet on the Western Front*, Graves's *Goodbye to All That* and Manning's *The Middle Parts of Fortune*. Borden does not suffer by comparison: here at last is a highly conscious literary modernist. In the preface, Borden calls her collection 'fragments': the shards of pockmarked bodies, landscape and memory that she dredges up cannot form a coherent narrative but are necessarily splintered into essays, stories and poems, combining reportage and literary invention. Phrases and similes connect the different narratives but perspectives shift and memories often contradict each other. Borden is one of the most visceral of the female war writers. In 'Rosa', the giant 'ox of a man' with thick curling bunches of red chest hair keeps tearing the bandage from his head in an attempt to die; in 'Enfant de Malheur', the beautiful body of the young patient – the object of desire – turns into a site of abjection emitting foul pus, odour and words; in 'Blind', an amputated knee is mistaken for mutton for casse croute.[52] The ceaseless metonymisation of the male body in Borden's narrative – eyes, lips, hair, shoulder blades, thighs – is grotesquely literalised in 'Moonlight' where the night sky is framed by the peaked roofs of the huts marked Abdomen, Gas Gangrene, Heads, Knees, Elbows and Thighs.

Lyricism and nostalgia are rare qualities in Borden's prose for they can be fatal, ushering in the moonlight that scalds as much as it caresses with memories of an idyllic pre-war life. Irony and satire are the twin tools of Borden's pacifist politics: men's bodies are like clothes to be mended, food to be cooked, metal to be beaten back to shape. Often, the chaos of the times puts the similes, metaphors and metonymies out of joint. Thus, men come out of the ambulances as 'loaves of bread are pulled out of the oven' only to 'be cooked back to life again' on the operating table;

---

51 See Higonnet (ed.), *Nurses at the Front*, for important details about the hospital unit. She juxtaposes Borden's text with La Motte's *Backwash*. For some other approaches to *The Forbidden Zone*, see Tylee, *Women's Consciousness*, 98–101; Higonnet, 'Women in the Forbidden Zone', 192–209; and Ariela Freedman, 'Mary Borden's Forbidden Zone: Women's Writing from No-Man's-Land', *Modernism/Modernity*, 9, 2 (January 2002), 108–24.

52 Borden, *FZ*, 101, 78, 153.

men are sent to the hospital as 'clothes to the laundry' but the chief surgeon is a 'wizard' working with his team of 'archangels'.[53] The hospital is a combination of an industrial factory, a grisly kitchen and a house of magic, throbbing and humming with the remaking of men: 'The hospital was going full steam ahead. I had a sense of great power, exhilaration and excitement. A loud wind was howling.'[54] 'Blind' is an extraordinary piece of writing: the heightened prose tries to keep pace with the frenetic activity – the steaming boilers and shining metal boxes and scuttling nurses – but the final howl of the blind man reveals the precipice between the exhilaration of service and the trauma of witnessing.

The seared sensibility of the woman – as witness, nurse and artist – is powerfully bared in 'Conspiracy' over the stripped body of the male patient:

We receive these bundles. We pull off a blanket. We observe that this is a man.
. . .

We lift him on to a table. We peel off his clothes, his coat and his shirt and his trousers and his boots. We handle his clothes that are stiff with blood. We cut off his shirt with large scissors. We stare at the obscene sight of his innocent wounds.
. . .

We confer together over his body and he hears us. We discuss his different parts in terms that he does not understand . . .

We conspire against his right to die. We experiment with his bones, his muscles, his sinews, his blood. We dig into the yawning mouths of his wounds. Helpless openings, they let us into the secret places of his body. We plunge deep into his body. We make discoveries within his body. To the shame of the havoc of his limbs we add the insult of our curiosity and the curse of our purpose, the purpose to remake him. We lay odds on his chances of escape, and we combat with death, his Saviour.[55]

The highly wrought, incantatory tone of the above passage teeters between recording the demands of professional service and a retrospective affective response. The plural 'we', in sharp contrast to the previous two operation scenes we examined, suggest a nursing community, transforming individual trauma into a medical discourse. The series of active verbs such as 'confer', 'discuss', 'dig' or 'experiment' suggest a process of acquiring scientific knowledge, assuming agency to a high degree, as evident in the project to 'remake' the soldier. Sentiments such as 'We make discoveries within his body' or phrases like 'Helpless openings' and

---

53 Borden, *FZ*, 148, 117, 147.     54 Borden, *FZ*, 146.     55 Borden, *FZ*, 119–20.

'combat' suggest an aggressively masculine enterprise of cognitive enquiry and bodily conquest. Is the operating theatre the ultimate site for the reversal of gender politics? The progress of medical science, the mysteries of the male anatomy and the power of the women: do they produce the 'excitement, exhilaration and power' Borden speaks of in 'Blind'?

Overriding the 'epistemophilic' vocabulary, what comes across is the sense of *shame*: the process of acquiring medical knowledge is compounded with the ignominy of bodily violation. The series of verbs suggesting cognitive control – experimenting, digging, plunging – point up the perversion of gender roles rather than a celebration of female autonomy or exploration. Early in the passage, 'obscene' – from Latin *obscenus* ('inauspicious', 'ill-omened') – is a word that leaps out of the page, taking us to the ethical core of the passage: in a world where the project to 'remake' the soldiers is to send them back to the trenches, death becomes the 'Saviour'. This final image brings with it the silent injunction of 'Noli me tangere', pointing up the violent infraction of the tremulous private body. Medical enquiry, instead of pointing the way towards exultation, is an 'insult' and the very 'purpose' of the duty – of repairing and sending the men back to the trenches – becomes a 'curse' that taints the profession of army nursing. The anaphoric repetition, by its very breathlessness and elongation, takes away the agency that individual verbs seem to confer: the actions become ritualised, compulsive. They take place within the protocol of a war machine whose relentless movements Borden's story suggests through its opening and closing statements: 'It is all arranged'. If the plural 'we' subsumed individual horror into a larger medical community, it also suggests the oppression of uniform and ideology, bringing the nurses rather close to the emasculated 'they' who are being treated: 'He is blind, deaf, dead, as I am – another machine just as I am'.[56] It is a shell-shocked collective voice as alienated from the previous, individual 'I' as is Remarque's Paul Bäumer or Manning's Bourne once they have crossed the forbidden zone. Similarly, the use of the present tense is peculiarly unnerving, combining the customariness of the inquisition and the particularity of the action. It is also the tense of the trauma victim, 'obliged to *repeat* the repressed material as a contemporary experience', just as the shell-shocked soldiers would return again and again to the trenches.[57]

56  Borden, *FZ*, 64.          57  Freud, 'Beyond the Pleasure Principle', *SE*, XVIII, 18.

In Borden's text, the trauma is of the order of both infliction (on soldiers) and victimisation (by war authorities): the 'obscene' gaze transfers the nakedness and the shame from the raw wounds to the probing eye. The staccato beat of the sentences almost hammers out an act of penance just as it relives most intimately the moment of original shame: for Borden, writing becomes a ritual of atonement. *The Forbidden Zone* is, in many ways, a 'traumatised' text *par excellence*: in the preface, Borden calls her work a 'collection of fragments' for 'they are fragments of a great confusion'.[58] Pieces such as 'Bombardment' or 'Moonlight' are like vivid snapshots, refusing assimilation into a linear narrative or a generic category. Identity is constructed through a series of negatives: 'I feel myself dying again. It is impossible to be a woman here. One must be dead.'[59] A fragmented modernist aesthetic becomes Borden's mode of recovering and transmitting traumatic memory, and in this, her disjointed narrative strategy resembles the gaps and ellipses in Price's *Not So Quiet*.

The imaginative power and literary qualities of the nurses' memoirs – in the fullness of their engagement with the human subject, with issues of memory, trauma and shame, and in the relentless questioning of the ideology of the military medical establishment – come out most powerfully if we contrast them with a slightly different kind of historical evidence: a medical record cum memoir by a woman doctor. Dr Flora Murray's *Women As Army Surgeons: Being the History of the Women's Hospital Corps in Paris, Wimereux and Endell Street, Sept. 1914 – October 1919*, as the title suggests, is a comprehensive record of the workings of the hospital, the daily duty of the doctors, the number of operations performed (which, Murray tells us, exceeded 7,000). At one point in this historical documentation, Murray gets excited by a new medical discovery, an antiseptic paste called 'Bipp': 'The surgeons relied on it so confidently that they never hesitated to operate on septic fractures or joints; and on one occasion a scalp abscess was evacuated, the skull trephined and a bullet extracted from the brain, in the complete assurance that Bipp would save the situation, as it did'.[60] 'Bipp' emerges very much the hero of the day as the patient is reduced to body parts and all human responses cancelled: an impersonal documentation of the

58 Borden, *FZ*, 'Preface', 1.    59 Borden, *FZ*, 60.

60 Flora Murray, *Women As Army Surgeons: Being the History of the Women's Hospital Corps in Paris, Wimereux and Endell Street, September 1914–October 1919* (London: Hodder and Stoughton Limited, 1920), 164–5.

body and its ailments and cures. The V.A.D. nurses – especially young, sensitive women such as Bagnold, Borden, La Motte – found themselves torn between the professional, detached world of medical science as exemplified by Flora Murray and a personal affective testimony that could too easily grasp the obscenity of many of the acts. While journals such *The Lancet* or official histories such as *Medical Services Surgery* give a scientific and factual documentation – as in the chapter, 'The Physiology of Wounds' with its list of 'Avulsing Wounds', 'Perforating & Fracturing Wounds' and 'Amputation Wounds'[61] – the nurses' memoirs provide us with an intimate account which is essential to a fuller understanding of First World War medical history.

Central to these nursing memoirs – something the texts cannot forget and that I have explored at greater length in the previous chapter – is the incommensurability of the body in pain: 'Sometimes they call to me 'Sister, Sister!' in the faint voices of faraway men, but when I go near them and bend over them, I am a ghost woman leaning over a thing that is mewing; and it turns away its face and flings itself back into the arms of Pain, its monster bedfellow'.[62] If pain reduces men – 'fathers and husbands and sons and lovers of men' – to pitiable mewing creatures, without individuality or dignity except the 'monster's' absolute reality, it strips the nurse of her own reality and subjectivity as well: she is rendered insignificant, unsubstantial, a 'ghost'. Pain has usurped the place of the woman. The helplessness of the witnessing subject generates its own peculiar brand of shame, something that recurs in the writers we have been considering. Locating shame as one of the key affects, the psychoanalytical writer, Silvan Tomkins, writes in *Affect, Imagery, Consciousness*: 'If distress is the affect of suffering, shame is the affect of indignity, of defeat, of transgression, and of alienation. Though terror speaks to life and death and distress makes of the world a vale of tears, yet shame strikes deepest into the heart'.[63] Shame is a recurrent affect in nurses' memoirs, an important corrective to the much mythologised flush of 'exultation' that Gubar and Gilbert turn into their central thesis about women and the First World War.

---

61 Major-General Sir W. G. Macpherson *et al.* (eds.), *Medical Services Surgery* (London: Printed and Published by His Majesty's Stationary Office, 1923), 32–77.
62 Borden, *FZ*, 61.
63 Eve Kosofsky Sedgwick and Adam Frank (eds.), *Shame and Its Sisters: A Silvan Tomkins Reader* (Durham, NC: Duke University Press, 1995) 134.

Freud linked shame almost exclusively to matters of sexual knowledge and exposure: a *Reaktionsbildung* serving as a defence against inappropriate scopophilic drives or wishes, something that Borden plays with in her two stories, 'Rosa' and 'Enfant de Malheur'. But most of the nurses' memoirs recount a different – perhaps a more fundamental – story of shame, as in the following account by Enid Bagnold: 'Rees, when he wakes, wakes sobbing and says, "Don' go away, nurse. . ." He holds my hand in a fierce clutch, then releases it to point in the air, crying, "There's the pain!" as though the pain filled the air and rose to the rafters.'[64] The transgression is not one of gender but of privacy, of having crossed frightful thresholds of intimacy without permission or even intention. Bagnold continues:

Pain. . .

To stand up straight on one's feet, strong, easy, without the surging of any physical sensation, by a bedside whose coverings are flung here and there by the quivering nerves beneath it. . .there is a sort of shame in such strength.[65]

The shame springs from the sense of well-being and health rather than from exposure: the 'indignity' that Tomkins speaks of is here of the order of contagion, of having watched, or touched the pitiful, shrieking human subject – the underside of the war hero – too intimately, of having known human vulnerability too closely. The 'defeat' is at once political and medical: to stop war, to put an end to pain. Witnessing and shame are linked in complex ways in the above scene. What is at issue here is not the 'essential dignity'[66] of the experiencing subject but that of the witnessed object: there is a frightful compromise which generates a sense of impropriety in the act of witnessing, of the nurse registering the shame of the patient at his awareness of the nurse's knowledge.

### TOUCH AND TESTIMONY

Speaking of testimony as a 'crisis' in witnessing, Shoshana Felman writes of the '*transformation*' of the subject who partakes of an '*apprenticeship in*

---

64 Bagnold, *Diary*, 89.     65 Bagnold, *Diary*, 22.

66 Tomkins, *Shame*, 136. Tomkins speaks primarily of shame as resulting from the sense of personal exposure and vulnerability, 'a sickness of the soul': 'It does not matter whether the humiliated one has been shamed by derisive laughter or whether he mocks himself. In either event he feels himself naked, defeated, alienated, lacking in dignity or worth' (133). I extend Tomkins's ideas to witnessing scenes of shame and its relation to one's sense of self.

*history* through an apprenticeship in witnessing'.[67] 'Apprenticeship' is a crucial word in connection to these V.A.D. nurses – young upper-middle-class women gaining an apprenticeship in nursing – encompassing, as it were, the emotional and the spiritual, an apprenticeship in pain, desolation and grief. Yet one of the problems of such 'apprenticeship in history' – something less often spoken about – is the issue of *owning* experience. After all, the nurses bear witness only to another's pain which is stubbornly resistant to everything outside its own absolute reality. Whose wounds are the nurses going to write about: the physical wounds they are bound to as duty, or their own mental wounds which seem to lose significance in comparison? How can they write about experiences that above all efface their own subjectivities, reduce them to a cipher: 'ghost of a woman'? There is thus a basic ethical and epistemological problem in testifying to another's wounds; the nurses' story is further fractured by the problem of knowledge inherent in all traumatic witnessing.

Moreover, will there be a sympathetic audience? 'I wonder if your metamorphosis has been as complete as my own', asks a sceptical Roland in a letter from the trenches to his beloved Vera, trapped as she is, or so he thinks, in a tranquil world of 'long wards and silent-footed nurses', 'an appalling whiteness in everything'.[68] Just before receiving the letter, Vera had concluded, 'I feel I shall never be the same person again and wonder if, when the War does end, I shall have forgotten how to laugh'. The 'apprenticeship' in history has been as traumatic, as profoundly transformative, as Roland's 'direct' participation but it is not acknowledged even by her beloved.[69] For the First World War nurse, writing a journal, testament or memoir becomes a ritual in owning experience as much to oneself in the solitude of recollection as to the rest of the world: it is the record of a subjectivity whose trauma and effacement are simultaneously inherent in the act of bearing witness to another's wound, and ignored by a less than empathetic world.

Writing about a different war, Albert Camus notes, 'In a civilization where murder and violence are already doctrines in the process of becoming institutions', the artist is by vocation 'Freedom's witness', in that

---

67 Felman and Laub, *Testimony*, 109–10.
68 Brittain, *Testament*, 216.
69 Felman notes, 'a narrator . . . learns something from the witnessing and from the telling, and his testimony takes stock of this knowledge. . . . The task of the testimony is to impart that knowledge: a firsthand, carnal knowledge of victimization,' *Testimony*, 111. See also the perceptive section titled 'The Physician's Witness', 111–13.

he 'testifies not to the Law, but to the body'.[70] As we have already seen in the case of Wilfred Owen, even within the act of body-witnessing history, there is a hierarchy: physical contact is the most immediate way of experiencing history, whether feeling the dead unknown soldiers in the dark or his dying servant, Jones. It is precisely in this zone, at the very centre of war's inscription – the physical wound – that the nurses would locate their narratives. Touching the wounds of soldiers is the most intimate way of body-witnessing history, witnessing in and through exposed flesh; repairing the wounds marks the female body with the knowledge of actually shaping that history though its underside is often helplessness and trauma. If wounding and pain cannot possibly be shared, the First World War nurses repeatedly dwell on acute body memories and knowledge to establish almost a *physical continuum, a bodily bridge, as it were, over an ontological impossibility.* Noting that 'psychoanalysis, like every psychology, in its attempts to dig to the depths must strike some-where on the rock of the organic', Ferenczi refers to memory-traces as 'scars, so to speak, of traumatic impressions . . .'.[71] Trying to transmit their mental scars, the First World War nurses obsessively return to the site of the physical wound: touch becomes the ground of both testimony and trauma.

Nursing and narration are integrally related in the project of reclaiming history as well as resisting its recurrence. At the core of each, in spite of the troubled and fractured ideology I have noted, is the impulse of preser-vation: just as the nurse sews up physical wounds and tries to save life, the narrator seeks to heal her mental wounds through the act of writing and preserve not just her subjectivity and experience but rather the memory and the knowledge of the cost of warfare. 'Writing to expose wounds', notes Higonnet, 'is surely a first step toward healing wounds'.[72] Writing the wounds at such a raw level and in such graphic details also becomes an act of political protest, an attempt to prevent new wounds. If Roland had doubted the metamorphosis of his beloved, Vera now directly addresses her readers: 'No sudden gift of second sight showed me the future months in which I should not only contemplate and hold, but dress unaided and without emotion, the quivering stump of a

70 Albert Camus, 'Actuelles' I, 188, 191, *Œuvres complètes d'Albert Camus*, v (Paris: Gallimard and Club de L'Honnête Homme, 1983), quoted in Felman and Laub, *Testimony*, 108.

71 Ferenczi, 'The Problem of Acceptance of Unpleasant Ideas', in *Further Contributions to the Theory and Technique of Psycho-Analysis*, ed. John Rickman (London: Hogarth, 1926), 377.

72 Higonnet (ed.), *Nurses at the Front*, xxxi.

newly amputated limb – than which a more pitiable spectacle hardly exists on this side of death'.[73] The nurses' memoirs act in themselves as traumatic objects: they evoke not only intense emotional experiences but physical responses. For all the now conventional scepticism about knowledge and representation, in reading the nurses' memoirs, we tighten, we crack, for in some obscure way that goes beyond literary affect, our bodies are touched. Like the shattered *poilus* in Mary Borden's preface, the mutilated body of the soldier in *Testament of Youth* looms behind Brittain's hand, touching hers, meeting ours as we turn the pages of the book – each alone.

73  *Testament*, 216.

# Afterword

On 7 June 1920, *The Times* reported: 'The French have a better term for what are described in this country as battlefield tours. They called them pilgrimages.' The language of sacralisation was an attempt by a devastated post-war generation to make meaning of the war. The article added that, while in pre-war tours to places such as Pompeii or Paris, 'we were merely spectators at a drama long played out', in the battlefields of France, 'we have a direct personal interest and too often an intimate share of sorrow'.[1] At the beginning of the twenty-first century, the personal resonance of the war is lost to most of us. Yet the battlefields continue to haunt and overwhelm us; the sheer scale of devastation seems to confront us with the inadequacy of a personal response.

In 1928, *Legionary* described the preserved trenches at Vimy Ridge as a place where 'a man can feel that he is back again in 1914–1918 . . . where he can stand at a sniper's post and fit the rotted butt of a rusted rifle to his shoulder as he peeps out between the bushes towards the German trenches'.[2] Though concrete sandbags and duckboards have changed much of the original character of Vimy Ridge, we still get an idea of the Allied and German frontline trenches zig-zagging in frightful proximity. Undetonated explosives still litter some of the fields pockmarked with mine craters; a large German trench mortar found here has been set up with other weapons scattered around. Led by Canadian student-guides, we enter the Grange tunnel built by the Royal Engineers with the help of the 7th Canadian Infantry Brigade, twenty to twenty-five feet underground. We inch our way through the narrow, dimly lit passageways in a single file, opening out into the cook room, the hospital and

---

1 'Battlefield Tour: On Holy Ground', in *The Times*, 7 June 1920, 13. For a survey of the highly successful battlefield tourism industry over the last eighty years, see David William Lloyd, *Battlefield Tourism* (Oxford: Berg, 1998).
2 *Legionary*, 11 (June 1928), 12.

ammunition dumps, and the commander's quarters which still has the disintegrating bed used by Lieutenant-Colonel Agar Adamson of Princess Patricia's (Canadian) Light Infantry. We realise the scale of the tragedy only when we visit the nearby cemetery, the endless series of white slabs, many of them simply marked, 'Known unto God'. In retrospect, we realise the horrors the twisting trenches and the underground hospital at Vimy Ridge must have held. The First World War battlefields and their enduring appeal exemplify, at the level of public consciousness, the physical devastation wrought by this war and our fantasised relationship to this ordeal.

In this book, I have argued how the bodily senses, particularly touch, define the texture of experience in the trenches and the hospitals, and how they inform and shape war writings. This study is a step towards a more affective and sensory record of the war that remains buried in personal and collective memory, narratives and artworks. Cinema is an important and particularly fruitful medium for examining the relation between sensory perception and representation in connection to the war. As Laura Marcus has recently noted, the relationship between World War I and cinema is a matter of 'historical and temporal concurrence', the two being the 'twin technologies of modernity'.[3] The British authorities realised, and started exploiting, the potential of the new medium for purposes of propaganda and education. *The Battle of the Somme* (1916), watched by some 80 per cent of the adult population in Britain, introduced many of its audiences at once to cinema and war: it brought home the scale of the war's devastation through images of bombed landscapes, ruined buildings and killed and wounded men.[4] One particular scene from the film, now held to be faked, haunted contemporary imagination: an English soldier, while preparing to go 'over the top', gets shot and collapses back into the trench while the rest of the army advances. The power of this image lay partly in its haptic quality: the soldier is seen to be gently sliding down, establishing an immediate bodily relationship between the viewer and the image. Rebecca West, recalling the film in her war novella, *The Return of the Soldier* (1918), writes that 'on the war films I have seen men slip down as *softly* from the trench

3 Laura Marcus, 'The Great War in Twentieth-century Cinema', in *Cambridge Companion*, 280 (280–301).

4 For a discussion of the film and its history, see Nicholas Reeves, *Official British Film Propaganda During the First World War* (London: Croom Helm, 1986), 101–4; Andrew Kelly, *Cinema and the Great War* (London: Routledge, 1997), 43–57.

parapet': it was the palpable substantiality of the falling bodies that troubled the mind.[5]

The 'most famous image to emerge from the re-creation of the 1914–1918 war in film', according to Jay Winter, is the final shot in Lewis Milestone's masterpiece *All Quiet on the Western Front* (1930): a close-up of Paul Bäumer's palm reaching out for a butterfly as he is shot by a sniper.[6] Delicate, sensuous and immensely moving, there is once more a manipulation of tactile aesthetics: we get to see the palm, outstretched, inviting, prehensile; the palm defines space in the shot, measuring the distance from the butterfly which symbolises the fragility of life. In First World War films, from popular reconstructions such as *The Battle of Jutland* (1921) to classics such as *All Quiet on the Western Front*, there is often a tactile visuality at work in the way the camera tries to draw us into the battlefield by focusing on the flooded trenches, barbed wire, duck-boards, blasted trees and the soldiers at close range – their clothes, contorted postures and damaged flesh. The aim is to elicit not only a visual but rather a visceral response from the audience. While the combination of the visual and the auditory makes cinema a particularly apt medium to capture what I have called the war's 'geographies of sense', this physical dimension drew the earliest film-makers to it and made them explore the full phenomenological complexity of their art to bring to life this 'great' war.

I have concentrated instead on the powers of language in my study. While considering the literature of the war, I have examined narratives produced by soldier-writers and nurses who served in the war and for whom the immediate, material circumstances were drastically and often irrevocably changed. Can the argument about the discourses of touch that we have noted in these accounts be extended to civilian war experience and writings? To do so would need a new book as well as a very different paradigm. The tangible materiality of the flesh that we have examined arises out of a very particular set of circumstances – a context of actual physical experience and extremity – and cannot be dissociated from them: to detect its traces in civilian war writings would involve questions of mediation, motive, and vicariousness, or exploring a very different

---

5 Rebecca West, *The Return of the Soldier* (London: Virago, 2003), 13–14. My italics.
6 Jay Winter, *The Experience of the First World War* (Oxford: Oxford University Press, 1995), 247. Milestone tried out various endings for the film and finally sought the help of the German cinematographer Karl Freund, and together they devised the closing shot of *All Quiet*. Freund shot the final scene with Milestone's hand substituting for Ayres who played the role of Bäumer.

set of issues and concerns.[7] Some civilian writers seemed to have a fantasised physical response to the war. Only a few days into the war, on 8 August 1914, Henry James wrote, 'My aged nerves can scarcely stand it, and I bear up as I can; I dip my nose, or try to, into the inkpot as often as I can; but it's as if there were no ink there, and I take it out smelling gunpowder, smelling blood'; similarly, D. H. Lawrence wrote to Lady Cynthia Asquith on 12 October 1917: 'But oh, the sickness that is in my stomach. . . . It is like being slowly suffocated in mud. . . . I have never known my heart so pressed with weight of mud.'[8] While both James and Lawrence went on to engage with the war in very original ways, many civilian writers sought to re-create combat experience by dwelling on the damaged, shell-shocked body in the trenches, as if it was the yardstick of the authenticity of their enterprise.

Yet, some of the most sensitive of the civilian war writings – often from women – draw upon touch to show how the war has reconfigured it within the domestic sphere: examples range from Helen Thomas's poignant description in *World without End* (1931) of the great physical tenderness with her husband Edward on the eve of his departure to France to Hilda Doolittle's thinly disguised account in her fictionalised memoir of the trauma at sleeping with her oversexed and strangely altered officer-husband, on leave from the trenches. In *Bid Me to Live* (1960), Julia feels that she has been physically contaminated with her soldier-husband's war neuroses: 'He had breathed a taint of poison-gas in her lungs, the first time he kissed her'. Later, she wakes up in the middle of the night with a 'muddle of poisonous gas and flayed carcasses in her head'.[9] This strong fantasised relation to the trenches, compounded with a sense of horror and repulsion, is brilliantly explored by the German writer Claire Goll in her short story, 'The Hand of Wax'. Here, a young, pacifist German housewife Ines is filled with horror at seeing her mutilated soldier-husband with

---

7  While civilian war trauma is usually taken to mean its emotional effects, the war did actually physically affect large groups of civilians: the female munition workers whose skin often turned yellow or the female labourers in coke works or other factories sometimes working for as long as seventy hours a week and carrying enormous loads on their backs; countless men, women and children who were geographically displaced in countries such as Belgium and Turkey; acute food shortages in Germany and Austro-Hungary in the final year of war where women were reduced to scavenging for food or in Eastern Europe where malnourished children were a common sight. See Jay Winter, *The Experience of World War I* (New York: Oxford University Press, 1995), 173–97, 215.

8  *The Letters of Henry James*, ed. Percy Lubbock (London: Macmillan, 1920), II, 402; *The Collected Letters of D. H. Lawrence*, ed. Harry T. Moore (London: Heinemann, 1962), I, 528.

9  H. D., *Bid Me to Live* (1960; London: Virago, 1984), 39.

his hand of wax as he proudly recounts the murderous exploits. As they lie in bed in the dark, she is haunted by this artificial hand which seems to reproach her with the 'solemn accusation of the dead': 'The hand began to creep up on her. Any moment now it was going to touch her. It was going to lie on top of her for the rest of the night, every night.'[10] Unable to bear it any longer, Ines is driven to suicide as Goll explores the relation between gender, war and trauma within a civilian context through a threatening moment of touch.

One civilian writer who was deeply affected by the war and whose writings are, perhaps more than any other writer in English, obsessed with the tremulousness of the flesh is D. H. Lawrence. Lawrence ecstatically and passionately championed the sense of touch as the supreme of the senses; to him it could rescue modern man from his cerebral, industrial crust, and put him back in contact with his inner, sensuous being.[11] Lawrence's ordeal during the war – suspected of being a spy, harassed by the war authorities and finally, during an examination for conscription, stripped naked, humiliated and declared unfit – forms the basis of the 'Nightmare' chapter in *Kangaroo* (1923) and is well documented by biographers who see the war as the defining trauma in his life and career.[12] In a letter to Cynthia Asquith, he writes, 'It kills me with speechless fury to be pawed by them. They shall *not* touch me again': the medical examination was for him the ultimate degradation of his most cherished sense.[13] In spite of his disgust and fury at the war, the male intimacy of the trenches seemed to have a positive value for Lawrence. In his late essay,

---

10 Claire Goll, 'Hand of Wax', trans. Agnes Cardinal in *Women's Writing on the First World War*, 249.

11 Lawrence's celebration of touch is scattered throughout his writings from *Sons and Lovers*, short stories such as 'You Touched Me' and poems such as 'Noli Me Tangere', 'Touch' and 'Touch Comes' in *Pansies* to *Fantasia of the Unconscious* and *Study of Thomas Hardy*. While analysing an ancient wall painting, he writes, 'That again is one of the charms of the Etruscan paintings: they really have the sense of touch; the people and the creatures are all really in touch. It is one of the rarest qualities, in life as well as in art.' (*Sketches of Etruscan Places and Other Italian Essays*, ed. Simonetta De Filippis, Cambridge: Cambridge University Press, 1992, 54). See also James C. Cowan, *D. H. Lawrence and the Trembling Balance* (Pennsylvania: Pennsylvania State University Press, 1990) which has a chapter titled 'Lawrence and Touch' (135–55).

12 For a historical record of Lawrence's war years, see Paul Delany, *D. H. Lawrence's Nightmare: The Writer and His Circle in the Years of the Great War* (Sussex: Harvester, 1979); for a more literary approach, see Hugh Stevens, 'Sex and the Nation: "The Prussian Officer" and *Women in Love*' in *The Cambridge Companion to D. H. Lawrence*, ed. Anne Fernihough (Cambridge: Cambridge University Press, 2001), 49–65.

13 *The Letters of D.H.Lawrence*, ed. James T. Boulton and Andrew Robertson (Cambridge: Cambridge University Press, 1981), III, 287.

'Nottingham and the Mining Countryside', he brilliantly evokes the underground community of miners and goes on to compare it with the masculine world of the trenches:

Under the butty system, the miners worked underground as a sort of intimate community, they knew each other practically naked, and with curious close intimacy, and the darkness and the underground remoteness of the pit 'stall', and the continual presence of danger, made the physical, instinctive, and intuitional contact between men very highly developed, a contact almost as close as touch, very real and very powerful. . . . He [my father] loved the contact, the intimacy, as men in the war loved the intense male comradeship of the dark days.[14]

In his war story, 'England, My England' (1915), the soldier-hero Evelyn feels that he 'seemed to have one physical body with the other men'; in *Lady Chatterley's Lover* (1928), the quintessential Lawrentian hero Mellors has the 'touch of tenderness' learnt from his battlefield experiences: 'I knew it with the men. I had to be in touch with them, physically, and not go back on it. I had to be bodily aware of them – and a bit tender to them – even if I put 'em through hell.'[15] Both passages resonate deeply with the discourses of male intimacy and touch that we have examined in the context of the First World War trenches. The most quirky and powerful exploration however occurs in the short story, 'The Blind Man'. Here, the returned and blinded soldier Maurice, suddenly fired by 'hot, poignant love, the passion of friendship', 'pressed' the quivering fingers of Bertie on his disfigured eye-sockets ('Touch my eyes, will you? – touch my scar'), a scene at once erotic and violent, charged with the kind of visceral thrill we have encountered in the poetry of Owen.[16] Similarly, the famous wrestling scene of Gerald and Birkin in *Women in Love* (1920) teeters on the fine edge between emotion, eroticism and extremity that we explored while discussing the kiss in the trenches, while Lilly's loving, lingering therapeutic massage of Aaron in *Aaron's Rod* (1922) is like a soldier caressing and resuscitating his dying comrade; incidentally both these novels, written during the war years when Lawrence was facing police persecution, are deeply haunted by the war

---

14 *Phoenix: The Posthumous Papers of D. H. Lawrence*, ed. Edward D.McDonald (London: Heinemann, 1936), 135–6.
15 'England, My England' (1915 version) in the collection, *England, My England and Other Stories*, ed. Bruce Steele (Cambridge: Cambridge University Press, 1990), 227; *Lady Chatterley's Lover, and A Propos of Lady Chatterley's Lover*, ed. Michael Squires (Cambridge: Cambridge University Press, 1993), 277.
16 'The Blind Man', in *England, My England*, 62.

though it does not figure directly in either.[17] Lawrence remains one of the most exciting figures in whose writings discourses of war, intimacy and the male body come together as he shows us, again and again, how touch gets under the guard of consciousness. However, to examine Lawrence in greater detail and to engage with his theory of 'blood-consciousness' would take us away from the actual, experiential dimension of warfare or nursing that is the focus of my book, and would require changing substantially the frame of reference. Instead, to retain the sense of contiguity, I would like to focus, by way of conclusion, on certain objects that bear a physical relation to the battlefields, its men and women, and engage directly with our senses.

Exhibitions on the First World War have emphasised the physicality of warfare and have even tried to simulate it with the help of modern technology. The exhibition, 'The Trench' (2002) in the Imperial War Museum aimed to evoke what Sassoon called 'sensuous frontline existence' not only through trench exhibits such as diaries and personal memorabilia of the 10th East Yorkshire Regiment but by constructing a maze of trenches, dug-outs and frontline quarters.[18] Loudspeakers blare out the sound of shelling while artificial lights simulate the bombardment in the horizon. The corridors give way to little enclaves, marking the officer's quarter (with a bed, desk and telephone set), a trench latrine or a section marked 'Gas' opening into the frontline, with its piled sandbags, barbed wire, duckboards and litter of picks and shovels. The exhibition stresses the importance of 'hands-on' experience: we are asked to try out the haversack weighing 20 lbs that the average soldier carried; to wear the British army tunics made from wool serge; to shoulder the .303 Mark III rifle; or, to crawl and lie in the dug-outs. There are interactive videos with 'TOUCH' printed on the screen; we pull open different boxes, including one that simulates the smell of mustard gas. While such reconstructions are interesting and playful, our curiosity for 'authenticity' is not satisfied: the physical simulacrum may satisfy our sense of adventure but fails to move us.

---

17 See Stevens, 'Sex and the Nation', 49–65; the introduction to *Aaron's Rod*, ed. Mara Kalnins (Cambridge: Cambridge University Press, 1988), xvii–xliv.

18 The exhibition was linked to the BBC 2 programme in which twenty volunteers were recruited from Hull to follow in the footsteps of the men who had joined the 10th Battalion East Yorkshire Regiment during the First World War. These volunteers spent some time in a trench system built near Cambrai to re-create the original war experience. In the absence of actual danger, the experience was bound to be radically different and comes across as rather mawkish but the effort however reveals the strong hold that the trench experience still has over us.

In contrast, the parallel exhibition titled 'Anthem for Doomed Youth: Twelve Soldier Poets of the First World War' (October 2002–April 2003) foregrounded the identity of these twelve men both as soldiers and as poets: diaries, letters, war papers, trench memorabilia, artefacts as well as manuscript poems and first editions of the books had been put together with a rare sympathy. The poets included not only well-known figures such as Owen and Sassoon but also men such as Grenfell, Ledwidge, Sorley and Gurney. Along with literary treasures such as the manuscripts of Brooke's 'Peace' and Owen's 'Dulce Et Decorum Est', Jones's own copy of the first edition of *In Parenthesis*, or the score of Gurney's setting of Thomas's poem, 'Lights Out', there were artefacts that are profoundly disturbing: a blood-stained map of Belgium found on the body of Julian Grenfell or the pocket watch of Edward Thomas. The hands of this watch are fixed at 7:36 am, a timeless testimony to Thomas's death by an explosion that left no visible marks on his body: a mute companion to the last, the clock had faithfully recorded the moment when its master's heart stopped beating. The tragedy of Ivor Gurney strikes us afresh as we read his letter to the London police begging for his release from the City of London Mental Asylum and it resonates in poems such as 'Pain'. We realise the grief of mothers as we look at Wilfred Owen's Military Cross which Susan Owen used to wear on a chain.

Why do these objects move and disturb us so much? These objects not only congeal time but also conceal processes of touch. The British Library reading room ticket of Brooke, the tunic worn by Blunden, the pocket watch of Thomas, the spectacles of Ledwidge or the hairbrushes of Wilfred Owen evoke the body of the user, traces of hands, quiescent but palpable. Like the manuscripts that we examined in the introduction, these objects have a precious, living quality for they are the archives of touch and intimacy – they have once held, protected or brushed against the bodies of their possessors in their youths or in the trenches and the hospitals, and through this intimate caress, these mute, insensate objects seem to have been touched to life, bequeathed with the very pulse of their owners' being. Their poignant materiality results from a constant frisson between presence and loss, between evoking the warm sensuousness of life – the inviolate contact with the users and owners – and mourning their absence. But unlike manuscripts, these objects preserved and exhibited behind glass-panels, cannot be handled. Susan Stewart, while analysing our charged relation to objects in her richly evocative study, *Poetry and the Fate of the Senses* (2002), writes that, in museums, 'the contagious magic of touch is replaced by the sympathetic magic of visual representation' and notes the 'constant play among deixis, tact, proximity, and negation' while looking at works of art.[19] Instead of assuming an inevitable triumph of the 'distantiated vision' in museums and exhibitions, what these objects do, she argues, is to blur the sharp distinction between our senses, bringing the tactile within the realm of the visual. Owen was acutely aware of this tactile dimension while looking at objects under glass, as he contemplated on the Roman ruins preserved in the Shrewsbury museum:

> And Samian jars, whose sheen and flawless shape
> Look fresh from potter's mould.
> Plasters with Roman finger-marks impressed;
> Bracelets, that from the warm Italian arm
> Might seem scarce cold;[20]

The objects in the present exhibition, so fittingly titled after one of Owen's poems, are often harrowing. Many of the items like the preserved lock of Brooke's hair or the sovereign carried by Owen in the Western Front are minute. In order to scrutinise and appreciate them, we have to lean and look at very close proximity. While these objects appeal to our immediate senses, our eyes soon wander to the labels beside them: the objects make more sense because of the accompanying information as well as our familiarity with the lives of these soldier-poets and their works.

If the objects are the sites of actual touch, we can gain access to the intimate encounter between people, places, objects and the emotions such meetings generate largely through language. The pressed flowers of Thomas touch us all the more because of our acquaintance with his pastoral verse; a nondescript cap gains immediate significance when we realise that it is the German cap found by Blunden and mentioned in *Undertones of War*. We sense how close the physical and the literary were intertwined in the experience of the First World War as we look at a Flemish copy of 'The Imitation of Christ' found by Sorley in a German-occupied trench, or the miniature edition of Shakespeare's *Cymbeline* that Thomas carried with him. Just as language preserves human memory,

---

19 Susan Stewart, *Poetry and the Fate of the Senses*, 174–5. The exhibition also has echoes of what Stephen Greenblatt has called the 'museum of resonance' in his powerful essay, 'Resonance and Wonder', in *Learning to Curse: Essays in Early Modern Culture* (New York: Routledge, 1990), 161–83. But the demarcation between 'resonance' and 'wonder' that Greenblatt suggests seems occasionally to collapse. When we examine the short poems in Wilfred Owen's manuscripts where looking and reading can be coterminous, the historical echoes blend with our wonder at the magic of form, of a poem coming together in front of our eyes.
20 Owen, 'Uriconium', *CP&F*, 66.

similarly memory can invest language with materiality. In *The Long Trail*, John Brophy and Eric Partridge provide a list of familiar trench terms, which they gloss using their knowledge and memory. In the concluding sentences of the 'Afterword', added to the revised edition of this wonderful book, Brophy notes:

Even in the two short syllables of *Dug-out* is suggested all the impetus of the spade-edge and the stiff resistance of the clay. It is a word you can feel in the palms of your hands and the sinews of your arms: the smell of broken soil lingers in it under the warm fuggy aromas of its later associations.[21]

Sound becomes sense, or a fusion of senses, cancelling the distance between the past and the present, the object and the signifier, the body and the world. Words become things, held and handled: the spade pressing against the hand or the soil in the hollow of the palm. Sweat and grime, labour and smell join the two syllables of 'Dug-out', a word so intimate that it is felt as part of the soldier's body. Brophy notes how 'the hardening of their [soldiers'] bodies and the sharpening of their physical faculties is clearly to be traced in the imagery, the onomatopoeia and the sensuous fidelity of many of these words'. We have not known the trenches, the stiff resistance of the clay or its lingering smell; we cannot ever grasp the full significance of what Brophy means by 'Dug-out'. But the inspired prose transforms the task of glossing into an act of recovery: the vivid nostalgia at work and the rustle of language, combined with our historical awareness of the 'sensuous' frontline existence, summon up for us not the remembrance but the imagining of things past, about to be felt.

21 John Brophy and Eric Partridge, *The Long Trail: What the British Soldier Sang and Said in the Great War of 1914–18* (1931; London: Andre Deutsch, 1965), 210. Desmond Graham, in *Truth of War*, 13–14, writes of Brophy turning from 'lexicographer to poet' and finds 'hope' in the poetic art of Owen, Blunden and Rosenberg to convey war experience.

# Bibliography

MANUSCRIPTS AND TYPESCRIPTS

Abraham, A. J. 'Memoirs of a Non-hero, 1914–18', P191. Imperial War Museum, London (hereafter IWM).

Acklam, W. R. 'Diary', 83/23/1. IWM.

Bennett, G. H. First World War Papers, Misc. 265. IWM.

Bennett, J. Diary, 83/14/1. IWM.

Block, R. Papers, 02/12/1. IWM.

Brown, M. A. Diary, 88/7/1. IWM.

Campbell, E. Notebook, Misc. 93 [1386]. IWM.

Christison, Philip. Memoirs, 82/15/1. IWM.

Cocker, Frank. Papers, 82/11/1. IWM.

Collins, W. Sound Archives, 9434/20. IWM.

Colyer, W. T. Memoirs, 76/51/1. IWM.

Connor, The Reverend. Diary, 87/10/1. IWM.

Cox, C. H. 'A Few Experiences of the First World War', 88/11/1. IWM.

Dalziel, T. Diary, 86/51/1. IWM.

Dent, Edward. Papers (Additional), 7973 S51–end. Cambridge University Library.

Dillon, J. Sound Archives, 4078/B/B. IWM.

Fenton, D. H. Papers, 87/13/1. IWM.

Fraser, J. 'Letters', 86/19/1. IWM.

Furse, Katherine. 'The Ideals of the VADs', Women's Work Collection, BRCS 10/1. IWM.

Gladstone, H. Diary, 86/2/1. IWM.

Goodman, Sam. 'Papers', 97/26/1, IWM.

Griffin, A. Sound Archives, AC9101. IWM.

Harry, Sybil. Memoirs, 84/41/1. IWM.

Hayman, G. W. Papers, 87/51/1. IWM.

Hunter, A. E. Papers, 94/11/1. IWM.

Ingle, R. G. Diary, 77/96/1. IWM.

17 King's Liverpool Battalion. 'Precis of Operations – 30 July to 3 August 1917', 30th Division War Diary May–August 1917, War Office 95/2312. Public Record Office, Kew.

Lawrence, D. H. 'Passages from Ecce Homo', Poetry Magazine Collection, Volume 34, Folder 4. Regenstein Library, Chicago.

Macdonald, Tom. 'Memories of 1914–1918 Great War'. 76/213/1, IWM.

McCann, Dorothy. 'The First World War Memoirs of Mrs D. McCann, V.A.D.', P371. IWM.

Mountfort, R. D. 'Papers', Con Shelf. IWM.

Nicol, Dorothy. 'Memoirs of a V.A.D. 1915–17', 81/1/1. IWM.

North, Katherine Hodges, 'Diary: A Driver at the Front', 92/22/1. IWM.

'Nurse's Autograph Book World War I'. Misc. 24 Item 464. IWM.

'Nurses' Autograph Book, Malta, 1915–1916', Misc. 154 Item 2396. IWM.

Okeden, Reverend Carl Parry. Papers, 90/7/1. IWM.

Owen, Wilfred. Wilfred Owen Manuscript Poems (Additional) 43720 and 43721. British Library, London.

Pemberton, E. B. Papers, 85/33/1. IWM.

Quinton, W. A. Memoirs, 79/35/1. IWM.

Raper, Major R. G. Papers, 83/50/1. IWM.

Reid, A. Diary, 87/8/1. IWM.

Rosenberg, Manuscripts, PP/MCR/C38. IWM.

Sargent, John. Sargent File, First World War Artists' Archive, 284 A/7. IWM.

Sassoon, Siegfried Loraine. 'The Last Meeting' 7973 S/75 (Additional Manuscripts). Cambridge University Library.

Simson, Arnold. 'First World War Note Book by a Royal Garrison Artillery Soldier', Misc. 41 Item 731. IWM.

Smith, R. I. Papers, 86/36/1. IWM.

Sulman, P. L. 82/29/1. IWM.

Thomas, M. A. A. 85/39/1. IWM.

Tisdall, C. E. Memoirs, 92/22/1. IWM.

Whitaker, Ruth. Papers, 76/123/1. IWM.

Williams, D. Papers, 85/4/1. IWM.


PRIMARY SOURCES

Ackerley, J. R. *My Father and Myself.* London: Bodley Head, 1968.

A. F. B. 'Smalley'. *The Third Battalion Magazine.* August 1918: 8–9.

Aldington, Richard. *War and Love: 1915–1918.* Boston: The Four Seas Company, 1919.

  *Images of War: A Book of Poems.* Westminster: C. W. Beaumont, 1919.

  *Death of a Hero.* 1929. London: Chatto and Windus, 1930.

  *Richard Aldington and H. D.: The Early Years in Letters.* Ed. Caroline Zilboorg. Bloomington: Indiana University Press, 1992.

Allen, Hervey. *Toward the Flame: A War Diary.* London: Victor Gollancz, 1934.

Asquith, Cynthia. *Diaries 1915–1918.* London: Hutchinson, 1968.

Auden, W. H. *Poems, Essays and Dramatic Writings 1927–1939.* Ed. Edward Mendelson. London: Faber, 1997.

Bagnold, Enid. *A Diary Without Dates.* 1918. London: Virago, 1979.

Baker, Kenneth. *The Faber Book of War Poetry.* London: Faber & Faber, 1996.

Barbusse, Henri. *Under Fire.* Trans. W. Fitzwater Wray. 1919. London: Dent, 1965. Originally published as *Le Feu (Journal d'une Escouade).* Paris: Ernest Flammarion, 1916.

    *Light.* Trans. W. Fitzwater Wray. London: Dent, 1919. Originally published as *Clarté.* Paris: Librarie Ernest Flammarion, 1919.

    *Under Fire* and *Light.* Trans. Fitzwater Wray. London: Dent, 1919.

    *Paroles d'un combatant.* Paris: Flammarion, 1920.

    *Lettres de Henri Barbusse à sa femme 1914–1917.* Paris: Flammarion, 1937.

Barker, Pat. *Regeneration.* 1991. Harmondsworth: Penguin, 1992.

    *The Eye in the Door.* 1993. Harmondsworth: Penguin, 1994.

    *The Ghost Road.* 1995. Harmondsworth: Penguin, 1996.

Bell, Charles. *The Hand, its Mechanisms and Vital Endowments as Evincing Design.* Bridgewater Treatises 4. London, 1833.

Bion, Wilfred. *The Long Week-End 1897–1919: Part of a Life.* 1982. London: Free Association Books, 1986.

Bishop, Alan and Mark Bostridge, eds. *Letters from a Lost Generation: First World War Letters of Vera Brittain and Four Friends.* London: Little, Brown and Company, 1998.

*Blast: Review of the Great English Vortex.* 2 vols. London: Kraus, 1914–15.

Blunden, Edmund. *Undertones of War.* 1928. Harmondsworth: Penguin, 1982.

    *Undertones of War.* 1928. Ed. and intro. Jon Stallworthy. London: Folio Society, 1989.

Bomberg, David. *Works by David Bomberg.* London: Chenil Gallery, 1914.

Borden, Mary. *The Forbidden Zone.* London: William Heinemann, 1929.

Bottomley, Gordon. *Poems and Plays.* London: The Bodley Head, 1953.

Bowser, Thekla. *The Story of British V.A.D. Work in the Great War.* London: Andrew Melrose, 1917.

Britnieva, Mary. *One Woman's Story.* London: Arthur Barker Ltd., 1934.

Brittain, Vera. *Chronicle Of Youth: Great War Diary 1913–1917.* Ed. Alan Bishop. 1981. London: Phoenix, 2000.

    *Testament of Youth.* 1933. London: Virago, 1999.

Brooke, Rupert. *The Collected Poems of Rupert Brooke, With a Memoir.* London: Sidgwick & Jackson, Ltd., 1929.

    *Collected Poems.* 1918. London: Papermac, 1992.

Brophy, John, ed. *The Soldier's War: A Prose Anthology.* London: Dent, 1929.

Brophy, John and Eric Partridge. *The Long Trail: What the British Soldier Sang and Said in the Great War of 1914–18.* 1931. London: Andre Deutsch, 1965.

Browning, Robert. *The Ring and the Book.* Ed. Richard Altick. Harmondsworth: Penguin, 1971.

Campbell, Phyllis. *Back of the Front: Experiences of a Nurse.* London: Newnes, 1915.

Cardinal, Agnes, Dorothy Goldman and Judith Hattaway, eds., *Women's Writing on the First World War.* Oxford: Oxford University Press, 1999.

Carpenter, Edward. *Some Friends of Walt Whitman: A Study in Sex-psychology.* London: J. E. Francis, 1924.

Carrington, Charles. *A Subaltern's War.* London: Peter Davies, 1929.

Céline, Louis Ferdinand. *Journey to the End of the Night.* Trans. Ralph Manheim. 1932. London: John Calder, 1983.

Choyce, Arthur Newberry. *Lips at the Brim: A Novel.* London: John Bale, 1920.

Cloete, Stuart. *A Victorian Son: An Autobiography 1897–1922.* London: Collins, 1972.

Cross, Tim. *The Lost Voices of World War I: An International Anthology of Writers, Poets and Playwrights.* London: Bloomsbury, 1988.

Davidson, Claudia, ed. *The Burgoyne Diaries.* London: Thomas Harmsworth, 1985.

De T'Serclaes, Baroness. *Flanders and Other Fields.* London: George G. Harrap, 1964.

Dolden, A. Stuart. *Cannon Fodder: An Infantryman's Life on the Western Front 1914–18.* Poole: Blandford Press, 1980.

Doolittle, Hilda (H. D.). *Bid Me to Live.* 1960. London: Virago, 1984.

Dorgelès, Raymond. *Wooden Crosses.* London: William Heinemann, 1920.

Duhamel, Georges. *The New Book of Martyrs.* Trans. Florence Simmonds. London: William Heinemann, 1918.

Farnam, Ruth S. *A Nation At Bay.* Indianapolis: Bobbs-Merrill Co., 1918.

Farrar, F. W. *Eric or Little by Little.* 1857–58. London: Ward Lock, n.d.

Fawcett, M. G. Introduction. *Questions for Women.* By H. Morten. London: A & C Black, 1899.

Featherstone, Simon, ed. *War Poetry: An Introductory Reader.* London: Routledge, 1995.

Ford, Madox Ford. *Parade's End.* 1924–8. Harmondsworth: Penguin, 1982.
  *Selected Poems.* Ed. Basil Bunting. Cambridge, Mass.: Pym-Randall Press, 1971.

Foot, Stephen. *Three Lives.* London: Heinemann, 1934.

Furse, Katharine. *Hearts and Pomegranates: The Story of Forty-five Years.* London: Peter Davies, 1940.

Goll, Claire. 'The Hand of Wax'. *Women's Writing on the First World War.* Ed. Agnes Cardinal, Dorothy Goldman and Judith Hattaway. Oxford: Oxford University Press, 1999.

Graham, Stephen. *A Private in the Guards.* London: Macmillan, 1919.
  *The Challenge of the Dead.* 1921. Manchester: Carcanet, 1991.

Graves, Robert. *Goodbye to All That.* 1929. Harmondsworth: Penguin, 1988.
  *Fairies and Fusiliers.* 1919. New York: Knopf, 1960.
  *But It Still Goes On.* London: Jonathan Cape, 1930.

Gurney, Ivor. *Severn and Somme and War's Embers.* 1917. Ed. R. K. R. Thornton. Manchester: Carcanet, 1987.
  *Selected Poems.* Ed. George Walter. London: Dent, 1996.
  *Collected Poems.* Ed. P. J. Kavanagh. Oxford: Oxford University Press, 1982.
  *Collected Letters.* Ed. R. K. R. Thornton. Manchester: Carcanet, 1991.

Haldane, Elizabeth. *The British Nurse in Peace and War*. London: John Murray, 1923.

Hankey, Donald. *A Student in Arms*. London: Andrew Melrose, 1918.

Hay, Ian. *The First Hundred Thousand: Being the Unofficial Chronicle of a Unit of 'K 910'*. London: William Blackwood and Sons, 1915.

Hemingway, Ernest. *A Farewell to Arms*. 1929. London: Vintage, 1999.

Herbert, A. P. *The Secret Battle*. 1919. London: Chatto & Windus, 1982.

Higonnet, Margaret R., ed. *Lines of Fire: Women Writers of World War I*. Harmondsworth: Penguin, 1999.

*Nurses at the Front: Writing the Wounds of the Great War*. Boston: Northeastern University Press, 2001.

Hughes, Thomas. *Tom Brown at Oxford*. London: Macmillan, 1889.

Hulme, T. E. *The Collected Works of T. E. Hulme*. Ed. Karen Csengeri. Oxford: Clarendon, 1994.

Jenkin, Arthur. *A Tank Driver's Experiences: Or Incidents in a Soldier's Life*. London: Elliot Stock, 1922.

Jones, David. *In Parenthesis*. 1937. London: Faber and Faber, 1961.

*Epoch and Artist: Selected Writings*. London: Faber and Faber, 1959.

Jünger, Ernst. *Storm of Steel*. 1920. Trans. Michael Hofmann. London: Allen Lane, 2003.

Keats, John. *John Keats: The Poems*. Ed. David Bromwich. London: Everyman's Library, 1992.

La Motte, Ellen N. *The Backwash of War: The Human Wreckage of the Battlefield As Witnessed by an American Hospital Nurse*. London: G. P. Putnam's Sons, 1919.

Lawrence, D. H. *The Collected Letters of D. H. Lawrence*. Ed. Harry T. Moore. Vol. I. New York: Viking, 1962.

*England, My England and Other Stories*. Ed. Bruce Steele. Cambridge: Cambridge University Press, 1990.

*Lady Chatterley's Lover*. 1928. Harmondsworth: Penguin, 1961.

Ledwidge, Francis. *Selected Poems*. Ed. Dermont Bolger and intro. Seamus Heaney. Dublin: New Island Books, 1992.

Lee, Vernon (Violet Paget). *Satan the Waster: A Philosophic War Trilogy with Notes and Introduction*. London: John Lane, 1920.

*Letters from the Front. Being a Record of the Part Played by Officers of the Canadian Bank [of Commerce] in the Great War 1914–19*. Toronto, 1920.

Lewis, Wyndham. *Blasting and Bombardiering: An Autobiography (1914–1926)*. 1937; London: John Calder, 1982.

Lewis, Wyndham, ed. *Blast: Review of the Great English Vortex*. Vols. I and II. London: Kraus, 1914–15.

MacDonald, Paul S., ed. *The Existentialist Reader: An Anthology of Key Texts*. Edinburgh: Edinburgh University Press, 2000.

McKee, Alexander. *Vimy Ridge*. London: Souvenir Press, 1966.

MacGill, Patrick. *The Great Push*. London: Herbert Jenkins, 1917.

Macmillan, Harold. *Winds of Change*. London: Macmillan, 1966.

Manning, Frederic. *The Middle Parts of Fortune*. 1929. London: Peter Davies, 1977.

Marks, Thomas Penrose. *The Laughter Goes from Life: In the Trenches of the First World War*. London: William Kimber, 1977.

Marlow, Joyce, ed. *The Virago Book of Women and the Great War 1914–1918*. London: Virago, 1998.

Masefield, John. *Collected Poems*. London: Heinemann, 1923.

Mott, Frederick Walter. *War Neuroses and Shellshock*. London: Oxford University Press, 1919.

Murray, Flora. *Women As Army Surgeons: Being the History of the Women's Hospital Corps in Paris, Wimereux and Endell Street, September 1914–October 1919*. London: Hodder and Stoughton Limited, 1920.

Nicols, Robert. *Ardours and Endurances*. London: Chatto & Windus, 1917.

*Aurelia and Other Poems*. London: Chatto & Windus, 1920.

Nicols, Robert, ed. *An Anthology of War Poetry*. London: Nicholson and Watson, 1943.

O'Flaherty, Liam. *Return of the Brute*. London: Mandrake Press, 1929.

*On the Anzac Trail. Being Extracts from the Diary of a New Zealand Sapper*. London: William Heinemann, 1916.

Orr, Boyd. *As I Recall*. London: Macgibbon & Kee, 1966.

Owen, Wilfred. *Wilfred Owen: Collected Letters*. Ed. Harold Owen and John Bell. London and Oxford: Oxford University Press, 1967.

*Selected Letters*. Ed. John Bell. Oxford: Oxford University Press, 1998.

*The Complete Poems and Fragments*. Ed. Jon Stallworthy. 2 vols. London: Chatto & Windus, Hogarth and Oxford University Press, 1983.

*The Poems of Wilfred Owen*. Ed. Jon Stallworthy. London: Chatto & Windus, 1990.

*War Poems*. Ed. Jon Stallworthy. London: Chatto & Windus, 1994.

Perduca, Maria Luisa. 'An Amputation'. Trans. Sylvia Notini from *Un anno D'ospedale: giugno 1915–novembre 1916: Note di un infermiera*. Milan: Fratelli Treves, 1917. *Lines of Fire*. Ed. Margaret R. Higonnet. 217–19.

Powell, Anne, ed. *A Deep Cry: First World War Soldier-Poets Killed in France and Flanders*. Thrupp: Sutton, 1993.

Rathbone, Irene. *We That Were Young*. 1932. New York: The Feminist Press, 1989.

Read, Herbert. *Collected Poems 1913–25*. London: Faber & Gwyer, 1926.

*Collected Poems 1919–1965*. London: Sinclair-Stevenson, 1966.

*The Contrary Experience: Autobiographies*. London: Secker & Warburg, 1963.

*In Retreat*. 1925. London: Imperial War Museum, 1991.

Reilly, Catherine, ed. *The Virago Book of Women's War Poetry and Verse*. London: Virago, 1997.

Remarque, Erich Maria. *All Quiet On the Western Front*. Trans. A. W. Wheen. 1929. Oxford: Heinemann New Windmills, 1990.

Roberts, David, ed. *Minds At War*. London: Saxon, 1996.

Romains, Jules. *Verdun*. Vol. VIII of *Men of Good Will*. Trans. Gerard Hopkins. 1938. London: Peter Davies, 1939.

Rosenberg, Isaac. *The Collected Works of Isaac Rosenberg: Poetry, Prose, Letters, Paintings, and Drawings.* Foreword by Siegfried Sassoon. Ed. Ian Parsons. London: Chatto & Windus, Hogarth, 1984.

*The Poetry and Plays of Isaac Rosenberg.* Ed. Vivien Noakes. Oxford: Oxford University Press, 2004.

Sandes, Flora. *An English Woman-Sergeant in the Serbian Army.* London: Hodder & Stoughton, 1916.

Sartre, Jean-Paul. *Nausea.* Trans. Robert Baldick. 1938. Harmondsworth: Penguin, 2000.

Sassoon, Siegfried Loraine. *Diaries 1915–1918.* Ed. Sir Rupert Hart-Davies. London: Faber & Faber, 1983.

*Diaries 1920–21.* Ed. Sir Rupert Hart-Davies. London: Faber & Faber, 1981.

*Collected Poems 1908–1956.* 1961. London: Faber & Faber, 1984.

*The War Poems.* Ed. Sir Rupert Hart-Davies. London: Faber & Faber, 1983.

*Memoirs of an Infantry Officer.* 1930. London: Faber & Faber, 1965.

*Sherston's Progress.* London: Faber & Faber, 1936.

*Siegfried's Journey.* London: Faber & Faber, 1945.

*The Complete Memoirs of George Sherston.* 1937. London: Faber & Faber, 1952.

Schilpp, Paul, ed. *The Philosophy of Gabriel Marcel.* Chicago: Open Court, 1969.

Silkin, Jon, ed. *The Penguin Book of First World War Poetry.* 1979. Harmondsworth: Penguin, 1996.

Silkin, Jon and Jon Glover, eds. *The Penguin Book of First World War Prose.* Harmondsworth: Penguin, 1989.

Shelley, Percy Bysshe. *Poetical Works.* Ed. Thomas Hutchinson. Oxford: Oxford University Press, 1970.

Sherriff, Robert Cedric. *Journey's End: A Play.* London: Samuel French, 1929.

Smith, Angela, ed. *Women's Writing of the First World War.* Manchester: Manchester University Press, 2000.

Smith, Helen Zenna (pseudonym of Evadne Price). *Not So Quiet . . . Stepdaughters of War.* 1930. New York: The Feminist Press, 1989.

Smith, Lesley. *Four Years Out of Life.* London: Allan, 1931.

Sorley, Charles Hamilton. *Marlborough and Other Poems.* Cambridge: Cambridge University Press, 1922.

*The Letters of Charles Hamilton Sorley.* Ed. Jean Moorcroft Wilson. London: Cecil Woolf, 1990.

Spearing, E. M. *From Cambridge to Camiers.* Cambridge: W. Heffer, 1917.

Stein, Gertrude. *Wars I Have Seen.* 1945. London: Brilliance Books, 1985.

Sturgis, Howard. *Tim.* London: Macmillan, 1891.

Tate, Trudi, ed. *Women, Men and the Great War: An Anthology of Stories.* Manchester: Manchester University Press, 1995.

Taylor, Martin, ed. *Lads: Love Poetry of the Trenches.* London: Duckworth, 1989.

Tennyson, Alfred. *The Poems of Alfred Tennyson.* Ed. Christopher Ricks. Essex: Longman, 1987.

Thomas, Edward. *Collected Poems of Edward Thomas.* Ed. R. G. Thomas. Oxford: Oxford University Press, 1981.

*Edward Thomas: Selected Letters*. Ed. R. G. Thomas. Oxford: Oxford University Press, 1996.

Thomas, W. Beach. *With the British on the Somme*. London: Methuen, 1917.

Tügel, Ludwig. 'Over the Top'. *Great First World War Stories*. 1930. Published originally as *Great Short Stories of the War*. London: Chancellor, 1994. 293–301.

Tylee, Claire, Elaine Turner and Agnes Cardinal, eds., *War Plays by Women: An International Anthology*. London: Routledge, 1999.

Ungaretti, Giuseppe. *Selected Poems*. Trans. Patrick Creagh. Harmondsworth: Penguin, 1971.

Vansittart, Peter, ed. *Voices from the Great War*. London: Pimlico, 1998.

Voigt, F. A. *Combed Out*. 1920. London: Jonathan Cape, 1930.

West, Arthur Graeme. *The Diary of a Dead Officer: Being the Posthumous Papers Of Arthur Graeme West*. London: George Allen & Unwin, 1919.

Whitman, Walt. *The Portable Walt Whitman*. Ed. Mark Van Doren. New York: Penguin, 1977.

Williamson, Henry. *The Wet Flanders Plain*. 1929. Norwich: Glidden Books, 1987.

*Wipers Times: A Complete Facsimile of the Famous Trench Newspapers, incorporating the 'New Church' Times, the Kemmel Times, the Somme Times, the B. E. F. Times and the Better Times*. Intro. Patrick Beaver. London: Peter Davies, 1973.

Woolf, Virginia. *The Years*. 1937. Oxford: Oxford University Press, 1992.

*The Essays of Virginia Woolf*. 3 vols. Ed. Andrew McNeillie. London: Hogarth, 1988.

*The Diary of Virginia Woolf 1920–24*. Ed. Anne Olivier Bell. London: Hogarth, 1978.

Yeats, W. B. *The Letters of W. B. Yeats*. Ed. Allan Wade. London: Rupert Hart Davis, 1954.

### SECONDARY SOURCES

Adamson, H. G. 'On the Treatment of Scabies and Some Other Common Skin Affections in Soldiers'. *The Lancet*, 10 February, 1917. i: 221–4.

Adamson, Joseph and Hillary Clark, eds. *Scenes of Shame: Psychoanalysis, Shame and Writing*. New York: State University of New York Press, 1999.

*About Cremation*. London: Cremation Society, 1923.

Aldersey-Williams, Hugh. *Experimental Lives: Science and Nationalism*. Work in progress.

Anzieu, Didier. *The Skin Ego: A Psychoanalytic Approach*. Trans. Chris Turner. New Haven: Yale University Press, 1989.

Aristotle. *The Complete Works of Aristotle*. Ed. Jonathan Barnes. Princeton: Princeton University Press, 1984.

*Art and Letters*. Spring, 1919: II.

Ashworth, Tony. *Trench Warfare 1914–18: The Live and Let Live System*. London: Macmillan, 1988.

Audoin-Rouzeau, Stéphane. *Men at War 1914–1918: National Sentiment and Trench Journalism in France during the First World War*. Trans. Helen McPhail. Oxford: Berg, 1992.

Bachelard, Gaston. *The Poetics of Space*. Trans. Maria Jolas. Boston: Beacon Press, 1969.

Backman, Sven. *Tradition Transformed: Studies in the Poetry of Wilfred Owen*. Lund: Gleerup, 1979.

Bailes, Sally M. and Robert M. Lambert. 'Cognitive Aspects of Haptic Form Recognition by Blind and Sighted Subjects'. *British Journal of Psychology*, 77 (1986), 451–8.

Banks, Arthur. *A Military Atlas of the First World War*. London: Leo Cooper, 1989.

Barham, P. *Forgotten Lunatics of the Great War*. New Haven: Yale University Press, 2004.

Baron-Cohen, Simon and John E. Harrison, eds. *Synaesthesis: Classic and Contemporary Readings*. Oxford: Blackwell, 1997.

Barrell, John. *The Dark Side of the Landscape: The Rural Poor in English Painting, 1730–1840*. Cambridge: Cambridge University Press, 1980.

   'Geographies of Hardy's Wessex'. *Journal of Historical Geography*, 8,4 (1982), 347–61.

Barrett, Deidre, ed. *Trauma and Dreams*. Cambridge, Mass.: Harvard University Press, 1996.

Barthes, Roland. *Image, Music Text*. Selected and trans. Stephen Heath. London: Fontana, 1977.

   *A Lover's Discourse*. Trans. Richard Howard. 1977. Harmondsworth: Penguin, 1990.

   *The Rustle of Language*. Trans. Richard Howard. Berkeley: University of California Press, 1989.

Bataille, Georges. *Visions of Excess: Selected Writings, 1927–1939*. Ed. and trans. Allan Stoekl. Minneapolis: University of Minnesota Press, 1985.

Baudry, Michael *et al.*, eds. *Advances in Synaptic Plasticity*. Cambridge, Mass.: MIT, 1999.

Beer, Gillian. 'Four Bodies on the Beagle: Touch, Sight, and Writing in a Darwin Letter'. *Textuality and Sexuality: Reading Theories and Practices*. Ed. Judith Still and Michael Worton. Manchester: Manchester University Press, 1993. 116–32.

   *Open Fields: Science in Cultural Encounter*. Oxford: Clarendon, 1996.

   *Virginia Woolf: The Common Ground. Essays by Gillian Beer*. Edinburgh: Edinburgh University Press, 1996.

Benjamin, Walter. *Illuminations: Essays and Reflections*. Ed. Hannah Arendt. New York: Schocken Books, 1968.

Benthien, Claudia. *Skin: On the Cultural Border between Self and the World*. Trans. Thomas Dunlap. New York: Columbia University Press, 2002.

Bergonzi, Bernard. *Heroes' Twilight: A Study of the Literature of the Great War*. 1965. Basingstoke: Macmillan, 1980.

Berry, Paul and Mark Bostridge. *Vera Brittain: A Life*. London: Chatto & Windus, 1995.

Bersani, Leo. *The Freudian Body: Psychoanalysis and Art*. New York: Columbia University Press, 1986.

  *Homos*. Cambridge, Mass.: Harvard University Press, 1995.

  *Caravaggio's Secrets*. Cambridge, Mass.: MIT Press, 1998.

Bet-el, Ilana R. *Conscripts: Lost Legions of the Great War*. Thrupp: Sutton, 1999.

Bois, Yves-Alain and Rosalind Krauss. *Formless: A User's Guide*. New York: Zone, 1997.

Booth, Allyson. *Postcards from the Trenches: Negotiating the Space between Modernism and the First World War*. New York: Oxford University Press, 1996.

Bourke, Joanna. *Dismembering the Male: Men's Bodies, Britain and the Great War*. London: Reaktion Books, 1996.

  *An Intimate History of Killing in Twentieth-Century Face-to-Face Warfare*. London: Granta, 1999.

Bradbury, Malcolm. 'The Denuded Place: War and Form in *Parade's End* and *U.S.A.*'. *The First World War in Fiction*. Ed. Holger Klein. London: Macmillan, 1976. 193–209.

Braybon, Gail. *Women Workers in the First World War: The British Experience*. London: Croom Helm, 1981.

Braybon, Gail, ed. *Evidence, History and the Great War: Historians and the Impact of 1914–18*. Oxford: Berghahn Books, 2003.

Brearton, Fran. *The Great War in Irish Poetry: W. B. Yeats to Michael Longley*. Oxford: Oxford University Press, 2000.

Breen, Jennifer. 'Wilfred Owen (1893–1918): His Recovery from Shell-Shock'. *Notes and Queries*, 23 (1976), 301–5.

*British Trench Warfare 1917–1918: A Reference Manual*. 1917; London: IWM, 1997.

Bridgewater, Patrick. *The German Poets of the First World War*. London: Croom Helm, 1985.

Bristow, Joseph. *Effeminate England: Homoerotic Writing after 1885*. Buckingham: Open University Press, 1995.

Brock, Arthur J. *Health and Conduct*. London: Williams and Norgate, 1923.

Brooks, Peter. *Body Work: Objects of Desire in Modern Narrative*. Cambridge, Mass.: Harvard University Press, 1993.

Brosman, Catharine Savage. *Images of War in France: Fiction, Art, Ideology*. Baton Rouge: Louisiana State University Press, 1999.

  'French Writing of the Great War', in *Cambridge Companion to the Literature of the First World War* (2004).

Brown, Malcolm. *Tommy Goes to War*. Charleston: Tempus, 1999.

Brown, William. 'The Treatment of Cases of Shell-shock In An Advanced Neurological Centre'. *The Lancet*, 1918. ii: 197–200.

Buitenhaus, Peter. *The Great War of Words: British, American and Canadian Propaganda and Fiction, 1914–1933*. Vancouver: University of British Columbia Press, 1987.

Butler, Judith. *Gender Trouble: Feminism and the Subversion of Identity*. New York: Routledge, 1990.

*Bodies that Matter: On the Discursive Limits of 'Sex'*. New York: Routledge, 1993.

Caesar, Adrian. *Taking It Like a Man: Suffering, Sexuality and the War Poets*. Manchester: Manchester University Press, 1993.

Campbell, James. 'Combat Gnosticism: The Ideology of First World War Poetry Criticism'. *New Literary History*, 30 (1999), 203–15.

Campbell, Patrick. *Siegfried Sassoon: A Study of the War Poetry*. North Carolina: McFarland, 1999.

Caruth, Cathy. *Unclaimed Experience: Trauma, Narrative, and History*. Baltimore: Johns Hopkins University Press, 1996.

Caruth, Cathy, ed. *Trauma: Explorations in Memory*. Baltimore: Johns Hopkins University Press, 1994.

Carver, Michael. 'A Surreal Mudbath'. *Times Literary Supplement* 12 January 2001. 36.

Caws, Peter. *Sartre*. London: Routledge, 1979.

Cecil, Hugh. *The Flower of Battle: British Fiction Writers of the First World War*. London: Secker & Warburg, 1998.

Charteris, Evan. *John Sargent*. London: William Heinemann, 1927.

Cheyette, Bryan and Laura Marcus, eds. *Modernity, Culture and 'the Jew'*. Oxford: Polity Press, 1998.

Classen, Constance. *Worlds of Sense: Exploring the Senses in History and Across Culture*. London: Routledge, 1993.

Classen, Constance, ed. *The Book of Touch*. Oxford: Berg, 2005.

Cohen, Debra Rae. *Remapping the Home Front: Locating Citizenship in British Women's Great War Fiction*. Boston: Northeastern University Press, 2002.

Cohen, Joseph. *Journey to the Trenches: The Life of Isaac Rosenberg*. London: Robson Books, 1975.

Cole, Sarah. *Modernism, Male Friendship and the First World War*. Cambridge: Cambridge University Press, 2003.

Connor, Steven. 'Making an Issue of Cultural Phenomenology'. *Critical Quarterly*, 42,1 (2000), 2–6.

*The Book of Skin*. London: Reaktion, 2004.

'Modernism and the Writing Hand.' 7 October, 2002. http://www.bbk.ac.uk/eh/eng/skc/modhand.htm.

'The Imagination of Flatness (Flat Life).' 15 October, 2002. http://www.bbk.ac.uk/eh/skc/flat.

'Skin: An Historical Poetics.' 15 October 2002. http://www.bbk.ac.uk/eh/skc/skinwalks.

Cooking, Miriam and Angel Woollacott, eds. *Gendering War Talk*. Princeton: Princeton University Press, 1993.

Cooper, Helen, Adrienne Auslander Munich and Susan Merrill Squier, eds. *Arms and the Woman: War, Gender and Literary Representation*. Chapel Hill: University of North Carolina Press, 1989.

Cork, Richard. *Vorticism and Its Allies.* 2 vols. London: Arts Council of Great Britain, 1974.

*David Bomberg.* New Haven: Yale University Press, 1987.

*A Bitter Truth: Avant-Garde Art and the Great War.* New Haven: Yale University Press, 1994.

Coroneos, Con. *Space, Conrad, Modernity.* Oxford: Oxford University Press, 2002.

Cru, Norton. *War Books: A Study in Historical Criticism.* Ed. and trans. Stanley J. Pincetl. San Diego: San Diego State University Press, 1976.

Danius, Sara. *The Senses of Modernism: Technology, Perception and Aesthetics.* Ithaca: Cornell University Press, 2002.

D'Arch Smith, Timothy. *Love in Ernest: Some Notes on the Lives and Writings of the English 'Uranian' Poets from 1889 to 1930.* London: Routledge, 1970.

Dansereau, P. *Inscape and Landscape: The Human Perception of the Environment.* New York, 1973.

Darrow, Margaret H. *French Women and the First World War: War Stories of the Home Front.* New York: Berg, 2000.

Das, Sashibhusan. *Wilfred Owen's 'Strange Meeting': A Critical Study.* Calcutta: Firma KLM Private, 1977.

David-Menard, Monique. *Hysteria from Freud to Lacan: Body and Language in Psychoanalysis.* Ithaca: Cornell University Press, 1989.

Davidson, Claudia, ed. *The Burgoyne Diaries.* London: Thomas Harmsworth, 1985.

Delany, Paul. *D. H. Lawrence's Nightmare: The Writer and His Circle in the Years of the Great War.* Sussex: Harvester, 1979.

*The Neopagans: Friendship and Love in the Rupert Brooke Circle.* London: Macmillan: 1987

Deleuze, Gilles. *Masochism: Coldness and Cruelty.* New York: Zone, 1991.

Dellamora, Richard. *Masculine Desire: The Sexual Politics of Victorian Aestheticism.* Chapel Hill: University of North Carolina Press, 1990.

Derrida, Jacques. *Of Grammatology.* Trans. Gayatri Chakravorty Spivak. Baltimore: Johns Hopkins University, 1976.

*Memoirs of the Blind: The Self-Portrait and Other Ruins.* Trans. Pascale-Anne Brault and Nichael Naas. Chicago: University of Chicago Press, 1993.

*Le Toucher, Jean-Luc Nancy.* Paris: Galilée, 2000.

'Le Toucher'. *Paragraph*, 16, 2 ( July 1993).

Diderot, Denis. *Thoughts on the Interpretation of Nature and Other Philosophical Works.* Manchester: Clinamen Press, 1999.

Dilworth, Thomas. *The Shape of Meaning in Poetry of David Jones.* Toronto: Toronto University Press, 1988.

Dollimore, Jonathan. *Sexual Dissidence: Augustine to Wilde, Freud to Foucault.* Oxford: Oxford University Press, 1991.

'Bisexuality, Heterosexuality, and Wishful Theory'. *Textual Practice*, 10, 3 (1996), 523–39.

Douglas, Mary. *Purity and Danger: An Analysis of the Concepts of Pollution and Taboo.* 1966. London: Routledge, 1984.

Dyhouse, Carol. *Girls Growing Up in Late Victorian and Edwardian England*. London: Routledge, 1981.

Eberle, Matthias. *World War I and the Weimar Artists: Dix, Grosz, Beckmann, Schlemmer*. New Haven: Yale University Press, 1985.

Eksteins, Modris. *Rites of Spring: The Great War and the Birth of the Modern Age*. New York: Bantham Press, 1989.

'In Hell Again', *Times Literary Supplement*, 27 April 2001. 27.

Elias, Norbert. *The Civilizing Process*. Trans. Edmund Jephcott. 1969. Oxford: Blackwell, 1994.

Elliot, Bridget and Jo-Ann Wallace. *Women Artists and Writers: Modernist (Im) positionings*. London: Routledge, 1994.

Ellis, Havelock. *Sexual Inversion*. Vol. I of *Studies in the Psychology of Sex*. London: University Press, 1897.

*Sexual Selection in Man*. Vol. IV of *Studies in the Psychology of Sex*. Philadelphia: F. A. Davies, 1920.

Ellis, John. *Eye-Deep in Hell: Life in the Trenches, 1914–1918*. Glasgow: Fontana, 1977.

Ellmann, Maud. *The Poetics of Impersonality: T. S. Eliot and Ezra Pound*. Brighton: The Harvester Press, 1987.

ed. *Psychoanalytic Literary Criticism*. London: Longman: 1994.

'Skinscapes in Lotus-Eaters'. *Ulysses: (En)Gendered Perspectives: Eighteen New Essays on the Episodes*. Ed. Kimberly J. Devlin and Marilyn Reizbaum. University of South Carolina Press, 1999. 51–65.

Elshtain, Jean Bethke. *Women and War*. Brighton: Harvester, 1987.

Fairbrother, Trevor. *John Singer Sargent: The Sensualist*. New Haven: Yale University Press, 2001.

Farwell, Byron. *The Great War in Africa, 1914–1918*. New York: W. W. Norton, 1986.

Felman, Shoshana and Dori Laub, M. D. *Testimony: Crises of Witnessing In Literature, Psychoanalysis, and History*. London: Routledge, 1992.

Fenton, James. *The Strength of Poetry*. Oxford: Oxford University Press, 2001.

Fenton, Norman. *Shell Shock and its Aftermath*. London: Henry Kimpton, 1926.

Ferenczi, Sándor. *The Clinical Diary of Sándor Ferenczi*. Ed. Judith Dupont. Trans. Michael Balint and Nicola Zarday Jackson. Cambridge, Mass.: Harvard University Press, 1988.

*Further Contributions to the Theory and Technique of Psychoanalysis*. Ed. John Rickman. Trans. Jane Isabel Suttie. London: Hogarth, 1926.

Ferguson, Niall. *The Pity of War*. Harmondsworth: Penguin, 1998.

Fidler, Florence G. *Cremation*. London: Williams and Norgate, 1930.

Field, Frank. *Three French Writers and the Great War: Barbusse, Drieu La Rochelle, Bernanos: Studies in the Rise of Communism and Fascism*. Cambridge: Cambridge University Press, 1975.

Finnegan, Ruth. *Communicating*. London: Routledge, 2002.

Fletcher, John and Andrew Benjamin, eds. *Abjection, Melancholia and Love: The Work of Julia Kristeva*. London: Routledge, 1990.

Flower, J. E. *Literature and the Left in France: Society, Politics and the Novel Since the Late Nineteenth Century*. London: Methuen, 1983.

Foster, Hal. *Return of the Real: The Avant-Garde at the End of the Century*. Cambridge, Mass.: October, 1996.

Foucault, Michel. *The Use of Pleasure, History of Sexuality*. Vol. II. Trans. Robert Hurley. Harmondsworth: Penguin, 1992.

Frantzen, Allen J. *Bloody Good: Chivalry, Sacrifice, and the Great War*. Chicago: Chicago University Press, 2003.

Freud, Sigmund. *The Standard Edition of the Complete Psychological Works*. Ed. and trans. James Strachey. 24 vols. London: Hogarth, 1953–74.

Friedman, Ariela. 'Mary Borden's Forbidden Zone: Women's Writing from No-Man's-Land'. *Modernism/Modernity*, 9, 2 (January 2002), 108–24.

Frijhoft, Willem. 'The Kiss Sacred and Profane, Reflections on a Cross-Cultural Confrontation'. *A Cultural History of Gesture, From Antiquity to the Present Day*. Ed. Jan Bremmen and Herman Roodenburg. Malden, Mass.: Polity Press, 1991.

Fuss, Diana, ed. *Inside/Out: Lesbian Theories, Gay Theories*. New York: Routledge, 1991.

Fussell, Paul. *The Great War and Modern Memory*. Oxford: Oxford University Press, 1975.

Gallop, Jane. *Feminism and Psychoanalysis: The Daughter's Seduction*. Basingstoke: Macmillan, 1982.

Gaselee, Stephen. 'The Soul in the Kiss'. *Criterion* 2 (April 1924), 349–59.

Gibson, J. *The Senses Considered as Perceptual Systems*. London: George Allen and Unwin, 1968.

Gilbert, Martin. *First World War*. London: Harper Collins, 1995.

Gilbert, Sandra. 'Soldier's Heart: Literary Men, Literary Women, and the Great War'. *Behind the Lines*. Ed. Margaret Higonnet. 197–226.

Gilbert, Sandra and Susan Gubar. *No Man's Land: The Place of the Woman Writer in the Twentieth Literature*. 3 vols. New Haven: Yale University Press, 1988–94.

Glover, Jon. 'Owen, Barbusse and Fitzwater Wray'. *Stand*, 21, 2 (1980), 22–32.

Goebel, Stefan. 'Re-membered and Re-Mobilized: The "Sleeping Dead" in Interwar Germany and Britain'. *Journal of Contemporary History*, 39, 4 (2004), 487–501.

'Forging the Industrial Home Front: Iron-nail Memorials in the Ruhr'. In Jenny Macleod and Pierre Purseigle, eds. *Uncovered Fields*. 159–78.

Goldman, Dorothy, ed. *Women and World War I*. Basingstoke: Macmillan, 1993.

Goldman, Dorothy with Jane Gledhill and Judith Hattaway. *Women Writers and the Great War*. New York: Twayne Publishers, 1995.

Goodway, David, ed. *Herbert Read Reassessed*. Liverpool: Liverpool University Press, 1998.

Gowing, Laura. *Common Bodies: Women, Touch and Power in Seventeenth-Century England*. New Haven: Yale University Press, 2003.

Graham, Desmond. *The Truth of War: Owen, Blunden and Rosenberg.* Manchester: Carcanet, 1984.

Grayzel, Susan R. *Women's Identities At War: Gender, Motherhood and Politics in Britain and France during the First World War.* Chapel Hill: University of North Carolina Press, 1999.

*Women and the First World War.* London: Longman, 2002.

Greenblatt, Stephen. *Learning to Curse: Essays in Early Modern Culture.* New York: Routledge, 1990.

'Touch of the Real'. *Representations,* 59 (1997), 14–29.

Gregory, Adrian. *The Silence of Memory: Armistice Day, 1919–1946.* Oxford: Berg, 1994.

Grosz, Elizabeth. *Sexual Subversions: Three French Feminists.* Sydney: Allen and Unwin, 1989.

*Volatile Bodies: Towards a Corporeal Feminism.* Bloomington: Indiana University Press, 1994.

Haggerty, George E. *Men In Love, Masculinity and Sexuality in the Eighteenth Century.* New York: Columbia University Press, 1999.

Hall, Lesley A. *Hidden Anxieties, Male Sexuality, 1900–1950.* Malden, Mass.: Polity Press, 1991.

Hall, Stanley. *Youth: Its Regimen and Hygiene.* New York: Appleton, 1906.

*Educational Problems.* Vol. II. New York: Appleton, 1911.

Halperin, David M. *One Hundred Years of Homosexuality and Other Essays on Greek Love.* New York: Routledge, 1990.

Hammond, Paul. *Love Between Men in English Literature.* London: Macmillan, 1996.

Harding, D. W. *Experience Into Words: Essays on Poetry.* Cambridge: Cambridge University Press, 1963.

Harrison, Charles. *English Art and Modernism, 1900–1939.* London: Indiana University Press, 1981.

Hartman, Geoffrey. *Saving the Text: Literature/Derrida/Philosophy.* Baltimore: Johns Hopkins University Press, 1980.

'On Traumatic Knowledge and Literary Studies'. *New Literary History,* 26 (1995), 537–63.

Harvey, Elizabeth D., ed. *Sensible Flesh: On Touch in Early Modern Culture.* Philadelphia: University of Pennsylvania Press, 2003.

Harvey, A. D. *A Muse of fire: Literature, Art and War.* London: Hambledon Press, 1998.

Haythornthwaite, Philip J. *The World War One Source Book.* London: Arms and Armour Press, 1994.

Heidegger, Martin. *Parmenides.* Trans. Andre Schuwer and Richard Rojcewicz. Bloomington: Indiana University Press, 1992.

Heller, Morton A., ed. *Touch, Representation and Blindness.* Oxford: Oxford University Press, 2000.

Hemmings, Clare. 'Resituating the Bisexual Body: From Identity to Difference'. *Activating Theory: Lesbian, Gay and Bisexual Politics.* Ed. Joseph Bristow and Angelia R. Wilson. London: Lawrence and Wishart, 1993. 118–38.

Hewitt, Nicholas. *The Life of Céline: A Critical Biography*. Oxford: Blackwell, 1999.

Hibberd, Dominic. *Owen-the Poet*. Basingstoke: Macmillan, 1986.
*Wilfred Owen: The Last Year, 1917–1918*. London: Constable, 1992.
*Wilfred Owen: A New Biography*. London: Weidenfeld & Nicolson, 2002.

Hibberd, Dominic, ed. *Poetry of the First World War: A Casebook*. London: Macmillan, 1981.

Hibbert, Christopher. *Nelson: A Personal History*. New York: Viking, 1994.

Higonnet, Margaret, R. 'Authenticity and Art in Trauma Narratives of World War I'. *Modernism/Modernity*, 9, 1 (2002), 91–107.
'Women in the Forbidden Zone: War, Women and Death', in Sarah W. Goodwin and Elisabeth Bronfen eds., *Death and Representation*. Baltimore: Johns Hopkins University Press, 1993. 205–8.
'Not So Quiet in No-Woman's Land', in *Gendering War Talk*, ed. Miriam Cooking and Angel Woollacott. Princeton: Princeton University Press, 1993. 205–26.

Higonnet, Margaret R., Jane Jenson, Sonya Michel and Margaret Collins Weitz, eds. *Behind the Lines: Gender and the Two World Wars*. New Haven: Yale University Press, 1987.

Hinde, Robert. *Biological Bases of Human Social Behaviour*. New York: McGraw-Hill, 1974.

Hirschfeld, Magnus. *The Sexual History of the World War*. 1930 New York: Cadillac, 1946.

Holloway, Sarah L., Stephan P. Rice and Gill Valentine. *Key Concepts in Geography*. London: Sage, 2003.

Holmes, Richard. *Tommy: The British Soldier on the Western Front*. London: Harper Collins, 2004.

Horne, John. *Labour at War: France and Britain, 1914–1918*. Oxford: Oxford University Press, 1991.

Hurd, Michael. *The Ordeal of Ivor Gurney*. Oxford: Oxford University Press, 1978.

Hurley, Kelly. *The Gothic Body: Sexuality, Materialism and Degeneration at the Fin de Siècle*. Cambridge: Cambridge University Press, 1996.

Hyde, H. Montgomery. *The Other Love*. London: Mayflower, 1972.

Hynes, Samuel. *A War Imagined: The First World War and English Culture*. London: Pimlico, 1990.

'Insanity and the War'. *The Lancet*, 4 September, 1915. ii: 553–4.

Irigaray, Luce. *This Sex Which Is Not One*. Trans. Catherine Porter. Ithaca: Cornell University Press, 1985.
*An Ethics of Sexual Difference*. Trans. Carolyn Burke and Gillian C. Gill. London: Althone, 1993.

Iversen, Margaret. *Alois Riegl: Art History and Theory*. Cambridge, Mass.: MIT Press, 1993.

Jacobus, Mary. *Reading Woman: Essays in Feminist Criticism*. London: Methuen, 1986.
*Psychoanalysis and the Scene of Reading*. Oxford: Oxford University Press, 1999.

Jacobus, Mary, Evelynn Fox Keller and Sally Shuttleworth, eds. *Body/Politics: Women and Discourses of Science*. London: Routledge: 1990.

Jameson, Frederic. *Sartre: The Origins of a Style*. New York: Columbia University Press, 1984.

Jay, Martin. *Downcast Eyes: The Denigration of Vision in Twentieth Century French Thought*. Berkeley: University of California Press, 1996.

   *Cultural Semantics: Keywords of Our Time*. Amherst: University of Massachusetts Press, 1998.

Jeffery, Keith. *Ireland and the Great War*. Cambridge: Cambridge University Press, 2000.

Johnson, J. H. *Stalemate: The Great Trench Warfare Battles of 1915–17*. London: Arms and Armour, 1995.

Johnston, John H. *English Poetry of the First World War: A Study in the Evolution of Lyric and Narrative Form*. Princeton: Princeton University Press, 1964.

Joliffe, John. *Raymond Asquith: Life and Letters*. London: Collins, 1980.

Jones, Nigel H. *Rupert Brooke: Life, Death and Myth*. London: R. Cohen, 1999.

Josipovici, Gabriel. *Touch*. New Haven: Yale University Press, 1996.

Julius, Anthony. *T. S. Eliot, Anti-Semitism and Literary Form*. Cambridge: Cambridge University Press, 1995.

Jupp, Peter. *From Dust to Ashes: The Replacement of Burial by Cremation in England, 1840–1867*. London: Congregational Memorial Hall Trust, 1990.

Keegan, John. *The Face of Battle: A Study of Agincourt (France), Waterloo and Somme*. London: Jonathan Cape, 1976.

   *The First World War*. London: Hutchinson, 1998.

Kent, William. *Encyclopaedia of London*. Revised by Godfrey Thompson. London: Dent, 1970.

Kern, Stephen. *The Culture of Time and Space 1880–1918*. London: Weidenfeld and Nicolson, 1983.

Kerr, Douglas. *Wilfred Owen's Voices: Language and Community*. Oxford: Oxford University Press, 1993.

Kerrigan, John. 'Touching and Being Touched'. *London Review of Books*, 24, 18 (19 September 2000), 19–22.

Khan, Nosheen. *Women's Poetry of the First World War*. Lexington: University of Kentucky Press, 1988.

King, James. *The Last Modern: A Life of Herbert Read*. London: Weidenfeld and Nicolson, 1990.

King, Jonathan. 'Henri Barbusse's *Le Feu* and the Crisis of Social Realism'. *The First World War in Fiction*. Ed. Holger Klein. London: Macmillan, 1976. 43–52.

Kittler, Friedrich A. *Discourse Networks 1800/1900*. Trans. Michael Metteer with Chris Cullens. Stanford: Stanford University Press, 1990.

Klein, Holger. *The First World War in Fiction*. London: Macmillan, 1976.

Kristeva, Julia. *Desire in Language: A Semiotic Approach to Literature and Art*. Trans. Thomas Gora, Alice Jardine and Leon S. Roudiez. Oxford: Blackwell, 1980.

*Powers of Horror: An Essay on Abjection.* Trans. Leon S. Roudiez. New York: Columbia University Press, 1982.

*Time and Sense: Proust and the Experience of Literature.* Trans. Stephen Bann. London: Faber, 1994.

Kruger, Lawrence. *Pain and Touch.* London: Academic Press, 1996.

Kwint, Marius, *et al.*, eds. *Material Memories: Design and Evocation.* Oxford: Berg, 1999.

LaCapra, Dominick, *Writing History, Writing Trauma.* Baltimore: Johns Hopkins University Press, 2001.

Lacqeuer, Thomas. *Making Sex: Body and Gender from the Greeks to Freud.* Cambridge, Mass.: Harvard University Press, 1990.

Lane, Arthur E. *An Adequate Response: The War Poetry of Wilfred Owen and Siegfried Sassoon.* Detroit: Wayne State University Press, 1972.

Laplanche, Jean and Pontalis, J. B. *The Language of Psychoanalysis.* Trans. Donald Nicholson-Smith. London: Hogarth Press, 1983.

Lawrence, Margot. *Shadow of Swords: A Biography of Elsie Inglis.* London: Michael Joseph, 1971.

'The Last Survivors'. *The Independent.* 5 August 2004. 1.

*Le Bochofage,* 26 March 1917.

Le Roux, Emmanuel. 'Exhibition Honours Jewish Soldiers in First World War'. *Le Monde.* Translated in *The Guardian,* 24 October 2002.

Lechte, John. *Julia Kristeva.* London: Routledge, 1990.

Leder, Drew. *The Absent Body.* Chicago: University of Chicago Press, 1992.

Leed, Eric. *No Man's Land: Combat and Identity in World War I.* Cambridge: Cambridge University Press, 1979.

*Legionary,* II (June 1928), 12.

Lehmann, John. *Rupert Brooke, His Life and His Legend.* London: Quartet, 1981.

Leighton, Angela, 'Touching Forms: Tennyson and Aestheticism', *Essays in Criticism,* 52, 1 (January 2002), 56–75.

Lerner, Paul Frederick. *Hysterical Men: War, Psychiatry, and the Politics of Trauma in Germany, 1890–1930.* Ithaca: Cornell University Press, 2003.

Levenson, Michael, ed. *The Cambridge Companion to Modernism.* Cambridge: Cambridge University Press, 1999.

Levin, David, ed. *Modernity and The Hegemony of Vision.* Berkeley: California University Press, 1993.

Leys, Ruth. *Trauma: A Genealogy.* Chicago: University of Chicago Press, 2000.

Liddle, Peter. *The 1916 Battle of the Somme: A Reappraisal.* London: Leo Cooper, 1992.

Liddle, Peter and Hugh Cecil, eds. *Facing Armageddon: The First World War Experienced.* London: Leo Cooper, 1996.

Lloyd, David William. *Battlefield Tourism.* Oxford: Berg, 1998.

Longley, Edna. 'The Great War, History, and the English Lyric'. *The Cambridge Companion to the Literature of the First World War,* 57–84.

Longridge, C. Nepean. 'A Note on the Cause and Prevention of Trench Foot'. *The Lancet.* 13 January 1917. i, 62–3.

Lynd, Robert. 'The Young Satirists'. *Nation,* 26, Supplement (6 December 1919), 351–2.

Macdonald, Lyn. *Roses on No Man's Land.* Basingstoke: Papermac, 1980.

MacDonald, Paul S., ed. *The Existentialist Reader: An Anthology of Key Texts.* Edinburgh: Edinburgh University Press, 2000.

McKee, A. *Vimy Ridge.* London: Souvenir Press, 1966.

Macleod, Jenny and Pierre Purseigle, eds. *Uncovered Fields: Perspectives in First World War Studies.* Leiden: Brill, 1984.

McPhail, Helen and Philip Guest. *Edmund Blunden.* London: Leo Cooper, 1999.

Macpherson, Major-General Sir W. G. *et al.,* eds. *Medical Services Surgery.* London: His Majesty's Stationary Office, 1923.

Marcus, Jane. 'Corpus/Corps/Corpse: Writing the Body in/at War'. Afterword. *Not So Quiet. . .Stepdaughters of War.* By Helen Zenna Smith. New York: The Feminist Press, 1989. 241–300.

'"The Asylums of Antaeus": Women, War and Madness – Is There a Feminist Fetishism'. *The New Historicism Reader.* Ed. Aram Veeser. New York: Routledge, 1989.

Marcus, Laura. 'The Great War in Twentieth-century Cinema'. *The Cambridge Companion to the Literature of the First World War,* 280–301.

Marks, Laura U. *Touch: Sensuous Theory and Multisensory Media.* Minneapolis: University of Minnesota Press, 2002.

Marsland, Elizabeth A. *The Nation's Cause: French, English and German Poetry of the First World War.* London: Routledge, 1991.

Marwick, Arthur. *Women at War 1914–1918.* London: Fontana, 1977.

McGreevy, Linda F. *The Life and Works of Otto Dix: German Critical Realist.* Michigan: UMI Research Press, 1975.

Mellor, Leo. 'Words from the Bombsites: Debris, Modernism and Literary Salvage'. *Critical Quarterly,* 46, 4 (2004), 77–90.

Mengham, Rod and Jana Howlett, eds. *The Violent Muse: Violence and the Artistic Imagination in Europe 1910–1939.* Manchester: Manchester University Press, 1994.

Merleau-Ponty, Maurice. *Phenomenology of Perception.* 1945. Trans. Colin Smith. London: Routledge, 2002.

*The Prose of the World.* Trans. John O'Neill. Ed. Claude Lefort. Heinemann: London, 1974.

Miller, William Ian. *The Anatomy of Disgust.* Cambridge, Mass.: Harvard University Press, 1997.

Mitchell, David. *Women on the Warpath: The Story of the Women of the First World War.* London: Cape, 1966.

Mitchell, Frank. *Tank Warfare: The Story of the Tanks of the Great War.* 1933. Stevenage: Spa Books, 1987.

*Modernism/Modernity (Men, Women and World War I)*. Vol. 9, No. 1 (January 2002).

Moeyes, Paul. *Siegfried Sassoon: Scorched Glory. A Critical Study*. Basingstoke: Macmillan, 1997.

Moi, Toril. 'Patriarchal Thought and the Drive for Knowledge'. *Between Psychoanalysis and Feminism*. Ed. Teresa Brennan. London: Routledge, 1989. 189–205.

   *Sexual/Textual Politics: Feminist Literary Theory*. London: Methuen, 1985.

Montagu, Ashley. *Touching: The Human Significance of the Skin*. New York: Columbia University Press, 1971.

Mort, Frank. *Dangerous Sexualities, Medico-moral Politics in England since 1830*. New York: Routledge, 1987.

Mosier, John. *The Myth of the Great War: A New Military History of World War I*. New York: HarperCollins, 2001.

Mosse, George L. *The Jews and the German War Experience, 1914–1918*. New York: Leo Baeck Institute, 1977.

Mott, F. W. 'The Effects of High Explosives Upon the Central Nervous System'. Published in three instalments (12 and 26 February and 11 March). *The Lancet*, 1916, 331–8, 441–9, 545–53.

   *War Neuroses and Shell Shock*. London: Hodder and Stoughton, 1919.

Murry, John Middleton. 'Mr Sassoon's War Verses'. *Nation*, 23 (13 July 1918), 398–400.

   'The Condition of English Poetry'. *Athenaeum* (5 December 1919), 1283–5.

Neu, J., ed. *The Cambridge Companion to Freud*. Cambridge: Cambridge University Press, 1991.

'Neurasthenia and Shell Shock'. *The Lancet*, 18 March 1916. 627–8.

Nicholls, Peter. *Modernisms: A Literary Guide*. Basingstoke: Macmillan, 1995.

Noble, George A. and P. Herbert Jones, eds. *Cremation in Britain*. 1909. London: Cremation Society, 1931.

Nyrop, Christopher. *The Kiss and Its History*. Trans. William Frederick Harvey. London: Sands, 1901.

Omissi, David, ed. *Indian Voices of the Great War: Soldiers' Letters, 1914–1918*. Basingstoke: Macmillan, 1987.

Ortony, Andrew, ed. *Metaphor and Thought*. Cambridge: Cambridge University Press, 1993.

Ouditt, Sharon. *Fighting Forces, Writing Women: Identity and Ideology in the First World War*. London: Routledge, 1994.

   *Women Writers of the First World War: An Annotated Bibliography*. London: Routledge, 2000.

Owen, Harold. *Journey From Obscurity*. 3 vols. London: Oxford University Press, 1963–5.

Page, Melvin, ed. *Africa and the First World War*. London: Macmillan, 1987.

Parfitt, George. *Fiction of the First World War*. London: Faber, 1988.

Parker, Peter. *The Old Lie, The Great War and the Public School Ethos*. London: Constable, 1987.

Pegum, John. 'Foreign Fields: Identity and Location in Soldiers' Writings of the First World War'. Ph.D. thesis, Cambridge University, 2005.

Perella, Nicolas James. *The Kiss Sacred and Profane: An Interpretative History of Kiss Symbolism & Related Religio-Erotic Themes*. Berkeley: University of California Press, 1969.

Peter, John. 'A New Interpretation of *The Waste Land*'. *Essays in Criticism*, 2 (1952), 242–66.

Phillips, Adam. *On Kissing, Tickling and Being Bored*. New York: Faber & Faber, 1993.

Pick, Daniel. *Faces Of Degeneration: A European Disorder*. Cambridge: Cambridge University Press, 1989.

    *War Machine: The Rationalisation of Slaughter in the Modern Age*. New Haven: Yale University Press, 1993.

Picker, John M. *Victorian Soundscapes*. Oxford: Oxford University Press, 2003.

Poliakov, Leon. *The History of Anti-Semitism: Suicidal Europe, 1870–1913*. Trans. George Klin. Oxford: Oxford University Press, 1985.

Porteous, J. D. *Landscapes of the Mind: Worlds of Sense and Metaphor*. Toronto: Toronto University Press, 1990.

'Poets, War-Poets and Poetasters'. *The Cambridge Magazine* (3 March 1917), 400–403.

Potter, Jane. 'A Great Purifier: The Great War in Women's Romances and Memoirs'. In Raitt and Tate, eds. *Women's Fiction and the Great War*. 85–106.

    *Boys in Khaki, Girls in Print: Women's Literary Responses to the Great War*. Oxford: Oxford University Press, 2005.

Powell, Anne, ed. *A Deep Cry: First World War Soldier-Poets killed in France and Flanders*. Guildford: Sutton, 1993.

Praz, Mario. *The Romantic Agony*. Trans. Angus Davidson. 1933. Oxford: Oxford University Press, 1988.

Prior, Robin and Trevor Wilson. *Passchendaele: The Untold Story*. New Haven: Yale University Press, 1996.

Quinn, Patrick, ed. *British Poets of the Great War: Brooke, Rosenberg, Thomas, A Documentary Volume*. Farmington: Gale, 2000.

    *The Great War and the Missing Muse: The Early Writings of Robert Graves and Siegfried Sassoon*. Selingrove and London: Susquehanna University Press and Associated University Press, 1994.

Rainey, Lawrence. *Institutions of Modernism*. New Haven: Yale University Press, 2000.

Ramazani, Jahan. *Poetry of Mourning: The Modern Elegy from Hardy to Heaney*. Chicago: Chicago University Press, 1994.

Ratcliff, Carter. *John Singer Sargent*. Oxford: Phaidon, 1983.

Reeves, Nicholas. *Official British Film Propaganda during the First World War*. London: Croom Helm, 1996.

Reilly, Catherine W. *English Poetry of the First World War: A Bibliography*. London: George Prior, 1978.

Ribot, Theodor. *The Psychology of the Emotions.* London: Walter Scott, 1897.

Rich, Adrienne. *Blood, Bread and Poetry: Selected Prose, 1979–85.* London: Virago, 1986.

Richards, Jeffrey. '"Passing the Love of Women": Manly Love and Victorian Society'. *Manliness and Morality, Middle-Class Masculinity in Britain and America, 1800–1940.* Ed. J. A. Mangan and James Walvin. Manchester: Manchester University Press, 1987. 92–120.

Richardson, John. 'The Green of the Spring'. Unpublished article quoted in Wilson, *Sassoon.*

Riegl, Alois. *Late Roman Art Industry.* 1927. Trans. Rolf Winkes. Rome: Giorgio Bretschneider Editore, 1985.

Rivers, W. C. 'Mr Yeats Analyses His Soul'. *The Cambridge Magazine,* 7, 15 (19 January 1918), 315–17.

Rivers, W. H. R. *Instinct and the Unconscious: A Contribution to A Biological Theory of the Psycho-neuroses.* 1920. Cambridge: Cambridge University Press, 1922.
*Conflict and Dream.* London: Kegan Paul, 1923.

Rodaway, Paul. *Sensuous Geographies: Body, Sense and Space.* London: Routledge, 1994.

Roper, Mike. 'Re-membering the Soldier Hero: The Composure and Re-composure of Masculinity in Memories of the Great War'. *History Workshop Journal,* 50 (2000), 181–205.
'Maternal Relations: Moral Manliness and Emotional Survival in Letters Home During the First World War'. S. Dudink, K. Hagerman and J. Tosh, eds. *Masculinities in Politics and War: Rewritings of Modern History.* Manchester: Manchester University Press, 2004, 295–315.
'Splitting in Unsent Letters: Writing as a Social Practice and a Psychological Activity', *Social History,* 26, 3 (October 2001), 318–40.

Rose, Gillian. *Feminism and Geography: The Limits of Geographical Knowledge.* Oxford: Polity Press, 1993.

Rose, Jacqueline. *Sexuality in the Field of Vision.* London: Virago, 1986.
*Why War?: Psychoanalysis and the Return to Melanie Klein.* Oxford: Blackwell, 1993.
'Bizarre Objects: Mary Butts and Elizabeth Bowen'. *Critical Quarterly,* 42, 1 (2000), 75–85.

Roshwald, Aviel and Richard Stites, eds. *European Culture in the Great War: The Arts, Entertainment and Propaganda 1914–1918.* Cambridge: Cambridge University Press, 1999.

Royle, Trevor. *The Great Crimean War, 1854–1856.* London: Little, Brown and Company, 1999.

Rutherford, Andrew. *The Literature of War: Five Studies in Heroic Virtue.* London: Macmillan, 1978.

Sartre, Jean-Paul. *Being and Nothingness.* Trans. Hazel E. Baines. 1943. London: Routledge, 1989.

Saunders, Anthony. *Weapons of the Trench War 1914–1918.* Sutton: Stroud, 1999.

Saunders, Nicholas J. *Trench Art.* Barnsley: Leo Cooper, 2001.

Saussure, Ferdinand. *Course in General Linguistics*. 1915. Ed. Charles Bally and Albert Sechehaye. Trans. Wade Baskin. London: P.Owen, 1960.

Scarry, Elaine. *The Body in Pain: The Making and Unmaking of the World*. Oxford: Oxford University Press, 1985.

Schama, Simon, *Landscape and Memory*. London: Fontana, 1996.

Schiff, William and Emerson Foulke, eds. *Tactual Perception: A Sourcebook*. Cambridge: Cambridge University Press, 1982.

Schmidt, Michael, ed. *The Harvill Book of Twentieth-Century Poetry*. London: Harvill Press, 1999.

Scott, Bonnie Kime, ed. *The Gender of Modernism: A Critical Anthology*. Bloomington: Indiana University Press, 1990.

Sebba, Anne. *Enid Bagnold: The Authorised Biography*. London: Weidenfield & Nicolson, 1986.

Sedgwick, Eve Kosofsky. *Between Men, English Literature and Male Homosocial Desire*. New York: Columbia University Press, 1985.

*Epistemology of the Closet*. Berkeley: University of California Press, 1990.

*Touching Feeling: Affect, Pedagogy, Performativity*. Durham, NC: Duke University Press, 2003.

Segal, Naomi. 'Entering the Skin of the Other'. Paper presented at the 'Psychoanalysis and Humanities' Seminar, Cambridge University, October 2004. Part of her forthcoming book, *Consensuality*.

Shephard, Ben. *A War Of Nerves*. London: Jonathan Cape, 2000.

Sherry, Vincent. *The Great War and the Language of Modernism*. New York: Oxford University Press, 2003.

Sherry, Vincent, ed., *The Cambridge Companion to the Literature of the First World War* Cambridge: Cambridge University Press, 2004.

Showalter, Elaine. *The Female Malady: Women, Madness and English Culture 1830–1980*. 1985. London: Virago, 1987.

'Rivers and Sassoon'. *Behind the Lines, Gender and the Two World Wars*. Ed. Margaret Higonnet *et al*. New Haven: Yale University Press, 1987. 61–9.

Sieg, Ulrich. 'Judenzählung'. In Gerhard Hirschfeld, Gerd Krumeich and Irina Renz, eds. *Enzyklopädie Erster Weltkrieg*. Munich: Ferdinand Schöningh, 2004.

Silk, Dennis. 'Isaac Rosenberg (1890–1918)'. *Judaism*, 14 (Fall 1965), 462–74.

Silkin, Jon. *Out of Battle: Poetry of the Great War*. 1972. Basingstoke: Macmillan, 1998.

Sillars, Stuart. *Structure and Dissolution in English Writing, 1910–1920*. Basingstoke: Macmillan, 1999.

Simpson, Andy. *Hot Blood and Cold Steel: Life and Death in the Trenches of the First World War*. London: Tom Donovan, 1993.

Sinfield, Alan. *Alfred Tennyson*. Malden, Mass.: Blackwell, 1986.

*The Wilde Century, Effeminacy, Oscar Wilde and the Queer Moment*. London: Cassell, 1994.

Smith, Angela. *The Second Battlefield: Women, Modernism and the First World War*. Manchester: Manchester University Press, 2000.

Smith, Leonard V., Stéphane Audoin-Rouzeau and Annette Becker. *France and the Great War, 1914–1918*. French sections trans. Helen McPhail. Cambridge: Cambridge University Press, 2003.

Sontag, Susan. *Regarding the Pain of Others*. Harmondsworth: Hamish Hamilton, 2003.

Stallworthy, Jon. *Wilfred Owen*. Oxford: Oxford University Press, 1974.

    *Wilfred Owen* (Chatterton Lecture On An English Poet: British Academy). From the Proceedings of the British Academy. London: Oxford University Press, 1970.

    'W. B. Yeats and Wilfred Owen'. *Critical Quarterly*, 11 (Autumn 1969), 119–214.

    *Anthem for Doomed Youth: Twelve Soldier Poets of the First World War*. London: Constable, 2002.

Staudt, Kathleen Henderson. *At the Turn of a Civilisation*. Ann Arbor: University of Michigan Press, 1994.

Strachan, Hew. *The First World War, Vol. I: To Arms*. Oxford: Oxford University Press, 2001.

Strachan, Hew, ed. *The Oxford Illustrated History of the First World War*. Oxford: Oxford University Press, 1999.

Sternlicht, Sanford. *Siegfried Sassoon*. New York: Twayne Publishers, 1993.

Stevens, Hugh. 'Sex and the Nation: "The Prussian Officer" and *Women in Love*'. *The Cambridge Companion to D. H. Lawrence*. Ed. Anne Fernihough. Cambridge: Cambridge University Press, 2001. 49–65.

    'Love and Hate in D. H. Lawrence'. *Men and Masculinities*, 4 (2002), 334–45.

Stevens, Hugh and Caroline Howlett, eds. *Modernist Sexualities*. Manchester: Manchester University Press, 2000.

Stewart, Susan. *On Longing: Narratives of the Miniature, the Gigantic, the Souvenir, the Collection*. Durham, NC: Duke University Press, 1993.

    *Poetry and the Fate of the Senses*. Chicago: University of Chicago Press, 2002.

Sturrock, John. *Journey to the End of the Night*. Cambridge: Cambridge University Press, 1990.

Summers, Anne. *Angels and Citizens: British Women as Military Nurses 1854–1914*. London: Routledge, 1988.

Sutherland-Gower, Ronald. *Cleanliness Versus Corruption*. London: Longmans, 1910.

Tate, Trudi. *Modernism, History and the First World War*. Manchester: Manchester University Press, 1998.

Tate, Trudi and Suzanne Raitt, eds. *Women's Fiction and the Great War*. Oxford: Oxford University Press, 1997.

Terry, Roy. *Women in Khaki: The Story of the British Woman Soldier*. London: Columbus, 1988.

Theweleit, Klaus. *Male Fantasies*. Trans. Stephen Conway. 2 vols. Cambridge: Polity Press, 1987.

Thiher, Allen. 'Céline and Sartre'. *Philological Quarterly*, 50, 2 (1971), 292–305.

Thom, Deborah. *Nice Girls and Rude Girls: Women Workers in World War I.* London: I. B. Tauris, 1998.

Tomkins, Silvan. *Shame and Its Sisters: A Silvan Tomkins Reader.* Ed. Eve Kosofsky Sedgwick and Adam Frank. Durham, NC: Duke University Press, 1995.

Trotter, David. *Paranoid Modernism: Literary Experiment, Psychosis and the Professionalization of English Society.* Oxford: Oxford University Press, 2001.

*Cooking With Mud: The Idea of Mess in Nineteenth-Century Art and Fiction.* Oxford: Oxford University Press, 2000.

'The British Novel and War' in *The Cambridge Companion to the Literature of the First World War.*

'Stereoscopy: Modernism and the "Haptic"'. *Critical Quarterly,* 46, 4 (2004), 38–58.

Tuan, Yi-Fi. *Space and Place: The Perspective of Experience.* Minneapolis: University of Minnesota Press, 1977.

*Passing Strange and Wonderful: Aesthetics, Nature and Culture.* Washington, DC: Island Press, 1993.

Tylee, Claire M. *The Great War and Women's Consciousness: Images of Militarism and Womanhood in Women's Writings 1914–1918.* Basingstoke: Macmillan, 1990.

'"Maleness Run Riot" – The Great War and Women's Resistance to Militarism'. *Women's Studies International Forum,* 11, 3 (1988), 199–210.

Tylee, Claire M., ed. *Women, the First World War, and the Dramatic Imagination: International Essays (1914–1999).* London: Edwin Mellen Press, 2000.

Vasseleu, Cathryn. *Textures of Light: Vision and Touch in Irigaray, Levinas and Merleau-Ponty.* London: Routledge, 1988.

Von Clausewitz, Carl. *On War.* 1832 Ed. and intro. Anatol Rapoport. Harmondsworth: Penguin, 1982.

'War Poems of Siegfried Sassoon'. *The London Mercury.* Vol. I (December 1919), 206.

'War Shock in the Civilian'. *The Lancet,* 4 March 1916. i: 522.

Watkins, Glenn. *Proof Through the Night: Music and the Great War.* Berkeley: University of California Press, 2003.

Watts, Philip. *Allegories of the Purge.* Stanford: Stanford University Press, 1998.

Webb, Barry. *Edmund Blunden: A Biography.* New Haven: Yale University Press, 1990.

Weeks, Jeffrey. *Coming Out, Homosexual Politics in Britain from the Nineteenth Century to the Present.* London: Quartet Books, 1977.

*Sexuality.* London: Tavistock, 1986.

*Sex, Politics and Society: The Regulation of Sexuality since 1800.* London: Longman, 1989.

*Between the Acts, Lives of Homosexual Men,* 1885–1967. London: Routledge, 1999.

Weizsacher, Victor V. 'Dreams in Endogenic Magersucht'. *Evolution of Psychosomatic Concepts: Anorexia Nervosa: A Paradigm.* Ed. M. Ralph Kaufman. London: Hogarth Press, 1964.

Welland, Dennis. *Wilfred Owen: A Critical Study.* London: Chatto & Windus, 1978.

Wertheimer, Jack. *Unwelcome Strangers.* New York: Oxford University Press, 1987.

Whaley, Joachim, ed. *Mirrors of Mortality: Studies in the Social History of Death.* London: Europa, 1981.

Wheeler R. H. and T. D. Cutsforth. 'Synaesthesia and Meaning'. *The American Journal of Psychology* 33 (July 1922), 361–84.

Williams, Merryn. *Wilfred Owen.* Glamorgan: Seren Books, 1993.

Wilson, Jean Moorcroft. *Isaac Rosenberg: Poet & Painter.* London: Cecil Woolf, 1975.

*Siegfried Sassoon, The Making of a War Poet, A Biography, 1886–1918.* London: Duckworth, 1998.

'Visions From the Trenches'. *The Guardian Review* (8 November 2003), 4–6.

Wilson, Stephen. *Ideology and Experience: Antisemitism in France at the Time of the Dreyfus Affair.* London: Fairleigh Dickinson University Press, 1982.

Winnicott, D. W. *Playing and Reality.* 1971. Harmondsworth: Penguin, 1974.

Winter, Dennis. *Death's Men: Soldiers of the Great War.* Harmondsworth: Penguin, 1978.

Winter, Jay. *The Great War and the British People.* London: Macmillan, 1985.

*The Experience of the First World War.* Oxford: Oxford University Press, 1995.

*Sites of Memory, Sites of Mourning: The Great War in European Cultural History.* Cambridge: Cambridge University Press, 1995.

'Shell-shock and the Cultural History of the Great War'. *Journal of Contemporary History,* 35, 1 (2000), 7–11.

Winter, Jay and Jean Louis-Robert. *Capital Cities at War: Paris, London, Berlin, 1914–1919.* New York: Cambridge University Press, 1997.

Woolf, Virginia. 'Mr Sassoon's Poems'. *Times Literary Supplement* (31 May, 1917), 259.

Wright, Colonel Sir Almroth E. 'Conditions which Govern the Growth of the Bacillus of "Gas Gangrene"'. *The Lancet,* 6 January 1917. i: 1–9.

# Index